12-29-93

Woods
RR1 BOX 223898
PALMYRA VA 22963
804-589-8460
842-3861

THE END OF THE BRONZE AGE

THE END OF
THE BRONZE AGE

CHANGES IN WARFARE AND THE
CATASTROPHE CA. 1200 B.C.

Robert Drews

PRINCETON UNIVERSITY PRESS

PRINCETON, NEW JERSEY

Library of Congress Cataloging-in-Publication Data

Drews, Robert.
The end of the Bronze Age: Changes in Warfare and the catastrophe
ca. 1200 B.C. / Robert Drews.
p.   cm.
Includes bibliographical references and index.
ISBN 0-691-04811-8
1. Bronze age—Mediterranean Region.   2. Warfare, Prehistoric—
Mediterranean Region.   3. Chariot warfare—Mediterranean Region.
4. Weapons, Prehistoric—Mediterranean Region.   5. Mediterranean
Region—Antiquities.   I. Title.
GN778.3.A1D74   1993   930'.09822—dc20   92-46511   CIP

CONTENTS

LIST OF ILLUSTRATIONS

ACKNOWLEDGMENTS

FOR PHOTOGRAPHS and permission to publish them in this book I am grateful to the Oriental Institute of the University of Chicago and to Princeton University Press. At the Oriental Institute my requests were very kindly expedited by John Larson and Lisa Snider. The photograph of the reconstructed "Battle Scene" fresco at Pylos was made for me by Tucker Blackburn, Research Associate in the Department of Classics at the University of Cincinnati. For the illustrations of "Shardana warriors" I am indebted to Vronwy Hankey, who promptly and graciously responded to my request for her matchless photographs of the Abydos reliefs of the Battle of Kadesh. The "Warrior Vase" illustration came from Marburg/Art Resource, of New York. For the drawing of figures 2–4 I thank Meg Coode Shannon.

Drs. Joanna Scurlock and Richard Beal provided me with much constructive criticism at a crucial stage of this manuscript. I thank them for saving me from errors large and small and exonerate them entirely from those that remain. I am also indebted, for various kindnesses and communications, to Professors Leonard Alberstadt, Frank Cross, Stuart Piggott, Anthony Snodgrass, and Stuart Wheeler. The editors at Princeton University Press have again been very helpful: for their good work and judgment I thank Lauren Osborne, Colin Barr, and especially Lauren Oppenheim.

For biblical passages, unless otherwise specified, I have used the RSV translation. The translations of occasional lines from Homer and other Greek authors are my own.

ABBREVIATIONS

ABSA	Annual of the British School at Athens
AJA	American Journal of Archaeology
ANET	J. B. Pritchard, ed., *Ancient Near-Eastern Texts Relating to the Old Testament*. 3d ed. Princeton: Princeton University Press, 1969
AR	Archaeological Reports
Arch. Anz.	Archäologischer Anzeiger
AS	Anatolian Studies
BASOR	Bulletin of the American Schools of Oriental Research
BIAL	Bulletin of the Institute of Archaeology (London)
Bib. Arch.	Biblical Archaeologist
BCH	Bulletin de Correspondance Hellénique
CAH	I.E.S. Edwards, C. J. Gadd, N.G.L. Hammond, and E. Sollberger, eds. *The Cambridge Ancient History*. 3d ed. Cambridge: Cambridge University Press, 1970–
CP	Classical Philology
CQ	Classical Quarterly
IEJ	Israel Exploration Journal
JAOS	Journal of the American Oriental Society
JARCE	Journal of the American Research Center in Egypt
JBL	Journal of Biblical Literature
JEA	Journal of Egyptian Archaeology
JHS	Journal of Hellenic Studies
JNES	Journal of Near Eastern Studies
JSOT	Journal for the Study of the Old Testament
JSS	Journal of Semitic Studies
MDAI	Mitteilungen des Deutschen Archäologischen Instituts
OA	Opuscula Atheniensia
Or. Ant.	Oriens Antiquus
PEQ	Palestine Exploration Quarterly
PPS	Proceedings of the Prehistoric Society
PRU	Charles Virolleaud, Jean Nougayrol, et al., eds., *Le Palais royal D'Ugarit publié sous la direction de Claude F.-A. Schaeffer*, vols. 2–6 (Paris: Librairie C. Klincksieck, 1955–70)
RE	A. Pauly, G. Wissowa, and W. Kroll, eds., *Real-Encyclopädie der klassischen Altertumswissenschaft* (1893–1978)
REG	Revue des Etudes Grecques

Rev. Bib.	*Revue Biblique*
Rev. Crit.	*Revue Critique d'Histoire et de Littérature*
RFIC	*Rivista di Filogia e d'Istruzione Classica*
UF	*Ugarit-Forschungen*
VT	*Vetus Testamentum*
ZA	*Zeitschrift für Assyriologie*
ZDMG	*Zeitschrift der Deutschen Morgenländischen Gesellschaft*

PART ONE

INTRODUCTION

Chapter One

THE CATASTROPHE AND ITS CHRONOLOGY

THE END of the eastern Mediterranean Bronze Age, in the twelfth century B.C., was one of history's most frightful turning points. For those who experienced it, it was a calamity. In long retrospect, however, the episode marked a beginning rather than an end, the "dawn time" in which people in Israel, Greece, and even Rome sought their origins. In certain respects that assessment is still valid, for the Age of Iron stands much closer to our own than does the world of the Bronze Age. The metallurgical progress—from bronze to iron—was only the most tangible of the innovations. More significant by far were the development and spread of alphabetic writing, the growth of nationalism, of republican political forms, of monotheism, and eventually of rationalism. These and other historic innovations of the Iron Age have been frequently noted and celebrated.

The bleaker objective of the present book will be a close look at the negative side. In many places an old and complex society did, after all, come to an end ca. 1200 B.C. In the Aegean, the palace-centered world that we call Mycenaean Greece disappeared: although some of its glories were remembered by the bards of the Dark Age, it was otherwise forgotten until archaeologists dug it up. The loss in Anatolia was even greater. The Hittite empire had given to the Anatolian plateau a measure of order and prosperity that it had never known before and would not see again for a thousand years. In the Levant recovery was much faster, and some important Bronze Age institutions survived with little change; but others did not, and everywhere urban life was drastically set back. In Egypt the Twentieth Dynasty marked the end of the New Kingdom and almost the end of pharaonic achievement. Throughout the eastern Mediterranean the twelfth century B.C. ushered in a dark age, which in Greece and Anatolia was not to lift for more than four hundred years. Altogether the end of the Bronze Age was arguably the worst disaster in ancient history, even more calamitous than the collapse of the western Roman Empire.[1]

The end or transformation of Bronze Age institutions is obviously a topic of enormous dimensions. From the modern perspective it is the disappearance of many of these centuries-old forms that gives the years ca. 1200

---

[1] For the comparison see Fernand Braudel, "L'Aube," in Braudel, ed., *La Méditerranée: l'espace et l'histoire* (Paris, 1977), 82–86. In Braudel's words, "la Méditerranée orientale, au xiie siècle avant J.-C., retourne au plan zéro, ou presque, de l'histoire."

B.C. their extraordinary importance. In this book, however, I shall deal with that topic only in passing. My subject here is much more limited and concrete: the physical destruction of cities and palaces. One might object that although the physical destruction was tragic for the occupants of the cities and palaces in question, in itself it need not and should not have entailed the collapse and disappearance of Bronze Age civilization. The razing of Athens in 480 B.C., after all, cleared the ground for the temples of the Periclean city, and the burning of Rome in 387 B.C. was followed directly by an unprecedented burst of Roman expansion. But although the sacking of cities ca. 1200 B.C. was not a sufficient condition for the disappearance of Bronze Age civilization in Greece, Anatolia, and southern Canaan, it was certainly a necessary condition. It is the destruction of sites that I shall therefore try to explain, and this topic is itself enormous. Within a period of forty or fifty years at the end of the thirteenth and beginning of the twelfth century almost every significant city or palace in the eastern Mediterranean world was destroyed, many of them never to be occupied again.

This destruction—which hereafter I shall refer to simply as "the Catastrophe"—I shall review in some detail in chapter 2. Before doing that, however, it will be useful to thread our way chronologically through the period in which the Catastrophe took place. For a chronology we must look to Egypt, since the only narrative history we can write for this period is Egyptian history. Most scholars would agree that there survives at least one documentary source on the Catastrophe, and that is an inscription that Ramesses III put upon the wall of his mortuary temple at Medinet Habu. This is the famous text, accompanied by pictorial reliefs, in which Ramesses III celebrates the victory that he won over the "Sea Peoples" in his eighth year.[2] Since Ramesses declares that before attacking Egypt the enemy had already ravaged Hatti, Alashia, and Amor, it is a reasonable assumption that the inscription furnishes a terminus ante quem for at least some of the destruction attested in these places.

---

[2] Wm. F. Edgerton and John Wilson, *Historical Records of Ramses III: The Texts in "Medinet Habu," Volumes I and II, Translated with Explanatory Notes* (Chicago, 1936), plate 46; Breasted, *AR*, vol. 4, nos. 59–82. Leonard H. Lesko, "Egypt in the 12th Century B.C.," in W. A. Ward and M. S. Joukowsky, eds., *The Crisis Years: The 12th Century B.C.* (Dubuque, 1992), 151–56, has argued that this inscription was cut for Merneptah's mortuary temple, that Ramesses III appropriated it for his own temple at Medinet Habu, and therefore that the events described in it occurred in the eighth year of Merneptah (1205 B.C.) rather than of Ramesses III. But the swath of destruction through "Amor" that the inscription mentions could hardly have taken place during Merneptah's reign, since the Levantine cities were still standing at the accession of Queen Twosret. In addition, the defensive posture that this inscription attributes to the Egyptian pharaoh is not easily reconciled with the offensive campaign that Merneptah claimed to have conducted in the southern Levant.

Dates for the reign of Ramesses III depend on the accession year chosen for Ramesses II, the illustrious predecessor whose name the young king adopted; and in this study I shall follow the "low" chronology that now seems to be accepted by most Egyptologists. On this chronology, Ramesses the Great ruled from 1279 to 1212, accounting—all by himself—for most of the Nineteenth Dynasty.[3] When the old king finally died, close to the age of ninety, he was succeeded by his oldest surviving son, his thirteenth, Merneptah. The latter was, at his accession, "a portly man already in his sixties."[4] As king, Merneptah lived another ten or eleven years and was in turn succeeded by one of his sons, either Seti II (whom Merneptah had designated as his successor) or Amenmesse. At any rate, Seti gained the throne not long after Merneptah's death.

For the first time in decades, Egypt was not ruled by an old man. But the middle-aged Seti II had an unexpectedly short reign. After ruling only six years, Seti died, leaving the succession in some confusion.[5] His principal wife had been Twosret, but the pair had no surviving son. In the event, Seti's nominal successor was Siptah, who was still a child or adolescent. Although Siptah was evidently the son of Seti, his mother was not Twosret but Tio, one of his father's secondary wives, and Siptah must have owed his elevation to the exertions of powerful mentors. Twosret survived the boy, and she herself ruled as pharaoh for at least two years, being only the fourth woman in almost two millennia of Egyptian history to reach the throne. During the reigns of Siptah and Twosret (a period of at least eight years), the power behind the throne seems to have been Bay, a Syrian who had risen to become "Great Chancellor of the Entire Realm." With the death of Twosret (the circumstances in which any of these people died are unknown), a man of uncertain origin, Setnakhte, drove "the Syrian" from his position as king-maker and established himself as king. Thus ended the Nineteenth Dynasty and began the Twentieth. Although Setnakhte ruled for only two years, Egypt was fortunate that the upstart had a son as capable as himself: this was the young Ramesses III, who faced the Catastrophe and survived to describe it.

---

[3] On the high chronology Ramesses II's accession year was 1304 B.C., on the middle chronology 1290. The high chronology has been generally abandoned by specialists. The low chronology was effectively advocated by E. F. Wente and C. C. Van Siclen, "A Chronology of the New Kingdom," in J. H. Johnson and E. F. Wente, eds., *Studies in Honor of George R. Hughes* (Chicago, 1976), 217–61. For other arguments see Paul Åström, ed., *High, Middle, or Low? Acts of an International Colloquium on Absolute Chronology Held at the University of Gothenburg 20th-22d August 1987* (Göteborg, 1987).

[4] K. A. Kitchen, *Pharaoh Triumphant: The Life and Times of Ramesses II* (Warminster, 1982), 207.

[5] The confusion, at once the bane and the delight of Egyptologists, was much clarified by Alan Gardiner, "Only One King Siptah and Twosre Not His Wife," *JEA* 44 (1958): 12–22.

Although the regnal dates for Ramesses III, his father, and their Nineteenth-Dynasty predecessors cannot be precisely fixed, the following seem to be approximately correct:[6]

Nineteenth Dynasty

Ramesses II	1279–1212 B.C.
Merneptah	1212–1203 B.C.
Amenmesse	1203–1202 B.C.
Seti II	1202–1196 B.C.
Siptah	1196–1190 B.C.
Twosret	1190–1188 B.C.

Twentieth Dynasty

Setnakhte	1188–1186 B.C.
Ramesses III	1186–1155 B.C.

On this reckoning, the terminus ante quem for much of the Catastrophe—the crucial eighth year of Ramesses III—will be 1179 B.C. That fits well enough with a recently discovered tablet indicating that Emar (on the Euphrates, downstream from Carchemish) fell in the second year of Melik-shipak, king of Babylon.[7] On J. A. Brinkman's Mesopotamian chronology, Emar must have been sacked in the 1180s.[8] An even more recent discovery, this time at Ras Shamra, shows that the rule of Hammurapi, the last king of Ugarit, began when Merneptah was ruling Egypt and extended into the reign of Siptah and Queen Twosret.[9] The synchronism proves that Ugarit was still standing in 1196 B.C., and suggests that the city was not destroyed before 1190.[10]

[6] Since in some cases only a terminus post quem for a monarch's death is available, various schemes have been proposed, and on the low chronology the accession of Ramesses III is placed anywhere from 1188 to 1182 B.C. For several possibilities see Wente and Van Siclen, "A Chronology of the New Kingdom," and K. A. Kitchen, "The Basics of Egyptian Chronology in Relation to the Bronze Age," in Åström, ed., *High, Middle, or Low?* 37–55.

[7] Daniel Arnaud, "Les textes d'Emar et la chronologie de la fin du Bronze Récent," *Syria* 52 (1975): 87–92. The tablet dated to Melik-shipak's second year is a short-term contract; Arnaud therefore concludes that only a very short time ("quelques semaines") elapsed between the writing of the contract and the destruction of the city.

[8] Brinkman, "Notes on Mesopotamian History in the Thirteenth Century B.C.," *Bibliotheca Orientalis* 27 (1970): 306–7; I am much indebted here to the explanations furnished by M. Bierbrier, "The Date of the Destruction of Emar and Egyptian Chronology," *JEA* 64 (1978): 136–37. At n. 2, Bierbrier notes that "Professor Brinkman now informs me that his latest date for year 2 is 1185±5 B.C."

[9] Jacques Freu, "La tablette RS 86.2230 et la phase finale du royaume d'Ugarit," *Syria* 65 (1988): 395–98. Tablets found at Ras Ibn Hani had already established that Hammurapi's reign overlapped that of Merneptah, and the new tablet indicates that Hammurapi was still on the throne when Bay, the "Grand Chancellor" for Siptah and Queen Twosret, held his office.

[10] Ibid., 398.

The relative chronology supplied by Mycenaean pottery must be fit into the absolute framework derived from Egypt. It now seems probable that the transition from LH IIIB to IIIC pottery occurred no earlier than the reign of Queen Twosret. On the low Egyptian chronology this would mean that IIIB pottery was still being produced ca. 1190 B.C.[11] Since that is only a terminus post quem, and since it is likely that a few years elapsed between the last of the IIIB wares and the resumption of pottery making in the Argolid, the earliest IIIC pots probably were not made before ca. 1185. The destruction at Tiryns and Mycenae may have occurred shortly before Ramesses III came to power. A few sites in the Aegean, on the other hand, seem to have been destroyed several decades before the end of the IIIB period, evidently while Ramesses the Great still reigned.

Altogether, then, the Catastrophe seems to have begun with sporadic destructions in the last quarter of the thirteenth century, gathered momentum in the 1190s, and raged in full fury in the 1180s. By about 1175 the worst was apparently over, although dreadful things continued to happen throughout the twelfth century. Let us now take a close look at the physical destruction that the Catastrophe entailed.

[11] For a discussion of all the evidence on the end of IIIB and the beginning of IIIC see Peter Warren and Vronwy Hankey, *Aegean Bronze Age Chronology* (Bristol, 1989), 158–62. The most important synchronism comes from a faience vase with Twosret's cartouche found in a shrine at Deir ʿAlla (ancient Succoth), along with a range of LH IIIB pottery. Warren and Hankey note that the pots were not heirlooms but functional vessels in the service of the sanctuary. The authors adopt Kitchen's slightly later dates for the last rulers of the Nineteenth Dynasty and so conclude (p. 161) that "we may place the boundary between IIIB and IIIC c. 1185/80 BC, the time of Tewosret or a few years later."

Chapter Two

THE CATASTROPHE SURVEYED

ANATOLIA

A T EVERY Anatolian site known to have been important in the Late
Bronze Age the Catastrophe left a destruction level.[1] Figure 1
shows a wide distribution of places in Asia Minor that ca. 1200
B.C. suffered what Kurt Bittel described as a "Brandkatastrophe." Four of
these sites are within the arc of the Halys River, the heartland of the Great
Kingdom of Hatti, and perhaps this region of Anatolia suffered more than
others. In the centuries following the Catastrophe the intra-Halys sites
seem to have been occupied only by squatters, and it is safe to say that for a
long time after 1200 there were no cities in the area.

Hattusas itself was plundered and burned at the beginning of the twelfth
century (since no Mycenaean pottery was found in the destruction level,
correlation with Aegean sites is problematic). The excavators found ash,
charred wood, mudbricks, and slag formed when mudbricks melted from
the intense heat of the conflagration. The nearby site of Alaca Höyük,
twenty kilometers to the northeast, suffered a similar fate: an ashy destruction level extends over the entire excavated surface. Southeast of Hattusas,
the Hittite city at Alishar—protected by a stout wall—was destroyed by
fire.[2] A hundred kilometers to the east, at Maşat Höyük, a palace that had
helped to anchor the frontier against the Kaskans went up in flames
early in the twelfth century. Here some LH IIIB pottery supplies a rough
synchronism.[3]

Between the Sangarios and the Halys three sites have been excavated, but
only one seems to have been destroyed in the Catastrophe. Gordion and
Polatli have yielded no evidence of destruction, but Karaoglan met a fiery
and violent end. Skeletal remains of the victims were found on the site.[4] On

[1] Kurt Bittel surveyed the evidence on Anatolia at the Zwettl symposium: cf. his "Die
archäologische Situation in Kleinasien um 1200 v. Chr. und während der nachfolgenden vier
Jahrhunderte," in Sigrid Deger-Jalkotzy, ed., *Griechenland, die Ägäis und die Levante während der "Dark Ages"* (Vienna, 1983), 25–47.

[2] H. H. von der Osten, *The Alishar Hüyük: Seasons of 1930–1932* (Chicago, 1937), 289.

[3] Bittel, "Kleinasien," 34, suggests that because Maşat is so distant from the Aegean we
should perhaps allow the pottery "einiges Nachlebens." If so, a date even later than 1190 will
not be excluded.

[4] Ibid., 31.

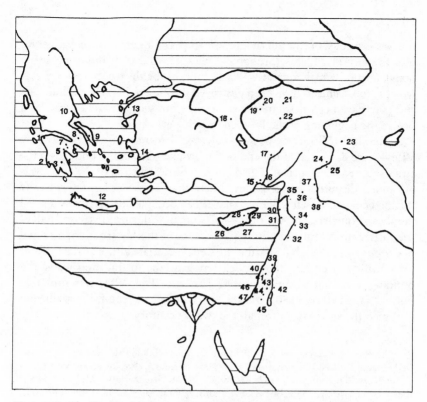

FIGURE 1. The Eastern Mediterranean: Major sites destroyed in the Catastrophe

GREECE

1. Teichos Dymaion
2. Pylos
3. Nichoria
4. The Menelaion
5. Tiryns
6. Midea
7. Mycenae
8. Thebes
9. Lefkandi
10. Iolkos

CRETE

11. Kydonia
12. *Knossos*

ANATOLIA

13. Troy
14. *Miletus*
15. Mersin

16. Tarsus
17. Fraktin
18. Karaoglan
19. Hattusas
20. Alaca Höyük
21. Maşat
22. Alishar Höyük
23. Norşuntepe
24. Tille Höyük
25. Lidar Höyük

CYPRUS

26. Palaeokastro
27. Kition
28. Sinda
29. Enkomi

SYRIA

30. Ugarit
31. Tell Sukas

32. Kadesh
33. Qatna
34. Hamath
35. Alalakh
36. Aleppo
37. *Carchemish*
38. Emar

SOUTHERN LEVANT

39. Hazor
40. Akko
41. Megiddo
42. Deir 'Alla
43. Bethel
44. Beth Shemesh
45. Lachish
46. Ashdod
47. Ashkelon

* At sites in italics destruction in the Catastrophe is probable but not certain.

the western coast of Anatolia a far more important Late Bronze Age center was the city of Miletus (probably Milawata, or Milawanda, in Hittite texts), around which a great wall was built in the thirteenth century B.C. Miletus too seems to have been destroyed during the LH IIIC period. The site may have been desolate for some time but was apparently resettled before the beginning of the Protogeometric period.[5]

At the site of Hissarlik two consecutive settlements—Troy VIh and Troy VIIa—were destroyed at the end of the Bronze Age, and in both cases the cities seem to have burned. The dates for the destruction of the two levels are much disputed, but it is now likely that Troy VI—an impressively fortified citadel, which is likely to have been occupied primarily by a royal family, its courtiers, and warriors—fell sometime during the second half of the thirteenth century B.C. In the aftermath of that destruction, a crowd of people—humbler, but sharing the same material culture as the lords of Troy VIh—moved into the citadel, repairing the fortification walls and building a warren of small houses. This city, Troy VIIa, was probably burned ca. 1190 or 1180,[6] but the survivors again rebuilt the walls and occupied the site (VIIb) through the twelfth century.

---

[5] The most lucid discussion of the evidence on Miletus is still that provided by Vincent Desborough, *The Last Mycenaeans and Their Successors: An Archaeological Survey c. 1200– c. 1000 B.C.* (Oxford, 1964), 162–63. Although Fritz Schachermeyr, *Mykene und das Hethiterreich* (Vienna, 1986), discussed at great length the Milawata of Hittite sources, he said nothing about the fate of Bronze Age Miletus.

[6] Blegen's argument that Troy VI was destroyed in the middle and Troy VIIa toward the end of the IIIB period is still widely accepted, but his dates—ca. 1275 and ca. 1240—are nowadays generally regarded as much too high (Blegen's dates were based on the high Egyptian chronology and on the assumption that LH IIIC began at the end of Merneptah's reign). The present excavator at Hissarlik, Manfred Korfmann, suggests that Troy VI was destroyed ca. 1250, and VIIa ca. 1180. See Korfmann, "Altes und Neues aus Troia," *Das Altertum* 36 (1990): 232. As noted in chapter 1, it now appears that the transition to LH IIIC can be placed no earlier than the reign of Queen Twosret. Even if one accepts Blegen's analysis of the pottery, but follows the Egyptologists' low chronology, one could date the fall of Troy VIIa as late as 1190, and of Troy VI as late as 1225. But even lower dates are probable. Studies of the pottery have convinced several specialists that VIIa was still standing in the IIIC period. For the arguments, see Michael Wood, *In Search of the Trojan War* (New York, 1985), 224; and D. Easton, "Has the Trojan War Been Found?" *Antiquity* 59 (1985): 189. If IIIC sherds were indeed found in VIIa levels, the destruction date for VIIa would be no earlier than ca. 1180, and Troy VI could have been destroyed in the last quarter of the thirteenth century. The most radical of the new schemes is that of Christian Podzuweit, "Die mykenische Welt und Troja," in B. Hänsel, ed., *Südosteuropa zwischen 1600 und 1000 v. Chr.* (Moreland, 1982), 65–88. Podzuweit reanalyzed the pottery from Troy VIh and VII and concluded that *late* LH IIIC pottery was used not only in the VIIa settlement but also in the VIh city. If one accepts Podzuweit's analysis, one would need to date the destruction of the great city—Troy VI—to the second half of the twelfth century. Podzuweit concludes that the much humbler settlement of Troy VIIa fell "in die ersten Jahrzente des 11. Jahrhunderts" (p. 83).

In southeastern Anatolia two important sites—Mersin and Tarsus—were burned during the Catastrophe, and here too there was recovery. Twelfth-century Tarsus was in fact a sizeable city, and a few pieces of LH IIIC pottery show that it was in sporadic contact with the Aegean. On the headwaters of the Seyhan River, two miles from the rock reliefs at Fraktin, unknown aggressors destroyed a Hittite town "durch eine grosse Brandkatastrophe," probably after 1190 B.C. (the date depends on a single LH IIIC1 stirrup jar found in the destruction debris).[7] Finally, on the upper Euphrates in eastern Anatolia other centers were burned in the Catastrophe: the excavations at Lidar Höyük (150 kilometers upstream from Carchemish) and at nearby Tille Höyük, as well as those at Norşuntepe (on the Murat Nehri, near Elazig) show that the Late Bronze Age structures there were destroyed in site-wide conflagrations.[8]

CYPRUS

Bronze Age Cyprus has become very interesting, since archaeological work on the island has in the last thirty years moved at a faster pace than in either Syria or Anatolia. The Catastrophe in Cyprus divides Late Cypriote II from LC III (LC III is thus contemporary with LH IIIC in Greece). Recent excavations have shown that the LC II period was one of general prosperity. Ashlar masonry, which had been regarded as an innovation of the post-Catastrophe period in Cyprus, now seems to have been employed in civic architecture for much of the thirteenth century.[9]

Among the major Cypriote cities that were sacked and burned at the end of LC II were Enkomi, Kition, and Sinda.[10] In fact each of the three sites may—like Troy—have been destroyed twice in the period of a few decades. The old view was that there were two waves of destruction, the first ca.

[7] Bittel, "Kleinasien," 31 and 34.

[8] Harald Hauptmann, *Arch. Arz.* 1991, 351, reports that Lidar Höyök was destroyed "in das 1. Viertel des 12. Jhs." On the 1989 salvage excavations at Tille Höyük, which discovered a "large burnt building" destroyed ca. 1200 B.C., see S. R. Blaylock, *AS* 41 (1991): 4–5. On Norşuntepe see Bittel, "Kleinasien," 33.

[9] Ashlar blocks have been found in LC II contexts at Ayios Dhimitrios and Palaeokastro. At Vournes, near Maroni, Gerald Cadogan has found an ashlar building that should be dated "probably to the earlier part of the 13th century." See Cadogan, "Maroni and the Late Bronze Age of Cyprus," in V. Karageorghis and J. Muhly, *Cyprus at the Close of the Late Bronze Age* (Nicosia, 1984), 8.

[10] James Muhly, "The Role of the Sea Peoples in Cyprus during the LC III Period," in Karageorghis and Muhly, *Cyprus*, 41. For a full survey of the Catastrophe in Cyprus see Vassos Karageorghis, *The End of the Late Bronze Age in Cyprus* (Nicosia, 1990); and the same author's "The Crisis Years: Cyprus," in Ward and Joukowsky, *Crisis Years*, 79–86.

1230 B.C. and the second ca. 1190 (those dates were predicated on the assumption that 1230 was the approximate date for the beginning of LH IIIC). Paul Åström has revised and compressed all this, dating the first set of conflagrations to ca. 1190 and the second to the eighth year of Ramesses III (1179). A more radical solution, advanced by James Muhly and accepted by Vassos Karageorghis, is to recognize only one wave of destructions in Cyprus and to date it to the end of LC IIC.[11] In any case, at all three sites— Sinda, in the interior, and Enkomi and Kition on the southern coast—there was reconstruction after the Catastrophe, and a sizeable community through the twelfth century.

Several smaller sites were not destroyed in the Catastrophe but abandoned. In a Late Cypriote IIC city at Ayios Dhimitrios (on the Vasilikos River, a few kilometers downstream from Kalavasos and some three kilometers up from the south coast) there is some trace of burning, but "the evidence does not suggest a great conflagration or deliberately destructive activities."[12] In addition to much Cypriote pottery, the site yielded LH IIIB but no IIIC imports. Another site abandoned during the Catastrophe was Kokkinokremos, in southeastern Cyprus, recently excavated by Karageorghis. This was a short-lived settlement, having been established not much earlier than ca. 1230. Karageorghis discovered that Kokkinokremos

> was abandoned suddenly, obviously as a result of an impending menace. The bronzesmith concealed his fragments of copper ingots and some of his tools and artefacts in a pit in the courtyard, the silversmith concealed his two silver ingots and some scrap metal between two stones of a bench, and the goldsmith carefully put away in a pit all the jewellery and sheets of gold which he had. They were all hoping, as happens in such cases, that they would return and recover their treasures, but they never did.[13]

That none of the three smiths returned to retrieve the hidden valuables suggests that they were killed or enslaved.

On the western coast of Cyprus, at Palaeokastro, Karageorghis unearthed more evidence of the Catastrophe. Here the excavations produced "a layer of thick ashes and débris attesting a violent destruction."[14] The city was rebuilt soon after the disaster, and LH IIIC:1b pottery appeared in the reoccupation level. The reoccupation seems to have lasted about a generation, after which the site was abandoned.[15]

[11] Muhly, "Sea Peoples," 51; Karageorghis, "Crisis Years," 82.

[12] Alison K. South, "Kalavasos-Ayios Dhimitrios and the Late Bronze Age of Cyprus," in Karageorghis and Muhly, Cyprus, 14.

[13] Karageorghis, "New Light on Late Bronze Age Cyprus," in Karageorghis and Muhly, Cyprus, 20.

[14] Ibid., 21.

[15] Catling, AR (1986–87): 71.

SYRIA

How terrible the Catastophe was in the Levant is attested both archae-
ologically and in the Medinet Habu inscription. Because the Levantine
sites were in relatively close contact with Egypt, several of the destruction
levels here have yielded artifacts dated by a royal Egyptian cartouche. The
same sites produced a quantity of Aegean pottery, especially LH IIIB ware,
and thus serve to tie together the ceramic chronology of the Aegean with
the dynastic chronology in Egypt.

The large city of Ugarit, which had been an important center in western
Syria since the Middle Bronze Age, was destroyed by fire at the end of the
Late Bronze Age and was not reoccupied.[16] The destruction level contained LH IIIB but no IIIC ware, and a sword bearing the cartouche of
Merneptah. Because the sword was "in mint condition" it was for some
time taken as evidence that Ugarit was destroyed during Merneptah's
reign. As we shall see in chapter 13, however, the sword is likely to have
been in mint condition primarily because it was unusable. At any rate, a
tablet discovered in 1986 establishes that the burning of Ugarit occurred
well after Merneptah's death and indeed after Bay became Great Chancellor (which he did, on the low chronology, in 1196 B.C.).[17] The last king of
Ugarit was Hammurapi, but although Hammurapi's reign certainly overlapped that of Suppiluliumas II in Hattusas, a more exact Hittite synchronism is not to be had. H. Otten supposed that the fall of Hattusas opened
the way for the destructive assaults on the Cypriote cities and on Ugarit,
while G. A. Lehmann concluded that Ugarit was destroyed *before* Hattusas.[18] The eighth year of Ramesses III is assumed by all to be the terminus
post quem non for the fall of Ugarit. On the chronology followed here, the
conflagration at Ugarit would have occurred sometime after 1196 but
before 1179.

When Ugarit was destroyed some hundred tablets were being baked in
the oven, and so from this site we have documents written on the very eve of
its destruction. One of these tablets "from the oven"—a letter from a
certain *Ydn* to "the king, his master"—mentions *prm* (*hapiru*), and requests that the king "equip 150 ships."[19] A tablet from the Rap'anu Ar-

[16] Marguerite Yon, "The End of the Kingdom of Ugarit," in Ward and Joukowsky, *The
Crisis Years*, 111–22.

[17] According to Freu, "Tablette," 398, "il faut donc abaisser la date de la destruction
d'Ugarit aprés 1195, sans doute pas avant 1190."

[18] On the relative sequence of the destruction of Ugarit and Hattusas see H. Otten, "Die
letzte Phase des hethitischen Grossreiches nach den Texten," in Deger-Jalkotzy, *Griechenland*,
21; and Lehmann's remarks in the discussion that followed Otten's paper (*Griechenland*, 22–
23).

[19] RS 18.148 = no. 62 (pp. 88–89) in *PRU*, vol. 5.

chive, and so somewhat earlier than the oven tablets, indicates the kind of threat that the last kings of Ugarit and Alashia faced (the tablet is a letter from the king of Ugarit to the king of Alashia):[20] "behold, the enemy's ships came (here); my cities (?) were burned, and they did evil things in my country. Does not my father know that all my troops and chariots (?) are in the Hittite country, and all my ships are in the land of Lycia? . . . Thus, the country is abandoned to itself. May my father know it: the seven ships of the enemy that came here inflicted much damage upon us." The king of Ugarit closes the letter with a plea that the king of Alashia send a warning, by any means possible, if he learns of other enemy ships in the vicinity. This letter is one of three from the Rap'anu Archive that were sent between Alashia and Ugarit, all concerned with "the enemy" who suddenly sail in, wreak havoc and raze cities, and then sail away.[21]

Not far from Ugarit, the coastal settlement at Ras Ibn Hani was destroyed at the same time as the capitol. Here, however, there is evidence that the site was re-used very soon after the destruction.[22] Tell Sukas, another coastal site, also shows a destruction level at this time.[23] The great inland cities of western Syria were also burned. Going upstream on the Orontes ca. 1200 B.C. one would have passed Alalakh, Hamath, Qatna, and finally Kadesh (Tell Nebi Mind, on the upper Orontes); apparently all four were sacked.[24] In his excavation of Tell Atchana, Leonard Woolley immediately came down upon the massive destruction level that effectively closed the life of ancient Alalakh.[25] "The burnt ruins of the topmost houses show that the city shared the fate of its more powerful neighbours."[26]

Cities in eastern Syria may have been less affected by the Catastrophe. Aleppo, lying midway between the Orontes and the Euphrates, was apparently sacked.[27] But Carchemish, on the Euphrates, may have escaped. Although included in Ramesses III's list of places destroyed by his opponents, there is reason to believe that Carchemish survived. Archaeological work done there early in this century did not identify a destruction level that could be assigned to this period. Tablets from Ugarit show that Talmi-

[20] RS 20.238, from the Rap'anu Archive. Translation from Michael Astour, "New Evidence on the Last Days of Ugarit," *AJA* 69 (1965): 255.

[21] The letters are RS 20.18, RS L1, and RS 20.238; these are, respectively, nos. 22, 23, and 24 in *Ugaritica*, vol. 5.

[22] See the summary by Annie Caubet, "Reoccupation of the Syrian Coast after the Destruction of the 'Crisis Years,'" in Ward and Joukowsky, *Crisis Years*, 124–27.

[23] R. D. Barnett, "The Sea Peoples," *CAH*, vol. 2, part 2, p. 370.

[24] See G. A. Lehmann, *Die mykenisch-frühgriechische Welt und der östliche Mittelmeerraum in der Zeit der "Seevölker"-Invasionen um 1200 v. Chr.* (Opladen, 1985), 14; Astour, "New Evidence," 254; Barnett, "The Sea Peoples," 370.

[25] Woolley, *A Forgotten Kingdom* (Harmondsworth, 1953), 156–64.

[26] Ibid., 164.

[27] Ibid.

Teshub, king of Carchemish and vassal of Suppiluliumas II, Great King of Hatti, was contemporary with Hammurapi of Ugarit. Recently published tablets indicate that after the destruction of Hattusas the kings of Carchemish began to use the title "Great King of Hatti."[28]

Whatever the fortunes of Carchemish may have been, recent excavations have shown that Emar, downstream from Carchemish on the Euphrates, was destroyed by fire during the Catastrophe.[29] And Emar is that rare site for which, as Annie Caubet has noted, we have "evidence for both the destroyers and the chronology."[30] Two tablets found here report that "hordes of enemies" attacked the city, the attack evidently occurring in the second year of Melik-shipak, king of Babylon (ca. 1185 B.C.). The dating formula employed on these two tablets shows that at Emar the year just concluded was described as "l'année où les *tarvu* ont affligé la ville," *tarvu* being translated by D. Arnaud as "hordes," or as masses for whom the scribes of Emar had no proper name or conventional designation.

THE SOUTHERN LEVANT

The Catastrophe took a heavy toll in Palestine and what in the Iron Age was called Israel. At Deir ʿAlla (ancient Succoth) a settlement was destroyed after 1190 B.C., since the destruction level yielded, along with much LH IIIB pottery, a vase bearing the cartouche of Queen Twosret.[31] Lachish may have been destroyed at the same time or a few years later. LH IIIB pottery was found throughout Stratum VI at Lachish, which underlies the destruction level, but there is some indication that Stratum VI did not end until the reign of Ramesses III. If that is so, LH IIIB wares were still being produced in the late 1180s, some years after they are generally supposed to have been superseded by LH IIIC. Trude Dothan, however, has proposed that after the destruction of Lachish a limited settlement, "probably an Egyptian garrison," was established above the ruins.[32] On this argument, the soldiers or squatters were there in the reign of Ramesses III, but the destruction of the city (and the last importation of LH IIIB pottery) had occurred before Ramesses' accession.

[28] J. D. Hawkins, "Kuzi-Tešub and the 'Great Kings' of Karkamiš," *AS* 38 (1988): 99–108.

[29] See Arnaud, "Les textes d'Emar," 87–92.

[30] Caubet, "Reoccupation," 129.

[31] H. J. Franken, "The Excavations at Deir ʿAlla, Jordan," *VT* 11 (1961): 361–72. Trude Dothan, "Some Aspects of the Appearance of the Sea Peoples and Philistines in Canaan," in Deger-Jalkotzy, *Griechenland*, 101, notes that the Twosret cartouche provides us with "the *terminus ad quem* for Myc. IIIB pottery."

[32] Dothan, "Sea Peoples and Philistines," 101; cf. her review of *Lachish*, vol. 4, in *IEJ* 10 (1960): 58–63.

The important centers along the Via Maris of Palestine, the route that led from Egypt to Syria (and more particularly from Gaza to Jaffa), were virtually all destroyed in the Catastrophe. Megiddo seems to have held out the longest, Stratum VII running without interruption from the thirteenth century until ca. 1150 B.C.[33] Among the earlier victims were Ashdod, Ashkelon, and Akko. For Ashdod no Egyptian synchronism is available, but the ceramics indicate an early twelfth-century date: the predestruction Stratum XIV produced LH IIIB pottery, and in the postdestruction Stratum XIII some LH IIIC:1b pottery was found. At any rate, Moshe Dothan excavated at Ashdod a "destruction layer (ca. 85 cm), containing ashes, which indicate that this stratum, in Area A–B, ended in a heavy conflagration."[34] At Akko, the destruction can be dated with some precision. In "the lowest ash refuse layer" of the destruction level was found a scarab with the name of Queen Twosret, evidence that places the destruction of Akko no earlier than 1190.[35] The city was rebuilt, and the excavators found that in the reoccupation the residents used a monochrome pottery closely related to Mycenaean IIIC ware.[36]

In addition to the major cities along the Via Maris, all of which would have been under Egyptian hegemony in the early twelfth century, smaller settlements were also destroyed in the Catastrophe. These little towns would surely have been vassals or dependencies of the major cities, and so would also have been protected, very indirectly, by Egypt's imperial majesty. Among the smaller sites destroyed in the Catastrophe were the towns at Tell Jemmeh, Tell Sippor, and Tell Jerishe.[37]

In the interior, the early twelfth-century destruction at Lachish and Deir ʿAlla has already been mentioned. Other inland sites destroyed at the same time were, from north to south, Tell el-Qedah (Hazor), Beitin (Bethel), Beth Shemesh, Tell el-Hesi (Eglon?), Tell Beit Mirsim (Debir or Eglon), and Khirbet Rabud (possibly Debir).[38] As everywhere else, these cities were burned, the destruction being either total or so extensive that archaeolo-

---

[33] William Dever, "The Late Bronze—Early Iron I Horizon in Syria-Palestine: Egyptians, Canaanites, 'Sea Peoples,' and Proto-Israelites," in Ward and Joukowsky, Crisis Years, 101.

[34] M. Dothan, "Ashdod at the End of the Late Bronze Age and the Beginning of the Iron Age," in Frank Cross, ed., Symposia Celebrating the Seventy-Fifth Anniversary of the Founding of the American Schools of Oriental Research (1900–1975) (Cambridge, Mass., 1979), 126.

[35] Trude Dothan, "Sea Peoples and Philistines," 104. Dothan goes on to say that the scarab "may provide a terminus ante quem for the destruction of the Late Bronze city." But it is a terminus post quem that the scarab actually gives us.

[36] Ibid., 103.

[37] Ibid., 108; for a tabular presentation of Palestinian sites destroyed and spared see Dever, "Late Bronze," 100.

[38] Paul Lapp, "The Conquest of Palestine in the Light of Archaeology," Concordia Theological Monthly 38 (1967): 283–300.

gists assume that virtually the entire city was destroyed. After the destruction, most of the sites in the interior were soon occupied by squatters: at Hazor, Succoth, and Debir there are traces of post-Catastrophe huts or small houses, storage silos, and crude ovens.[39] Some cities near the coast, on the other hand, were substantially rebuilt. At Tell Ashdod and Tell Mor there is evidence for considerable occupation after the Catastrophe.[40]

A few settlements, finally, were spared. There is evidence for continuous occupation from the thirteenth century through all or most of the twelfth at a number of major sites: Beth Shan, Taanach, Jerusalem, Shechem, Gezer, and Gibeon. Still other sites show no destruction in the late thirteenth or early twelfth century because they were unoccupied at that time: paradoxically, Jericho and Ai, two of the cities whose destruction is dramatically described for us (Joshua 6–8 celebrates the slaughter of all the inhabitants of Jericho and Ai, and the burning of the two cities), were deserted tells at the time of the Catastrophe.[41]

MESOPOTAMIA

The closest the Catastrophe came to Mesopotamia was the destruction of Norşuntepe, in eastern Anatolia, and of the Syrian cities of Emar and—possibly—Carchemish. Emar was destroyed by nameless "hordes" and perhaps the same can be assumed for Norşuntepe. The Euphrates river and the Jezirah may have furnished something of a barrier to protect the Mesopotamian cities from the devastation experienced in the Levant, but it is also likely that the kingdom of Assur served as a deterrent. Generally, Mesopotamian history in the late thirteenth and twelfth centuries follows the pattern of earlier times.[42] Wars were common, but they were between perenniel rivals. It was primarily the palaces at Babylon and Assur that competed for primacy, with the kingdom of Elam playing a major role from time to time.

It is instructive to see what the kings of Assur were able to accomplish before, during, and after the Catastrophe. Tukulti-Ninurta I (1244–1208 B.C.) was perhaps the greatest of the Middle Assyrian kings. After subduing the barbarians who lived to the east, in the Zagros mountains, he marched

---

[39] Norman Gottwald, *The Tribes of Yahweh: A Sociology of the Religion of Liberated Israel, 1250–1050 B.C.E.* (Maryknoll, N.Y., 1979), 195.

[40] Moshe Dothan, "Ashdod," 127–28.

[41] William Stiebing, Jr., *Out of the Desert? Archaeology and the Exodus/Conquest Narratives* (Buffalo, 1989), 80–86.

[42] For the history of Mesopotamia see the relevant chapters by J. M. Munn-Rankin, D. J. Wiseman, and René Labat in *CAH*, vol. 2, part 2; for a summary directly pertinent to the present study see Richard L. Zettler, "Twelfth-Century B.C. Babylonia: Continuity and Change," 174–81, in Ward and Joukowsky, *Crisis Years*.

through the mountains of Kurdistan and reached the district of Lakes Van and Urmia. His greatest triumph may have come in 1235, when he defeated the Kassite king of Babylon; soon thereafter he captured Babylon, and his underlings governed there for perhaps seven years. When Tukulti-Ninurta was murdered by his son, Assyrian power was riven in faction and Assur's dominion rapidly receded, but Assur and the other cities of the Assyrian heartland came through the Catastrophe unscathed. Ashur-dan I defeated Babylon in 1160 and took from it several frontier cities. His successors apparently had no difficulty maintaining their rule over the Assyrian heartland in the second half of the twelfth century, but they did have to do battle against Akhlamu and Aramu warriors (both names probably refer to Aramaic-speaking tribesmen) who threatened on the north and west of Assyria. Still more serious was an invasion by twenty thousand warriors from Mushki, under five chieftains, who crossed the Taurus mountains and raided the lands around the upper Tigris. But the Mushkians were beaten by Tiglath-Pileser I (1115–1077) in a great battle in the mountains of Kurdistan.

In southern Mesopotamia the Kassite line reestablished itself in Babylon after its interruption by Tukulti-Ninurta and enjoyed another forty years of dominion. Apparently it was while Melik-shipak ruled at Babylon (1188–1174) that so many cities in the Levant were destroyed, but neither Melik-shipak nor his son seems to have experienced serious trouble. Trouble did come in 1157, when the city of Babylon was stormed and parts of it were burned by the Elamites. Although this incident might be reminiscent of the Catastrophe, the "sacking" of Babylon in 1157 seems to have been relatively limited and fits quite well within the normal expectations of Mesopotamian history: three years after having been beaten and humiliated by Ashur-dan, a weak Kassite king was defeated by Shutruk-Nahhunte, the king of Elam, and his large army. The Elamite king allowed his troops to plunder parts of the city—razing some sections in order to teach the occupants a lesson—and he then removed the statue of Marduk to Elam. Although Shutruk-Nahhunte put an end to the Kassite dynasty, he made no effort to subjugate Babylon permanently and certainly did not destroy the city. Soon after his departure a new Babylonian dynasty was established by a warlord from Isin. Babylon not only recovered its independence but also established some control over towns as far north as the Diyala river.

EGYPT

Like Mesopotamia, Egypt was spared the destruction of its centers during the Catastrophe. It was not, however, spared the fear of destruction, for between 1208 and 1176 the pharaohs had to battle repeatedly against invaders who threatened to do in Egypt what had already been done in Anatolia and the Levant. Because the kingdom of Egypt survived the Catastrophe we have Egyptian inscriptions advertising what happened there during the years in which so many other lands lost their principal cities and palaces.

In some respects, it is true, Egypt did not survive the Catastrophe. Although prosperous and secure during the long reign of Ramesses the Great, after the accession of Merneptah Egypt entered upon a time of troubles that effectively ended its long history as the dominant power in the Near East. Merneptah and Ramesses III were able to repel the attacks upon Egypt and then celebrate their accomplishments in a princely fashion, but they were virtually the last of the great pharaohs. The successors of Ramesses III were hard-pressed to maintain any Egyptian presence in the Levant. Under Ramesses IV (1155–1149) there may still have been Egyptian garrisons at Beth Shan and a few other strategic posts in southern Canaan, but they must soon have been overrun or withdrawn.[43] The last evidence of Egyptian power so far north is the name of Ramesses VI (1141–1133) inscribed on a bronze statue base at Megiddo.[44] At home, the last kings of the Twentieth Dynasty left few architectural or inscriptional monuments, and in the Twenty-First Dynasty royal power in Egypt reached a low ebb.

The victories of Merneptah and Ramesses III were thus the swan song of the Egyptian New Kingdom. Merneptah celebrated his triumphs in various places, but especially in the Great Karnak Inscription and on the Hymn of Victory Stele (sometimes referred to as the "Israel Stele"), found across the river, at Thebes.[45] For our purposes, however, the inscriptions of Merneptah and Ramesses III are important not so much because they are a final celebration of pharaonic power but because they illuminate the nature of the dangers that Egypt and many other kingdoms faced in the Catastrophe. Merneptah's troubles began in his fifth year, 1208 B.C., when a Libyan king named Meryre attacked the western Delta. Meryre brought with him an enormous army, most of his men being from Libya itself but a fair number being auxiliaries from "the northern lands." They are identified by Merneptah's scribe as *Ekwesh, Lukka, Shardana, Shekelesh,* and *Tursha*.[46] The Libyan warlord also brought with him his wife, children, and even his throne, obviously intending to set himself up as ruler of the west-

[43] James Weinstein, "The Collapse of the Egyptian Empire in the Southern Levant," in Ward and Joukowsky, *Crisis Years,* 142–50.

[44] Weinstein, "Collapse," 144; Itamar Singer, "Merneptah's Campaign to Canaan and the Egyptian Occupation of the Southern Coastal Plain of Palestine in the Ramesside Period," *BASOR* 269 (1988): 6.

[45] For the Great Karnak Inscription see Breasted, *AR,* vol. 3, nos. 572–92; for the Hymn of Victory Stele, see nos. 602–17. Lesko, "Egypt," 153–55, has argued that the "year 5" and "year 8" inscriptions of Ramesses III at Medinet Habu were originally cut for Merneptah's mortuary temple.

[46] Breasted, *AR* 3, no. 574.

ern Delta. Against the invaders Merneptah mustered all his forces, and on the third day of the third month of summer he defeated them at Periri, the precise location of which is disputed. It was undoubtedly a long and difficult battle. According to the inscription on the Athribis stele, Merneptah's army slew over 6000 Libyans, as well as 2201 *Ekwesh*, 722 *Tursha*, and 200 *Shekelesh* (how many *Lukka* and *Shardana* were killed cannot be determined).[47] The Libyan king fled in disorder and disgrace.

The Hymn of Victory Stele, although primarily celebrating the victory over the Libyans and their allies, shows that Merneptah also conducted a major campaign in Canaan.[48] He claims here to have "plundered" and "pacified" various places, including several cities (Ashkelon and Gezer; Yanoam too was evidently a city). The land of Canaan and the peoples of Israel and Hurru were chastised.[49] Until recently Merneptah's claims to have campaigned in southern Canaan were dismissed as mere propaganda; but Frank Yurco discovered that wall reliefs, which were once attributed to Ramesses II and in which the capture of Ashkelon is portrayed, were actually commissioned by Merneptah.[50] It now seems that Ashkelon and Gezer must have declared their independence from Egypt at the outset of Merneptah's reign and were brought to heel by this elderly but surprisingly energetic pharaoh.[51] The trouble presented by men of Israel must have been something new. Here Merneptah was dealing not with the cities that had traditionally been Egypt's concern but with uncivilized tribesmen. Merneptah evidently battled against them and inflicted some casualties: "their seed is not," he announced. Since the offense of the tribesmen of Israel was not the withholding of tribute or the renunciation of allegiance to Merneptah, it is likely to have been something indirect, such as an assault against one or more of the pharaoh's vassal cities in southern Canaan.

From the reigns of Merneptah's ephemeral successors we have no record of foreign conflicts. That certainly does not mean that barbarians on both

---

[47] Ibid., no. 601 (in the Karnak Inscription the figures are slightly different).

[48] The text of this stele has also been translated by Wilson, *ANET*, 376–78.

[49] For a recent treatment of this much-debated text see J. J. Bimson, "Merenptah's Israel and Recent Theories of Israelite Origins," *JSOT* 49 (1991): 3–29.

[50] In 1977, while working on his doctoral dissertation, Yurco examined the reliefs that flank the "Peace Treaty Text" and discovered that the original cartouches (underlying those of Seti II) belonged not to Ramesses II, as had been assumed, but to Merneptah. See Yurco, "Merenptah's Canaanite Campaign," *JARCE* 23 (1986): 189–215; and the same author's "3200-Year-Old Picture of Israelites found in Egypt," *Bib. Arch. Rev.* 16 (1990): 20 ff. See also Lawrence Stager, "Merenptah, Israel, and Sea Peoples: New Light on an Old Relief," *Eretz-Israel* 18 (1985): 61–62. For objections to the identification see D. Redford, "The Ashkelon Relief at Karnak and the Israel Stele," *IEJ* 36 (1986): 188–200; for Yurco's reply see "Once Again, Merenptah's Battle Reliefs at Karnak," *IEJ* (forthcoming).

[51] Singer, "Merneptah's Campaign," 3.

frontiers had ceased to cause problems or to insult Egyptian interests. Dreadful things were beginning to happen in the 1190s, and in Canaan especially Egypt's vassals must have been crying for assistance. But the last representatives of the Nineteenth Dynasty—Seti II, Siptah, and Twosret—had all to do to keep a feeble grasp on the throne.

With the establishment of the Twentieth Dynasty our documentation resumes,[52] and it is obvious that the situation has become more parlous than it had been under Merneptah. Ramesses III faced no less than three attacks upon the Delta in his first eleven years. In his fifth year (1182 B.C.) a Libyan force that must have been counted in the tens of thousands (Ramesses claimed to have slain 12,535 of the invaders) attacked the western Delta. Three years later, in 1179, a force consisting mostly of Philistines and *Tjekker*, but assisted by men whom his scribe identified as *Shekelesh*, *Denyen*, *Weshesh*, and apparently *Tursha*, attacked from the east. Ramesses bested the invaders in a land battle at Djahi, somewhere in the southern Levant, and defeated another contingent of the same coalition in a sea battle. Finally, in his eleventh year (1176) Ramesses had to face yet another Libyan invasion. The inscriptions credit Ramesses with the slaughter of 2175 *Meshwesh* tribesmen (and the capture of another 1200) on this occasion.[53] Altogether, the assaults upon Egypt in the reign of Ramesses III seem to have constituted the most serious external threat that Egypt had faced since the invasion of the *hyksos* in the seventeenth century B.C.

GREECE AND THE AEGEAN ISLANDS

None of the palaces of Late Helladic Greece survived very far into the twelfth century B.C.[54] The nature of the Catastrophe here has been well defined by Richard Hope Simpson and Oliver Dickinson: "By the end of LH IIIB almost all the great mainland centres had been destroyed by fire, several being deserted thereafter. The destructions seem to concentrate at sites where there were palaces or comparable large buildings, or fortifications."[55] Since a great deal of archaeological work has been done in

[52] Breasted, *AR*, vol. 4, nos. 21–138.

[53] Edgerton and Wilson, *Historical Records of Ramses III: The Texts in "Medinet Habu," Volumes I and II, Translated with Explanatory Notes* (Chicago: University of Chicago Press, 1936), plate 75.

[54] The standard survey of the Catastrophe in Greece is Vincent Desborough's *The Last Mycenaeans and Their Successors: An Archaeological Survey c. 1200–c. 1000 B.C.* (Oxford, 1964). R. Hope Simpson and O.T.P.K. Dickinson, *A Gazetteer of Aegean Civilisation in the Bronze Age*, vol. 1: *The Mainland and Islands* (Göteborg, 1979), provide an excellent site-by-site summary.

[55] Hope Simpson and Dickinson, *Gazetteer*, 379.

Greece, hundreds of Bronze Age sites from the mainland and the islands are known. The following survey will focus on the destruction of the principal IIIB sites. But because we are fortunate to have considerable material evidence for Greece in the period immediately following the Catastrophe, we may also note the several places that became important communities (some of them deserving to be called cities) in the IIIC period.

In Greece the northernmost evidence for the Catastrophe (see figure 1) comes from the settlement and "palace" at Iolkos. Unfortunately, the site has not been well published, and one cannot be sure what happened here. The palace (from which fresco fragments and much pottery was recovered) was evidently burned, probably early in the LH IIIC period. Iolkos may, however, have continued to be occupied after the destruction of the palace, for a considerable amount of IIIC pottery was found at the site. Although there is evidence for a Protogeometric settlement at Iolkos, it is not clear whether habitation was continuous from IIIC to Protogeometric times.[56]

One of the first of the Greek palaces to be sacked was apparently the Theban palace, well before the end of LH IIIB. It may have been rebuilt, only to be destroyed for a second time at the end of IIIB. From the IIIC period chamber tombs but no buildings have been found.[57] It is therefore doubtful that Thebes was a significant settlement in the middle of the twelfth century.

On the Euboean coast a town at Lefkandi (or more precisely at "Xeropolis," a few hundred yards east of Lefkandi) was destroyed at least once during the Catastrophe. No evidence for destruction at the end of LH IIIB has been found, but that may be because early in the IIIC period there was much new building at the site (whatever the IIIB settlement may have been, the IIIC settlement was considerably larger and deserves to be called a city). This city was "destroyed in a great conflagration" during the IIIC period; but it was immediately rebuilt and continued to be occupied until ca. 1100, when it was finally abandoned.[58]

For Athens, the only conclusion now possible is a *non liquet*. Since there are no remains of an LH IIIB palace, we cannot know what may have happened to it in the early twelfth century. It is likely, however, that the IIIC settlement at Athens was much smaller than the preceding settlement, since the IIIB houses on the north slope of the Acropolis were unoccupied in the later period, and very few IIIC burials have been found in the Agora.[59]

[56] Desborough, *Last Mycenaeans*, 128–29; Hope Simpson and Dickinson, *Gazetteer*, 273.

[57] Hope Simpson and Dickinson, *Gazetteer*, 244–45; see also Fritz Schachermeyr, *Griechische Frühgeschichte* (Vienna, 1984), 119–22 ("Palastkatastrophe in Theben").

[58] M. R. Popham, L. H. Sackett, et al., eds., *Lefkandi I: The Dark Age* (London, 1980), 7.

[59] Desborough, *Last Mycenaeans*, 113; Hope Simpson and Dickinson, *Gazetteer*, 198–99.

Perhaps the largest community in Attica during the IIIC period was on Attica's east coast. At Perati, on the north side of the Porto Rafti bay, a cemetery of more than two hundred chamber tombs from the IIIC period has been excavated. The town was undoubtedly near the cemetery but has not yet been found. The Perati tombs furnish much of what is known about IIIC Attica.[60]

On the Corinthian Isthmus attention focuses on a fortification wall, built late in the thirteenth century B.C. Apparently intended to span the entire isthmus, the wall may never have been completed. It is usually assumed that it was built by Peloponnesians who feared an attack from the north.[61] Almost nothing is known of Corinth in this period, but at nearby Korakou—on the Corinthian Gulf—there is evidence for an LH IIIB settlement (the houses were excavated by Blegen). Although it was once thought that Korakou survived intact into the IIIC period, it is possible that the place may have suffered some damage and was briefly abandoned at the end of IIIB. At any rate, it was certainly reoccupied in IIIC and enjoyed a period of some prosperity before a final destruction and abandonment.[62]

In the northeast Peloponnese almost a hundred Bronze Age sites have been identified, although many of these are known only from surface finds.[63] At those Argolid sites that have been excavated the pattern is clear: shortly after 1200 the site was either destroyed or abandoned. Prosymna and Berbati—both in the interior—were evidently evacuated without being destroyed,[64] and the same was probably true of Lerna. The little unwalled settlement at Zygouries, also in the interior, was apparently destroyed at the end of LH IIIB and was not reoccupied in IIIC.[65]

In his excavations at Mycenae, Wace found evidence for a destruction at the end of LH IIIB, but only in the houses outside the citadel ("House of the Wine Merchant," "House of the Oil Merchant," etc.). His excavations also showed that at the end of LH IIIC the entire site—including everything within the citadel—was burned. On the basis of these findings, the scholarly consensus until the 1960s was that enemies attacked Mycenae ca. 1230 B.C. (the old date for the end of LH IIIB) but were unable to penetrate the citadel itself; and that the citadel was not sacked until the *end* of the

---

[60] Spyridon Iakovides, "Perati, eine Nekropole der Ausklingenden Bronzezeit in Attika," in H.-G. Buchholz, ed., *Ägäische Bronzezeit* (Darmstadt, 1987), 437–77.

[61] Desborough, *Last Mycenaeans*, 85.

[62] For the earlier view see Desborough, *Last Mycenaeans*, 85–86. Jeremy Rutter's dissertation, "The Late Helladic IIIB and IIIC Periods at Korakou and Gonia" (University of Pennsylvania, 1974), pointed out that although no evidence for destruction at Korakou was found, the argumentum ex silentio has little significance since the site provides no stratigraphic record of the transition from IIIB to IIIC.

[63] Hope Simpson and Dickinson, *Gazetteer*, 27–74 (nos. A 1 through A 94a).

[64] Desborough, *Last Mycenaeans*, 77.

[65] Ibid., 84; but cf. Podzuweit, "Mykenische Welt," 70.

twelfth century. This view was shown to be incorrect by George Mylonas, whose twenty years of excavation at that site began in 1958. Mylonas found that the earlier destruction—now dated to the early twelfth century—had indeed included the citadel itself. At that time masonry structures within the fortification walls melted in a fire of great intensity. The LH IIIC pottery from the site thus represents a rebuilding and reoccupation of the citadel settlement.[66]

At Tiryns the citadel itself, along with everything outside it, was burned at the end of LH IIIB. Here too there was a reoccupation, and through the LH IIIC period there was a large town between the citadel walls and the coastline some two hundred meters to the south (today the coastline is a mile from the citadel).[67] At Midea, a two-hour walk from Tiryns, there was likewise destruction by fire at the end of the IIIB period. Unlike Mycenae and Tiryns, Midea was not reoccupied after the destruction.[68]

At Asine, on the gulf coast, Desborough concluded that "habitation in LH IIIB was meagre in the extreme."[69] In the IIIC period, on the other hand, the population of Asine was considerable, and a fair number of houses from this period have been excavated. At Iria, down the coast from Asine, there was a small settlement that had been continuously occupied for at least five centuries; but excavations show that it was destroyed by fire "at the very beginning of LH IIIC, and that the site was abandoned shortly afterwards."[70]

In Laconia the most important LH IIIB site was the Menelaion, on the left bank of the Eurotas, near what would later be Sparta. A large and "palatial" building on this site went up in flames at the end of LH IIIB, after which the site seems to have been abandoned until the eighth century B.C.[71] In post-Catastrophe Laconia the only significant site thus far discovered lies on the east coast, near Monemvasia. Chamber tombs attest to the presence of a IIIC community here (the settlement is supposed to have occupied the acropolis of Epidauros Limera). The quantity of IIIC pottery found in the tombs "suggests that this site was an important survivor in that period."[72]

Between 150 and 200 settlements, most of them tiny, are known from

[66] S. Iakovides, "The Present State of Research at the Citadel of Mycenae," *BIAL* (1977): 99–141.

[67] Klaus Kilian, "Zum Ende der mykenischen Epoche in der Argolis," *Jahrbuch des Römisch-Germanischen Zentralmuseums Mainz* 27 (1980): 166–95.

[68] Paul Åström, "Die Akropolis von Midea um 1200 v. Chr.," in Eberhard Thomas, ed., *Forschungen zur aegaeischen Vorgeschichte: Das Ende der mykenischen Welt (Akten des Internationalen Kolloquiums 7.-8. Juli 1984 in Köln)* (Cologne, 1987), 7–10.

[69] Desborough, *Last Mycenaeans*, 82; cf. Hope Simpson and Dickinson, *Gazetteer*, 49.

[70] Hope Simpson and Dickinson, *Gazetteer*, 50.

[71] Ibid., 107–8.

[72] Ibid., 117; cf. Desborough, *Last Mycenaeans*, 89.

LH IIIB Messenia, and 90 percent of these were abandoned after the burning of the "Palace of Nestor" at Pylos.[73] Most of the abandoned places are known only from a scattering of pottery, and are likely to have been either single homesteads or small clusters of houses. The palace at Pylos was not the only place in Messenia that was destroyed in the Catastrophe. Two towns northeast of the palace—Mouriatadha and Malthi—were destroyed by fire, as was Nichoria on the Messenian Gulf. The date of these destructions can hardly be much later than ca. 1190 B.C., since of the thousands of pots found at Pylos it is questionable whether any have IIIC features.[74]

There is little stratigraphic evidence for the LH III period in Elis, but the pottery found in the area suggests a fairly dense population in IIIB times and a sharp decline in IIIC.[75] The Mycenaean period in Arcadia is even more obscure. It is often assumed, perhaps correctly, that Arcadia was of marginal importance before the Catastrophe. A large cemetery of chamber tombs indicates that in the IIIC period a community of some size was established at Palaiokastro, a few miles east of Andritsana.[76]

For Achaea we do have evidence for sites destroyed by fire during the Catastrophe. But Achaea was also one of the areas to which people moved after the Catastrophe, and a fair number of IIIC settlements are known from their cemeteries (most of which are backed up against the Panachaikon mountain range).[77] At two coastal sites the settlements themselves have been found. In westernmost Achaea, on Cape Araxos, Teichos Dymaion was burned at the end of LH IIIB, but was reoccupied in IIIC and was at that time protected by a fortification wall.[78] At Aigeira, a *Burgberg* facing the Corinthian Gulf, the Austrians have excavated a IIIC settlement.[79]

---

[73] Pia de Fidio, "Fattori di crisi nella Messenia della Tarda Età del Bronzo," in John Killen et al., eds., *Studies in Mycenaean and Classical Greek Presented to John Chadwick* (Salamanca, 1987; *Minos* supplement), 127–28.

[74] Desborough, *Last Mycenaeans*, 94, accepted Blegen's IIIC classification of a dozen Pylos pots; Hope Simpson and Dickinson, *Gazetteer*, 129, believe that the vases which Blegen's team assigned to early LH IIIC "can hardly be placed so late."

[75] Desborough, *Last Mycenaeans*, 91–93.

[76] Hope Simpson and Dickinson, *Gazetteer*, 83.

[77] Emily Vermeule, "The Mycenaeans in Achaea," *AJA* 64 (1960): 1–21.

[78] Cf. the description by Hope Simpson and Dickinson, *Gazetteer*, 196: "A fine acropolis strategically placed on the Araxos promontory at the NW tip of the Peloponnese; the sea would once have covered the present marshes on the SW flank. . . . The site appears to have suffered destruction by fire in LH IIIB, but was reoccupied in strength in LH IIIC, to which the bulk of the finds belong, to be destroyed again and thereafter deserted until LG."

[79] On the situation of the site cf. Gerhard Dobesch, "Historische Fragestellungen in der Urgeschichte," in Deger-Jalkotzy, *Griechenland*, 205n.74: "Aigeira war von Natur aus gut geeignet als Stützpunkt und Wachtposten gegen Seeräuber, die von den Meeren westlich von Griechenland kamen."

Moving to the islands of the Aegean, we find that evidence for the Catastrophe and its aftermath is limited but occasionally quite informative. Recent excavations on the island of Paros have shown that at a citadel now known as Koukounaries there was an extensive LH IIIB complex, possibly deserving to be described as a "palace." The complex was sacked and burned, and the excavators found not only a great deal of ash but also the skeletons of some of the victims. According to D. Schilardi, director of the excavations, "preliminary study indicates that the destruction of Koukounaries is slightly later than the disasters which afflicted the mainland. The pottery should be classified in the transition of LH IIIB2 to LH IIIC."[80] After this destruction in the early twelfth century, the settlement was rebuilt in IIIC and was protected by a fortification wall.[81] In general, however, the Cyclades were not hard hit in the Catastrophe, at least in its early stages. The few major Mycenaean sites on islands in the central and western Aegean (Phylakopi on Melos, Ayia Irini on Kea, and Grotta on Naxos) seem to have survived until late in the IIIC period.[82]

For Rhodes and the other islands of the southeast Aegean evidence comes almost exclusively from tombs, and it is therefore uncertain what did or did not happen to settlements ca. 1200 B.C. The continuity of the cemeteries, however, suggests the essential continuity of population from IIIB to IIIC.[83] On the other hand, there is reason to believe that very new settlement patterns appeared in the twelfth century. The tombs suggest that the city of Ialysos, on the northern coast of Rhodes, enjoyed a fivefold increase in population, and considerable prosperity, while some sites in the southern part of the island were abandoned.[84] On Kos, a settlement has been excavated—the Seraglio site—and here there seems to have been continuous occupation until well down into the IIIC period.[85]

CRETE

What happened on Crete during the Catastrophe is a matter of vigorous debate. There is reason to believe that during the Catastrophe the island suffered as much as did the Greek mainland, but how much evidence there

[80] From D. Schilardi's report on Koukounaries, included in H. Catling's "Archaeology in Greece, 1980–81," in *AR* (1980–81): 36.

[81] See the summaries by H. Catling, *AR* (1988–89): 90; and E. French, 68.

[82] Hope Simpson and Dickinson, *Gazetteer*, 305, 314, 325–26; to which add Catling, *AR* (1986–87): 47.

[83] Hope Simpson and Dickinson, *Gazetteer*, 348.

[84] Colin Macdonald, "Problems of the Twelfth Century BC in the Dodecanese," *ABSA* 81 (1986): 149–50.

[85] Desborough, *Last Mycenaeans*, 153 and 227; Hope Simpson and Dickinson, *Gazetteer*, 360.

is here for physical destruction is disputed. The palace at Knossos, possibly the most splendid and extensive palace of the Late Bronze Age, was at some time destroyed, but the date of Knossos's destruction has conventionally been set in the early fourteenth century B.C. rather than in the early twelfth. How credible the conventional chronology is can best be judged after a survey of the rest of the island in the LM IIIB and IIIC periods.

It has long been known, on the basis of evidence from sites other than Knossos, that economic and cultural activities on Crete did not decline drastically after 1400. In Pendlebury's words, architecture and pottery from Cretan sites other than Knossos indicate that in LM III "Minoan culture continued unbroken but on a lower level."[86] But the picture of fourteenth- and thirteenth- century Crete has become much rosier than it was in Evans's and Pendlebury's books. It is now clear that the Cretans of both the LM IIIA and IIIB periods were "prosperous and enterprising."[87] In fact, thanks to Philip Betancourt's survey, we can now say that the thirteenth century was the golden age of the Minoan ceramic industry.[88] The pots—especially the kraters and the thousands of stirrup jars— suggest a lively export of some liquid (wine, olive oil, or possibly an ointment or perfumed oil).[89] Some of the pots demonstrate what had always been suspected anyway: Linear B continued in use on Crete until ca. 1200 B.C. In addition to inscribed LM IIIB pots found in Crete itself, stirrup jars exported from Crete have been found at five mainland sites, and on the jars are Linear B legends that were painted on before firing.[90]

In western Crete there appears to have been an important thirteenth-century center at Khania (classical Kydonia), now being excavated by a Greek-Swedish team. A great deal of LM IIIB pottery was evidently shipped from this site. A number of vases found at Khania bear inscriptions

---

[86] J.D.S. Pendlebury, *The Archaeology of Crete* (London, 1939), 243.

[87] A. Kanta, *The Late Minoan III Period in Crete: A Survey of Sites, Pottery, and Their Distribution.* Studies in Mediterranean Archaeology, vol. 58 (Göteborg, 1980), 313. Kanta, who accepts the orthodox dating (ca. 1380) of the "final destruction" of the Knossos palace, found little sign of decline thereafter in the island as a whole. Cf. her conclusion at p. 326: "Art and life in Crete are best summarised as having continued at a reasonably high level after LM III A 2, and the relative material well being of the average Cretan did not deteriorate in the wake of the destruction of Knossos."

[88] Philip Betancourt, *The History of Minoan Pottery* (Princeton, 1985). At p. 159 Betancourt observes that in terms of volume, "the third Late Minoan period is a time of increased production and expanded commercial enterprise. Mycenaean pottery reaches both the Near East and the West in increasing quantities, vivid testimony to the thriving Aegean economy. Crete, well within the Mycenaean sphere, has a good share in this profitable trade." Tablet K700, which inventories over 1800 stirrup jars, "is a good example of the new performance expected from LM III potters." As for the quality of the pots, "technically, LM IIIB is the high point of Minoan potting and pyrotechnology" (p. 171).

[89] Kanta, *Late Minoan III Period*, 296.

[90] Betancourt, *History of Minoan Pottery*, 173.

referring to a *wanax*, and perhaps we may assume that the *wanax* in question resided somewhere on the island.[91] Whether there was a palace in Kydonia itself is unclear, although Linear B tablets of LM IIIB date have recently been found there.[92] At any rate, Kydonia was destroyed ca. 1200 B.C., presumably sharing the same fate that overtook cities and palaces all over the eastern Mediterranean.[93]

There is evidence that at the beginning of LM IIIC numerous sites in central and eastern Crete were abandoned. Amnisos, the harbor town for Knossos, seems to have been mostly unoccupied in LM IIIC, although a fountain-house and a shrine did continue in use.[94] At Mallia there may have been some burning, but most of the site seems to have been simply abandoned soon after 1200.[95] On the eastern tip of the island, the evidence from Palaikastro indicates abandonment at the end of LM IIIB, with transfer to a site on Kastri hill in IIIC.[96] Finally, excavations in 1987 revealed that from LM I to LM IIIB there was a large settlement at Aghios Phanourios, near Mirabello Bay, and that this city was also deserted early in the twelfth century.[97]

The most noticeable feature of habitation shifts in Crete, however, was the sudden preference, ca. 1180, for relatively large settlements in remote and well-protected places. A recent survey of the Late Bronze Age sites in eastern Crete concluded that during LM IIIB there were a great many settlements, with many people living either in hamlets or in isolated houses. In LM IIIC, on the other hand, such small sites are unattested: in this period people lived in larger villages or in towns. The IIIC sites, continuing into the Iron Age, cover approximately one hectare.[98]

The IIIC towns were typically placed high in the mountains. Three excavated sites, all in eastern Crete, have commonly been referred to as "cities of refuge," since they were apparently founded by people who sought security

[91] Louis Godart, "La caduta dei regni micenei a Creta e l'invasione dorica," in Domenico Musti, ed., *Le origine dei Greci: Dori e mondo egeo* (Rome, 1990), 174–76.

[92] Louis Godart and Yannis Tzedakis, "Les nouveaux textes en Linéaire B de la Canée," *RFIC* 119 (1991): 129–49.

[93] Godart, "La caduta," 185.

[94] Veit Stürmer, "Das Ende der Wohnsiedlungen in Malia und Amnisos," in Thomas, ed., *Forschungen*, 33–36.

[95] Stürmer, "Ende," 34, says that at the end of LM IIIB all parts of the city "endgültig verlassen werden."

[96] Kanta, *Late Minoan III Period*, 192.

[97] Catling, *AR* (1988–89): 107.

[98] Donald C. Haggis, "Survey at Kavousi, Crete: The Iron Age Settlements," *AJA* 95 (1991): 291: "Iron Age sites are fewer in number, but are large settlements, certainly villages or small towns, and occupy new locations. . . . One question is whether there is a significant population decrease at the end of LM IIIB or rather, a nucleation of settlement in the Kavousi highlands in LM IIIC. . . . The Iron Age settlements are large in size, usually about 1 ha, and occupy locations in close proximity to arable soil and water supplies."

from city-sackers. Karphi is a mountain aerie some six airline miles inland from Mallia, on a peak thirteen hundred feet above the Lasithi plain (which is itself twenty-eight hundred feet above sea level).[99] For understandable reasons nobody lived there in the LM IIIB period, but in the IIIC period there was a sizeable town at Karphi.[100] A second "city of refuge" was Vrokastro, little more than a mile from the western corner of Mirabello Bay, but high on a precipitous peak. The town on Vrokastro peak was constructed at the same time that the settlement at Aghios Phanourios, in the plain below Vrokastro, was abandoned.[101] The third of the LM IIIC mountain sites in eastern Crete is Kavousi, which is actually a double site (the "lower" settlement near Kavousi is Vronda, while Kastro is perched still higher on the mountain).[102] Although excavations here are still continuing, it is once again very clear that these twin sites were established at the beginning of LM IIIC.

For the building of towns in such appalling locations a powerful motivation must be imagined. This flight to the mountains early in the twelfth century was very likely precipitated by a particularly frightening instance of the Catastrophe nearby: whatever security the Cretans had relied upon in the IIIB period was now gone, and the population was left to defend itself as best it could. One can hardly avoid the conclusion that the regime by which the eastern half of the island had been ruled and protected in the LM IIIB period was routed and annihilated shortly after 1200. If Evans was correct in dating the final destruction of the Knossos palace to ca. 1400, then one must assume that in the fourteenth and thirteenth centuries B.C. central and eastern Crete had been administered from some palace yet to be discovered; and that when this other palace is discovered, with its stocks of provisions and its Linear B tablets, it will prove to have been destroyed in the early twelfth century.

SUMMARY

Destruction by fire was the fate of the cities and palaces of the eastern Mediterranean during the Catastrophe. Throughout the Aegean, Anatolia, Cyprus, and the Levant dozens of these places were burned. Although

[99] Pendlebury et al., "Excavations in the Plain of Lasithi. III," *ABSA* 38 (1938–39): 57–145.

[100] Desborough, *Last Mycenaeans*, 175, concluded that Karphi was founded in "the middle or latter part of LH. IIIC." Cf., however, Kanta, *Late Minoan III Period*, 121: "It is now clear that the town of Karphi was first inhabited during a relatively early stage in LM III C."

[101] Catling, *AR* (1988–89): 107.

[102] For the most recent report on these two sites see G. C. Gesell, L. P. Day, and W. D. Coulsen, "The 1991 Season at Kavousi, Crete," *AJA* 96 (1992): 353.

many small communities were not destroyed, having been simply abandoned in the early twelfth century B.C., the great centers went up in flames. In fact, in all the lands mentioned it is only in the interior of the southern Levant that one can find at least a few significant centers that were *not* destroyed by fire at least once during the Catastrophe.

In the aftermath of destruction many centers were rebuilt, and a surprising number of them were on or within sight of the seacoast. Tiryns, Troy, Ialysos, Tarsus, Enkomi, Kition, Ashdod, and Ashkelon are the best-known of these twelfth-century coastal settlements, but there were many others. Another expedient, favored especially by the survivors of the Catastrophe in eastern Crete, was to locate new towns high in the mountains. Small, unfortified settlements were far less common in the middle of the twelfth century than they had been a century earlier.

Egypt escaped the Catastrophe, inasmuch as no Egyptian cities or palaces are known to have been destroyed, although after Ramesses III pharaonic power and prestige entered a sharp decline. And in Mesopotamia the Catastrophe seems to have done little damage: the kings of Assur remained strong through the twelfth century, and Babylonia's troubles were of a conventional kind. But in all other civilized lands, the Catastrophe was synonymous with the burning of rich palaces and famous cities.

PART TWO

ALTERNATIVE EXPLANATIONS
OF THE CATASTROPHE

Chapter Three

EARTHQUAKES

THE PRESENT STUDY makes the case that the Catastrophe was the result of a new style of warfare that appeared toward the end of the thirteenth century B.C. The new warfare, it is argued here, opened up new and frightening possibilities for various uncivilized populations that until that time had been no cause for concern to the cities and kingdoms of the eastern Mediterranean. Archaeologists have long known that it was ca. 1200 that the Naue Type II sword—perhaps along with certain types of defensive armor—came to the eastern Mediterranean. Historians, however, have scarcely investigated the change in warfare that the new artifacts imply. So far as I know, the Catastrophe has never been explained squarely in terms of revolutionary military innovations. The reason for this omission is perhaps that several other (and initially plausible) explanations have been available. Let us therefore, before exploring a new hypothesis, examine those already at hand.

The Catastrophe—which is to say, the destruction of palaces and cities all over the eastern Mediterranean ca. 1200 B.C.—is not invariably attributed to human agency. Although most scholars do hold that the cities were destroyed by men, a minority has explained the Catastrophe (or at least the most conspicuous instances of it) as the result of a terrible "act of God." Specifically, six archaeologists concluded that their Late Bronze Age sites were destroyed by earthquakes. In addition, two of the archaeologists have claimed that the quakes that destroyed their sites were also responsible for the fires that burned many other famous sites. In this view, the Catastrophe was an "act of God" of proportions unparalleled in all of history.

That such was indeed the case was proposed by C.F.A. Schaeffer, the distinguished excavator of Ugarit.[1] Schaeffer contributed so much to our knowledge of the Bronze Age that one hesitates to charge him with leading us astray on what for him was perhaps a problem of secondary importance. But that problem is what this book is about, and so we shall have to look closely at Schaeffer's solution of it. For most of his forty years of excavation at Ras Shamra, Schaeffer held the conventional view that Ugarit had been destroyed by "the Sea Peoples." His change of mind was not the result of

[1] C.F.A. Schaeffer, "Commentaires sur les lettres et documents trouvés dans les bibliothèques privées d'Ugarit," *Ugaritica*, vol. 5 (= *Mission de Ras Shamra*, vol. 16.) (Paris, 1968), 753–68.

any new physical evidence for an earthquake but followed from his interpretation of a tablet (RS 20.33) from the Rap'anu Archive, found at Ugarit
in 1955, which suggested to Schaeffer that ca. 1200 B.C. Ugarit was hostile
to Egypt and therefore, one could assume, on good terms with "the Sea
Peoples."[2] Now if Ugarit was allied with "the Sea Peoples," it could not
have been destroyed by them, but neither was it destroyed by Ramesses III,
since his inscriptions make no mention of such a feat. Therefore, Schaeffer
concluded, Ugarit must have been the victim of a natural disaster—an
earthquake. Schaeffer suggested that the same fate must have overtaken
many cities in Syria and Asia Minor—Alalakh, Hattusas, Alishar, Alaca
Höyük, and other centers—that were ruined at about the same time as
Ugarit.[3] All this destruction, Schaeffer argued, could not have been
wrought by invaders, because invaders would have had nothing to gain and
much to lose by burning cities in which they themselves might comfortably
have lived. Therefore, the ruin of all the Anatolian cities ca. 1200 must have
been caused by a natural disaster:

> Est-il vraisemblable qu'un conquérant de la capitale et des autres centres urbains
> contemporains de l'Anatolie hittite, ait pu tirer quelque avantage de livrer aux
> flammes, outre le palais et les fortifications, également les habitations privées de
> ces villes où il comptait s'établir?

> Pour toutes ces raisons, il est plausible d'admettre que les destructions massives
> qui firent disparaître, au temps de Suppiluliuma, l'empire hittite, sa capitale et
> nombre d'autres villes importantes en Hatti, ne sont pas imputables à des actions
> guerrières, mais à de désastreux tremblements de terre dont l'Asie Mineure, l'une
> des régions du globe les plus éprouvées par les séismes, a été si souvent le
> théâtre.[4]

This theory, so casually advanced, was not the first in which an excavator
argued that his famous site was destroyed by an act of God rather than by

---

[2] For the text, transliteration, and translation of the letter see Jean Nougayrol, "La 'Lettre
du Général,'" in ibid., 69–79. Schaeffer's commentary and exploration of the letter's implications appear on pp. 640–90 of the same volume.

[3] The suggestion that the great fortress at Hattusas was ruined in an earthquake has been
unequivocally rejected. Cf. Kurt Bittel, "Die archäologische Situation in Kleinasien," 26:
"Dass auch hier [i.e., just outside the fortification wall to the south of Hattusas], wie an vielen
anderen Stellen des Stadtgebietes, *absichtlich herbeigeführte Vernichtung die Ursache war*, ist
nicht zu zweifeln. Brandschutt, bestehend aus verkohltem Holz und verbrannten, manchmal
durch die Glut geradezu verschlackten Lehmziegeln von Oberbau des Stadtmauer und der
Turme bezeugen das ganz eindeutig" (my italics). For a much earlier statement to the same
effect see Bittel, *Grundzüge der Vor- und Frühgeschichte Kleinasiens* (2d ed., Tübingen,
1950), 73: "Alle Bauten, grosse und kleine, offizielle und private, der Hauptstadt Hattuscha
(zeigen) eindrucksvolle Spuren einer grossen Feuerbrunst, die, *absichtlich nach der Einnahme
gelegt*, die ganze Stadt der Vernichtung preisgab" (my italics). See also G. A. Lehmann, "Der
Untergang des hethitischen Grossreiches und die neuen Texte aus Ugarit," *UF* 2 (1970): 40.

[4] Schaeffer, "Commentaires," 755–56.

anonymous aggressors. A pioneering theory of this sort was constructed for Knossos by Sir Arthur Evans. To the fire that destroyed the Knossos palace and baked the Linear B tablets in its archives, Evans wrote, "it seems best to assign a seismic cause." In his reconstruction of events, ca. 1400 a moderate earthquake (which left little evidence at neighboring sites) happened to strike Knossos on a March day, when the south wind called the Notios was blowing; lamp fires were upset, other open fires were disrupted, and the Notios fanned them into a blaze that destroyed so much of the palace that the king and his court decided to abandon it and set up their administration on the Greek mainland, at Mycenae.[5]

The same sort of natural catastrophe was posited by Carl Blegen for Troy VIh, the "royal" city at Hissarlik that preceded the more populous but humbler settlement known as VIIa. Blegen dated the catastrophic earthquake and its attendant fires to ca. 1275 B.C.[6] Today, as noted in chapter 2, the destruction of Troy VIh is usually put in the second half of the thirteenth century. But although his chronology has been revised, Blegen's explanation remains influential. Even while radically redating its destruction to ca. 1150, Christian Podzuweit assumed without argument that Troy VIh succumbed to an earthquake.[7]

Most recently, an earthquake has been identified as the cause for the Catastrophe in the Peloponnese. During his long romance with the site of Mycenae, George Mylonas imagined that the destruction at the end of the LH IIIB period was a material record of the turmoil caused by Aigisthos's murder of Agamemnon and by the even bloodier coup eight years later, when Orestes slew Aigisthos and Klytemnestra.[8] Not surprisingly, this interpretation was not accepted in all quarters. In 1977 Spyridon Iakovides, who had also spent many years excavating at Mycenae, declared his conviction that the destruction at Mycenae was the result of earthquake fires.[9] Since 1977 Iakovides's fiery quake has spread far beyond its original

[5] Evans, *The Palace of Minos at Knossos*, vol. 4 (London, 1935), 943–45.

[6] Carl W. Blegen et al., *Troy: Excavations Conducted by The University of Cincinnati*, vol. 3, part 1 (Princeton, 1953), 330–32.

[7] Podzuweit, "Mykenische Welt," devotes ten pages of close argument to the ceramic evidence for the date of the destruction but passes over the cause in one line (p. 82): "Bekanntlich wurde die Siedlung durch ein Erdbeben zerstört."

[8] Mylonas, *Mycenae and the Mycenaean Age* (Princeton, 1966), 224–27. Mylonas argued at some length that the destruction of Mycenae could not have been wrought by the Dorians or by other invaders from the north: there was no indication of newcomers in the IIIC period. The legends, so far as Mylonas was concerned, held the key: the assassinations of the royal family, together with "the tumultuous conflicts which must have followed the appalling deeds" (p. 226). At the other end of the Peloponnese, however, poor Pylos was undoubtedly destroyed by "a successful piratical attack by people who remain unknown" (p. 227).

[9] Wace had found evidence for destruction and burning only outside the citadel wall; scholars of his generation therefore assumed that at the end of LH IIIB Mycenae was attacked, but the aggressors did not enter the citadel itself. But Mylonas, Iakovides, and their associates found evidence for destruction both inside and outside the wall. Iakovides, "The Present State

epicenter. In 1980 Klaus Kilian, director of the excavations at Tiryns, made a case that the Catastrophe at Tiryns and in all of the Argolid was the result of an earthquake: although at Pylos and Paros and elsewhere in the eastern Mediterranean the Catastrophe was evidently wrought by human hand, the destruction of the three great Argolid sites—Tiryns, Mycenae, and Midea—was caused by a quake and the fires that it ignited.[10] By April of 1983 Kilian had extended the quake through all of the Peloponnese, now proposing that the Menelaion in Laconia and even the Pylos palace, a hundred miles from Mycenae, fell victim to the same quake that destroyed Tiryns.[11] Kilian's conclusion was in large part based upon his discovery that in the early LH IIIC period the *Aussensiedlung*, the settlement just outside the walls of the citadel at Tiryns and reaching down to the coastline, was larger than it had ever been, covering slightly more than twenty-four hectares.[12] At the same time, the *Unterburg*, or the northward extension of the citadel itself, was surrounded by new fortifications, apparently to serve as a shelter for the large population now living in the *Aussensiedlung*. There must have occurred, soon after 1200 B.C., a centralization here at Tiryns of a population that through the LH IIIB period had been scattered among several small communities in the Argolid. The most reasonable explanation for this *synoikismos*, according to Kilian, is that a massive earthquake destroyed the Argolid towns, and that the survivors banded together to create the large city below Tiryns.[13]

The thesis of Iakovides and Kilian has been accepted by a number of scholars and was incorporated in Podzuweit's important article on the

---

of Research at the Citadel of Mycenae," *BIAL* (1977): 134, with note on p. 140, vigorously insisted that the new evidence pointed to earthquake fires as the cause of destruction:

> During the last quarter of the 13th century BC a violent earthquake, signs of which have been noticed both inside and outside the citadel, overthrew the palace and many other buildings and started fires which caused the total destruction of many of them. The importance of these observations for the history of the site, and, indeed, for the development of Mycenaean civilisation cannot be stressed too emphatically. Based on firm, incontrovertible excavation evidence, they provide, to the belief of the present author, the only satisfactory explanation for the general destruction which overtook Mycenae at the end of LH IIIB, but did not disrupt the evolution of its culture, nor bring about any appreciable change in it. This is a no less incontestable fact, which none of the explanations put forward so far has succeeded in answering convincingly.

[10] At "Zum Ende," 193, Kilian conceded the likelihood of armed violence as the cause of destruction at Pylos and Paros.

[11] At the colloquium "Dori e mondo egeo," held at the University of Rome on 11–13 April of 1983, Kilian expanded his earlier thesis to include all the Peloponnesian sites: cf. Kilian, "La caduta dei palazzi micenei continentali: aspetti archeologici," in D. Musti, ed., *Le origini dei Greci: Dori e mondo egeo* (Rome, 1990), 74–75.

[12] Kilian, "Zum Ende," 171–73.

[13] Kilian has restated this conclusion in "Ausgrabungen in Tiryns 1982/83," *Arch. Anz.* (1988): 150.

destruction of Troy.[14] It was given a significant boost when Paul Åström, director of the excavations at Midea, accepted it as the explanation for the ruin of his site.[15] Åström had earlier held out for the traditional explanation that Midea—and the other Argolid sites—had been destroyed by human hand.

In addressing the earthquake explanation for the Catastrophe it will be unnecessary to examine all the sites destroyed ca. 1200. Although Schaeffer and Kilian proposed, for example, that Alalakh, Hattusas, and Pylos were the victims of earthquake fires, that was not the opinion of the archaeologists (Woolley, Bittel, and Blegen) who excavated these sites. Because, in estimating what happened at any given site, most scholars accept the verdict of the excavator, few have believed that an earthquake destroyed Alalakh, Hattusas, and Pylos. On the other hand, the same authority of the excavator has convinced many historians and archaeologists that earthquakes were indeed what ruined Ugarit, Knossos, Troy, Mycenae, Tiryns, and Midea, and we shall therefore need to look at these six sites in some detail.

That each of these places suffered much damage from earthquakes is almost certain. All six sites lie in zones of high seismicity. It is likely that Troy VI (like LM Knossos) experienced at least one major quake in the five centuries of its existence: Troy III, IV, and V also were damaged by quakes, and in our own century lands within a sixty-mile radius of Troy have experienced four quakes measuring at least 6.0 on the Richter scale.[16] Since in plate tectonic theory the pressure generated by the shifting of plates is relatively constant, one must assume that the incidence of catastrophic quakes in the eastern Mediterranean was approximately the same in the thirteenth and twelfth centuries as it has been in better documented times.[17]

[14] For restrained endorsement see, for example, Muhly, "Sea Peoples," 52. Podzuweit, "Die mykenische Welt und Troja," 67–68, accepts Kilian's view that the Argolid sites were destroyed by an earthquake soon after 1200. At p. 82 Podzuweit goes on to suggest that Troy VI was also destroyed by an earthquake, although not until the second half of the twelfth century.

[15] Åström returned to Midea in 1983 and concluded that it too had been ruined by a quake: Åström, "The Sea Peoples in the Light of New Excavations," *Centre d'Etudes chypriotes* 3 (1985): 6–7. See also Åström, "Die Akropolis von Midea," 7–10: "Die bisherige Ergebnisse scheinen die Beobachtungen in Mykene und Tiryns zu bestätigen, dass wir am Ende der Phase SH III B 2 mit einem Erdbeben zu rechnen haben, das sein Epizentrum in der Nähe von Mykene, Midea und Tiryns hatte und diese Burgen zu derselben Zeit zerstört hat."

[16] Wood, *Trojan War*, 225–26.

[17] The classic work is B. Gutenberg and C. F. Richter, *Seismicity of the Earth and Associated Phenomena* (Princeton, 1954). For a map of epicenters of moderate (over 4.5 on the Richter scale) to great quakes in the eastern Mediterranean over a ten-year period see B. A. Bolt, *Earthquakes* (New York, 1988), 90.

Damage is one thing, however, and destruction another. In all of antiquity only a very few cities are known to have been destroyed by an "act of God." Whatever may have happened to Sodom and Gomorrah, we do know that Thera and Pompeii were covered by volcanic eruptions. And very occasionally we do hear of a city *destroyed* (rather than damaged) by an earthquake. What was perhaps the most terrible quake in ancient Greece struck the Corinthian Gulf on a winter night in 373 B.C., utterly destroying the cities of Helike and Bura (Helike sank and was covered by the enlarged gulf). The general rule in antiquity, however, as in modern times, was that after a quake the survivors repaired the damage done to their city. The large city of Patrai was struck three times between A.D. 23 and 62, and Smyrna twice during the reign of Marcus Aurelius, but both cities revived and prospered.[18] The notices of Byzantine chroniclers suggest that Constantinople suffered a major earthquake once or twice a century (and tremors every few years), but of course the city was never destroyed by a quake. In the several hundred ancient quakes about which we are informed one assumes the same pattern: the dead were buried, the buildings rebuilt, and the city lived on. One is therefore reluctant to believe that ca. 1200 B.C. a number of the most important places in the eastern Mediterranean were hit by a quake from which they could not recover.

There is, of course, no documentary evidence for a catastrophic earthquake ca. 1200. Because Ramesses III states that the aggressors who attacked Egypt in 1179 had earlier destroyed places from Hatti through Alashia and Amor, and because tablets from Hattusas, Ugarit, and Emar show that those cities were under attack by raiders or "hordes," what little documentation we have indicates that the Catastrophe was wrought by men. Nor is there any archaeological evidence that any of our six sites was at the epicenter of a catastrophic quake. At each site buildings clearly collapsed, upper stories falling to floor level, or single-story houses subsiding into the streets. At none of the sites, however, was any displacement of surface levels reported. Vertical displacement, one would suppose, should have resulted in a stratigraphic step, with all the prequake strata (at Troy, for example, from VI down to I) shifted here and there to a point measurably above or below their normal altitude. Horizontal displacement would have shown up in the lateral jamming of what had once been a continuous surface.

It appears in fact that the destruction levels at the six problematic sites are very similar to destruction levels at sites outside the seismic zone. For the Palestinian coast, for example, Moshe Dothan has reported destruction levels ranging from one to two meters at Ashdod and Akko.[19] Here too, the

[18] W. Capelle, "Erdbebenforschung," *RE*, Supplementband 4, cols. 350 and 353.
[19] M. Dothan, "Ashdod," 126.

destruction level consisted mainly of collapsed buildings, ash (from site-wide fires), pottery, and very few artifacts or valuables. The archaeological novice would therefore assume that the cities of Palestine must have suffered the same fate as did those in the seismic zone to the north.

Another surprising fact is that in each of the six sites the killer quake resulted in a fire or fires that raged over much or all of the site. Over the several millennia of ancient history thousands of villages, towns, and cities were burned, but in almost all cases the fires were set deliberately: sackers of cities routinely burned a place after they had looted it. Earthquakes, on the other hand, were in antiquity not associated with devastating fires, presumably because there were no gas mains or electrical cables, and most cities and towns consisted primarily of masonry structures. In his discussion of earthquakes Pliny does not even mention the danger of fire.[20] Lamps or cooking fires could of course be disturbed; in describing the terrible quake that in A.D. 17 shattered twelve cities in the Roman province of Asia, Tacitus says that because it occurred at night the survivors could see "fires shining out from among the ruins."[21] But there is no indication that on this or any other occasion fire devastated a whole city: of the several hundred ancient earthquakes that W. Capelle cataloged from literary sources, none is known to have ignited a city-wide fire.[22] It therefore strains credulity to suppose that a single earthquake should have resulted in conflagrations at three sites in the Argolid—Mycenae, Tiryns, and Midea—and that similar fires should have been set by this or other quakes at Knossos, Troy, and Ugarit.

Still more surprising is the fact that none of the six quakes, presumably the most severe that those particular sites ever suffered, resulted in casualties. The absence of skeletons could be explained in a city sacked by intruders. If given any kind of warning, the occupants of an unwalled place such as Knossos or Pylos would probably have fled long before the sackers arrived at the palace, and even the residents of a fortress such as Mycenae or Hattusas may have elected to leave, especially if they knew that in the long run the sackers were likely to prevail. Not even those who chose to stay in a city or palace against which raiders were moving are likely to have been killed in situ. Ancient conquerors normally removed the occupants from a city—executing some and enslaving the rest—before setting fire to it: so, for example, when the Persians burned Miletus, when Alexander burned Thebes and Tyre, and when the Romans burned Corinth and Carthage. In earthquakes, however, the victims are interred at the site, and the general experience in ancient times, as in modern, was that when a city was shaken

[20] *Nat. Hist.* 2.81–86.
[21] *Annales* 2.47.
[22] Capelle, "Erdbebenforschung," cols. 346–61, presented a region-by-region catalog of all the earthquakes reported for the eastern Mediterranean in the period 600 B.C.–A.D. 600.

in a major earthquake the casualties were numerous. When Sparta was hit by a quake in the 460s, buildings collapsed from their foundations and more than 20,000 Spartans died.[23] Justin (40.2.1) reports that 170,000 people were killed when an earthquake jolted Syria during the reign of Mithridates Eupator. The Asian earthquake of A.D. 17 may have claimed almost as many lives, since Pliny called it the worst quake in the memory of mankind.[24] Recent excavations at Kourion, in Cyprus, have disclosed a city that was actually destroyed by an earthquake (apparently the great quake that struck the northeast corner of the Mediterranean on 21 July of A.D. 365).[25] In the few rooms thus far cleared at Kourion, the excavators have come upon the skeletons of two women, a young girl and a horse. The bones are cracked and crushed. How Mycenae, Tiryns, Midea, Knossos, Troy, and Ugarit could have experienced quakes sufficient to destroy these sites completely, but without loss of human or animal life, is difficult to imagine. Nor can it be argued that casualties may have been high at the sites in question but that the bodies of the victims were retrieved by their loved ones: at none of the sites has an excavator reported evidence for such mining operations.

Most amazing of all is that at none of the six sites claimed to have been destroyed by an earthquake ca. 1200 B.C. was anything of value buried by the collapsing buildings. As the tomb of Tutankhamon or the Shaft Graves at Mycenae show so spectacularly, palaces in antiquity must have been treasuries of precious artifacts. In the palaces, after all, people did live like kings and queens. It goes without saying that a palace that was plundered and then burned, as presumably happened at the Menelaion or Pylos or Hattusas, could not be expected to yield to archaeologists anything so elegant as the *corredo* found in tombs. But palaces instantaneously destroyed by earthquakes should have been a series of bonanzas for modern excavators. Yet at none of the six sites supposedly so destroyed was there any such haul. What gold, silver, and bronze items archaeologists found in these cities had been secreted in pits or hidden in wall caches.

The claims that six famous Late Bronze Age sites were destroyed by earthquakes, we may conclude, must as a class be set aside. But one can also challenge each of them individually. So far as Evans's scenario for Knossos is concerned, it may be sufficient to note that even those who defend Evans's date (ca. 1400 B.C.) for the destruction at Knossos do not

[23] Diodorus 11.63.1.

[24] *Nat. Hist.* 2.86.

[25] D. Soren, "An Earthquake on Cyprus. New Discoveries from Kourion," *Archaeology* 38 (1982): fascicle 2, pp. 52–59. For an account of the earthquake in 365 see Ammianus 26.10.15–19.

accept his explanation.[26] Evans's theory on this point was one of the few that Pendlebury flatly rejected: "Everything," Pendlebury concluded, "points to a deliberate sacking on the part of enemies."[27] Among the growing number of scholars who date the destruction at Knossos to ca. 1200 there is of course no inclination whatever to see an earthquake as the cause. In this view Knossos was destroyed by the same violence that destroyed Pylos and the other Aegean sites.

Blegen's dogma that Troy VI was destroyed by an earthquake is still orthodox, but heresy grows. The pre-Blegen view, put forward by Wilhelm Dörpfeld, was that Troy VI had been sacked. Dörpfeld had found evidence for fire or fires at various places in the destruction level of Troy VI and had interpreted the destruction as the work of men. Blegen acknowledged the evidence for fire at the destruction of Troy VI but argued that this proud settlement was the victim of a catastrophic earthquake; the humdrum VIIa, on the other hand, was destroyed by attackers. Blegen's arguments were long accepted without much question but were given close scrutiny and much publicity in Michael Wood's *In Search of the Trojan War*.[28] Following up some of Wood's ideas, Donald Easton reviewed in detail the arguments on which Blegen based his theory that Troy VI was the victim of an earthquake. Easton's conclusion was that there is little or no evidence for such a quake.[29]

To some extent, Blegen's conclusions about VI may have been forced upon him by his identification of VIIa as the "Homeric" city. Dörpfeld's view had been that the city destroyed by the Achaeans was Troy VI. Since Blegen concluded that Troy VIIa was the city sacked by the Achaeans, he had little choice but to attribute the destruction of Troy VI to something other than enemy aggression (it was improbable that the capture of nondescript VIIa could have resulted in the *Iliad*, while a sacking of majestic VI was never celebrated). But there is no reason why city-sackers could not have been responsible for the fall of both VI and VIIa. Blegen's dates for the

---

[26] In discussing the palace's destruction John Boardman, "The Date of the Knossos Tablets," in Palmer and Boardman, *On the Knossos Tablets* (Oxford, 1963), speaks only about fire and does not mention an earthquake or earthquake damage. At p. 87 Boardman assumes that the palace was burned "through insurrection or attack from abroad."

[27] Pendlebury, *Archaeology of Crete*, 229.

[28] Wood, *Trojan War*, 225–30.

[29] Easton, "Has the Trojan War Been Found?" *Antiquity* 59 (1985): 188–95. Easton argues that the tilt of the citadel wall and the cracks in the wall next to two towers could as easily have been caused by subsidence as by a quake. "When during VIIa the fill behind the wall subsided, there was shifting of the VIIa houses and floors built over it and of the citadel wall resting on it; the towers cracked as a result. If this is correct, then there will be no compelling reason, if any reason at all, to attribute the end of Troy VI to an earthquake" (p. 190).

destruction of both cities are now regarded by even conservative critics as at least thirty or forty years too high. Although relatively little Mycenaean pottery was found in Troy VIIa levels, it now seems that some of the pottery found in those levels must be assigned to the LH IIIC period.[30] How long the improvised city of VIIa had lasted is uncertain, but few observers have credited it with more than a generation. Its royal predecessor, Troy VI, may therefore have been destroyed as late as ca. 1220, and the fall of that citadel may have marked the beginning of the Catastrophe. It was presumably destroyed in the same way that so many other cities were destroyed in the years that followed.

Schaeffer's hypothesis that Ugarit was destroyed by an earthquake has been criticized from several quarters. His reconstruction of the final episode in that city's diplomatic history was immediately and effectively attacked by G. A. Lehmann[31] and is incompatible with documentary evidence that has subsequently been found. As indicated in chapter 1, recently published tablets show that on the eve of its destruction Ugarit was on good terms with Bay, the "Grand Chancellor" of Egypt under Siptah and Queen Twosret. Even before the correspondence with Bay was discovered, Schaeffer's reconstruction of Ugarit's diplomatic history was generally rejected.[32]

Archaeologists have also insisted that Ugarit was destroyed by human hand. The present excavators at Ras Shamra, under the direction of Marguerite Yon, do not accept the explanation put forward by Schaeffer in 1968, and instead see the destruction and abandonment of Ugarit as "une conséquence de l'invasion des 'Peuples de la Mer.'"[33] At the Brown Conference the fate of Ugarit was vividly summarized by Professor Yon:[34]

> Violent fighting seems to have taken place throughout the city; the presence of numerous arrow-heads dispersed throughout the destroyed or abandoned ruins

[30] Podzuweit, "Die mykenische Welt und Troja," 75–80, argues in detail that LH IIIC ware was present not only in VIIa but also in VIh levels. Cf. Wood, Trojan War, 224: "Blegen asserted that 'not a single piece' of LH III C pottery was found in Troy VIIa. However, it is now clear that several pieces of LH III C were found in Troy VIIa, and that it was probably destroyed around 1180 BC. This is confirmed by the appearance of another kind of pottery, the so-called 'Granary Class,' in the next phase of Troy, VIIb 1." For the pottery cf. Blegen, Troy, vol. 4, part 2, plates 277–79.

[31] Lehmann, "Untergang," 67–71.

[32] For a balanced presentation of the documents bearing on Ugarit's diplomatic history immediately before its destruction see Nancy Sandars, The Sea Peoples: Warriors of the Ancient Mediterranean 1250–1150 BC (London, 1978), 141–43; August Strobel, Der spätbronzezeitliche Seevölkersturm (Berlin, 1976), 55–61; and M. Liverani, Antico Oriente: storia società economia (Rome, 1988), 635.

[33] Marguerite Yon, Annie Caubet, and Joël Mallet, "Ras Shamra-Ougarit 38, 39 et 40e campagnes (1978, 1979 et 1980)," Syria 59 (1982): 170.

[34] Yon, "The End of the Kingdom of Ugarit," in Ward and Joukowsky, Crisis Years, 117.

(and not in orderly deposits as if they had been stockpiled weapons) provides evidence of this. . . . On the whole, the inhabitants seem either to have left in great haste, or to have been surprised in their homes by the invaders and plunderers. This is the impression conveyed by certain rooms where objects of no value such as kitchen utensils and domestic equipment were overturned.

In short, there is every reason to believe that Ugarit was sacked and razed by marauders, and no reason to accept Schaeffer's argument that it was destroyed by an earthquake fire.

That LH IIIB Mycenae was destroyed by an earthquake was proposed by Iakovides and was stated as fact by Kilian[35] but was not the conclusion of Wace, Mylonas, or others who had been associated with the site. Åström states that "the destruction of Mycenae is now also considered by the British excavators as possibly having been due to an earthquake," and cites W. D. Taylour to that effect.[36] That is not, however, exactly what Taylour concluded. According to Taylour, building phase VII of the Citadel House area at Mycenae "was brought to a close by a minor fire or possibly an earthquake" late in the LH IIIB period.[37] But this relatively minor misfortune was followed by alterations and rebuilding, and the IIIB period did not end until the destruction at the end of building phase VIII. In describing this second—and major—disaster Taylour mentions not even a "possible" earthquake: "The whole of the Citadel House area was destroyed in an intense conflagration which frequently reduced mudbrick and stone to calcined debris."[38] In his 1983 revision of The Mycenaeans Taylour canvassed several possible explanations (the Dorian Invasion, internecine wars, drought and famine, the Sea Peoples) for the fall of Mycenae, but an earthquake was not one of them.[39]

A specific objection to the earthquake thesis for the Argolid is that so much masonry at all three sites came through this killer quake unscathed. The tholoi at Mycenae and Midea, with their corbeled courses of masonry, show no sign of having been at the epicenter of a killer quake; nor do other sophisticated structures such as the gallery at Tiryns, the cistern stairway at Mycenae, or the Lion Gate. Nor in fact do the massive fortification walls at any of the three sites seem to have been disturbed. The only masonry affected by the quake, apparently, was in the bearing-walls of houses and

[35] Kilian, "Zum Ende," 182: "Am Ende von SH IIIB litten Burg wie Aussensiedlung von Mykene stark unter einem Erdbeben, dessen verderbliche Wirkung durch begrenzt ausbrechende Feuerbrünste erhöht wurde."

[36] Åström, "The Sea Peoples," 5. On Mycenae, Åström refers to Taylour, Well-Built Mycenae: The Helleno-British Excavations within the Citadel at Mycenae, fascicle 1 (Warminster, 1981), 9.

[37] Taylour, Well-Built Mycenae, 9.

[38] Ibid., 10.

[39] Taylour, The Mycenaeans, 2d ed. (New York, 1983).

other buildings. At Midea, Åström reports that some stone walls "are not quite straight, but concave or convex" and that one wall "was discovered in a tilted position." Such dislocations, however, are perhaps not surprising in buildings destroyed by fire. Åström has shown beyond any doubt that Midea was destroyed in a conflagration (ash deposits were found everywhere, with an ash layer 40 centimeters thick near the interior of the Cyclopean wall).[40]

The main argument that the Argolid was smashed by an earthquake at the beginning of the twelfth century B.C. comes from Kilian's excavation of the *Aussensiedlung* and the *Unterburg* at Tiryns. That there was so large an LH IIIC settlement at Tiryns is a highly significant discovery and should shed a great deal of light on the Catastrophe. As Kilian recognized, the settlement argues against both the old view that the citadels in the Argolid were destroyed by a Dorian invasion and the new view that because of a drought the Argolid was all but deserted in the twelfth century. The deflation of these two possibilities, however, does not much improve the credentials of the earthquake hypothesis. A much more obvious possibility remains undimmed, and even strengthened, by Kilian's discoveries at Tiryns: the Argolid sites were destroyed in raids, and in the aftermath the survivors from the several sites banded together in one large community, for purposes of self-defense.[41]

As was pointed out in chapter 2, a great many of the post-Catastrophe settlements were sited on the coast. Elsewhere on the coasts of the Peloponnese there were IIIC cities at Korakou, Aigeira, Teichos Dymaion, Monemvasia, and Asine. Perati on the east coast of Attica and Lefkandi on Euboea's west coast are also analogous. Another coastal city, created quite suddenly in the early twelfth century B.C., is attested by a cemetery at Ialysos on Rhodes. On Cyprus, similar urban settlements seem to have been built at the coastal sites of Enkomi and Kition immediately after the destruction that ended the LC II period. Even more remarkable is the city that Åström has recently explored at Hala Sultan Tekke (on an inlet of the sea near Larnaca), for which Åström estimates a population "between 11,000 and 14,000 people."[42] Anatolian coastal cities with increased pop-

---

[40] Åström, "The Sea Peoples," 5.

[41] Kilian argued at great length ("Zum Ende," 187–91) against the possibility that the Catastrophe in the Argolid could have resulted from the Dorian Invasion. On the other hand, Kilian acknowledged the possibility that the Catastrophe might have been the work of raiders, but he passsed over that possibility so quickly ("Zum Ende," 191) that I repeat his discussion of it here in full: "Die Möglichkeit einer Bedrohung durch Piraten, ähnlich dem Auftreten der Seevölker in der Levante, wie sie für Pylos aus dem Aufstellen von Küstenwachen erschlossen wird, böte eine Einklärung der Palastzerstörung, wenngleich der Nachweis eines direkten Zusammenhanges auch in Pylos aussteht."

[42] Åström, "The Sea Peoples," 10. On Enkomi and Kition see Knapp, *Copper Production*, 46–47. At both Enkomi and Hala Sultan Tekke the city seems to have been laid out on a grid plan.

ulation in the twelfth century were Troy, Miletus, and Tarsus. In the eleventh century the Ionian settlements on the coast of Asia Minor and the Phoenician cities in the Levant were also of the new centralized type.

Undoubtedly the centralized coastal city offered a security not available in the small and isolated communities ten or twenty kilometers inland. The security that the new cities promised, however, would hardly have been against earthquakes. Earthquakes under the oceans or the Mediterranean Sea normally result in tsunamis, or seismic sea waves (popularly called "tidal waves"), which batter and sometimes destroy coastal settlements. In reviewing the evidence for destruction wrought by tsunamis, Bruce Bolt notes that after the 1956 earthquake off Amorgos, "wave heights of 25 to 40 meters were reported" (though not necessarily believed), and the tsunami inflicted damage on Patmos, Crete, and Melos as well as on Amorgos itself.[43] Ancient writers' accounts of earthquakes show that people in antiquity were as aware as are people today of the special dangers that earthquakes posed for cities on the sea. The coastal location of settlements built after the Catastrophe of ca. 1200 B.C. suggests very strongly that the security sought by the inhabitants was against aggressors who came by sea: the coast offered the best vantage point, and the best defense, against seaborne marauders.

Schaeffer argued that the cities destroyed ca. 1200 would not have been deliberately destroyed, because invaders would not wish to destroy cities in which they themselves might live. This focus on "invaders" obscures entirely the fact that ancient cities were normally destroyed by raiders or by enemies who had homes of their own to which they intended to return. History readily shows that when cities were destroyed in antiquity they were almost invariably razed by men. Razing a city involved both demolition and burning, with many structures collapsing in the flames (the enemy had to go to great lengths to "prepare" the city for burning).[44] The object was to make the place uninhabitable and thus a monument to the ferocity of its assailants. In the classical world one recalls how Xerxes made an example of Eretria, the Carthaginians razed four Sicilian cities (Selinus, Akragas, Himera and Gela) in five years, Alexander burned Thebes, the Gauls burned Rome, the Romans razed both Carthage and Corinth in the same year, and in another banner year (A.D. 407) the Vandals and Alans sacked and set fire to cities all over Gaul ("uno fumavit Gallia tota rogo").

The same thing had been happening since prehistoric times, as indicated by the destruction levels found at sites everywhere in Anatolia at the end of EB II, or in Greece after EH II and MH. Most cities razed by their enemies were eventually rebuilt (although Carthage and Corinth lay desolate for a

---

[43] Bolt, *Earthquakes*, 91.

[44] On the practical requirements for burning a settlement see D. H. Gordon, "Fire and Sword: The Technique of Destruction," *Antiquity* 27 (1953): 149–52.

century), but others remained an uninhabited ruin after having been torched. In legend, that is what happened after the Achaeans burned Troy, or Joshua burned Jericho and Ai. In fact, many famous Near Eastern cities were never again inhabited after having been sacked and burned by their enemies. The list runs from Lagash and Akkad in the third millennium to Assur and Nineveh in the first. Far more numerous are the obscure names that appear only in the obituaries written by Assyrian kings: "I destroyed, I devastated, I burned with fire. . . . Their cities I burned with fire."

That this sort of atrocity was committed late in the second millennium is clear from several sources. A vivid example is the Amelekite raid on Ziklag, David's town in the Negeb in the days when David was still a captain of freebooters and Saul was king of Israel (1 Samuel 30.1–3): "They had overcome Ziklag, and burned it with fire, and taken captive the women and all who were in it, both small and great; they killed no one, but carried them off, and went their way. And when David and his men came to the city, they found it burned with fire, and their wives and sons and daughters taken captive." A far greater city, Hazor, was sacked ca. 1200 B.C., and this sacking was long remembered in Israel (the Song of Deborah was a part of the oral tradition). One of the largest cities in Canaan, Hazor is said (Joshua 11.11) to have been destroyed and burned by the men of Israel, and Yigael Yadin's excavations showed that the city was indeed razed at the end of the Late Bronze Age.[45] An Aegean parallel has recently been found on the island of Paros. Early in the twelfth century a site-wide fire, preceded by the violent death of many inhabitants, occurred at a Parian citadel called Koukounaries. The skeletons found at Koukounaries show that the Catastrophe was wrought by human hand.[46] According to the excavator, D. Schilardi "The fire that devastated the entire plateau was not accidental or caused by earthquake. That human and animal skeletons were found in the destroyed rooms shows that the Mycenaean inhabitants were anticipating the attack."[47]

Ramesses III reports that his enemies in 1179 B.C. had destroyed cities from Hatti through Alashia and the Levant. From Hattusas, Ugarit, and Emar there are documents declaring that these cities were threatened by attack, and in his letter to the king of Alashia the king of Ugarit directly

[45] On the date see Yadin, "The Transition from a Semi-Nomadic to a Sedentary Society in the Twelfth Century B.C.E.," in Cross, *Symposia*, 57–68.

[46] Catling, *AR* (1982–83): 47: "In a narrow path leading to the N entrance of the building a confused mass of human and animal bones was found in an ash layer. . . . In the second apotheke lay a woman's skeleton, her skull damaged by the violent blow that killed her. Her death is seen as a consequence of a violent assault on the site. Another group of skeletons was found near the stairwell on the W entrance of the building. . . . Pottery evidence places this catastrophe early in LH IIIC."

[47] Schilardi, *AR* (1980–81): 36.

states that unnamed enemies who came in ships burned some of his cities. It is about as clear as such things can be that the cities destroyed in the Catastrophe were destroyed by human hand. Theories that an act of God destroyed many of the most important eastern Mediterranean cities ca. 1200 not only are unsupported by archaeological evidence but go against the historical evidence for both antiquity as a whole and for the period ca. 1200 specifically.

Chapter Four

MIGRATIONS

THE MOST popular explanation for the last century has been that the Catastrophe was the result of massive migrations. Most recently, Ekrem Akurgal, Gustav Lehmann, and especially Fritz Schachermeyr argued that *Volkswanderungen* are what brought down the Bronze Age world.[1] Even many scholars who believe that the underlying cause of the Catastrophe was a systems collapse or a drought assume that the immediate cause of the destruction of so many cities was the violent passage of bellicose migrants through the eastern Mediterranean. Thus August Strobel's *Seevölkersturm* concluded that a drought occasioned the Catastrophe, and Nancy Sandars's *The Sea Peoples* found the chief factor to have been a systems collapse in the eastern kingdoms; but both books presented the actual destruction of sites as the work of peoples who had been uprooted from their original homelands and were not yet settled into new ones.

THE EGYPTIAN EVIDENCE

The thesis that a great "migration of the Sea Peoples" occurred ca. 1200 B.C. is supposedly based on Egyptian inscriptions, one from the reign of Merneptah and another from the reign of Ramesses III. Yet in the inscriptions themselves such a migration nowhere appears. After reviewing what the Egyptian texts have to say about "the Sea Peoples," one Egyptologist recently remarked that although some things are unclear, "eins ist aber sicher: Nach den ägyptischen Texten haben wir es nicht mit einer 'Völkerwanderung' zu tun."[2] Thus the migrations hypothesis is based not on the inscriptions themselves but on their interpretation.

[1] Of Schachermeyr's numerous publications on the subject see *Griechische Frühgeschichte*, and especially *Die Levante im Zeitalter der Wanderungen: vom 13. bis zum 11. Jahrhundert v. Chr.* (Vienna, 1982). The second chapter of *Die Levante*, entitled "Grundsätzliches zu Völkerwanderungen," argues that folk migrations played a very important role throughout ancient history and distinguishes between short migrations ("Verschiebungen") and long ones ("Fernwanderungen"). For Lehmann's reconstruction of "the migrations of the Sea Peoples" see his *Mykenische Welt*, 37–49. For Akurgal's views see his "Das dunkle Zeitalter Kleinasiens," in Deger-Jalkotzy, *Griechenland*, 70–72.

[2] Wolfgang Helck, "Die Seevölker in den ägyptischen Quellen," in H. Müller-Karpe, *Geschichte des 13. und 12. Jahrhunderts v. Chr.: Frankfurt Colloquium, Feb. 1976* (Munich, 1977), 18.

The first of the inscriptions appears on the inside of the eastern wall of the main Karnak temple, and commemorates a great victory that Merneptah won over Libyan invaders and their allies in his fifth year (1208). The inscription is lengthy, running to eighty lines on the wall and to nineteen paragraphs in Breasted's translation, but only three of these paragraphs make regular appearances in discussions of "the Sea Peoples." The first relevant paragraph consists of the opening lines of the inscription:[3] "[Beginning of the victory that his majesty achieved in the land of Libya] ——i, Ekwesh, Teresh, Luka, Sherden, Shekelesh, Northerners coming from all lands." After a long apostrophe on Merneptah's valor, the inscription reports that a messenger had come during "the third season, saying: 'The wretched, fallen chief of Libya, Meryey, son of Ded, has fallen upon the country of Tehenu with his bowmen —— Sherden, Shekelesh, Ekwesh, Luka, Teresh, taking the best of every warrior and every man of war of his country. He has brought his wife and his children —— leaders of the camp, and he has reached the western boundary in the fields of Perire.' " We then hear how Merneptah led a great army against Meryre, how he utterly defeated him, capturing Meryre's wives, silver, gold, throne, and all the other possessions that he had brought with him. Merneptah and his army returned in triumph, "driving asses before them, laden with the uncircumcised phalli of the country of Libya, together with the hands of every country that was with them" (the Egyptian practice being to cut off the penis of a slain enemy as a trophy; if the enemy was circumcised, his right hand was cut off). A count of all the penises and hands somehow resulted in the following breakdown of enemy casualties:[4]

Libyans	6359
Shekelesh	222
Tursha	742
Ekwesh	2201
(*Lukka? Shardana?*)	200

There is general agreement about the decoding of the names borne by the Libyan king's foreign allies, the "northerners, from all lands." The names are in one way or another related to what were in fact the most important lands and islands on Egypt's northern horizon. Soon after the Great Karnak Inscription was first read in the early nineteenth century, Egyptologists identified the *Lukka* with Lycia, the *Ekwesh* with "Achaea," the *Tursha* with "Tyrsenia" (i.e., Tyrrhenia, the southern and western coasts of Italy), the *Shekelesh* with Sicily, and the *Shardana* with Sardinia. Although the inscription leaves no doubt that the Libyan king and his court hoped to

---

[3] Breasted, *AR*, vol. 3, no. 574.
[4] Cf. ibid., nos. 588 (Karnak) and 601 (Athribis stele).

settle in Egypt, there is no indication that any of the "northern" contingents were migrating nations. In fact, careful readers of the Great Karnak Inscription have all along observed that the low number of casualties among Meryre's northern allies indicate that what Merneptah was facing here were mercenary contingents.[5] The evident import of the Great Karnak Inscription is that in 1208 King Meryre of Libya invaded the western Delta, with intentions of seizing at least parts of it, and toward that end had secured the services of warriors from many northern lands: Sardinia, Sicily, western Italy, Greece, and southern Anatolia.[6]

The second inscription usually cited as evidence for a migration of Sea Peoples at the end of the Bronze Age comes from Medinet Habu, the mortuary temple of Ramesses III, the walls of which were cleared by Auguste Mariette in the early 1850s. The walls were found to be covered with inscriptions and illustrative reliefs commemorating every victory with which Ramesses could conceivably be credited.[7] Some of these are bogus: his purported victory over the Hittite kingdom was borrowed from Ramesses II, and his Nubian campaign was lifted from some other pharaoh's mortuary temple. And there is some repetition: sentences that are met for the first time under Year Five appear again under Year Eight. Nevertheless, it seems that Ramesses III did fight three major campaigns and win three significant victories, in his fifth, eighth, and eleventh year. In his fifth year (1182 B.C.) Ramesses defeated a Libyan invasion of the western Delta. At that time Egypt was threatened by a large force of Libyans and *Meshwesh* (often identified with the area around Tunis, where Herodotus locates people whom he calls "Maxyes"). Philistines and *Tjekker*

---

[5] Along with other Egyptologists in the nineteenth century, Gaston Maspero, *The Struggle of the Nations* (New York, 1896), 432, assumed that the people mentioned in the Great Karnak Inscription "followed the occupation of mercenary soldiers, and many of them hired out their services to the native princes." It was therefore not surprising that "Maraiu brought with him Achaeans, Shardana, Tursha, Shagalasha, and Lycians in considerable number when he resolved to begin the strife." Among recent Egyptologists who stress the mercenary character of the Libyan king's auxiliaries see G. Hölbl, "Die historischen Aussagen der ägyptischen Seevölkerinschriften," in Deger-Jalkotzy, *Griechenland*, 125. With some despair F. Schachermeyr noted that one need only read the texts to see that what Merneptah faced were *Söldnerkontingente* rather than migrating nations; see especially his *Die Levante*, 41–43: "Dass das noch lange keine Völkerwanderung bedeutete, habe ich immer wieder und wieder betont, doch hat man es durch lange Zeit nicht gelten lassen. Man braucht aber nur die Texte zu lesen, um zu erkennen, dass die Scharen, welche unter dem Begriff 'Seevölker' in den Berichten Merneptahs auftreten, hier eine völlig andere Rolle spielten als nachher um 1200 zur Zeit von Ramses III die eigentlichen Wandervölker."

[6] That *Lukka* was the name for southwestern and south-central Asia Minor is fairly certain (classical Lycia and Lycaonia both seem to reflect the Bronze Age name). See Trevor Bryce, "Lukka Revisited," *JNES* 51 (1992): 121–30.

[7] I shall use the translation furnished by Wm. Edgerton and John Wilson, *Historical Records of Ramses III* (the texts are listed as plates 1–130). For an earlier translation see Breasted, *AR*, vol. 4, nos. 1–150.

may also have made trouble in 1182, on both land and sea, and if they did so their attack was undoubtedly coordinated with that by the Libyans and *Meshwesh*.[8] Ramesses met the Libyan invaders in the western Delta, where the Egyptians slew no fewer than 12,535 of the Libyans and their allies (the reliefs show five piles of hands and foreskins, and the inscriptions at three of the piles attest 12,535 specimens).[9] Six years later—in 1176—Egypt was once again threatened by Libyans. This time the number of casualties was smaller: 2,175 Libyan warriors were slain and another 1,205 captured. In both Year Five and Year Eleven the Libyan king was evidently intent upon establishing himself permanently in the Delta, since some of his warriors shouted, "We will live in Egypt!" and a considerable number of women and children accompanied the warriors. Ramesses reports that in his second Libyan battle he captured 558 women and girls and 283 boys.[10]

Between the two Libyan invasions, Ramesses III had to face another invasion, this one from the Levant and so threatening the eastern Delta. This is the famous campaign of Year Eight (1179 B.C.). The inscription that tells about it is accompanied by reliefs depicting a land battle and a naval battle (see plates 6 and 7). The paragraph thought to attest to a migration of Sea Peoples is the following:[11]

> As for the foreign countries, they made a conspiracy in their isles (*rww*). Removed and scattered in the fray were the lands at one time. No land could stand before their arms, from Hatti, Kode, Carchemish, *Yereth*, and *Yeres* on, (but they were) cut off at [one time]. A camp [was set up] in one place in Amor. They desolated its people, and its land was like that which has never come into being. They were coming, while the flame was prepared before them, forward toward Egypt.

> Their confederation was the Peleset, Theker, Shekelesh, Denye(n), and Weshesh, lands united. They laid their hands upon the lands to the very circuit of the earth, their hearts confident and trusting: "Our plans will succeed."

Ramesses assembled a great army as well as a naval force and met the invaders on both land and sea, winning two glorious battles (the site of the land battle was Djahi, somewhere in southern Canaan). No casualty figures are given for this campaign. Ramesses' opponents in 1179 B.C. may also have included Tyrsenians, since on a stele from Deir el Medineh he boasts of having defeated *Peleset* and *Tursha* who attacked Egypt.[12]

[8] Edgerton and Wilson, *Historical Records of Ramses III,* plates 27–28 (p. 30).
[9] Ibid., plate 22.
[10] Ibid., plate 75.
[11] Ibid., plate 46 (p. 53). For a later translation by Wilson see *ANET,* 262. For Breasted's translation of this text see Breasted, *AR,* vol. 4, no. 64.
[12] Lepsius, *Denkmäler,* vol. 3, 218c.

The inscription nowhere mentions or even suggests a migration, but the reliefs show four ox carts, laden with women and children, accompanying the Philistine and *Tjekker* warriors in the land battle. One may therefore conclude that at least some of these two groups intended to establish themselves in Egypt. The Sicilians (and perhaps Tyrsenians) who joined in the attack on Egypt in 1179 evidently fought in the naval battle, but the reliefs of the naval battle portray no women and children in the enemy ships.

The Medinet Habu inscriptions and reliefs for Year Eight show us that in 1179 Egypt was invaded from the Levant by a force of Philistines and *Tjekker*,[13] who were supported by ships from Sicily and other places, and that some of the Philistine and *Tjekker* invaders presumably intended to settle in Egypt. Where did these invaders come from? In the opening line, "As for the foreign countries, they made a conspiracy in their *rww*," the word *rww* is usually translated as "islands," implying that in 1179 the Philistines and *Tjekker* lived on islands. But the translation appears to be somewhat misleading. Egyptologists have explained that the Egyptian language had no word or concept that matched our "islands," and the two Egyptian words that sometimes mean "islands" are frequently used for continental coasts.[14] A less prejudicial translation of the line would therefore be "As for the foreign countries, they made a conspiracy in their sealands." In locating the sealands where the Philistines and *Tjekker* lived one ought to start with the assumption that the Philistines came from Philistia, which is to say the original Palestine—the coast of the Levant between Gaza and Joppa. And since *Tjekker* are known only as inhabitants of the coastland south of Mt. Carmel,[15] one should assume that those

[13] The name has never been Anglicized and is variously transliterated (*Tkr, Theker, Sikkar, Tjeker, Zakkala*). Its bearers have been identified with various peoples, from Teucrians to Sicilians. It has been argued that this name in Egyptian inscriptions is the same as the *Sikalayu* recently read in Ugaritic texts, Egyptian *r* being the equivalent of either *r* or *l* in Semitic. See L. Stager, "When Canaanites and Philistines Ruled Ashkelon," *Bib. Arch. Rev.* 17 (1991): 43n.23; and Gregory Mobley, "The Identity of the *Sikalayu* [RS 34.129]," *BASOR* (forthcoming). But since the Medinet Habu Inscription mentions both *Shekelesh* and *Tjekker* as participants in the "confederation," we must insist on the separate identities of these two groups.

[14] A. Nibbi, *The Sea Peoples and Egypt* (Park Ridge, N.J.: 1975), 48, observes that "every student of Egyptology is taught that there is no determinative indicating 'island.'" At p. 65 she refers to "the common use in Egyptian of 'isles' (*iww* and *rww*) for inland areas and for Asiatic settlements." The Hebrew word *'i* likewise is ambiguously "coastland" or "island." For an Akkadian parallel see J. Brug, *A Literary and Archaeological Study of the Philistines* (Oxford, 1985), 34: "The Assyrian term *qabal tamtim* which has traditionally been translated 'in the midst of the sea' has a fairly broad usage. It should be translated 'on an island,' 'on the sea coast,' or 'at sea' depending on the context. This usage may be partly explained by the lack of a distinct Assyrian term for 'island.'"

[15] In "The Journey of Wen-Amun to Phoenicia," the hero says, "I reached Dor, a town of the Tjeker" and goes on to mention the *Tjekker* betimes (*ANET*, trans. Wilson, 26).

Tjekker who in 1179 attempted to force their way into Egypt had come from the *rww* directly north of Philistia. As has recently been observed, the phrases in which the Egyptian documents refer to Philistines "are appropriate of nearby adversaries" rather than "of enemies arriving from a distance."[16] This identification of the Philistines and *Tjekker* of 1179 as people from the Levant is reinforced by the frequent description of them as "Asiatics" (*St ty*), a term often used for Egypt's Levantine neighbors.[17] Another inscription praises Ramesses for having cowed the Philistines and the Temeh, people of eastern Libya: "The heart of the land of Temeh is removed, the Peleset are in suspense hidden in their towns."[18] The inscription seems to suggest that the "towns" of the Philistines are no farther away than the land of Temeh. In still other texts Ramesses claims to have added to Egypt land that had belonged to the Philistines and *Tjekker* and to have overthrown "the land of Peleset."[19] Finally, it is also relevant that even in the reign of Merneptah there was enough trouble from various people in Palestine and its interior that Merneptah fought a campaign there. He claimed to have defeated Ashkelon, Gezer, Yenoam, and Israel, and recent evidence suggests that his claim must be taken seriously.[20]

In short, the Medinet Habu inscriptions and reliefs indicate that in Year Eight of Ramesses III invaders from Palestine, supported by shipborne adventurers from Sicily (and perhaps Italy), headed for Egypt, intending to sack whatever they could and to appropriate some of the fertile Delta lands. The "migrations" toward the eastern Delta in 1179 were evidently analogous to the Libyan incursions into the western Delta in 1208, 1182, and 1176 B.C. Although the pressure from Egypt's Libyan and Palestinian neighbors was apparently far more severe during the years 1208–1176 than it had been since the Second Intermediate Period, such pressures were a chronic difficulty all through Egyptian history. The Egyptian inscriptions in no way attest to a transmarine *Volkswanderung* in the decades before and after 1200 B.C.

THE ORIGINS OF THE THESIS

Current beliefs that vast migrations were partly or wholly responsible for the ruin of Bronze Age civilization do not in fact rest on documentary evidence. They are instead the residue of a radical and imaginative conjecture that was launched late in the nineteenth century. The migrations thesis is largely the creation of Gaston Maspero, who developed his thesis in the

---

[16] Brug, *Philistines*, 20.
[17] Edgerton and Wilson, *Historical Records of Ramses III*, plates 31, 43, 44, 46.
[18] Ibid., plate 29.
[19] Ibid., plate 46 (p. 56) and plate 107.
[20] See pp. 19–20.

1870s and promoted it in his popular *Histoire ancienne des peuples de l'orient classique*.[21] The thesis was thus formulated when the excavation of Mycenae, Tiryns, Pylos, Knossos, Hattusas, Ugarit, and the many Levantine sites was still in the future and when it was not yet known that the *Tjekker* lived near Mt. Carmel.[22] What Maspero intended his thesis to explain, then, was not the Catastrophe, whose occurrence had not yet been perceived, but the unsuccessful assaults upon Egypt in the reigns of Merneptah and Ramesses III.

Already in the 1840s Egyptologists had debated the identity of the "northerners, coming from all lands," who assisted the Libyan King Meryre in his attack upon Merneptah. Some scholars believed that Meryre's auxiliaries were merely his neighbors on the Libyan coast, while others identified them as Indo-Europeans from north of the Caucasus. It was one of Maspero's most illustrious predecessors, Emmanuel de Rougé, who proposed that the names reflected the lands of the northern Mediterranean: the *Lukka, Ekwesh, Tursha, Shekelesh,* and *Shardana* were men from Lycia, Achaea, Tyrsenia (western Italy), Sicily, and Sardinia.[23] De Rougé and others regarded Meryre's auxiliaries—these "peuples de la mer Méditerranée"—as mercenary bands, since the Sardinians, at least, were known to have served as mercenaries already in the early years of Ramesses the Great.[24] Thus the only "migration" that the Karnak Inscription seemed to suggest was an attempted encroachment by Libyans upon neighboring territory.

Nor was this view much changed by the Medinet Habu inscriptions, with their references to *Peleset*, which were discovered in the 1850s.[25] Egyptologists concluded that these people were Philistines, but in the 1850s the Philistines were still considered to have been living on the coast

[21] For Maspero's first suggestions see *Revue Critique d'Histoire et de Littérature* (1873): 85–86, elaborated in *Rev. Crit.* (1878): 320, and ibid. (1880): 109–10. For the full reconstruction see Maspero, *Histoire ancienne des peuples de l'orient classique*, vol. 2 (Paris, 1895), subtitled *Premières Mêlées des Peuples* and translated into English as *The Struggle of the Nations*, ed. A. H. Sayce, trans. M. L. McClure (New York, 1896).

[22] The Golenischeff papyrus, with its Wen-Amun story, was published in 1891.

[23] On pp. 23–25 of a thirty-six-page pamphlet, *Extraits d'un mémoire sur les attaques dirigées contre l'Egypte par les peuples de la mer Méditerranée vers le xxve siècle avant notre ère* (Paris, 1867).

[24] Even as late as 1893 Eduard Meyer, who knew the inscriptions firsthand, was still interpreting the names as locality-names. In the first edition of his *Geschichte des Alterthums*, vol. 2 (Stuttgart, 1893), 208–9, Meyer identified the *Schardana* as "Sardinians" (the "Namensgleichheit" shows "dass die Insel Sardinien ihre Heimath sei") and noted that Sardinians had served in Egypt as mercenary soldiers, alongside Libyans and Kushites, from the beginning of the Nineteenth Dynasty. In this first edition, Meyer also saw *Turscha* merely as an equivalent for "Etrusker" from Italy (cf. p. 502 of the same volume).

[25] The first analysis of the Medinet Habu Inscription was de Rougé's *Notice de quelques textes hiéroglyphiques récemment publiés par M. Greene* (Paris, 1855).

north of Gaza for many centuries prior to the Israelite conquest of Canaan. It was understood, however, that the Philistines were not autochthonous: according to the Hebrew prophets, Yahweh had "brought up" the Philistines from Caphtor, just as he brought up the Israelites from Egypt and the Syrians from Kir, and so it had been suggested that originally the Philistines may have been Pelasgians from Crete (this view was first put forward in 1747 and had been espoused by Semiticists such as Gesenius and Renan). But the Pelasgian exodus from Crete to Canaan was supposed to have occurred before the days of the Patriarchs, since in Genesis there were references to Abimelech, king of the Philistines, as a contemporary of Abraham and Isaac, and since the Old Testament consistently implied that the Philistines had been in their promised land well before the Israelites reached theirs. Thus to scholars in the 1860s the Medinet Habu references to *Peleset* seemed to record an attack upon Egypt by its Palestinian neighbors, who were supported (exactly as the Libyans had been) by mercenaries from Sicily, Italy, and other northern lands in or along the Mediterranean Sea. W. Max Müller, de Rougé, and others who studied the inscriptions did not yet imagine that Merneptah and Ramesses had faced a tide of migratory peoples.

A slight shift occurred in 1872, when F. Chabas published the first translation of all the texts relating to the wars of Merneptah and Ramesses III. Chabas found it strange that the *Peleset* shown in the reliefs were armed and garbed in the same manner as "European" peoples such as the Sicilians and Sardinians, and he therefore argued that these *Peleset* were not from Philistia after all but were Aegean Pelasgians.[26] It was this unfortunate suggestion that triggered Maspero's wholesale revision of the entire episode.

In his 1873 review of Chabas's book, Maspero agreed that the *Peleset* of Medinet Habu were accoutred more like Europeans than Semites and also agreed that they were Aegean Pelasgians. But he proposed that it must have been at this very time—in the reign of Ramesses III—that these Pelasgians became Philistines. The *Peleset* of the Medinet Habu inscriptions, that is, were a European nation reaching the end of a long migration. Having been expelled from the Aegean, perhaps by the Dorians, they first tried to settle in Egypt; and being unsuccessful there, they settled next door and came to be known as Philistines.[27]

This novel identification of Ramesses' Philistine opponents as a migrating nation, on the verge of settling in the land that would ever after bear their name, underlies the entire migrations thesis. The specific provenance

---

[26] Chabas, *Etudes sur l'Antiquité historique d'après les sources égyptiennes et les monuments réputés préhistoriques* (Paris, 1872), 292–96.

[27] Maspero, *Revue Critique* (1873): 85.

of the Philistines was not all that important to the thesis. Although in 1873 Maspero identified the Philistines as erstwhile Pelasgians, he soon found a better match. Once he had made all his "Sea Peoples" natives of Asia Minor, he located the original Philistines there too. In Maspero's *Histoire ancienne* the Philistines move first from Crete to Caria, and then from Caria to the Levant. Thus their migration to Canaan proceeded from southern Anatolia rather than from Crete, an altogether more likely trip for a nation in ox carts. But otherwise their situation remained as Maspero had sketched it in 1873.

If the *Peleset* of the Medinet Habu inscriptions stood for a nation embarked on a migration from afar, so—Maspero proposed—did all the other names in the Karnak and Medinet Habu inscriptions. Whereas other Egyptologists interpreted the names in a straightforward sense—as Libyans, Sardinians, Sicilians, and so forth—Maspero interpreted the names as pregnant with history: ca. 1200 B.C. these were not yet the local names so familiar from Mediterranean geography but exotic *ethnica* that were about to be conferred upon lands and islands. In order to convey this distinction Maspero chose to attach definite articles to the names, and then to transliterate rather than to translate them. Whereas "Sicilians" may be random individuals and must be inhabitants of Sicily, "les Shekelesh" are a corporate entity and can be assigned a home anywhere on the globe.

Thus "the Libu" were not simply Egypt's Libyan neighbors but a mysterious and migrating nation, originally resident in the central Balkans. For them Maspero had to devise a circuitous route of migration. They must have reached the western Delta by land, having trekked two thousand miles westward from the Balkans to Gibraltar; on crossing to Africa they turned sharply, now marching eastward for another two thousand miles, thus to arrive at Egypt's doorstep in the fifth year of Merneptah. Rebuffed by that king, the Libu settled down on Egypt's western border and became Libyans, just as the defeated Peleset became Philistines.

As Maspero saw it, nations in the Balkans and Asia Minor, coming under pressure in their own homelands, resorted first to raiding and mercenary service, and then finally to migration, intending to settle in Egypt. Only the Achaeans and Lycians were in the end able to maintain their original locations. Since Herodotus (1.94) had told a story of Prince Tyrsenos leading a migration from Lydia to Italy, Maspero concluded that the *Tursha* of Merneptah's time were these very emigrants from western Anatolia. And if the *Tursha* were migrating at that time and from that place, so may have been the *Shardana* and *Shekelesh*.[28] Lacking any literary or

[28] At *Revue Critique* (1873): 86, Maspero states this as a logical deduction:

> Hérodote attribuait à une migration lydienne l'origine des Tyrséniens; les Sardiniens et une partie des populations Sicules passaient également pour être d'origine asiatique. Il

documentary evidence for migrations from Lydia to Sicily and Sardinia, Maspero found his evidence in the "derivation" of toponyms, even today a favorite hunting ground when all else has failed. As their name suggested, the *Shardana* must have come from Sardis, while the *Shekelesh* and the *Zakkala* will have come from Sagalessos (a town on the upper Maeander). Upon their eviction from Lydia, these nations spent years sailing the high seas in search of new lands in which to live. It was in this transitional phase, as "peuples de la mer," that they tried to establish themselves in Egypt.[29] Failing that, the "peuples de la mer" settled for second best and rebounded from the Delta to the western Mediterranean. In summary, "the Sea Peoples" during the reign of Ramesses III "proceeded in a series of successive detachments from Asia Minor and the Aegean sea to the coasts of Italy and of the large islands; the Tursha into that region which was known afterwards as Etruria, the Shardana into Sardinia, the Zakkala into Sicily."[30] Maspero seems to have regarded western Italy, Sicily, and Sardinia as virtually uninhabited before the migrants arrived. Thus refugees from a single Anatolian city were able to appropriate and name an island or territory covering thousands of square miles.

Maspero's "migration of the Sea Peoples," which stands on its head the ostensible meaning of the Egyptian inscriptions, ultimately rests on Herodotus's story that the cities of Etruria were founded by Tyrsenos, son of the king of Lydia. Critical historians and philologists in the nineteenth century had dismissed the Herodotean story of Prince Tyrsenos and his followers (Niebuhr and Mommsen, for example, thought the Lydian foundation of the Etruscan cities to be no less fictitious than the Arcadian or Trojan foundations in Latium). Maspero, however, took Herodotus at his

---

serait donc fort naturel de voir dans les peuples qui attaquèrent l'Egypte au temps de Menephtah et de Rhamsès III les tribus asiatiques des Tyrséniens, Sardiniens et Sicules, alors en pleine migration et qui, avant d'aller chercher un asile sur les côtes lointaines de l'Italie, essayaient de s'établir sur les rivages moins éloignés de la Syrie et de l'Egypte.

As we shall see presently, Maspero stated this more dogmatically in his *Histoire ancienne*.

[29] Whereas his predecessors had referred to them as "peuples de la mer Méditerranée," Maspero dropped the adjective and called them simply "peuples de la mer." The earlier sobriquet was more prosaic and less misleading, since the people in question did live on the coasts or islands of the Mediterranean. Maspero's term, which gave rise to the unfortunate "Sea Peoples," was intended to suggest that at the moment of their aggression against Egypt these people *had* no homes other than their ships. In fact, there is every reason to believe that Maspero's "Sea Peoples" were landlubbers, who took to the sea with misgivings and rarely headed out from the shoreline to the open sea. Some raiders must have crossed to Crete, but perhaps only because on that island there was a palace eminently worth sacking. Otherwise, the safest places in the Aegean during the Catastrophe were the Cyclades and Dodecanese islands. One thinks of the endless troubles that Odysseus and the other Achaeans are said to have encountered on their return home after sacking Troy.

[30] Maspero, *Struggle*, 587.

word and supposed that references to Tyrsenians in the inscriptions of Merneptah and Ramesses III reflected the chaotic period when Tyrsenos was attempting to translate his followers from Lydia to Italy. Unfortunately, one must evaluate critically whatever information Herodotus gives us about events that happened long before the time of Herakles. Analysis shows that before Herodotus published it, neither Greeks nor Lydians had heard the story of the Lydian Prince Tyrsenos and his colonization of Etruria; this etiological explanation for the cities of Etruria was evidently put together and given to Herodotus by a Lydian *logios* resident in Athens.[31]

Maspero explained his "migration of the Sea Peoples" as the result of an earlier migration—a Phrygian migration from Europe to Asia Minor. As he presented it, the exodus of the Phrygians from the Balkans into western Anatolia caused an upheaval there, expelling the entire lot of "the Sea Peoples."[32] The Lycians too were disturbed by the arrival of the Phrygians and so for a time tried to move to Egypt; but ultimately they were able to hold their ground against the intruders. Maspero's belief in a Phrygian migration from Europe was based, once again, on Herodotus and other writers of the Classical period.[33]

Finally, in Maspero's scheme there was a primary migration—an Illyrian migration into the Balkans—that set in motion the Phrygians, the Dorians, and the *Libu*. The possibility of an Illyrian migration (although not at that time) had already been raised by some of Maspero's contemporaries, who supposed that the Dorians may have migrated—in 1104 B.C., traditionally—because of pressures from the north. Maspero accepted such an explanation for the Dorian migration, placed it somewhat earlier than 1104, and concluded that during most of the second millennium the Dorians, Phrygians, and *Libu* had all inhabited the central Balkans. But ca. 1200 the three nations were driven out by the Illyrians: the Illyrian nation, having tardily left its Indo-European homeland in northern Europe, reached and appropriated the Balkans, sending the Phrygians southeast across the Dardanelles, the Dorians south into Greece, and the *Libu* westward on their interminable tour to Egypt. This Illyrian migration into the Balkans depended neither on a Herodotean tag nor any other text from a

[31] R. Drews, "Herodotus 1.94, the Drought ca. 1200 BC, and the Origin of the Etruscans," *Historia* 41 (1992): 14–39.

[32] When Maspero first proposed a Phrygian migration as the reason for the departure of "the Sea Peoples" he did so with some diffidence: in *Revue Critique* (1878): 320, he stated that the *Tursha* etc. were forced to leave western Anatolia by "une cause inconnue, peut-être l'arrivée des Phrygiens, des Bithyniens, des Maryandiniens et des autres peuplades d'origine thrace."

[33] Herodotus 7.73; Xanthus (no. 765 in Felix Jacoby, *Die Fragmente der griechischen Historiker* [Berlin and Leiden, 1923–58], no. 765), frags. 14 and 15.

classical author and was never more than an inference. Nevertheless, Maspero stated it with confidence. By the time of Merneptah,

> The movement of great masses of European tribes in a southerly and easterly direction was beginning to be felt by the inhabitants of the Balkans, who were forced to set out in a double stream of migration—one crossing the Bosphorus and the Propontis towards the centre of Asia Minor, while the other made for what was later known as Greece Proper, by way of passes over Olympus and Pindus. The nations who had hitherto inhabited these regions now found themselves thrust forward by the pressure of invading hordes, and were constrained to move towards the south and east by every avenue which presented itself. It was probably the irruption of the Phrygians into the high table-land which gave rise to the general exodus of these various nations.[34]

Thus Maspero invented or gave shape to three great migrations in the reigns of Merneptah and Ramesses III. In the primary migration, Illyrians came from their Indo-European homeland in northern Europe to the Balkans. This set off the secondary migrations, in which Dorians, Phrygians, and Libu were expelled from the Balkans. The arrival of the Phrygians in western Anatolia, finally, resulted in the tertiary migrations of "the Sea Peoples."

The picture sketched by Maspero in the 1870s was not immediately accepted, but neither was it seen as absurd, probably because in the late nineteenth century it was widely supposed that prehistoric peoples had a penchant for migrating. Maspero's scheme became attractive with the discovery of the "Lemnos stele" in 1885.[35] This funerary stele (apparently set up ca. 510 B.C.) bears inscriptions in dialectal Etruscan. Although the stele might have been seen as evidence that several hundred Etruscan colonists had come to Lemnos in the seventh or early sixth century, it was instead seen as evidence that the entire Etruscan nation had originated in Lemnos and its environs. In the wake of the stele's discovery, critical scholars were chastened for having dismissed Herodotus's story about the Lydian migration to Tyrsenia. Although Eduard Meyer initially protested that it was "methodisch unzulässig" to see the Lemnian inscriptions as a vindication of Herodotus,[36] the overwhelming consensus was that that is exactly what they were, and eventually Meyer himself subscribed to the new orthodoxy: the Etruscans were descended from Tyrsenians who had migrated to Italy

[34] Maspero, *Struggle*, 461–62.

[35] G. Cousin and F. Durrbach, "Bas-relief de Lemnos avec inscriptions," *BCH* 10 (1886): 1–6; for the inscriptions and the relief see Giuliano and Larissa Bonfante, *The Etruscan Language: An Introduction* (New York, 1983), 51 and n. 4. On the role of the inscription in Etruscological scholarship see Drews, "Herodotus 1.94," 24–28.

[36] Meyer, "Die Pelasger," in his *Forschungen zur alten Geschichte*, vol. 1 (Halle, 1892), 27.

from the eastern Aegean. The date of the migration remained controversial. Although orientalists, with Maspero's "Sea Peoples" in mind, tended to date it to ca. 1200 B.C., Etruscologists preferred to date the migration ca. 700 because that seemed to be the date, according to the archaeological evidence, that "Etruscan civilization" began. But whatever date one preferred for the migration, it was agreed all around that the *Tursha* who so troubled Merneptah came from the eastern Aegean.

With that decided, the *Shardana* and *Shekelesh* were readily consigned to the same bailiwick. In 1901 H. R. Hall rejected de Rougé's notion that the *Shardana* and *Shekelesh* had come from Sardinia and Sicily, on the grounds that these islands were "too far off to the west" to have had anything to do with Egypt; Maspero's suggestion that these were nations from Sardis and Sagalassos, on the other hand, "absolutely hits the right nail on the head."[37] As for the Philistines, they too must have originated in Asia Minor (Caria, Pamphylia, or Cappadocia), and it was agreed that the Medinet Habu reliefs depicted their migration to southern Canaan. In his Schweich lectures on the Philistines, given in 1911, R. A. Macalister expressed the new consensus:[38]

> We are thus to picture a great southward march through Asia Minor, Syria and Palestine. Or, rather, we are to imagine a double advance, by land and by sea: the landward march, which included two-wheeled ox-carts for the women and children, as the accompanying picture indicates; and a sea expedition, in which no doubt the spare stores would be carried more easily than on the rough Syrian roads. Clearly they were tribes accustomed to sea-faring who thus ventured on the stormy Mediterranean; clearly, too, it was no mere military expedition, but a migration of wanderers accompanied by their families and seeking a new home.

The definitive statement of the migrations thesis was perhaps the twelfth chapter (appropriately titled "Die grossen Wanderungen") of the revised second volume of Eduard Meyer's *Geschichte des Altertums*, published in 1928. Here Meyer reviewed the decline of Egypt, the end of the Hittite kingdom and the destruction of so many sites in Greece and the Near East.[39] All of this he now attributed to the folk migrations that Maspero

---

[37] Hall, "Keftiu and the Peoples of the Sea," *ABSA* 8 (1901–2), 181.

[38] R. A. Macalister, *The Philistines: Their History and Civilization* (London, 1914), 22. At p. 25 Macalister followed Maspero in deriving "the *Sherdanu* from the town of Sardis. These are the future Sardinians. . . . The inland Pisidian town of Sagalassus finds its echo in the *Shekelesh*."

[39] Meyer discussed the period initially in *Geschichte des Altertums*, vol. 2 (1893), but the discoveries at Hattusas, Knossos, and elsewhere required him to write de novo a much expanded history of the period from 1600 to 1200. The "Erste Abteilung" of the revised volume (*Geschichte des Altertums*, vol. 2, part 1 [Stuttgart and Berlin, 1928]) is devoted entirely to the period of the Egyptian New Kingdom. The close of that age is described on pp.

had proposed (it is noteworthy that Meyer nowhere credits the reconstruction to Maspero, probably because by the 1920s Meyer regarded it as fact rather than a speculative hypothesis). According to Meyer, the original homes of "die Seevölker" were beyond any doubt to be found "im Bereich des Ägaeischen Meeres."[40] And the migration of "die Seevölker" could only be understood within the wider context of ethnic movements in the twelfth century: the Dorians' descent upon Greece, the Phrygians' migration from Europe (where they had occupied the lands between the Strymon and the Adriatic) to Asia Minor, and the movement of the Italic peoples—the Latins, Sicels, Ausonians, and others—from the Balkan to the Italic peninsula. Again like Maspero, Meyer declared that the cause of this colossal upheaval in the Balkans, and so of "die grosse Wanderungen des 12. Jahrhunderts," was an Indo-European volkswanderung into the lands south of the Danube: "We cannot recover in detail the course of events, but the main lines are clear enough. It appears that the primary impetus came from the arrival of a new Indo-European nation, the Illyrians, in the northwest of the Balkan peninsula. With that, all of the peoples who had been situated in that area were set into motion."[41]

Thus the migrations hypothesis, sprung from a rash conjecture made by Maspero in 1873, was by the 1920s no longer a hypothesis but a generally accepted historical fact. Subscribed to by archaeologists, historians, Old Testament scholars, and even Egyptologists, it has seemed a self-evident "reading" of the Egyptian inscriptions. And few remember that until Maspero read his folk migrations between the lines, the inscriptions made perfect sense as a record of Egypt's battles with Libyan and Palestinian invaders, aided by warriors recruited from all the northern lands.

ARCHAEOLOGICAL AND HISTORICAL CONSIDERATIONS

Even though Maspero's overall reconstruction has not been challenged, parts of it have come to seem unlikely and so have disappeared from discussion. Maspero's primary migration—the Illyrian invasion of the Balkans—seemed dubious already in the 1920s, and has almost no advo-

---

544–607: "Die grossen Wanderungen: Ausgang der mykenischen Zeit, Ende des Hethiterreichs und Niedergang Aegyptens."

[40] Geschichte, vol. 2, part 1, 556.

[41] Ibid., 567: "Den Verlauf im einzelnen können wir nicht ermitteln; aber die Grundzüge lassen sich deutlich genug erkennen. Der Anstoss ist, so scheint es, von dem Eindringen eines neuen indogermanischen Volksstammes, der Illyrier, in den Nordwesten der Balkanhalbinsel ausgegangen. Dadurch sind alle hier·ansässigen Volksstämme in Bewegung geraten."

cates today.[42] Fritz Schachermeyr still believed that it was the Illyrians who set "the migration of the Sea Peoples" under way, but even Schachermeyr spoke more in terms of Illyrian expansion than Illyrian migration.[43] The difficulty with the Illyrian hypothesis was that when archaeological work in the Balkans commenced there turned out to be no material evidence that ca. 1200 B.C. a great nation crossed the Danube and took control of the Balkans.[44]

Likewise, "the migration of the Libu" from the Balkans to Egypt's western frontier has long been abandoned. Maspero had described the *Libu* as "men tall of stature and large of limb, with fair skins, light hair and blue eyes: everything, in fact, indicating their northern origin."[45] Needless to say, no archaeological evidence for the migration was ever turned up, and close analysis showed that the physical characteristics of the Libyans were traceable in Libya itself far back into the Bronze Age.[46] Today, so far as I know, no scholar holds that the Libyans who fought Merneptah and Ramesses III were a nomadic European nation. As a result, unfortunately, the Libyans have become less interesting and in some discussions of the Catastrophe have virtually disappeared.

The case of the Dorians is more complicated. Until late in the nineteenth century, scholars supposed—following the lead of Classical and Hellenistic Greek writers—that in 1104 B.C. the Dorians came to the Peloponnese and Crete from the mountains that fringe the Thessalian plain and that their arrival was not especially destructive. As reconstructed by Maspero, the migration became an invasion, was retrojected to the decades from Merneptah to Ramesses III, and was derived from the central Balkans, several hundred kilometers north of the starting point indicated by Her-

[42] V. Gordon Childe, *The Danube in Prehistory* (Oxford, 1929) found little evidence for an Illyrian invasion ca. 1200. The possibility was not even mentioned by Peter Wells, "Crisis Years? The 12th Century B.C. in Central and Southeastern Europe," in Ward and Joukowsky, *Crisis Years*, 31–39.

[43] See especially Schachermeyr, *Griechische Frühgeschichte*, 36ff. Most recently, G. Lehmann has argued that "the Sea Peoples" originated in Illyria, but Lehmann has not explicitly argued that they moved out of Illyria because other people were moving in (Lehmann, *Mykenische Welt*, 42–49).

[44] See, for example, T.G.E. Powell, "The Inception of the Final Bronze Age in Middle Europe," *PPS* 29 (1963): 233: "What then can be said of *Die Grosse Wanderung*, the great migration of Danubian Europeans, allegedly Illyrians, who are so frequently credited with the final overthrow of the Hittites, the sacking of Syrian cities, and the great raids on Egypt? From the European side it is increasingly difficult to find any evidence for an evacuation on such a scale from the populous lands of the Middle Danube, and not anyway in a southerly direction. In Danubian Serbia, which should be a crucial area for this matter, cultural continuity indicates a largely undisturbed population for the whole of the period under review."

[45] Maspero, *Struggle*, 430.

[46] G. Möller, "Die Aegypter und ihre libyschen Nachbarn," *ZDMG* 78 (1924): 36ff.

odotus. By the early twentieth century historians and archaeologists alike held the "Dorian Invasion" responsible for the destruction of Mycenae, Tiryns, and other Bronze Age sites.

Today the Dorians tend to be once again what they were before Maspero revamped them. The majority view of specialists in Greek dialectology is that the Dorians were descended from North-Greek speakers, who in the Late Helladic period lived in the Pindus and other mountain ranges north and west of Boeotia (in the first millennium Northwest Greek dialects were spoken by the Locrians, Phocians, and Aetolians).[47] Many of these North Greeks would then have come into the Peloponnese and Crete after the departure of South Greeks for Cyprus, but probably before other South Greeks moved to the coast of Asia Minor and became Ionians. Although this Dorian migration from northern to southern Greece has been dated as late as the tenth century B.C., it is more commonly placed toward the end of the twelfth or beginning of the eleventh.[48]

The old view—that the Dorian Invasion proceeded from the central Balkans, and that it occurred ca. 1200—is now maintained by only a few archaeologists and against increasing evidence to the contrary. Kilian's excavations at Tiryns have shown that at that site (as at Mycenae itself) "Mycenaean" Greeks occupied the lower city until, at the end of the IIIC period, there was further destruction and then abandonment.[49] Iron Age innovations that were once attributed to invaders from the Balkans— geometric pottery, cremation burials, and ironworking itself—have long since been seen to date from well after 1200 and to have come from other sources. The case for a Dorian invasion from the Balkans ca. 1200 has therefore been recently based on the Danubian antecedents for a number of the artifacts that turn up in the Aegean and western Asia Minor early in the twelfth century: handmade burnished ware ("barbarian ware"), violin-bow fibulae, and especially the Naue Type II sword.[50] But the "barbarian"

---

[47] On the linguistic evolution see Ernst Risch, "La posizione del dialetto dorico," in Musti, *Origini dei Greci*, 13–35. John Chadwick's proposal that the Dorians had been living in the Peloponnese and Crete throughout the second millennium, forming a lower class to a South-Greek–speaking aristocracy, has not been generally accepted; see Chadwick, "I Dori e la creazione dei dialetti greci," in Musti, *Origini dei Greci*, 3–12, and the objections, on linguistic grounds, of R. A. Crossland, Carlo de Simone, Ernst Risch, and Peter van Soesbergen on pp. 335–40 and 359–67 of the same volume. My own objections, on historical grounds, are stated in *Coming of the Greeks*, 208–13.

[48] See especially Desborough, *The Greek Dark Ages* (New York, 1972), 64–79; D. Musti, "Continuità e discontinuità tra Achei e Dori nelle tradizioni storiche," in Musti, *Origini dei Greci*, 60, also argues for a "migrazione dorica della fine del TE III C."

[49] Kilian, "Caduta dei palazzi," 73–115.

[50] The German-language scholarship (G. von Merhart, W. Kimmig, J. Bouzek, and others) is cited by Lehmann, *Mykenische Welt*, 43–44 (esp. n. 86). On the pottery see J. Rutter,

pottery has been found not only in the Peloponnese but also at Lekfandi, in Asia Minor, and most recently in Cyprus.[51] Although it can hardly be explained as a result of trade (it is too crude and coarse to have had any commercial value), it is hardly the pottery of an immigrant Dorian population, since its location does not correlate with "Dorian" Greece and since it represents an infinitesimal fraction of twelfth-century B.C. Greek pottery.[52] Even in the earlier excavations the quantity of this "barbarian ware" at any site was minute (at Korakou, for example, sixteen sherds). And now, as Podzuweit points out, the excavations at Tiryns not only confirm that "barbarian ware" was a negligible commodity in the LH IIIC period, but also that its use began before the Catastrophe rather than after it.[53] Nor do the new metal artifacts (which point as much to Italy as to the central Balkans) indicate a migration. The best explanation for the fibulae seems to be, as Desborough argued, that they were first brought from the Balkans (or Italy) to Greece over trade routes, or by individuals and small groups, and eventually were copied and produced by Mycenaean artisans.[54] The Naue Type II sword, we shall see in chapter 13, is undoubtedly a central European and northern Italian type, but the specimens found in Greece in LH IIIC contexts came from "Greek" tombs and were accompanied by "Greek" pottery. One would therefore suppose that Greek-speakers had acquired the swords and learned how to use them. Or, as Hector Catling suggested, one might imagine these Naue Type II swords in the hands of mercenaries who had joined the service of Helladic kingdoms or communities.[55] In short, there may have been movement of people from the Balkans into Greece and western Asia Minor during and shortly after the Catastrophe, just as there had always been, but what movement there was

---

"Ceramic Evidence for Northern Intruders in Southern Greece at the Beginning of the Late Helladic IIIC Period," *AJA* 79 (1975): 17–32; E. French and J. Rutter, "The Handmade Burnished Ware of the Late Helladic IIIC Period: Its Historical Context," *AJA* 81 (1977): 111–12; Sigrid Deger-Jalkotzy, "Das Problem der 'Handmade Burnished Ware,'" in Deger-Jalkotzy, *Griechenland*, 161–68.

[51] Cf. Ian Todd's review, in *AJA* 95 (1991): 548, of the excavation report on Maa/Palaeokastro.

[52] For a balanced discussion of the "barbarian" ware and its ramifications see A. F. Harding, *The Mycenaeans and Europe* (London, 1984), 216–27. Harding sees no link with the Danube or the central Balkans and concludes (p. 227) that "by far the strongest case for a connection with alien ceramic traditions can be made for Italy and north-western Greece."

[53] Podzuweit, "Die mykenische Welt und Troja," 69: at Tiryns, where a great deal of twelfth-century pottery was uncovered, "dürfte der Anteil an der gesamten unbemalten Keramik unter 0,1% liegen, also einem völlig unerheblichen Anteil an der Gesammtmasse ausmachen." Podzuweit also notes its occurrence in IIIB levels at Tiryns.

[54] *Last Mycenaeans*, 54–58.

[55] Catling, "A New Bronze Sword from Cyprus," *Antiquity* 35 (1961): 121: "The distribution suggests that these mercenaries may have travelled overland south to the Adriatic, and thence by sea up the Gulf of Corinth—they may even have been shipped in Mycenaean hulls."

must have been limited to individuals, families, and small groups of families. There is no evidence for a general migration, to say nothing of a migration responsible for the destruction of the IIIB sites.[56]

Although many historians continue to believe in a Phrygian migration from Europe to Asia Minor ca. 1200 B.C., the idea has been generally abandoned by Anatolian archaeologists. Maspero's Phrygian migration was widely accepted when excavations first showed that Hattusas, Alishar, and other Hittite sites were destroyed ca. 1200. Eventually, however, it became clear that at none of the Hittite sites was there any evidence for newcomers after the destruction. As a result, by the 1960s Hittitologists were generally agreed that no "new people" had brought down the Hittite empire.[57] The history of western Anatolia is less clear, but the evidence that has been advanced for a new population there is exiguous. A few sherds of "barbarian ware" have been found at Troy (VIIb2) and at Gordium, but the sherds are too few and too late to serve as an argument that a Phrygian invasion from the Balkans was responsible for the Catastrophe in western Anatolia. At most, the sherds may indicate—as Kenneth Sams has argued—that in the aftermath of the Catastrophe immigrants from Europe squatted in the ruins of Troy.[58] After his last review of the pottery from the period, even Schachermeyr abandoned the idea that it was a Phrygian migration from Europe that set "the Sea Peoples" in motion.[59] The lack of archaeological support for a Phrygian migration from Europe ca. 1200 is hardly surprising since, as noted previously, Maspero's thesis rested entirely on statements by two Greek authors of the fifth century. Analysis will show that the statements in question—one from Herodotus and one from the *Lydiaka* of Xanthus—have no value as evidence for Bronze Age history. Contradicting the earlier Greek view that the Phrygians had "always" lived in Phrygia, the texts seem to have been occasioned by a late fifth-century controversy about the identity of the legendary King Midas.[60] Although we can be quite certain that "the Phrygian migration from Europe" was first postulated in the Age of Pericles, Maspero assumed that it was a fact, faithfully transmitted from the thirteenth century to Her-

---

[56] Wells, "Crisis Years?" 38: "There is no question that lively contact existed between the regions and it probably took the form of trade, among other mechanisms. But direct participation on any substantial scale by northern groups in Mediterranean palace destructions seems unlikely."

[57] See, for example, G. Walser, "Alte Geschichte und Hethiterforschung," in Walser, ed., *Neuere Hethiterforschung* (Wiesbaden, 1964), 10; cf. Bittel, "Kleinasien," 37 and 45.

[58] G. Kenneth Sams, "Observations on Western Anatolia," 58, in Ward and Joukowsky, *Crisis Years*, suggests that settlers from Thrace came to Phrygia after "the fall of the Anatolian Bronze Age establishments" had removed "barriers to penetration and resettlement."

[59] See his remarks in Deger-Jalkotzy, *Griechenland*, 257.

[60] I argue this in detail in "Myths of Midas and the Phrygian Migration from Europe" (forthcoming in *Klio*).

odotus's and Xanthus's own day. And on this "fact" he based his "Phrygian migration from Europe" shortly before the reign of Ramesses III. There is no reason to doubt that the Phrygian language spoken in western Anatolia during the Iron Age was descended from a proto- Phrygian spoken there in the Late Bronze Age.

Maspero's tertiary migrations still have many advocates but no more foundation now than when they were first proposed. There is, first of all, no archaeological evidence for migrations into Sicily and Sardinia in the early twelfth century. The "Nuragic culture" on Sardinia continued without significant interruption from the thirteenth century B.C. through the twelfth.[61] Sicilian archaeology is no more forthcoming: a migration to the island at this time, whether of Sicels from Italy or of *Shekelesh* from Asia Minor, has "no material support," and classical authors' statements that Trojan refugees settled in Sicily may be dismissed as learned conjectures.[62] So far as "Tyrsenia"—the name the Greeks seem to have used initially for the southern and western coast of Italy is concerned, there is a school of thought that "the Urnfielders" came to Italy in the twelfth century and brought in the Protovillanovan culture (the other school, of course, is that Protovillanovan evolved from local roots). But whatever external ties the Urnfield cemeteries may have had seem to be with temperate Europe rather than with the Aegean or Asia Minor.[63] From Maspero onward, the real basis for the belief that "the Tursha" came to Italy from the east has not been archaeological but literary—Herodotus's story about the Lydian colonization of Tyrsenia. As I have argued elsewhere in detail, that story is an etiology constructed shortly before Herodotus wrote.[64]

[61] Giovanni Lilliu, *La civiltà nuragica* (Sassari, 1982), 113: "I secoli nei quali si svolgono le vicende dei *Sherdanw* e dei confederati . . . sono quelli che vedono le comunità nuragiche guidate dai loro principi toccare il massimo splendore nell'architettura e sviluppare un consistente e organizzato vivere civile, economicamente prospero. Sono i secoli XIII-XII." Lilliu finds it entirely reasonable that some of the "pirates" who joined in the attack on Egypt came from Sardinia and finds no evidence for an invasion of the island between his Fase II (1500–1200) and Fase III (1200–900).

[62] D. Trump, *The Prehistory of the Mediterranean* (New Haven, 1980), 214; cf. Ross Holloway, *Italy and the Aegean 3000–700 B.C.* (Louvain-la-Neuve, 1981), 102.

[63] J. M. Coles and A. F. Harding, *The Bronze Age in Europe: An Introduction to the Prehistory of Europe c. 2000–700 BC* (New York, 1979), 425, note that "the scientific world is divided into those who favour an indigenous development for Protovillanovan and those who see it as intrusive," the latter group emphasizing links between Italy and Europe beyond the Alps. See also M. A. Fugazzola Delpino, "The Proto-Villanovan: A Survey," in D. and F. Ridgway, eds., *Italy before the Romans: The Iron Age, Orientalizing, and Etruscan Periods* (London, 1979), 31–51. On the links between Hungary and northern Italy in the Protovillanovan period see Powell, "Inception," 234.

[64] Drews, "Herodotus 1.94," 33–38. On the parallel story of exiles from Greece founding cities in Latium and Etruria see Dominique Briquel, *Les Pélasges en Italie. Recherches sur l'histoire de la légende* (Paris, 1984).

Let us turn, finally, to Canaan and to Maspero's thesis of a "Philistine" invasion ca. 1200. Archaeological arguments have traditionally been advanced for a massive invasion by a new nation in the twelfth century, but they do not seem to be very strong.[65] The bichrome "Philistine ware" seems to have evolved from a Palestinian imitation (locally manufactured) of Aegean LH IIIC pottery, which after 1190 B.C. was evidently difficult to obtain.[66] The anthropoid coffins found in burials at various sites have often been hailed as a sign of the arrival of "the Philistines" early in the twelfth century, but the recent discovery of such coffins at Deir-el-Balaḥ greatly weakens the argument. As James Muhly has pointedly remarked, that the anthropoid coffins had little or nothing to do with a Philistine invasion ca. 1200 "was apparent a long time ago, but now, with the material from Deir el-Balah, has become inescapable. Here was a site with something on the order of 50 burials in anthropoid coffins, a 'Philistine' site par excellence. The only problem is that the site dates to the LBA, the 14th and 13th centuries B.C., is purely Egyptian in character, has nothing whatsoever to do with the Philistines and is related to the Aegean only because, like Beth Shan, Aegean pottery was in use at the site."[67]

In short, the archaeological evidence by itself would hardly lead any observer to conclude that ca. 1200 Philistia was overrun by an immigrant nation. The belief that "the Philistines" at that time descended upon Canaan from western Asia Minor (Caria has frequently been mentioned as the point of departure) is a modern revision of the Hebrew prophets' assertion that the Philistine nation had been delivered to Canaan from Crete (Caphtor). The prophets' statements (Amos 9.7, Jeremiah 47.4) seem to have rested on at least a slender historical basis. Much earlier biblical texts

---

[65] The arguments are set out fully by Trude Dothan, *The Philistines and their Material Culture*, rev. ed. (New Haven, 1982) and by John Brug, *A Literary and Archaeological Study of the Philistines* (B.A.R. International Series, no. 265, 1985); Dothan argues for two invasions, one by the "Sea Peoples" and a slightly later one by the "Philistines." Brug finds no compelling reason to believe in any significant influx of new people. Meyer, *Geschichte*, vol. 2, part 1, 560, noted that the invaders "haben Gefässe der spätmykenischen Zeit mitgebracht." For the identification of this pottery as "Philisterkeramik" Meyer cited Thiersch, *Arch. Anz.* (1908): 378ff.

[66] Dothan, "Sea Peoples and Philistines," 103, notes for example that at Ashdod LH IIIC: 1b pottery is dominant in Stratum XIIIb, but in the subsequent Stratum XIIIa "it coincides with the appearance of typical Philistine bichrome pottery. Trace element analysis has shown that both the monochrome Myc. IIIC: 1 pottery and the bichrome Philistine pottery were of local manufacture." Although Dothan herself believes that the LH IIIC: 1b pottery was brought in by "the Sea Peoples," and the bichrome pottery by "the Philistines," it seems more reasonable to suppose that both types were made by the population that had been living at Ashdod all along (perhaps with some help from Aegean refugees who fled eastward after the mainland Greek centers had been destroyed).

[67] Muhly, "Sea Peoples," 46; cf. Trude Dothan, "Anthropoid Clay Coffins from a Late Bronze Age Cemetery near Deir el-Balaḥ," *IEJ* 23 (1973): 129–46.

imply that in the tenth century there was a small Cretan enclave in Philistia: David employed both "Pelethite and Cherethite" guards, and in Saul's reign there was a "*negeb* of the Cretans" northeast of Gaza (1 Samuel 30.14; cf. Deuteronomy 2.23). The likeliest explanation for that term, and for David's "Cretan" guards, is that refugees from one of the Cretan cities had settled in Palestine during the Catastrophe or in its aftermath, when life was perceived to be even more precarious in the Aegean than on the Levantine coasts. That some South-Greek speakers from Crete might have fled to southern Canaan—rather than to the mountain aeries of Kavousi, Vrokastro, and Karphi—is not entirely surprising. The popularity of Greek pottery in Late Bronze Age Palestine (the Mycenaean ware was much better than anything produced in the Levant) suggests that there was regular traffic between the Aegean and the coastal cities of Palestine in the thirteenth century. It is thus possible that a flight from Crete to Canaan paralleled the flight from Greece to Cyprus and, eventually, to Ionia. But whatever settlement there was must have been on a comparatively tiny scale. Whereas a South-Greek dialect was transplanted from the Aegean to Cyprus and Ionia, the Cretans who came to Philistia were evidently too few to have made any noticeable linguistic impression.

The drama of the refugees' flight, however, seems to have made a deep impression and was eventually appropriated by the general population of Philistia. Just as the people of all Israel and Judah came to treasure the myth that their ancestors—six hundred thousand fighting men—had escaped from Egypt, so by the middle of the first millennium people in Gaza, Ashkelon, and the other cities of Philistia were regarded (and undoubtedly regarded themselves) as "the remnant from Caphtor" (Jeremiah 47.4). In fact the population of Philistia, as of Israel and Judah, had predominantly local roots. The name "Philistia" (or "Palestine") seems to have been nothing more than a place-name, without ethnic connotations.[68] Since the inhabitants of Philistia worshiped Canaanite gods, and since the language of the area in the first millennium was Northwest Semitic, one must assume that the overwhelming majority of Iron Age Palestinians were descended from Palestinians of the Late Bronze Age.[69] Nevertheless, regardless of how

---

[68] At *Philistines*, 47, Brug concluded that "on the basis of the evidence presently available it does not appear that the term 'Philistine' is primarily an ethnic or linguistic term. It has geographic and political connotations connected with southwestern Palestine."

[69] Cf. ibid., 196: "There is at present no clear evidence that there was a distinct Philistine language." Belief in a "Philistine" intrusion into southern Canaan ca. 1200 has always been embarrassed by the fact that Iron Age Philistia has yielded nothing but Northwest Semitic inscriptions. The linguistic evidence remains uncompromising. At p. 200 Brug observes that "there is at present no decisive evidence for the general use of a non-Semitic language among the Philistines at any stage of their history. It appears that they used a dialect similar to the people around them."

much it was exaggerated and distorted, there does seem to have been at least a thin basis in fact for the ancient myth that the Philistines were a "remnant from Caphtor."

For the modern myth that has replaced it, however, there is none. Instead of questioning the story of the Philistines' Cretan origins, in an attempt to locate a core of historical probability, Maspero took the story at face value and proceeded to inflate it to fantastic dimensions. Believing that the Medinet Habu reliefs, with their ox carts, depict the Philistine nation on the eve of its settlement in Canaan, Maspero imagined a great overland migration. The Philistines moved first from Crete to Caria, he proposed, and then from Caria to Canaan in the time of Ramesses III. Whereas Amos and Jeremiah derived the Philistines directly from Crete, a five-day sail away, Maspero's myth credited them with an itinerary that, while reflecting badly on their intelligence, testified to prodigious physical stamina: the Philistines sail from Crete to Caria, where they abandon their ships and their maritime tradition; the nation then travels in ox carts through seven hundred miles of rough and hostile terrain until it reaches southern Canaan; at that point, far from being debilitated by their trek, the Philistines not only conquer the land and give it their name but come within a hair's breadth of defeating the Egyptian pharaoh himself. Not surprisingly, for the migration from Caria to Canaan imagined by Maspero there is no evidence at all, whether literary, archaeological, or documentary.

Since none of Maspero's national migrations is demonstrable in the Egyptian inscriptions, or in the archaeological or linguistic record, the argument that these migrations did indeed occur has traditionally relied on place-names. These place-names are presented as the source from which were derived the *ethnica* in Merneptah's and Ramesses' inscriptions. We have already noted Maspero's Anatolian etymologies for "Sardinians," "Sicilians," and "Tyrsenians": Sardis, Sagalassos, and Tyrrha, respectively. The thesis that Asia Minor was the homeland of all "the Sea Peoples" depended in part, however, on the credibility of a Phrygian invasion, since otherwise there would have been no explanation why these peoples should have left Asia Minor for new homelands in the west. When it began to appear, in the 1950s and 1960s, that a Phrygian migration was not responsible for the Catastrophe in Asia Minor, it was less credible that Asia Minor was the original home of "the Sea Peoples." Some migrationists have therefore looked for a new starting point for "the Sea Peoples" and have located their original home in the Balkans. According to Lehmann, Schachermeyr, and Liverani,[70] the *Tursha* and Lycians came from Asia Minor, but the

---

[70] In Deger-Jalkotzy, *Griechenland*, see Lehmann's article, "Zum Auftreten von ‚Seevölker'-Gruppen im östlichen Mittelmeerraum—eine Zwischenbalanz," 79–92, and es-

Shardana, Shekelesh, and *Peleset* came from the Adriatic coast of the Balkans. Lehmann's onomastic evidence for a Balkan provenance comes from classical authors: the Philistines' name recalls the town of Palaeste, on the Albanian coast; further north, according to Pliny the Elder and Claudius Ptolemy, there lived a community of Siculi; the same authors knew of Sardeates near Salonae (near modern Split), and in the interior were Serdoi or Sardoi (ancient Serdica is now Sofia). These Balkan names are perhaps as convincing as the Anatolian names cited by Maspero. But of course there is a much more obvious source for the names. If the name *Shardana,* for example, does indeed have something to do with the island of Sardinia, the natural explanation should be that the *Shardana* warriors who fought against Ramesses came neither from Sardis nor Serdica but from Sardinia.

The notion that ca. 1200 "the *Shekelesh*" and "the *Shardana*" were on their way *to* Sicily and Sardinia—which they would name after themselves—made little sense when Maspero proposed it and makes less today. A minor objection is that we now know (as Maspero did not) that Sicily and Sardinia—to say nothing of Italy and Palestine—were too important throughout the Late Bronze Age to have remained nameless. Any theory holding that the names of Sardinia and Sicily came from the *ethnica* of "the Sea Peoples," and were not conferred upon the islands before the twelfth century B.C., must also therefore hold that in the Bronze Age the Levantine and Aegean traders had other names for these islands and that these (unknown) traditional names were somehow replaced and utterly obscured by the new *ethnica.*[71]

When Merneptah boasted of having turned back an attack by a Libyan king who was supported by "northerners, from all lands," he went on to specify who exactly these northerners were. The *ethnica* were presumably given in order to impress the reader or listener, and that could only have been accomplished if the appended names were meaningful. The names

---

pecially his remarks on pp. 175–78 of that volume; see also Lehmann's fuller and more recent presentation, *Mykenische Welt,* 42–49. Schachermeyr, *Griechische Frühgeschichte,* 162, accepts Lehmann's identifications. Liverani likewise derives the marauders from the "penisola balcanica" (cf. *Antico Oriente,* 632).

[71] For an attempt along these lines see, for example, M. Dothan, "Sardina at Akko?" in M. Balmuth, ed., *Studies in Sardinian Archaeology,* vol. 2 (Ann Arbor, 1986), 105–15. Dothan suggests that the *Shardana* who settled on the island in the twelfth century were a tiny group but that it was this tiny group that Phoenician merchants happened upon when they discovered the island in the ninth century. Mistaking the *partem pro toto,* the merchants called the entire island *srdn* (the name attested in the Nora Stone). This argument works only if between the twelfth century B.C. and the ninth the very existence of Sardinia had been forgotten in Levantine ports, maps, and onomastica. That is extremely unlikely, and instead it is beginning to appear that "Phoenician merchantmen were plying the western Mediterranean in the metal trade no later than the eleventh century" (Frank Cross, "Phoenicians in the West: The Early Epigraphic Evidence," in Balmuth, *Sardinian Archaeology,* vol. 2, 124).

were hardly meant to introduce the listener to peoples hitherto unknown but to celebrate the fact that the pharaoh had defeated a Libyan king who was supported by a force drawn from places that an Egyptian would recognize as exotic but important lands on the northern rim of the world: precisely such lands as Lycia, Greece, Italy, Sicily, and Sardinia. The *ethnica* of the Egyptian inscriptions argue against the migrations hypothesis rather than for it.

The most serious argument against the hypothesis that the adversaries of the Egyptians were migratory peoples, about to take over huge chunks of the Mediterranean world, is a historical argument. The hypothesis assumes, first of all, national entities for which there is no other evidence. For Maspero, in nineteenth-century France, nationalism was the "natural" ideology of people all through history. But nationalism was as alien to the Bronze Age as it was characteristic of nineteenth-century Europe, and there is no reason to believe that in antiquity "the Sicilians" or "the Sardinians" (or, for that matter, "the Etruscans" or "the Achaeans") were *ever* a cohesive group, a "peuple" with a shared history, pursuing a common goal and acting with a common purpose. When Phoenician merchants established a refinery at Sardinian Nora in the ninth century B.C., and when Carthaginians and Greeks came to Sicily in the eighth, they had to deal with those particular Sardinians and Sicilians who lived in the vicinity of the new emporia or colonial cities. But they certainly did not have to deal with a Sardinian or a Sicilian nation.

Even if one grants that in the Bronze Age there were proto-Sardinian and proto-Sicilian nations, and that for one reason or another the national cohesion disintegrated between the twelfth century and the eighth, Maspero's thesis would still run aground on historical arguments. His thesis assumes, on the one hand, that nations materialized out of an assortment of places (whether in Anatolia, the Balkans, or the Levant) so minuscule and obscure that they can only be located with the help of classical geographers and gazetteers; and, on the other hand, that once released from their confinement these nations were large enough to cover all of Sardinia, Sicily, Etruria, and Palestine. The supposed military fortunes of these nations are extraordinary. Although too weak to maintain themselves in their own hometowns, after their expulsion they conceived the ambition to conquer Egypt, the greatest kingdom in the world. After being defeated by Ramesses on land and sea, they found themselves so formidable that they dispensed with their coalition, and each nation went its own way to effect a magnificent and historic conquest (although, strangely, a conquest that left no archaeological trace). One nation took over Sicily, a project that in historical times proved too difficult for either the Greeks or the Carthaginians. Another nation took over Sardinia, which at the time was at a peak of prosperity that in antiquity it had never reached before and would never reach again. A third nation took over Etruria, which the Romans spent most of the Early Republic trying to reduce. Finally, a fourth nation took over Palestine, an area that even David did not annex. The achievement of any one of these four projects by the entire and undefeated coalition would have been remarkable enough. That all four projects could have been simultaneously achieved after the coalition had been soundly defeated by Ramesses, and had broken up into its original minuscule and obscure components, is so remote a possibility that it must be dismissed. If the names *Shardana*, *Shekelesh*, *Tursha*, and *Peleset* have something to do with Sardinia, Sicily, Tyrsenia, and Palestine (and they very likely do), the names can only mean—quite simply—"people from Sardinia, Sicily, Italy, and Palestine." The names themselves are not evidence for migrations from anywhere to anywhere. The only "migrations" that contributed to the Catastrophe are the encroachments of Libyans and Palestinians on the Egyptian Delta.

Chapter Five

IRONWORKING

MANY HAVE SEEN "the migration of the Sea Peoples" as the proximate cause of the Catastrophe but have understood the underlying and ultimate cause to be something very different. One such explanation for the Catastrophe that was once popular in the English-speaking world (even outside the circles of professional historians) but is now out of favor is that the Catastrophe was ultimately the result of a technological innovation: the invention of ironworking. This hypothesis in some ways anticipates my own, since it presents the Catastrophe as the work of men who prevail on the battlefield because of an advantage in weaponry. But in what we may call the "ironworking hypothesis" no change in the art of war was envisaged: the types of weapons and the tactics employed ca. 1200 B.C. were what they had always been, with the only change being in the material from which the weapons are made. The innovation was therefore more metallurgical than military.

The ironworking hypothesis emerged in embryonic form early in this century, when belief in a massive Indo-European migration into the Balkans was still unshaken. In this early form of the hypothesis, the Phrygians and Dorians were sent southward by an Illyrian expansion, but they were able to conquer western Anatolia and Greece because they were armed with iron (they had learned of this metal, at great cost, from the Illyrians who expelled them). That the Sea Peoples themselves—the Shardana, Shekelesh, Tursha, and the rest—used iron was not so clear. A passage in the Old Testament (1 Samuel 13.19–21) was taken to mean that "the Philistines" were ironworkers, even though the passage did not mention iron, but how they and the other peoples of Anatolian provenance had managed to learn about iron was a problem.

A quite different form of the ironworking hypothesis appeared in 1942. In his *What Happened in History* V. Gordon Childe presented a picture of the Catastrophe in which an Indo-European migration played a very small role, and the development of ironworking a very big one.[1] Childe, whose investigation of Balkan prehistory had turned up little evidence for either the supposed migration or for ironworking there ca. 1200 B.C., concluded that ironworking was not a central or northern European innovation after all but was developed in Asia Minor in the thirteenth century (the Hattusas tablets contained several references to iron artifacts and even to an iron

[1] Childe, *What Happened in History* (Harmondsworth, 1942), 175–79.

throne). But the new art, in Childe's reconstruction, remained a "secret" of the Hittites until the end of that century. At that point, the subject peoples who had been obliged to produce the metal began to take it into their own hands. With iron weapons, the Anatolian rebels were able to overturn the Hittite monarchy. They then took to the sea and, along with other barbarian peoples, attacked and overran most of the other Bronze Age kingdoms.

In Childe's reconstruction, the Catastrophe became something of a blessing in disguise. The destruction of palaces and cities was regrettable, but it cleared the decks for advances of all kinds. Along with iron weapons came iron tools, and for the first time the lower classes were able to afford metal plowshares, hoes and saws. The new technology thus brought about not only the destruction of the old centers of power but also the most important shift in the class struggle in the five thousand years between the Urban Revolution and the Industrial Revolution. So far as "the Sea Peoples" were concerned, Childe was content to see them as natives of Asia Minor who eventually settled in Italy, Sicily, Sardinia, and Palestine.[2] But these secondary migrations, like the Dorian Invasion of Greece, had been occasioned not by an Indo-European *Volkswanderung* from central Europe but by a technological innovation within the civilized world itself.

It is doubtful that any treatment of the Catastrophe, in any language, has been so broadly influential as Childe's. Although widely ignored by specialists in Egyptology, Assyriology, and Aegean or Near Eastern archaeology, it had an immediate and lasting impact in the more progressive disciplines of the social sciences, especially in Britain and America. The first edition of *What Happened in History* was reprinted four times, and the revised edition of 1954 was even more successful. Although Childe was evidently wrong about the role of ironworking in the Catastrophe, his suggestions on other matters have been quite helpful. Most importantly, Childe insisted on the difference in character between the Bronze Age and the Iron Age: whereas the earlier period was dominated by its kings and its professional elites, in the Iron Age the common man counted for something.

A variation on Childe's reconstruction was put forward by George Mendenhall.[3] Mendenhall supposed that the secret of ironworking was brought to Canaan (and perhaps to Greece) late in the thirteenth century by immigrants from Anatolia. Thanks to their iron, the Anatolians were able to make themselves an elite in the Levantine cities. This alien domination, however, was resented by the Canaanite natives, and ca. 1200 B.C. they rose in revolt, in the process destroying many of the cities from which their

---

[2] Childe, *Prehistoric Migrations in Europe* (Cambridge, Mass., 1950), 180.

[3] Mendenhall, *The Tenth Generation: The Origins of the Biblical Tradition* (Baltimore, 1973).

ironworking masters ruled.[4] Mendenhall thus turned Childe's hypothesis on its head and presented the Catastrophe (or at least the Canaanite segment of the Catastrophe) as a social revolution directed against an ironworking elite.

The most recent work in which a vestige of the ironworking hypothesis appears is Norman Gottwald's *The Tribes of Yahweh*.[5] In Gottwald's presentation, as in Mendenhall's, iron was "introduced into Canaan from Anatolia in the thirteenth or early twelfth century." The innovation upset Levantine power-relationships, and soon "armies equipped with iron chariots, spears, swords, and daggers acquired greatly increased striking power over opponents equipped with equivalent weapons in bronze."[6] A social revolution ensued, culminating in the termination of the old order. Although in Gottwald's reconstruction the twelfth-century Israelite peasants had few iron weapons, they did have iron tools. With iron axes, spades, and plows they began to cultivate land far more productively than their ancestors had a century earlier. Thus they were able to build up surpluses and lay the foundations of a very new society.

The ironworking hypothesis has been undone by archaeological excavations and by metallurgical analyses. Although in conventional terminology the "Iron Age" commenced with the Catastrophe, it is now quite clear that iron did not come into regular use until well over a century after the Catastrophe ended. Although there were premonitions of this discrepancy all along,[7] it was demonstrated conclusively in the 1960s. Anthony Snodgrass's survey of early Greek weaponry showed that few iron weapons were used in twelfth-century Greece.[8] Although areas to the east may have been slightly in advance of Greece in ironworking, in the twelfth century iron weapons were also rare in the Near East. According to the tabulations of Jane Waldbaum, of all the weapons and armor found in twelfth-century contexts in the eastern Mediterranean, only a little more than three percent are iron while over 96 percent of them are bronze (for the eleventh century the proportions are 80 percent bronze and 20 percent iron, and for the tenth century 46 percent bronze and 54 percent iron).[9] It now appears that

[4] Ibid., 147–49.

[5] Gottwald, *The Tribes of Yahweh: A Sociology of the Religion of Liberated Israel, 1250– 1050 B.C.E.* (Maryknoll, N.Y., 1979).

[6] Ibid., 655.

[7] Against the view that ironworking may not have begun until the tenth century, George E. Wright, "Iron: The Date of Its Introduction into Palestine," *AJA* 43 (1939): 458–63, showed that in Palestine there was evidence for at least a few twelfth-century artifacts of iron.

[8] Snodgrass, *Early Greek Armour and Weapons: From the Bronze Age to 600 B.C.* (Edinburgh, 1964).

[9] Waldbaum, *From Bronze to Iron: The Transition from the Bronze Age to the Iron Age in the Eastern Mediterranean*, Studies in Mediterranean Archaeology, vol. 54 (Göteborg, 1978). Waldbaum first presented her survey in 1968, in her Harvard University Ph.D. dissertation.

the technical progress that culminated in the production of carburized iron extended from the late thirteenth to the ninth century B.C., and it may be that a good deal of the progress occurred on Cyprus.[10]

In short, the Catastrophe may somehow or other have contributed to the development of an ironworking technology. But it could not have been the other way around.

[10] A. Snodgrass, "Cyprus and the Beginnings of Iron Technology in the Eastern Mediterranean," in J. D. Muhly, R. Maddin, and V. Karageorghis, eds., *Early Metallurgy in Cyprus, 4000–500 B.C.* (Nicosia, 1982), 289–95. The technical progress has been carefully documented by scholars at the University of Pennsylvania and their collaborators. See, for example, T. A. Wertime and J. D. Muhly, eds., *The Coming of the Age of Iron* (New Haven, 1980); J. D. Muhly, R. Maddin, T. Stech, and E. Özgen, "Iron in Anatolia and the Nature of the Hittite Iron Industry," *AS* 35 (1985): 67–84; and P. Åström, R. Maddin, J. D. Muhly, and T. Stech, "Iron Artifacts from Swedish Excavations in Cyprus," *Opuscula Atheniensia* 16 (1986): 27–41.

Chapter Six

DROUGHT

A S THE IRON WORKING hypothesis lost its credibility, archaeologists and historians in the English-speaking world began to explore other possible reasons for the Catastrophe. One of the most attractive alternatives has been the drought hypothesis: the upheaval ca. 1200 B.C. was the result of a drought of unprecedented proportions. This hypothesis is not entirely new, since it was at least mentioned more than a century ago.[1] But the present-day hypothesis is obligated especially to the argument put forward by Rhys Carpenter in the 1965 J. H. Gray lectures at Cambridge University and published the following year.[2]

Carpenter's thesis was that the Bronze Age centers of Greece fell victim to an intense and prolonged drought and to the disorders occasioned by the drought. The thesis was inspired by the facts that (as Vincent Desborough had shown in 1964) there was no evidence for a migration into Greece ca. 1200 B.C., and that many places were not destroyed but *abandoned* at that time. Arguing from these facts, and from Plato's demythologized interpretation of the Phaethon myth, Carpenter proposed that ca. 1200 the eastern Mediterranean suffered a drought so severe that many people were forced to leave their homes. As for those places that were destroyed, Carpenter suggested that because they were storehouses of grain and other foodstuffs they fell victim to a "final resort to violence by a drought-stricken people."[3] Sites destroyed a generation or two after 1200 may have caught fire because of lightning strikes or other random accidents.

Carpenter's little book became an immediate bestseller by scholarly standards and brought the drought hypothesis to the forefront in English language scholarship on the Catastrophe. Among European scholars the hypothesis has been less popular: although occasionally admitted (as, for example, by Strobel) as a "triggering factor" for folk migrations,[4] drought

---

[1] Cf. Sayce's note, at Maspero, *Struggle*, 462: "W. Max Müller (*Asien und Europa*, p. 359) believes that the invasion was caused by the famine, during which Mineptah supplied the Khati with corn."

[2] Carpenter, *Discontinuity in Greek Civilization* (Cambridge, 1966). My references are to the Norton paperback edition of 1968.

[3] Ibid., 69.

[4] Strobel, *Seevölkersturm*, 173–74: "Es scheint, dass zum ausgehenden 13. Jh. v. Chr. im östlichen Mittelmeergebiet eine längere Dürre katastrophale Auswirkungen zeitigte, die zahlreiche Volksgruppen zum Aufbruch nötigte."

was hardly mentioned by the fifteen participants in the Zwettl symposium. But in Britain, Canada, and the United States the drought hypothesis has been extended to account for the end of Bronze Age civilization in general. Perhaps contributing to this extension was Claude Schaeffer's surprising deduction that the earthquake that ruined Ugarit had been preceded by many years of abnormally hot and dry weather.[5] At any rate, climatic explanations for the end of Bronze Age civilization have been prevalent in English-language scholarship on both the Aegean and the Near East for the last twenty years: drought has been found responsible for the Catastrophe in the Levant and Hittite Asia Minor and even for the subsequent decline of Mesopotamia.[6] Most drought hypotheses assume that hungry people—whether violent locals, raiders, or migrating nations—were the proximate cause of the destruction of cities and palaces. Some introduce a "systems collapse" (see chapter 7) as the second term in the sequence, the final term being either an internal uprising or an attack from the outside.

Although it may be that drought was a precipitating factor for the Catastrophe, whatever role it played is likely to have been too early and limited to warrant the conclusion that the Catastrophe was in any way the "result" of a drought. Despite an intense search, evidence for a radical change in weather patterns over all of the eastern Mediterranean in the late thirteenth and early twelfth century has not yet been found. Arguments have been made that in the period 1400-900 the entire northern hemisphere was hotter and drier than normal, the arguments being based on the tree-rings of California's bristlecone pines and on the evidence for fall of lake levels in Switzerland and for the advance and recession of glaciers in the Himalayas.[7] Contrarily, it has been maintained that from a peak of aridity ca. 1500 B.C. the weather became colder and rainier for the next three centuries, culminating ca. 1200 in a "little ice age."[8] Whichever of these diamet-

---

[5] Schaeffer, "Commentaires," 760–62. Schaeffer based his opinion on the presence of a yellow and powdery sand that permeated the destruction level (which in places was two meters thick) all over the site at Ras Shamra. The pale powder bathed everything "qui reste des bâtiments ravagés par les tremblements de terre et les incendies de la fin d'Ugarit." The import of this was very clear: the "couche de poussière jaunâtre ou blanchâtre. . . témoigne, sans aucun doute possible, d'une période d'extrême chaleur et de sécheresse à la fin de l'existence d'Ugarit." The yellowish powder is more conventionally seen as a result of the burning of brick and stone structures.

[6] B. Weiss, "The Decline of Late Bronze Age Civilization as a Possible Response to Climatic Change," *Climatic Change* 4 (1982): 172–98; Baruch Halpern, *The Emergence of Israel in Canaan* (Chico, Calif., 1983), 96–99; J. Neumann and S. Parpola, "Climatic Change and the Eleventh–Tenth-Century Eclipse of Assyria and Babylonia," *JNES* 46 (1987): 161–82; Ronald L. Gorny, "Environment, Archaeology, and History in Hittite Anatolia," *Biblical Archaeologist* (1989): 78–94; and William H. Stiebing, Jr., *Out of the Desert?* 182–87.

[7] Stiebing, *Out of the Desert?* 183–84.

[8] M. Liverani, "Variazioni climatiche e fluttuazioni demografiche nella storia siriana," *Or.*

rically opposite scenarios is preferred, the geographical and chronological frames of reference are here so vast that they do not help very much.

A more promising possibility is that shortly before 1200 isolated regions—parts of Anatolia, and perhaps Libya's north coast—experienced one of the "normal" droughts that can be expected at least once in every generation. Some documentary support for such a possibility comes from Merneptah's Great Karnak Inscription, which celebrates Merneptah's victory over Meryre and his Libyans.[9] Merneptah says here that Meryre and his warriors "spend the day roaming the land and fighting to fill their bellies daily; they have come to the land of Egypt to seek food for their mouths." Although Merneptah's complaint could mean nothing more than that Meryre's soldiers had no source of livelihood other than their weapons, it could also indicate that there were food shortages in Libya. In the same inscription, Merneptah reports that he had sent grain to the king of Hatti, "to keep alive that land of Kheta." A bit of physical evidence pointing to an Anatolian drought has been produced from Gordion: a series of narrow tree-rings in a juniper log unearthed at that site suggests that western Anatolia may have had several dry years ca. 1200.[10] It therefore may be that in 1208 a shortage of food was a factor in Meryre's aggression. His objective may have been to take over part of the western Delta and so to be in control of a major source of grain at a time when grain was unusually valuable.

A moderate drought in Anatolia and possibly elsewhere ca. 1208, however, cannot be directly linked to the destruction of cities from 1225 to 1175. Appropriation of fertile fields was evidently not on the agenda of whoever it was who sacked Troy, Mycenae, Pylos, Hattusas, and Ugarit, since apparently none of these places was taken over by new settlers. If there was an Anatolian famine shortly before 1200, it was localized enough that adjacent areas were hardly affected. For Greece itself no botanical or geological evidence has yet been found for a drought.[11] This point was

---

Ant. 7 (1968): 81–82, cites climatologists' conclusions that in southwestern Asia there were "due periodi più freddi e piovosi, due 'piccole età glaciali' culminanti verso il 2300 e verso il 1200."

[9] Breasted, *AR*, vol. 3, no. 580.

[10] P. I. Kuniholm, "Dendrochronology at Gordion and on the Anatolian Plateau," *Summaries of Papers, 76th General Meeting, Archaeological Institute of America* (New York, 1974), 66.

[11] Environmentalists and climatologists R. A. Bryson, H. H. Lamb, and David L. Donley, "Drought and the Decline of Mycenae," *Antiquity* 48 (1974): 46, welcomed Carpenter's thesis and hoped to support it. Although they offered no evidence for an early twelfth-century drought, they did point out that in the winter of 1954–55 Greece experienced a drought pattern very much like that which Carpenter had postulated for the years ca. 1200 B.C. Whether the parallel strengthened or weakened the appeal of Carpenter's thesis is unclear. For an archaeologist's rebuttal to both the article and the Carpenter thesis on which it

made by a historical climatologist as early as 1968 and is apparently still valid.[12]

Recent excavations have in fact shown that Carpenter's picture of drastic depopulation in the twelfth-century Argolid was incorrect. We have seen in chapter 2 that scores of small towns, hamlets, and isolated houses in Greece were abandoned early in the LH IIIC period and that their inhabitants seem to have taken up residence in large towns, especially on the coasts. In the Argolid this resulted in the *Aussensiedlung* that Kilian excavated at Tiryns, which in the first half of the twelfth century was far larger than it had been in the thirteenth.[13] Other relatively large settlements of the twelfth century have been found, as noted, on Crete, Rhodes, Cyprus, and the coasts of Asia Minor.[14] We may therefore generalize that after the Catastrophe people in the Aegean and on Cyprus began collecting themselves into centralized or defensible locations. The abandonment of small communities in these areas is therefore not attributable to a drought.

Nor can legend be made to produce evidence for a catastrophic drought in Greece. Homer and Hesiod seem unaware of any tradition that the Age of Heroes ended in a famine. Several scholars have cited Herodotus 1.94 as a memory of a calamitous drought in Lydia ca. 1200 B.C. But there is little chance that the eighteen-year Lydian famine, which Herodotus dates to the reign of King Atys (a mythical figure who lived many generations before Herakles), is any more real than the Lydian accomplishments that it is intended to explain.[15]

For a drought in Greece ca. 1200 Carpenter referred to a passage in Plato's *Timaeus*. The "tradition" on which Carpenter relied has no connection with Greek oral tradition but came from the "book of the Egyptian priests" that Critias, one of Plato's literary characters, was wont to cite when about to embark on a story about Athens and Atlantis in the days

---

rested, see Oliver Dickinson, "Drought and the Decline of Mycenae: Some Comments," *Antiquity* 48 (1974): 228–29. In turn, H. H. Lamb responded (pp. 229–30) that he and his co-authors "were not trying to explain the decline" of the Mycenaean world but had intended only to show that "Carpenter's proposed drought pattern was possible."

[12] H. E. Wright, Jr., "Climatic Change in Mycenaean Greece," *Antiquity* 42 (1968): 125, concluded that in Messenia and in the few other areas of the Aegean (and western Anatolia) for which palaeoecological data was available "the pollen curves show no significant inflexion around 1200 BC." For a recent assessment see Gordon Shrimpton, "Regional Drought and the Economic Decline of Mycenae," *Echos du Monde Classique* 31 (1987): 142. Shrimpton, who believes that drought was indeed a major factor in the decline of the Mycenaean world, concedes that "there is no geological or ecological evidence for an abnormal drought" in Greece ca. 1200 and therefore advocates a systems collapse as the most important factor in the decline.

[13] Kilian, "Zum Ende," 171–73.

[14] For the fivefold growth of Rhodian Ialysos and the parallel with Tiryns see Macdonald, "Problems," 149.

[15] Drews, "Herodotus 1.94," 15–16 and 28–33.

before the Flood.[16] The entire story is one of Plato's elaborate literary fictions, but if one were to date the *ekpyrosis* to which Plato's Critias' priests refer one would need to put it ca. 17,500 B.C.[17] Nor does the Phaethon myth, to which Plato's Critias's Egyptian priests appeal, have anything to do with a drought (it was an etiological myth explaining why Africans had black skin). Israelite legend is no more forthcoming about a drought in southern Canaan. The story of Joseph and his brethren does include a drought, but Joseph cannot be made into a contemporary of the Catastrophe. More pertinent would be the story that when—four hundred years after Joseph's time—the progeny of the Twelve Patriarchs departed from Egypt, the land toward which they headed was a land flowing with milk and honey.

Documents written immediately before the destruction of the Late Bronze Age palaces make it quite clear that the lands subject to the palaces were not then suffering from a drought or famine. The tablets from Pylos and Knossos indicate that on the eve of the Catastrophe the inventories in those palaces were large and varied, flour-grinders and bread-bakers were at work, and rations were being regularly dispensed to a great many people. These rations were by no means scanty: according to a recent calculation, when the last tablets at Pylos were inscribed the women and children of Pylos were receiving, on average, 128 percent of their daily caloric requirement.[18] The animals of Messenia were also thriving, to judge by the thousands of sheep, goats, and cattle that the tablets locate in the countryside. At Ugarit there was no less to be thankful for: the tablets mention not only many small numbers of cattle, sheep, and birds but also a few large ones (400 geese in one poultryman's flock, 440 in another, and in the care of one Ewir-Sharruma a herd of possibly 2000 horses). A tablet "from the oven" at Ugarit shows us that immediately before that city was destroyed a tunic cost as much as three sheep, and for the price of three tunics you could buy an ox.[19] That is not a rate of exchange that one expects to find in ancient cities in time of famine.[20]

---

[16] According to Plato's Critias, his family had a text of Egyptian history reaching back over nine thousand years. The history had been composed by the priests of Egypt and had been translated into Greek by Solon, during his sojourn in Egypt. On his return to Greece, Solon had given the precious text to Critias's great-grandfather. For fourth-century Greek authors' fondness for claiming Egyptian, Persian, or "Chaldaean" sources for their fictions cf. Drews, *The Greek Accounts of Eastern History* (Washington, 1973), 103–21.

[17] At *Timaeus* 23E and *Critias* 108E Critias cites the priests' testimony that the Fire and the Flood alternate in nine-thousand-year cycles, and that eight thousand years have passed since the Flood that destroyed the ideal Athens and Atlantis.

[18] Ruth Palmer, "Subsistence Rations at Pylos and Knossos," *Minos* 24 (1989): 89–124.

[19] RS 18.24 (no. 101 in *PRU*, vol. 5, pp. 124–26).

[20] Peter Garnsey, *Famine and Food Supply in the Graeco-Roman World* (Cambridge, 1988), 3ff., quotes Ps-Joshua the Stylite (*Chronicle*, 39) on the famine that scourged Edessa in

In Anatolia itself there was evidently no shortage of food by the time Hattusas and all the other centers within the Halys arc were destroyed. In the tablets from Hattusas there is no mention of either drought or famine. A few scholars believe that one of the Ugaritic tablets "from the oven" (RS 18.38) testifies to a famine in Syria and Hatti. This letter from Suppiluliumas II, Great King at Hattusas, upbraids Hammurapi, his Ugaritic vassal, for having failed to appear before him in more than a year and for omitting to send him "the food tablet."[21] The expression is not entirely clear; possibly the reference is to a special shipment of grain, but it is more likely that the Great King meant only to chide Hammurapi for having neglected the ordinary duties of a vassal to his lord.

Even if one were to argue that there were food shortages in Anatolia on the very eve of the Catastrophe, one would still need to propose a reasonable link between famine and the burning of cities and palaces. To this end, the drought hypothesis has been coupled with the migrations hypothesis. Strobel, as we have seen, proposed that a severe drought in Asia Minor expelled from there "the Sea Peoples," who first destroyed the eastern Mediterranean sites and then moved on to the better climate of the western Mediterranean. Other proposals are less precise about the direction of migrations (Ronald Gorny, for example, speaks only of "mass movements of peoples in search of less affected regions").[22] We have already seen, in chapter 4, the liabilities of the migrations hypothesis.

If the people who destroyed the eastern Mediterranean sites were not outsiders, they were insiders. And that is what the drought hypothesis has traditionally assumed. Carpenter suggested "a final resort to violence by a drought-stricken people" and quoted with approval the generalization that "always there comes a time, a homicidal moment, when the famished cannot longer endure the sight of the well-nourished."[23] But in recent centuries no city has been destroyed by famished citizens or neighbors, and in fact Carpenter offered no example—whether ancient or modern—of a starving mob burning down a city. If such a thing ever did occur in antiquity, it is not reported in our sources. Of the three kinds of "food riots" isolated in modern scholarship, the only one attested for antiquity is what Peter Garnsey calls "urban market riots, a reaction to shortage of grain for

---

A.D. 499–500: chickpeas sold for 500 numia a kab, and lentils for 360 numia a kab, but "everything that was not edible was cheap."

[21] For the text of RS 18.38 see *PRU*, vol. 5, pp. 84–86. Charles Virolleaud there translates lines 17–20 as follows: "Et la tablette des vivres, quand tu l'as eu envoyée au Soleil, ton maître, alors il n'y a plus eu de vivres pour ta subsistance." For a similar translation see Liverani, *Storia di Ugarit*, 133: "E la tavoletta del cibo (cioè concernente il vettovagliamento), poiché hai scritto al Sole, tuo signore, che non c'è cibo (neanche) per la tua vita."

[22] Gorny, "Environment, Archeology, and History," 91.

[23] Carpenter, *Discontinuity*, 69.

sale."[24] For the sake of argument, however, let us imagine the inhabitants of villages around Tiryns—for example—becoming so hungry that they assemble and march en masse against the city. But what do we imagine next? As I shall show in chapter 11, the villagers could have posed no military threat. They had no weapons of their own, no chariots, no defensive armor, and no military training. Against the chariots and professional infantrymen of the palace, the villagers would have fared no better than any civilian population has ever fared against an army. And even if we can imagine the villagers somehow overpowering all the king's horses and men, penetrating the stout citadel wall, and so gaining control of the citadel, we will hardly be able to imagine why—after finally having appropriated it—they proceeded to raze it. These are the actions not of a starving, unarmed, local, civilian population but of robust enemies who have come from some distance away, who enjoy some sort of military superiority, and who take pleasure in seeing a great but alien city burn.

And that is exactly what the documents indicate. The drought hypothesis produces an obscure phrase about a "food tablet" in RS 18.38 as proof of a devastating famine but ignores the rest of the tablet, which witnesses far more clearly to a military than to an alimentary emergency: the brunt of the Hittite king's message is a request for men and supplies to help him against an enemy attack ("allo scopo di fronteggiare il nemico").[25] Virolleaud translated these important lines from Suppiluliumas's letter as follows:[26]

l'ennemi est monté contre (?) moi.
et le nombre (des ennemis) n'est pas. . .
(tandis que?) notre nombre est. . .
Ce qu'il y a, cherche(-le)
et envoie(-le) moi.

Although RS 18.38 is the latest of the texts pertinent to Hatti's military emergency, it is not the only one. Other texts found at Ugarit pertain to Hittite requests to the king of Ugarit for ships and for shipment to Hatti of chariots and troops sent from Carchemish.[27] A Hittite tablet also speaks of Suppiluliumas II's victory in a naval battle (the first to be fought by a Hittite king) off Alashia.[28]

[24] Garnsey, *Famine and Food Supply*, 29; cf. his remark on p. 30: "My impression is that peaceful protest was much more common than riot, and that only in the city of Rome itself in certain periods was the food riot a phenomenon of any significance." Needless to say, no ancient food rioters are known to have set fire to their cities.

[25] Liverani, *Storia di Ugarit*, 133.

[26] RS 18.38 = no. 60 (pp. 84–86) in *PRU*, vol. 5.

[27] RS 20.237 and RS 20.141b, nos. 31 and 34 respectively, in *Ugaritica*, vol. 5; see also Schaeffer's commentary at p. 737.

[28] On this see Lehmann, "Der Untergang," 61–63; cf. Strobel, *Seevölkersturm*, 27–28.

As was noted in chapter 3, tablets show that the last king of Ugarit was also beset by enemies: seaborne raiders who burned towns and ravaged the kingdom. And at Emar on the Euphrates a text shows that the city was imperiled by "hordes of enemies." Whatever shortage of food there may have been in Hatti and Syria in the early twelfth century B.C. is likely to have been the result of the raiders' activity rather than the other way around.

At many of the Greek sites destroyed in the Catastrophe there is in fact evidence that the arsonists must have been looking for something other than food. The destruction levels at these sites yielded carbonized remains of wheat, barley, olive pits, and grape seeds and evidence that the enemy destroyed pithoi and stirrup jars without emptying them of their contents.[29] That storerooms of food were burned to the ground by starving mobs would be surprising. What we see in the eastern Mediterranean ca. 1200 is a general pattern of destruction by fire, and both logic and data indicate that the sites were razed by well-armed enemies. At both Pylos and Ugarit texts indicate that these were enemies from abroad, whose ships had been sighted or were rumored to be off the coast. Both the Libyans and the Palestinians against whom Merneptah and Ramesses fought intended to appropriate fields in the Delta, but that is hardly surprising: all through antiquity the Delta's neighbors tried to encroach upon this fabulously fertile area. But elsewhere the Catastrophe was evidently not motivated by a desire for land or food. One would suppose that the men who sacked Pylos, Ugarit, Troy, and a score of other great centers did so for the booty that these centers held: precious artifacts and textiles, silver and gold, children and women.

[29] For references on carbonized remains see Isabelle Erard-Cerceau, "Documents sur l'agriculture mycénienne: peut-on concilier archéologie et épigraphie?" *Minos* 23 (1988): 185. Too late to be included in Erard-Cerceau's list are "the carbonized remains of figs, horsebeans and olivepits" that Paul Åström found at Midea; see Åström, "The Sea Peoples," 5. Åström also notes (p. 6) that the stirrup jars found at the site "are often grey, as if they had been burnt when soaked in perfumed oil."

Chapter Seven

SYSTEMS COLLAPSE

ACCORDING to an article published in 1990, historians are now convinced that Bronze Age society in the eastern Mediterranean was undone by shifts in the patterns of production:

There is now a general consensus linking the collapse of many Near Eastern palace organizations (noticeably in Anatolia and Syria-Palestine) and the substantial decline of other political entities (primarily Egypt) with a change in long established trade networks and patterns of production, a change that both caused the crisis, and eventually the end of the bronze industry, and at the same time fostered the introduction of iron as an alternative metal.[1]

The consensus is not complete, however, and skeptics might go so far as to question whether there is any evidence at all that the Catastrophe was the result of the factors proposed in the analysis here quoted.

Childe emphasized that the Late Bronze Age kingdoms had many shortcomings. The priestly, scribal, and military elites of a typical kingdom furnished their king with a far shallower base of power than did the "democratic" societies of the Iron Age. Although the Late Bronze Age kingdoms were linked by overland and seaborne trade and can almost be said to have shared in a single "international" economy, they were centralized and stratified, and economic benefits seldom trickled down from the wealthy to the lower classes. As Childe saw it, the Bronze Age kingdoms were fatally flawed by what a Marxist would call "contradictions," and it was not surprising that an innovation such as ironworking could have swept away the Bronze Age world and established an entirely new society on a new economic base.

Although the ironworking hypothesis proved to be incorrect, Childe's focus on the internal weaknesses and contradictions of the Late Bronze Age kingdoms has obviously not been abandoned. The approach is in fact favored by many scholars not only in the English-speaking world but also and especially in Europe. For this school of thought the emphasis is on the fragility of the Mycenaean, Hittite, Ugaritic, and Egyptian kingdoms. Their collapse ca. 1200 B.C. was possibly related to the actions of "the Sea Peoples," but whatever the latter did is of less interest than the internal

---

[1] Carlo Zaccagnini, "The Transition from Bronze to Iron in the Near East and in the Levant: Marginal Notes," *JAOS* 110 (1990): 496–97.

reasons for the collapse. The priority is stated quite frankly by Mario Liverani:

> In general, I belong to that group of scholars who consider (both on a theoretical level, and in the case of the Late Bronze Age crisis) internal factors of socio-economic dynamics to be pre-eminent, and the external (migratory) factors to be rather limited from a quantitative point of view. They represent the result more than the cause of the crisis, coming as part of a response with a sort of "multiplier" effect.[2]

The internal factors that Liverani singled out included such things as plague, famine, and wars between states. Social problems, however, were "la causa prima de tutto il collasso."[3] Among these were depopulation, alienation of land, the breakup of villages, debt slavery, and a "distacco incolmabile tra classe dirigente e classe produttiva."[4] When all of this deterioration had reached frightening proportions, the coup de grace was supplied either by an earthquake or—in Liverani's scenario—by an "urto migratorio" by peoples from the Balkans (they had perhaps left the Balkans because of some development or shortage in that peninsula).[5] The earthquake or the foreign invasion was the straw that broke the camel's back, and the tottering kingdoms of the Mycenaean world, Hatti, Ugarit, and many other places collapsed. Liverani says nothing about any military advantage that Balkan migrants may have had or, in fact, about warfare at all.

In other systems-collapse theories "the Sea Peoples" are more correctly characterized as pirates and raiders rather than as the populations of migratory nations. Here too, however, they come in toward the end: after the economic and social systems of a kingdom have already broken down, "the Sea Peoples" or other outsiders sense an easy victory and come in to loot and plunder. Thus A. B. Knapp concluded that "the movements of the 'Sea Peoples' represent the outcome of wide-reaching socio-economic breakdown, the end of a demographic chain reaction."[6] Whether effected by raiders or migratory peoples, the actual destruction of cities and palaces is of much less significance than the collapse of the kingdom's various sys-

---

[2] Liverani, "The Collapse of the Near Eastern Regional System at the End of the Bronze Age: The Case of Syria," in M. Rowlands, M. Larsen, and K. Kristiansen, eds., *Centre and Periphery in the Ancient World* (Cambridge, 1987), 69.

[3] Liverani, *Antico Oriente*, 630.

[4] Ibid., 631.

[5] What impelled the migrants to leave the Balkans is not of great interest: "Le cause della loro irruzione nel Mediterraneo orientale dovranno ricercarsi in qualche processo o vuoto nell'area balcanica (ed europea in generale), la cui precisazione non è agevole, e non riguarda comunque la presente trattazione" (ibid., 638).

[6] A. B. Knapp, *Copper Production and Divine Protection: Archaeology, Ideology, and Social Complexity on Bronze Age Cyprus* (Göteborg, 1986), 99.

tems. These hypotheses hold that even if the "Sea Peoples" did burn down the city of Ugarit, for example, the kingdom ought to have survived, just as Rome survived the Gallic sack in 387 B.C. That the kingdom did not survive is witness to the hollowness and artificiality of its institutions.

Thus the sackers of the cities do not play much of a role in systems-collapse hypotheses. The decisive factors were internal, and many hypothetical possibilities have been proposed. The factors may have been climatic and environmental (drought, plague, shrinkage of arable land), or sociopolitical (increase of nomadism, revolt of peasants, defection of mercenaries), or both.[7] A drought or some other disruption of agriculture may have made it impossible for a kingdom to export grain or olive oil and therefore to import necessities from distant lands.[8] A widely held view (though probably not the "consensus" claimed by Carlo Zaccagnini) is that interference in maritime trade—by pirates, for example—may have cut off supplies of copper and tin, bringing to a halt the production of bronze. In an economy so centralized, a shortage or stoppage in one sector would entail the breakdown of all. Or a demographic crisis may have been at fault: one hypothesis holds that the collapse in Syria resulted from serious depopulation, and another concludes, contrarily, that overpopulation was ultimately responsible for the collapse of the Pylos kingdom.[9]

[7] Philip Betancourt, "The End of the Greek Bronze Age," *Antiquity* 50 (1976): 44, argued that in the LH IIIB period the population of Messenia reached approximately one hundred thousand and that "too high a percentage of their agriculture may have been based on just a few items, especially grain. Thus a failure in one crop could not be alleviated by good harvests in others which would mature a little later. . . . The highly specialized system could have held the seeds of its own collapse." A somewhat different analysis is developed by Pia de Fidio, "Fattori di crisi," 127–36: De Fidio emphasizes the extent to which arable plots were abandoned, and she suggests that the cultivators (perhaps "gruppi di origine allogena" who had been assigned land in return for military service) left because of dissatisfaction with their treatment by the palace. Nancy Sandars, *Sea Peoples*, 197, also suggests that along with the marauding of the Sea Peoples one must also reckon with a systems collapse as the cause of the catastrophe: in Greece, "an essentially artificial way of life, which had been cultivated in the great political centres, was unable to take the strain. Collapse was gradual, lasting through several generations."

[8] Shrimpton, "Regional Drought," 143–45, offers a systems collapse hypothesis along these lines: in the late thirteenth and early twelfth centuries B.C. Greece may have experienced a "normal" drought, no worse than other droughts that periodically afflict the region (three or four such droughts must have occurred during the half-millennium of the Late Helladic period). What was different in the drought ca. 1200, Shrimpton suggests, was that the Mycenaean Greek economy had by that time become heavily dependent upon the export of wine and olive oil. Thus, when these commodities were adversely affected (not only in quantity, but also and perhaps especially in quality), the Mycenaean centers had nothing to export and consequently went into a steep economic decline. The physical destruction of various LH IIIB sites would have been a result of this decline since "raids, invasions and political turmoil may be provoked and their effects aggravated by adverse economic conditions" (137).

[9] On Syria see Liverani, *Antico Oriente*, pp. 629–30, and John Strange, "The Transition

The systems-collapse hypotheses usefully focus attention on the differences between Bronze Age and Iron Age societies and on the defects of the former. The Linear B tablets have been especially illuminating in this regard, showing as they do how ponderous and stifling was the palace bureaucracy that managed—or tried to manage—every aspect of life in Messenia and Knossos. That systems so complex and centralized collapsed under even slight pressures is not surprising. But although the systems-collapse hypothesis has moved us closer to an understanding of the Late Bronze Age economies and societies, it does not finally explain the Catastrophe. Its analysis does not seem to relate directly to the question "How and why were so many cities and palaces destroyed ca. 1200 B.C.?" There is no doubt whatever that many institutions of the Bronze Age did not survive into the Iron Age. And one may agree that the Bronze Age kingdoms were indeed hollow and unusually vulnerable. The fact remains, however, that these bureaucratic dinosaurs were remarkably long-lived. There is little reason to think that they were any more fragile or artificial ca. 1200 than they had been two centuries earlier. We may grant that not much of a "precipitating factor" was needed to send the Bronze Age kingdoms crashing down, but we must also recognize that for a very long time no such factor did so.

And it now appears that some systems must have survived, at least for a short time, the destruction of the palaces. This was not the case, obviously, at Hattusas, Ugarit, and Pylos. But at Tiryns, Mycenae, Troy, and in several centers on Cyprus there was apparently enough organization in the LH IIIC period to allow some productive activity and even, perhaps, a modest prosperity. Since after the destruction of their citadel at the beginning of the twelfth century the Mycenaeans rebuilt and reoccupied it, and proceeded to manufacture and decorate a great deal of LH IIIC pottery, it is difficult to believe that the destruction had been brought about by the collapse of their economic and social systems.

Simply stated, the systems-collapse hypothesis does not address the essence of the Catastrophe. That essence is not economic or social but physical: the palaces were destroyed, the cities burned. On this essential fact, the systems-collapse hypothesis is of no help. From its perspective, the destruction of sites is merely an event, and therefore incidental; what is of interest is not events but process and structure. Thus while historians focus their systems-collapse hypotheses on the "important" development—the decay and collapse of structures—they delegate to others the explanation of the "incidental" events—the destruction of cities and palaces. For explaining

from the Bronze Age to the Iron Age in the Eastern Mediterranean and the Emergence of the Israelite State," *Scandinavian Journal of the Old Testament* 1987: 1–19. On Messenia see Betancourt, "End," 42.

such "incidental" events, the earthquake hypothesis is made to order. In the coupling of systems-collapse hypotheses with earthquake hypotheses, earthquakes are identified as the cause of the physical destruction, and systems collapse is made responsible for the society's inability to rebound from the damage done by the quake. Thus in Iakovides's scenario for the end of Mycenaean civilization, a massive earthquake starts the fires that burn down the Argolid centers ca. 1200; Mycenaean society and civilization survive the fiery quake but collapse later in the twelfth century, primarily because Mycenae's trade connections with the Levant have in the meantime been reduced by piracy.[10]

But as argued above, it is utterly improbable that the conflagrations at the Argolid sites ca. 1200 were started by an earthquake. And without the earthquake hypothesis to account for the physical destruction, the systems-collapse hypothesis is conspicuously incomplete. In lieu of earthquakes, Liverani supposed that migrating hordes, which happened to be passing through, administered the coup de grace. Knapp's more promising analysis attributes the destruction to raiders but does not explain why the raiders were successful. Important though it is to look at the internal weaknesses of the Bronze Age kingdoms, the Catastrophe cannot be understood simply (or even essentially) as an internal development—the consequence of deterioration in internal systems. There was an active as well as a passive side to the Catastrophe, and although the victims were in part "responsible" for their fate we must not overlook the role of their attackers. If one wishes to tell the story of Peru in the early sixteenth century one would do well to discuss in detail the strengths and weaknesses of Incan society, but that would be only half of the matter, and not necessarily the most important half: the other half, in which the actual story lies, is the attack by Juan Pizarro and his defeat of the Incas. Just as Pizarro would never have marched to Peru had he not known the limitations of Incan power, so it must be conceded that the Catastrophe would not have occurred had the aggressors not believed that the eastern Mediterranean kingdoms were weak and vulnerable. But a persuasive reconstruction of the Catastrophe must establish not only the weakness of the victims but also the motivations, resources, and acts of the aggressors.

The kind of weakness that these aggressors attended to—and which we must therefore attend to—was above all military. No matter how socially or economically reprehensible the Bronze Age regimes may have been, they were still functioning quite well on the eve of the Catastrophe. Liverani was able to make his critique of Ugarit's socioeconomic health in the early twelfth century because the palace scribes continued to do their work (as the tablets "from the oven" so starkly show) until the day of destruction.

[10] Iakovides, "Present State of Research," 139–40.

The oven tablets show no sign of a systems collapse. As Marguerite Yon has summarized it, they show us a Ugarit "frozen by its destruction, in a state reflecting a rich and prosperous society, not a decadent and impoverished one."[11] Similarly, we know something about the bureaucracy at Pylos because it was still going about its meticulous business as disaster struck. The weakness of the Bronze Age kingdoms was certainly one of the reasons they fell. But weakness and collapse are not the same thing. So far as our evidence allows us to see, the *collapse* of a kingdom, and of all its systems, was everywhere a consequence of the Catastrophe, and not a cause. It seems that at those sites for which we have some documentation— Hattusas, Pylos, Emar, and Ugarit—the kingdom's systems must have collapsed in the few hours or days that elapsed between the arrival of enemy forces and the burning of the palace.

So far as it goes, then, the systems-collapse hypothesis is useful in exploring the social and economic weaknesses of the eastern kingdoms. And when paired with what we may call the "raiders hypothesis" it provides a partial explanation of what happened ca. 1200 B.C. But what we must finally address is a military question: why were the armies of the Bronze Age kingdoms unable to defend the cities and the palaces? Even if one assumes that their economies were top-heavy and calcified, and their kings unloved, these kingdoms had survived for centuries. How did it happen that ca. 1200 they were one after another overwhelmed and overrun?

[11] Yon, "End of the Kingdom of Ugarit," 114.

Chapter Eight

RAIDERS

H ERE WE REACH a hypothesis that is undoubtedly correct but that in its present form is incomplete. Most historians have sup-posed that raiding and piracy troubled the eastern Mediterranean before, during, and after the Catastrophe. Systems-collapse hypotheses, for example, have frequently found a role for pirates in the Catastrophe. They present this role as peripheral, however, and as limited to the final scene of the tragedy. Nancy Sandars, for example, suggested that "Aegean corsairs" looking for spoil were responsible for some of the destruction, and to illustrate the generalization pointed to the seven ships that worried the king of Ugarit shortly before the city's fall. But Sandars was reluctant to assign the raiders more than a small part in the Catastrophe: the corsairs "were not a cause of the general breakdown, they were one of its results."[1] Bernard Knapp concluded—quite correctly, I believe— that "the motley group known to modern scholarship as 'the Sea Peoples' " was in fact an agglomeration of raiders and city-sackers.[2] But Knapp, too, regarded the formation of these raider-bands as not a cause but a result of the general breakdown of social and economic systems.

Conversely, migrations hypotheses assign a limited role to pirates in the earliest stage of the Catastrophe. Although Eduard Meyer eventually regarded the Catastrophe as the result of folk migrations, he did not forget that "die Schardana" had served Ramesses II as mercenaries and that in the fourteenth and early thirteenth centuries they and the Lycians had raided the coasts of Egypt and Cyprus respectively.[3] Meyer thus saw "the Sea Peoples" as anticipating the behavior of barbarians on the borders of the Roman Empire: when the Goths first appear in history—in the third century A.D.—they are raiders, but soon they are mercenaries, and by the end of the fourth century they have become a migrating nation. Other historians have drawn the same analogy between "the Sea Peoples" and the

---

[1] Sandars, *Sea Peoples*, 186.

[2] Knapp, *Copper Production*, 98–99.

[3] *Geschichte*, 457 and 545. When writing his first (1893) edition, Meyer did not yet believe in *Volkswanderungen* as the cause of Ramesses III's troubles and so was even more emphatic in attributing them to rogue mercenaries. See his excellent summary in *Geschichte des Altertums*, 1st ed., vol. 2, 212: "Den Söldnerschaaren, die in den Diensten des Pharao ihr Brot suchen, den kleinasiatischen Kriegern, welche dem Chetakönig Heerfolge leisten, folgen kühne Abenteurer, welche auf eigene Hand die Schätze des Orients zu gewinnen trachten." It is hard to improve on this, and the revised edition certainly does not.

Goths, the Saxons, and the Vikings. Recently Gerhard Dobesch, in tracing the symbiosis between a *Hochkulturgebiet* and the barbarian peoples on its periphery, noted that often in antiquity a civilized state exploited its barbarian neighbors by hiring them as cheap soldiers; but the barbarians soon learned to supplement their earnings by plunder and eventually appropriated outlying sections of the civilized world. The relationship between "the Sea Peoples" and the high civilization of the eastern Mediterranean, Dobesch suggests, fits this pattern very well.[4] Apart from its assumptions about "the migrations of the Sea Peoples," there is much in this analysis that is useful.

A few historians have recognized raiding as the very essence of the Catastrophe. As noted above, this was Eduard Meyer's first view, before he embraced the migrations hypothesis. H. A. Ormerod knew nothing of a systems collapse and believed that only a small part of the Catastrophe was the result of migrations. Although he supposed that during the reign of Ramesses III "the Philistines and Thekel" migrated from some northern home to Palestine, he supposed that the rest of "the Sea Peoples" were simply raiders. The name *Shekelesh*, he thought, had no connection with Sicily, nor the names *Shardana* and *Tursha* with Sardinia and Tyrrhenia.[5] These were and remained Anatolian peoples, Ormerod believed, who made their living as mercenary soldiers, an occupation that regularly alternated with raiding (as Odysseus's speech in *Odyssey*, book 14 shows). Another student of ancient seamanship, Lionel Casson, also saw the Catastrophe as a series of attacks by sea-raiders, coordinated with the Philistine and Tjekker migration on land.[6] An Egyptologist, Wolfgang Helck, concluded that the inscriptions of Merneptah and Ramesses III speak not of "Sea Peoples" but of pirates, wasting everything within their reach.[7] This characterization has most recently been endorsed, at the Brown Conference, by Robert Merrillees.[8]

An overland invasion by raiders has occasionally been suggested. Desborough's *Last Mycenaeans* concluded that the Greek mainland was overrun by barbarian raiders who came south from the Balkan peninsula;

[4] Gerhard Dobesch, "Historische Fragestellungen," 179–230.

[5] For his doubts about a Sardinian and Sicilian connection see H. A. Ormerod, *Piracy in the Ancient Mediterranean: An Essay in Mediterranean History* (Liverpool, 1924), 86–88, with notes. Ormerod did, however, assume that "the Philistines and the Thekel" were migratory nations: "The migratory character of the movement is clearly shown by the pictures of the ox-carts carrying women and children. . . . Thekel and Peleset may well have reached their later homes in Palestine as the result of this migration" (ibid., 85).

[6] Lionel Casson, *The Ancient Mariners: Seafarers and Sea Fighters in the Mediterranean in Ancient Times* (New York: 1959), 31–36.

[7] Helck, "Die Seevölker," 17–18.

[8] Merrillees, "The Crisis Years: Cyprus. A Rejoinder," in Ward and Joukowsky, *Crisis Years*, 90–91.

swept through Boeotia, across the Corinthian isthmus, and into and all through the Peloponnese; and then returned to their homelands in temperate Europe.[9] Sandars briefly entertained the same hypothesis. Although in her book she opted for a systems collapse as the overall cause of the Catastrophe, fifteen years earlier she supported Desborough's suggestion that the Greek mainland was plundered by hit-and-run raiders who came from and returned to the Balkans.[10]

By itself the raiders hypothesis is incomplete and so has necessarily appeared as a component of a more complex hypothesis. There must be a reason, that is, why raiders enjoyed such uniform success in the period ca. 1200, after four centuries in which they had been little more than a nuisance. Iron weapons were once identified as the raiders' edge. Lately the systems-collapse hypothesis has provided the necessary explanation: toward the end of the thirteenth century B.C. the eastern kingdoms collapsed from within and so became suddenly vulnerable to motley and otherwise unimpressive collections of pirates and raiders. As I have argued in the preceding chapter, however, the eastern kingdoms did not in fact collapse until *after* they were attacked. The raiders hypothesis, I would therefore insist, needs to be completed in some other way. Instead of arguing that the Catastrophe occurred because the eastern kingdoms were suddenly weakened at the end of the thirteenth century, let us see whether it may have occurred because at that time the raiders suddenly became formidable. A military explanation seems to provide all that is necessary. Shortly before 1200, barbarian raiders and pirates discovered a way to overcome the military forces on which the eastern kingdoms relied. With that discovery, they went out into the world and made their fortunes.

[9] Desborough, *Last Mycenaeans*, 220–29.

[10] Sandars, "The Last Mycenaeans and the European Late Bronze Age," *Antiquity* 38 (1964): 258–62.

PART THREE

A MILITARY EXPLANATION
OF THE CATASTROPHE

Chapter Nine

PREFACE TO A MILITARY EXPLANATION
OF THE CATASTROPHE

THE CATASTROPHE can most easily be explained, I believe, as a result of a radical innovation in warfare, which suddenly gave to "barbarians" the military advantage over the long established and civilized kingdoms of the eastern Mediterranean. We shall see that the Late Bronze Age kingdoms, both large and small, depended on armies in which the main component was a chariot corps. A king's military might was measured in horses and chariots: a kingdom with a thousand chariots was many times stronger than a kingdom with only a hundred. By the beginning of the twelfth century, however, the size of a king's chariotry ceased to make much difference, because by that time chariotry everywhere had become vulnerable to a new kind of infantry.

The infantries that evidently defeated even the greatest chariot armies during the Catastrophe used weapons and guerrilla tactics that were characteristic of barbarian hill people but had never been tried en masse in the plains and against the centers of the Late Bronze Age kingdoms. The Medinet Habu reliefs indicate that the weapons of Ramesses' opponents were javelins and long swords, whereas the traditional weapon of the chariot corps was the bow. Neither the long sword nor the javelin was an invention of the late thirteenth century: a long slashing sword had been available in temperate Europe for centuries, and the javelin everywhere for millennia. Until shortly before 1200 B.C., however, it had never occurred to anyone that infantrymen with such weapons could outmatch chariots. Once that lesson had been learned, power suddenly shifted from the Great Kingdoms to motley collections of infantry warriors. These warriors hailed from barbarous, mountainous, or otherwise less desirable lands, some next door to the kingdoms and some far away.

Before attempting to demonstrate these generalizations, I must make some apologies. Warfare in the preclassical world is a subject on which we evidently will never know very much. We have some idea what warfare was like in fifth-century Greece, and a few Roman battles can be reconstructed in detail. By extension, we can imagine at least the outlines of battles fought by Archaic Greeks and Romans. But beyond ca. 700 questions begin to multiply, and about the second millennium we are grossly ignorant. After surveying what is known and can be known about warfare at Ugarit, Jean

ıgayrol concluded that "malheureusement, nous ne savons pratique-
ıt rien sur l'armée qu'Ugarit pouvait alors mettre sur pied."[1] On many
questions one can only guess, and since guessing seems unprofessional,
historians do as little of it as possible. The result, however, is that for lack of
evidence one of the most important things about the preclassical world is
largely ignored. There is good reason to think that the evolution of warfare
made and unmade the world of the Late Bronze Age. Even though we
cannot be certain about this evolution, and especially about its details, it is
time that we begin to guess.

The description of Bronze Age and early Iron Age warfare would ordinarily be the task of the military historian. For some time, however, military history has been of little interest to professional scholars. During its
golden age, in the late nineteenth and early twentieth centuries, the subject
was utilitarian and pragmatic, written by and for men who had considerable military experience. One studied it in order to win wars. The study of
ancient military history culminated in Germany, with the first volume of
Hans Delbrück's *Geschichte der Kriegskunst* and the magisterial works
of Johannes Kromayer and Georg Veith.[2] Since World War II military
history has been—quite understandably—in bad odor in most academic
circles.

Even if military history remained a vigorous discipline, it is doubtful that
today's scholarly officers would find Bronze Age and early Iron Age warfare
intelligible enough to extract from it lessons useful for cadets. Since there is
no Xenophon, Caesar, or Vegetius to serve as a *Wegweiser* to the Near East,
the military history of this region is frustratingly opaque. Written records
contain hundreds of references to weapons and military personnel, but
more often than not the meaning of the words is uncertain. Even in Hebrew,
which is relatively intelligible, it is not entirely clear when the word *parashim* means "horses" and when it means "cavalrymen." In Egyptian, Hittite, Hurrian, Ugaritic, Akkadian, and Mycenaean Greek the situation is
far worse. Here the study of military history is stuck at the lexicographical
stage, since there are uncertainties about even the most basic and elementary terms. The general plight of scholars attempting to illuminate all this
darkness is described by Timothy Kendall, condemned to extract from the
Nuzi tablets what they had to say about military matters: "The Nuzi texts
pertaining to military personnel and supplies contain a vast nomencla-
ture. . . . As one begins to read these texts, he immediately finds himself
confronted by this strange new vocabulary and to his discouragement he

---

[1] J. Nougayrol, "Guerre et paix à Ugarit," *Iraq* 25 (1963): 117.

[2] Delbrück, *Geschichte der Kriegskunst im Rahmen der politischen Geschichte*, vol. 1:
Das Altertum (Berlin, 1900); Kromayer and Veith, *Antike Schlachtfelder*, 4 vols. (Berlin,
1903–31); and *Heerwesen und Kriegsführung der Griechen und Römer* (Munich, 1928).
There was nothing remotely comparable in English or French.

soon discovers that a fair number of these terms have been inadequately treated or little understood even by the editors of the most up-to-date Akkadian lexicons."[3] Even when all the words are understood, problems remain. Lengthy inscriptions advertise pharaohs' victories at Megiddo and Kadesh, but the course of the battles can barely be reconstructed out of the bombast. Perhaps our most informative and least misleading sources of information on military matters are Mycenaean vase paintings and Near Eastern royal reliefs, but the latter tend to cluster in a few periods and places (especially New Kingdom Egypt and imperial Assyria).[4]

Surprisingly little illumination has come from *in corpore* evidence. In the Near East, first of all, archaeologists have found considerably fewer weapons and pieces of armor than have their counterparts at work in the Aegean or in prehistoric Europe (the discrepancy perhaps reflects the difference between tells and tombs as sources of the material record). And for both the Aegean and the Near East, what has been found has received less attention than it deserves. Although specialists have cataloged the weapons of the Bronze and early Iron Age, they have seldom ventured to speculate— on the basis of the particulars—about the evolution of warfare during this period. And few other scholars have found the catalogs of any interest at all. Until 1964, when Anthony Snodgrass published his *Early Greek Armour and Weapons*, discussion of these objects was largely restricted to out-of-print dissertations written in Germany early in this century.[5] The situation today is very much better. The Bronze Age swords of the Aegean were cataloged by Nancy Sandars in the early 1960s, and the spearheads and arrowheads by Robert Avila in 1983.[6] The swords of prehistoric Italy are also now classified and published, and A. F. Harding has cataloged those from Yugoslavia.[7] Serious study of Near Eastern weaponry peaked in 1926, when two little books—Walther Wolf's on Egypt, and Hans Bon-

[3] Kendall, *Warfare and Military Matters in the Nuzi Tablets* (Ph.D. dissertation, Brandeis University, 1975), 74.

[4] The Egyptian reliefs are best seen in W. Wreszinski's collection of photographs and in the line drawings based on them. Although "published" before World War II, the photographs were quite inaccessible until their recent reprinting, by Slatkine Reprints, in two boxed sets. See now Walter Wreszinski, *Atlas zur altägyptischen Kulturgeschichte* (Geneva and Paris, 1988).

[5] Snodgrass, *Early Greek Armour and Weapons: From the End of the Bronze Age to 600 B.C.* (Edinburgh, 1964); for the dissertations see Snodgrass, *Arms and Armour of the Greeks* (Ithaca, N.Y., 1967), 131. Snodgrass's *Early Greek Armour and Weapons* itself began as a dissertation.

[6] Sandars, "The First Aegean Swords and Their Ancestry," *AJA* 65 (1961): 17–29; "Later Aegean Bronze Swords," *AJA 67 (1963): 117–53*. Avila, *Bronzene Lanzen- und Pfeilspitzen der griechischen Spätbronzezeit*, Prähistorische Bronzefunde, part 5, vol. 1 (Munich, 1983).

[7] V. Bianco Peroni, *Die Schwerter in Italien/Le Spade nell'Italia continentale*, Prähistorische Bronzefunde, part 4, vol. 1 (Munich, 1970); on the publication of the Yugoslavian swords see Harding, *Mycenaeans and Europe*, 163.

net's on the rest of the Near East—sketched an elementary typology.[8] Detailed typologies of Near Eastern axes, daggers, swords, and spears have since been published but have been seldom used or even mentioned.[9]

Chariots have been of greater interest, and it is encouraging to note that recently their technical aspects have received expert attention.[10] An understanding of the military applications of the chariot, on the other hand, lags far behind.[11] Several assumptions about the role of the chariot on the battlefield seem to be quite mistaken, and we have apparently ignored the extent to which warfare in the Late Bronze Age was "chariot warfare."

In addition to the archaeological and typological studies of weaponry and armor, we now have detailed analyses—several of them in doctoral dissertations at American universities—of texts dealing with military matters. Focusing especially on the technical terminology used in the documents of this or that kingdom, these studies provide kingdom-by-kingdom surveys of things military at Mari, Nuzi, Hatti, Ugarit, Israel, Egypt, Pylos, and Knossos.[12]

[8] Hans Bonnet, *Die Waffen der Völker des alten Orients* (Leipzig, 1926); Walther Wolf, *Die Bewaffnung des altägyptischen Heeres* (Leipzig, 1926). Although both surveys remain useful today, neither sheds any light on the changes in warfare that occurred from the Late Bronze Age to the Iron Age or even acknowledges that changes occurred at that time. Wolf's format is broadly chronological, but stops with the Nineteenth Dynasty. Bonnet's presentation is weapon-by-weapon. Thus although he was concerned to show the differences between chariot lances and infantry spears, Bonnet nowhere discussed the role of the chariot in battle. How the nature of ancient warfare was changed with the advent of chariotry, and what changes were associated with the obsolescence of chariotry, are thus questions that could not be answered on the basis of his information.

[9] Much of this was done by Rachel Maxwell-Hyslop, who began her typological research in the late 1930s. See her "Daggers and Swords in Western Asia," *Iraq* 8 (1946): 1–65; "Western Asiatic Shaft-Hole Axes," *Iraq* 11 (1949): 90–129; and "Bronze Lugged Axe- or Adze-Blades from Asia," *Iraq* 15 (1953): 69–87. On spears see Alessandro de Maigret, *Le lance nell'Asia anteriore nell'Età del Bronzo* (Rome, 1976).

[10] Mary Littauer and Joost Crouwel, *Wheeled Vehicles and Ridden Animals in the Ancient Near East* (Leiden, 1979); Crouwel, *Chariots and Other Means of Land Transport in Bronze Age Greece* (Amsterdam, 1981); Stuart Piggott, *The Earliest Wheeled Transport: From the Atlantic to the Caspian Sea* (Ithaca, N.Y., 1983).

[11] Good beginnings have been made by Elena Cassin, "A propos du char de guerre en Mésopotamie," in J. Vernant, ed., *Problèmes de la guerre en Grèce ancienne* (Paris, 1968), 297–308; by Littauer and Crouwel, *Wheeled Vehicles*, 91–93; and by P. S. Moorey, "The Emergence of the Light, Horse-Drawn Chariot in the Near East c. 2000–1500 B.C.," *World Archaeology* 18 (1986): 196–215.

[12] Alan Schulman, *Military Rank, Title and Organization in the Egyptian New Kingdom* (Berlin, 1964; Ph.D. dissertation, University of Pennsylvania, 1962); Albert Glock, *Warfare in Mari and Early Israel* (Ph.D. Dissertation, University of Michigan, 1968); Michel Lejeune, "La civilisation mycénienne et la guerre," in Vernant, *Problèmes de la guerre*, 31–51; J. Nougayrol, "Guerre et paix à Ugarit," *Iraq* 25 (1969): 110–23; Jack Sasson, *The Military Establishments at Mari* (Rome, 1969); Timothy Kendall, *Warfare and Military Matters in the Nuzi Tablets* (Ph.D. dissertation, Brandeis University, 1975); Adele Franceschetti, "Armi e

The synthesis of these specialized studies, and their conversion into a diachronic account of military history, has barely begun. While surveys of classical military history appear with some frequency, the first and last military history of the ancient Near East was Yigael Yadin's. In the long tradition of a military practitioner writing military history, General Yadin did a signal service to the academic world in writing a colorful and lucid story—a diachronic account, that is—of warfare in the ancient Near East.[13] His *Art of Warfare in Biblical Lands* was not only a remarkable pioneering achievement but remains fundamental for anyone interested in the subject. It is not annotated, however, having been written as much for the general public as for professional historians; and, given its enormous range and the impenetrable nature of its subject, it has not surprisingly turned out to be wrong or misleading on many points. Israeli interest in military history has produced a number of books, narrower in topic than Yadin's but more popular in approach, recounting the victories of ancient kings in Israel and Judah.[14] More recently, Nigel Stillman and Nigel Tallis have collaborated to produce a thoroughly expert survey of what is known about ancient Near Eastern weapons and military organization (their format, unlike Yadin's, is not diachronic but kingdom-by-kingdom, or people-by-people).[15] Although Stillman's and Tallis's book is not annotated and has the flavor of a military manual, the quality of their scholarship is high, and it is unfortunate that their survey has not been reviewed or acknowledged in scholarly journals.

Since a general survey of preclassical military history is so novel and difficult an undertaking, it is not surprising that the subject is ignored even in some books whose subject is ostensibly "war in the ancient world."[16] Scholars venturesome enough to write on Near Eastern military history must expect to be embarrassed by occasional pratfalls. A case in point is the fairly recently published *Warfare in the Ancient World*, edited by General

---

guerra in testi micenei," *Rendiconti dell'Accad. di Archeologia, Lettere e Belle Arti di Napoli* 53 (1978): 67–90; Michael Heltzer, *The Internal Organization of the Kingdom of Ugarit* (Wiesbaden, 1982), esp. chap. 6 ("The Military Organization and the Army of Ugarit"); Philo Houwink ten Cate, "The History of Warfare According to Hittite Sources: The Annals of Hattusilis I," part 1, *Anatolica* 10 (1983): 91–110, and part 2, *Anatolica* 11 (1984): 47–83; and Richard Beal, *The Organization of the Hittite Military* (Ph.D. dissertation, University of Chicago, 1986).

[13] Yadin, *The Art of Warfare in Biblical Lands*, 2 vols. (New York, 1963).

[14] See for example Chaim Herzog and Mordecai Gichon, *Battles of the Bible* (New York, 1978).

[15] N. Stillman and N. Tallis, *Armies of the Ancient Near East, 3000 BC to 539 BC* (Worthing, Sussex, 1984).

[16] Y. Garlan's, *War in the Ancient World: A Social History* (London, 1975) is limited to the classical world. In J. Harmand, *La guerre antique, de Sumer à Rome* (Paris, 1973) there are references to the Near East, but no systematic treatment.

Sir John Hackett.[17] Each chapter of this very useful book is written by a scholar of high distinction. The eight chapters beginning with Archaic Greece and ending with the Later Roman Empire cover ground that has been trod for centuries and is now quite exquisitely mapped, but the two chapters on the pre-Persian Near East—by prehistorian Trevor Watkins and Assyriologist D. J. Wiseman—explore what to a great extent is still a terra incognita.[18] Here one encounters, amid a variety of archaeological illuminations and Assyriological clarifications, a few impossible items: bows with a range up to 650 meters, Bronze Age chariots pulled by four-horse teams, and Assyrian chariots with iron undercarriages. Nevertheless, the overviews furnished by pioneers such as Watkins and Wiseman far outweigh the occasional mistake on particulars.

Having no credentials as a military historian, I shall undoubtedly furnish future scholars with ample opportunity for mirth and correction. But a generalist of the rankest order, with no inhibitions against guessing when evidence fails, should be in as good a position as anyone to reconstruct the general evolution of warfare at the end of the Bronze Age and beginning of the Iron Age. Because the Catastrophe was followed by a dark age, productive of neither written nor pictorial evidence, the military history of this period is especially obscure. In both the Aegean and the Near East, the period between the reign of Ramesses III and Ashurnasirpal II is pictorially almost a total blank, relieved only by the stelae of "Neo-Hittite" kings in northern Syria.[19] Yet there is reason to believe that the decades around and after 1200 B.C. were among the very most important in the evolution of warfare in the ancient world. The next chapters will accordingly attempt to sketch in at least its broad outlines how warfare changed at the end of the thirteenth century and the beginning of the twelfth.

Some innovations in weaponry at the end of the Bronze Age have been noticed, especially by scholars who work closely with the material record. Archaeologists have known for a long time that at the end of the IIIB period

---

[17] Hackett, ed., *Warfare in the Ancient World* (London, 1989).

[18] Watkins, "The Beginnings of Warfare," 15–35; and Wiseman, "The Assyrians," 36–53. The bibliography included for Watkins's chapter (*Warfare*, 250) contains three items: Yadin's *Art of Warfare*, Breasted's *Ancient Records of Egypt*, and Luckenbill's *Ancient Records of Assyria and Babylonia*. In contrast, ten works—all studies in military history meant for the professional scholar—are listed for Lazenby's chapter on the Greek hoplite.

[19] On the absence of artistic evidence on military matters in the Aegean during this period see Desborough, *The Greek Dark Ages*, 306: "Between the early twelfth century and the eighth there exists no figure or figurine of a warrior, nor any representation of such in vase painting, with the single exception of the two confronted archers at Lefkandi." Nor are things much better for the Near East. The lack of evidence there almost persuaded Yadin to "write off" the Iron I period as "a kind of transitional period about which nothing on warfare could be known" (*Art of Warfare*, vol. 2, 291; cf. p. 247: "Our sole source for the first part of the period is the many reliefs of Rameses III.").

several items of defensive armor—greaves, certainly, and a smaller shield—proliferate in the Aegean, as did the Naue Type II sword (on the Near Eastern side, where the transformation in warfare was radical, there has been less attention to it). Jeremy Rutter has in fact noted that in the post-palatial Aegean "the changes in virtually all forms of offensive and defensive weaponry . . . are remarkable for the comprehensiveness of their range and the rapidity with which they are effected."[20] But although these material changes have been recognized, their historical significance is too little appreciated, apparently because the nature of warfare in the Late Bronze Age is so imperfectly understood. Tentative suggestions have occasionally been made. Nancy Sandars, for example, alluded to "a new form of attack introduced with the flange-hilted sword,"[21] and James Muhly observed that the appearance of greaves and slashing swords points to "the introduction of a new style of fighting. The tactics now were not just to thrust but also to cut or slash, especially at the legs of your opponent."[22] If the changes in weaponry and tactics are fully explored, and especially if their impact upon chariot warfare is imaginatively assessed, I believe that they will furnish as good an explanation for the Catastrophe as we are likely to find.

[20] Rutter, "Cultural Novelties in the Post-Palatial Aegean World: Indices of Vitality or Decline?" in Ward and Joukowsky, *Crisis Years*, 67.

[21] Sandars, *Sea Peoples*, 92.

[22] Muhly, "The Role of the Sea Peoples," 42. Catling, with whom the idea originated, temporarily abandoned it when the Dendra greaves (dating ca. 1400) were found; see Catling, "A New Bronze Sword from Cyprus," *Antiquity* 35 (1961): 122.

Chapter Ten

THE CHARIOT WARFARE OF THE LATE BRONZE AGE

THE THESIS of the present study is that the Catastrophe came about when men in "barbarian" lands awoke to a truth that had been with them for some time: the chariot-based forces on which the Great Kingdoms relied could be overwhelmed by swarming infantries, the infantrymen being equipped with javelins, long swords, and a few essential pieces of defensive armor. The barbarians—in Libya, Palestine, Israel, Lycia, northern Greece, Italy, Sicily, Sardinia, and elsewhere—thus found it within their means to assault, plunder, and raze the richest palaces and cities on the horizon, and this they proceeded to do.

In order to place this thesis in perspective, it will be necessary to recall some familiar facts about chariots on the battlefield and to bring a few others out from obscurity. Although to the general public the chariot has always seemed one of the more interesting things about antiquity, few historians have devoted much time or thought to the subject. In the last few years, however, Mary Littauer, Joost Crouwel, and Stuart Piggott have given us scholarship of the first order on chariots and chariotry. Their writings on the subject combine a mastery of the ancient evidence with an equestrian's expertise on horses, harnessing, and horse-drawn vehicles.[1] It has thus become possible to glimpse at least the outlines of a phenomenon hitherto almost unrecognizable—chariot warfare.

THE BEGINNINGS OF CHARIOT WARFARE

Although carts and wagons had been used in Mesopotamia from the beginning of the third millennium B.C., these were ponderous, solid-wheeled vehicles, and were much more easily drawn by oxen than by equids. The chariot was a technological triumph of the early second millennium. Made of light hardwoods, with a leather-mesh platform on which the driver could stand, the entire vehicle weighed not much more than thirty kilograms. The wheels were, shall we say, the revolutionary element: the heat-bent spokes provided a sturdy wheel that weighed only a tenth as much as the disk wheels of the third millennium. With such a vehicle one could

---

[1] For their treatments of chariotry in this period see Littauer and Crouwel, *Wheeled Vehicles*, 74–98; Crouwel, *Chariots*; Piggott, *Earliest Wheeled Transport*, 91–104.

begin to exploit the horse as a draft animal: whereas an ox cart traveled only two miles in an hour, a team of chariot horses could cover ten.

The recent scholarship on technical aspects of the chariot permits us to establish approximately when chariots became militarily significant. The era of the war chariot, as I have elsewhere argued in detail, began in the seventeenth century B.C.[2] Before that time, chariots seem to have been of little or no importance on the battlefield, even though they had been used for rapid transportation, for amusement, and for royal display as early as 1900. It is likely that in Mesopotamia, at least, kings had all along ridden to the battlefield—on stately, heavy wagons in the third millennium and in chariots after the development of the spoked wheel. The chariot of the early second millennium, however, was apparently only a prestige vehicle and not yet a military instrument. That is not to say that in the time of Hammurabi of Babylon a king did not occasionally shoot an arrow from his chariot with hostile intent. Perhaps there were even battles in which a royal entourage of four or five chariots may have made a tiny contribution to the outcome. But in the Age of Hammurabi, as analysis of the Mari documents has shown,[3] battle still meant the clash of two infantries. By the standards of later antiquity these infantries of the Middle Bronze Age were not very formidable. In Twelfth-Dynasty Egypt, the army seems to have consisted of alternating formations of archers and close-formation spearmen.[4] The archers used the simple or self bow, which must have had an effective range of only fifty or sixty meters, and their arrows apparently helped only to "soften up" the enemy's formation of massed spearmen as it approached their own. After this preliminary phase, the battle proper began, with the opposing phalanxes attacking each other with axes and thrusting spears.

Then came a revolution in ancient warfare. Since no documents describe it, we have no other recourse but to imagine it: a traditional infantry marches out to do battle with an opposing infantry but instead finds itself attacked by several score of archers mounted on chariots and armed with composite bows, the archers shooting arrows with impunity until the traditional infantry formation is broken and routed. Each chariot carried two young men with excellent reflexes: the charioteer drove the horses while the chariot warrior shot arrow after arrow against the relatively stationary enemy formations, the chariots keeping just outside the range of the opposing infantry's bowmen. Essentially, the chariot became militarily significant when it was combined with another intricate artifact, the composite bow, which also had been known for a long time but had until then been a

---

[2] Drews, *The Coming of the Greeks: Indo-European Conquests in the Aegean and the Near East* (Princeton, 1988), especially 74–120; see also Cassin, "Char de guerre," 298; Littauer and Crouwel, *Wheeled Vehicles*, 63–65; and Moorey, "Emergence," 205.

[3] Glock, *Warfare in Mari and Early Israel*, 144.

[4] Stillman and Tallis, *Armies*, 54.

luxury reserved for kings or the very rich. Early in the seventeenth century it must have occurred to someone (who perhaps had himself enjoyed using his chariot and composite bow for hunting exploits) that several score of chariots, each manned by an expert driver and a "hunter" armed with a composite bow, would be able to overcome a conventional army of infantrymen.

The earliest chariot warfare seems to have occurred in Asia Minor. Troy VI may have been established soon after 1700 B.C. by chariot warriors, and there is evidence that by ca. 1650 chariots were used by the king of Hatti, by Umman Manda at Aleppo, and by the *hyksos* who took over Egypt.[5] The *hyksos*, an assortment of Semitic, Hurrian, and Aryan adventurers, set up at Avaris a regime known to Manetho as Egypt's Fifteenth Dynasty. As another pioneer of the new warfare, Hattusilis I not only made himself Great King of all Hatti—a remarkable accomplishment—but also raided as far as Aleppo and Alalakh. By 1600 chariot warriors were in control at Mycenae and elsewhere in Greece, and not long thereafter charioteers took over northwestern India.

CHARIOTRIES: NUMBERS AND COSTS

Chariot forces in the middle of the seventeenth century were relatively small and possibly numbered no more than a hundred vehicles.[6] At this time, the chariots were presumably used against infantries of the old style. As chariotries proliferated, the target of a chariot archer was increasingly the horses and crewmen of the opposing chariotry, and it became important for a king to have more chariots than his opponent had. Thutmose III's account of his victory at the Battle of Megiddo shows that by the middle of

[5] In *Coming of the Greeks*, 102–5, I presented evidence for the use of war chariots by Hattusilis I and by the "Great Hyksos" rulers of Egypt in the second half of the seventeenth century, but overlooked two other very early instances of its use. First, it is certain that chariots were used by Yarim-lim III of Aleppo, one of Hattusilis's adversaries. Yarim-lim's chariots, evidently one hundred in number, are indicated by the "Zukrasi text," an Old Hittite tablet: "Zaludis, the commander of the Manda-troops, (and) Zukra(s)sis, the commander of the heavy-armed (?) troops, of the Ruler (?) of Aleppo came down from Aleppo with his foot-soldiers and his charioteers." For this translation see Houwink ten Cate, "History of Warfare" 58; for the number, see Beal, *Organization*, 58. Second, it now seems probable (as I argue in "Myths of Midas") that the Troad was the first area to be taken over by chariot warriors (soon after 1700 B.C.) and that they built Troy VI.

[6] See Beal, *Organization*, 343. An epic text, "The Siege of Urshu," mentions forces of thirty and eighty chariots in the campaign of Hattusilis I against Urshu; in the wars between Hattusilis and Yarim-lim III of Aleppo two hundred chariot fighters (implying a hundred chariots) are mentioned. At pp. 432–45, however, Beal discusses a text referring to a pair of officers who were called "Overseers-of-one-thousand-chariot-fighters." In private correspondence Beal informs me that the text dates to the reign of either Hattusilis I or Mursilis I.

the fifteenth century B.C. a Great King could deploy at least a thousand chariots. At the beginning of the next century the Great Kingdom of Mitanni seems to have had at its disposal a chariotry numbering several thousand, since the Nuzi tablets indicate that one of the minor vassals of the Great King of Mitanni could all by himself have supplied his lord with over three hundred chariots.[7] At the same time, however, an Attarissiyas (whose name has often been compared with the Achaean "Atreus") caused trouble in western Anatolia with only a hundred chariots.[8]

Chariotries in the thirteenth century likewise ranged from a few hundred to a few thousand. At Kadesh, the Hittite king is said to have deployed thirty-five hundred chariots, twenty-five hundred of these being his own and one thousand being supplied by vassals.[9] Since Ramesses II emerged from the battle with some dignity, if not with victory, the Egyptian chariotry was probably about the same size.[10] At the end of the century the kings of Hatti and Egypt are likely to have been able to field chariotries of several thousand, since even a Hittite vassal—the king of Ugarit—seems to have had close to one thousand chariots.[11]

Perhaps a more typical palace at the end of the thirteenth century maintained a chariotry numbered in the low or middle hundreds. This, at least, seems to have been the situation at Pylos. Although the excavators at Pylos did not turn up "chariot tablets" such as those found at Knossos, they did recover approximately thirty "wheel tablets" detailing the disposition of at least two hundred pairs of wheels. Another text mentions the purchase of wood for 150 axles.[12] Since these spare parts constituted the palace's

---

[7] Kendall, *Warfare*, 67. Since the "mayor" of Nuzi was an underling of the king of Arrapaha, who in turn was the vassal of the Great King of Mitanni, we may suppose that the Nuzi forces were a very small fraction of the total that the Great King could muster.

[8] On the Madduwattas text and its date see Hans Güterbock, "The Hittites and the Aegean World: Part 1. The Ahhiyawa Problem Reconsidered," *AJA* 87 (1983): 133–34.

[9] For the texts see Alan Gardiner, *The Kadesh Inscriptions of Ramesses II* (Oxford, 1960), P130–35 and P150–55. Beal, *Organization*, 702, accepts the figures as reasonable for the Hittite army at full strength.

[10] Ramesses does not state how many chariots he had at Kadesh, but his predecessors seem to have maintained thousands of chariots. Amenhotep II, who admittedly was very fond of horses, brought back 730 chariots from one Asiatic campaign and 1092 from another. See Wilson's translation of his annals in *ANET*, 246 and 247.

[11] Twice in Ugaritic texts we find references to two thousand horses, or at least to *hn alpm* (in Israel, an *'eleph* was—like a Roman century—sometimes merely a "division" rather than a precise number). Cf. Astour, "New Evidence," 257, and B. Cutler and J. Macdonald, "Identification of the *na'ar* in the Ugaritic Texts," *UF* 8 (1976): 255. A tablet analyzed by Heltzer, *Internal Organization*, 194, lists teams of chariot horses, and Heltzer concludes that "at least 200 pairs of horses were counted originally in this text." Heltzer's estimate is "that the chariotry of Ugarit numbered at least 700–1000 chariots." This is also the estimate of Nougayrol, "Guerre et paix à Ugarit," 117n.47.

[12] Lejeune, "La civilisation mycénienne et la guerre," 49.

reserve, we are probably justified in imagining that the Pylos palace could put several hundred chariots into the field.

The Knossos archive gives us our most detailed information about numbers of chariots in a Late Bronze Age kingdom. Here the chariotry may have numbered as many as a thousand. The relevant tablets at Knossos are all from no more than eight scribal hands, and these scribes seem to have "specialized" in keeping a full and meticulous record of the chariots available to the palace.[13] That all the relevant tablets have survived, however, is not very likely, and on some surviving but damaged tablets the numerical notations on the right-hand side are illegible. The figures we have are therefore only a minimum for the chariot strength of the Knossos palace. According to Michel Lejeune's computation,[14] the Knossos tablets refer to more than 150 complete (*CURR ideogram) war chariots that were already distributed to individuals, and to another 39 chariots of the same type "en magasin." Most of these *CURR chariots appear in the 140 tablets of the "Sc series," each tablet in this series being the record of a single charioteer to whom an assignment of horses and equipment has been made.[15] Other tablets indicate the numbers of incomplete chariots, or chariot parts, stored in the magazine. Here, arranged in multiples of four,[16] were approximately 550 chariot boxes (*CAPS ideogram), and at least as many pairs of wheels (apparently any set of wheels was immediately adaptable to any chariot box).[17] With so many replacements stored in the magazine, it would seem that the field strength of Knossos's chariotry must have been somewhere between five hundred and one thousand.

Other information on the Knossos tablets, however, suggests that the number of chariots that could take the field may have been far lower than the number "on paper." Of the tablets in the Sc series, twenty-eight are

13 J.-P. Olivier, *Les scribes de Cnossos* (Rome, 1967), identified the scribes and their places of work. Michel Lejeune, "Chars et roues à Cnossos: Structure d'un inventaire," *Minos* 9 (1968): 9–61, used Olivier's conclusions as a point of departure for a thorough analysis of how the scribal bureaucracy worked. Lejeune described the responsibilities of three offices ("Bureaux I, II, III") in the matter of chariots. At p. 15 Lejeune notes that the scribes who worked in these offices "paraissent avoir eu chars et roues comme affectation unique." Because these scribal hands show up in no other tablets, John Chadwick suggested that they were apprentices and that the "chariot tablets" are merely scribal exercises; see his "The Organization of the Mycenaean Archives," in A. Bartoněk, ed., *Studia Mycenaea. Proceedings of the Mycenaean Symposium, Brno, April 1966* (Brno: 1968), 1–15. Why a palace would have kept such student exercises in an archive, while preserving none of the chariot records kept by professional scribes, is difficult to imagine.

14 Lejeune, "Chars," 47; and "Civilisation," 49–51.

15 Lejeune, "Civilisation," 50.

16 John T. Killen, "Notes on the Knossos Tablets," in John T. Killen et al., *Studies in Mycenaean and Classical Greek Presented to John Chadwick*, 319–23.

17 Lejeune, "Civilisation," 49, says that the magazine held "plus de mille paires de roues," but the figures he presents at "Chars," 47, indicate a total of 550.

preserved well enough that Mycenologists can confidently inventory what these twenty-eight charioteers did and did not have. The pattern is not very encouraging: One charioteer has horses but no vehicle, another has a vehicle but only one horse, and still another has both horses and a vehicle but no defensive armor. In fact, only six of the twenty-eight charioteers (that is, 21 percent) had all of the equipment necessary to take the field.[18] If one believes, with Chadwick, that the "chariot tablets" are merely scribal exercises, one could suppose that the actual condition of the Knossos chariotry was much better than the tablets indicate. But comparison with records elsewhere suggests that the figures for the chariotry at Knossos are real, for they are no worse than those for Alalakh and Nuzi and somewhat better than those for Assur in Neo-Assyrian times.[19] Another possibility may be that both at Knossos and elsewhere the tablets indicate not what a charioteer actually had but what the palace furnished to him. A tablet itemizing the chariot and single horse of a particular charioteer would in that case indicate only that the charioteer received a chariot and one horse from the palace, and we would presume that he had another horse of his own.[20] But this solution is speculative, and it is certainly possible that at any given time only a fraction of a kingdom's chariotry would be in condition to fight. If indeed a Great King could count on only some 20 percent of his chariotry to be battle-ready, then we must suppose that when Muwatallis put twenty-five hundred of his own chariots into the field at Kadesh the "paper strength" of his chariotry was over ten thousand.

Whatever discrepancy there may have been between the size of a chariotry on paper and that of one in the field, it must be observed that even the largest Late Bronze Age chariotry was small, relative to the size of the population it had to defend. Although a thousand chariots at Knossos might initially seem an impressive number, there must have been well over one hundred thousand Cretans whose security depended on them.[21] The proportions were no less steep at Pylos: if we assign the Pylos chariotry a field strength of five hundred vehicles (an optimistic number), there was probably not more than one chariot for every two hundred souls in Mes-

[18] Alexander Uchitel, "Charioteers of Knossos," *Minos* 23 (1988): 48–50.

[19] Ibid., 53–58.

[20] Along this same line, Uchitel, in ibid., 48, suggests that the "EQU 1 *e-ko* 1" of Tablet Sc 226 "can possibly mean that he (*i.e.* the charioteer, *ti-ri-jo-qa*) 'has' one horse of his own, and another one is supplied by the state."

[21] Pendlebury, *Archaeology of Crete*, 303n.3, observed that at its height in both Byzantine and modern times the island's population was about half a million. Evans estimated that Knossos itself had one hundred thousand people. Kanta, *Late Minoan III Period*, refrains from estimating how many people lived in Crete during that period but notes (p. 322) that "finds, especially those belonging to LM III B, are thickly spread all over the island. It is evident that there was a population explosion in Crete at this time."

senia.[22] In Egypt, even if the pharaoh had as many as forty-five hundred chariots, the number of his subjects was possibly a thousand times greater.[23]

The limitations on the size of a chariotry were imposed most of all by the enormous expense of maintaining one. Solomon is said (1 Kings 10.29) to have paid 150 shekels of silver for each of his chariot horses, and 600 shekels for each chariot. That was a considerable outlay, since it was also said (2 Samuel 24.24) that for fifty shekels of silver David bought a team of oxen and a threshing floor, and since Exodus 21.32 fixed liability damages for the death of a slave at thirty shekels of silver. The Papyrus Anastasi ridicules the young Egyptian who mortgages his grandfather's property to buy a chariot pole for three deben, and a chariot for five. Composite bows were also notoriously expensive. Such a bow was a very effective weapon, having double or triple the range of a self bow, but its manufacture was costly and difficult (the layering and lamination of wood, horn, and sinew was done at long intervals, and a properly aged bow would leave a bowyer's shop five or ten years after he had brought in the raw materials from which it was made).[24]

Defensive armor for the chariot crew (and sometimes even for the horses) was a major expense. As Yadin pointed out, the development of the mail corslet resulted from the use of chariots in battle.[25] Until the Hittites added a shield-bearer to the crew, corslets were the only protection that the driver and the warrior had. In the *Mahabharata* both crewmen regularly wear a corslet. So Uttara, for example, clowning for the benefit of his sister and her friends, "put on his coat of mail upside down, and the wide-eyed maidens giggled when they saw him. . . . Uttara himself tied the costly armor on Brhannada. Himself wearing a superb coat of mail which shone like the sun, and raising his lion standard, he ordered the other to handle his chariot."[26] In the Near East and the Aegean corslets are attested from the very beginning of the Late Bronze Age (scales found in the Shaft Graves at Mycenae may have come from a corslet), the time at which chariot

[22] Betancourt, "The End of the Bronze Age," 42, notes that population estimates for Messenia at the time the palace was destroyed range between 50,000 and 120,000.

[23] On the basis of data in the Harris Papyrus, John Wilson, *The Culture of Ancient Egypt* (Chicago, 1951), 271, guessed that the population of Egypt in the twelfth century was about 4,500,000.

[24] Wallace McLeod, "An Unpublished Egyptian Composite Bow in the Brooklyn Museum," *AJA* 62 (1958): 400.

[25] *Art of Warfare*, vol. 1, 84. For a comprehensive presentation on the Late Bronze Age corslet see Catling, "Panzer," in H.-G. Buchholz and J. Wiesner, *Kriegswesen, Teil 1*, Archaeologia Homerica I E (Göttingen, 1977), 74–118.

[26] *Mahabharata* 4 (47) 35.19–21. The translation comes from J.A.B. van Buitenen, *The Mahabharata* (Chicago, 1978).

warfare began. The "chariot tablets" from Knossos itemize the distribution of a pair of knee-length corslets to each chariot crew.[27] The corslet may also appear in ceremonial chariot scenes on LH IIIA and IIIB pottery: men in or alongside the chariots carry swords in tassled scabbards and wear long and dot-covered "robes" that Catling has tentatively identified as corslets.[28] Much of what is known about Late Bronze Age corslets was learned at Nuzi. Copper scales from corslets were found there in great quantity, and the Nuzi tablets make frequent reference to corslets.[29] The typical Nuzi charioteer's corslet, or *sariam* (a Hurrian word, borrowed by Hittite, Akkadian, and Northwest Semitic speakers), was a long, cumbersome, and expensive affair. Its basis was a leather (usually goatskin) tunic, partially sleeved and reaching down to the knees or to midcalf. Approximately five hundred large copper scales were sewn to the torso and skirt of the *sariam*, and another several hundred small scales were sewn to the arms. The head and neck of the chariot crewman was protected by a *gurpisu*, a leather helmet covered with long strips of bronze or copper (since the *gurpisu* extended to the collar, the crewman was entirely covered except for the face, the lower arms, and the lower legs). The several Nuzi corslets that can be reconstructed are estimated to have weighed between thirty-seven and fifty-eight pounds.[30]

At Nuzi and occasionally in other kingdoms the horses also wore coats of mail.[31] A very few Egyptian chariot horses are shown wearing such things, and an ivory carving from Cyprus shows—oddly—a hunting scene in which both the chariot archer and his horses are draped with scale corslets.[32] Possibly the Mycenaean kingdoms regularly issued horse-armor: Catling has argued that two of the Linear B ideograms refer to horse-coverings of some sort rather than to crewmen's corslets.[33] The horse-armor was undoubtedly very costly, and how effective it was is difficult to guess (horses wearing heavy cloaks were less vulnerable, but surely also much slower).

Apart from the expense of purchasing all these items, and of hiring all the necessary specialists (charioteers, chariot warriors, trainers, grooms, veterinarians, carpenters), there was the matter of food: Stuart Piggott has estimated that eight to ten acres of good grain-land would have been re-

[27] Catling, "Panzer," 107ff.; Franceschetti, "Armi e guerra," 77 and 80.

[28] Catling, "Panzer," 96.

[29] The fullest discussion of the Nuzi evidence is in Kendall, *Warfare*, 263–86.

[30] Ibid., 278; cf. Catling, "Panzer," 89–90.

[31] Kendall, *Warfare*, 223–25 and 242–45.

[32] For the Enkomi ivory see H.-G. Buchholz and V. Karageorghis, *Prehistoric Greece and Cyprus* (London, 1973), no. 1749.

[33] Catling, "Panzer," 108–16.

quired to feed one team of chariot horses.[34] If Hammurapi of Ugarit did indeed have more than two thousand horses, they must have represented a sizeable fraction of that king's wealth, and the cost of maintaining them would have been enormous: in addition to all the professional and specialized personnel, they would have required—on Piggott's formula— almost ten thousand acres of grain-land.

Given the extraordinary expense of maintaining a chariotry, it is no surprise to find that the chariotry was a palace's chief concern. Keeping track of the chariots and charioteers required a small bureaucracy of clerks and quartermasters. This is shown most clearly at Knossos, but in Egypt too there are references to the "scribe of the stable," "scribe of horses," and "scribe of the chariotry."[35] Everywhere the charioteers have names, while infantrymen are merely numbered. In the Greek world, the palace furnished everything: each tablet in the Knossos Sc series was devoted to one charioteer, being a record of the vehicle, team, harness, and corslet (or corslets) allocated to him. In Egypt and the Levant, the charioteer may have "owned" his own chariot, with the palace supplying arms, armor, and horses.[36] Nougayrol thought that at Ugarit the *maryannu* were "sans doute propriétaires de leurs chars" but that other individuals may have been furnished with vehicles by the palace.[37] In Egypt it likewise was a charioteer's responsibility to provide his own chariot, while the pharaoh supplied the horses.[38]

Throughout the civilized world in the thirteenth century charioteers and chariot warriors were thus a privileged elite. The king and the men in his chariot corps were closely interdependent, the king supplying much or all of the expensive equipment that the chariot crews needed and the chariot crews providing for the king's and the kingdom's security. Often the men of the chariotry were given land by the king, to be held in fief. At Ugarit land allotments were made to the *maryannu*, and apparently a son inherited both the allotment and his father's military obligation.[39] Arrangements in the Mycenaean world were probably much the same, but details are lack-

---

[34] Piggott, "Horse and Chariot: The Price of Prestige," *Proceedings of the Seventh International Congress of Celtic Studies, Held at Oxford from 10th to 15th July, 1983* (Oxford, 1986), 27.

[35] Alan Schulman, "Egyptian Chariotry: A Re-Examination," *Journal of the American Research Center in Egypt* 2 (1963): 95. Lejeune, "Chars et roues," 14–15, identifies in the Knossos palace three separate "bureaus" whose scribes specialized in the chariot inventories and are not known (from their distinctive hands) to have inscribed anything other than "chariot tablets."

[36] At Nuzi, for example, Kendall, *Warfare*, 130, concluded that many charioteers owned their own vehicles but were supplied with horses by the palace.

[37] Nougayrol, "Guerre et paix à Ugarit," n. 47.

[38] Schulman, "Egyptian Chariotry," 87, citing Papyrus Anastasi III, vs. 6, 7–8.

[39] A. F. Rainey, "The Military Personnel at Ugarit," *JNES* 24 (1965): 19–21.

ing.[40] At Nuzi there were "imperial" charioteers whose livelihood was apparently supplied by the Great King of Mitanni, and local charioteers who depended directly on the "mayor" of Nuzi; but both groups were part of an aristocracy closely connected to the palace.[41]

How Chariots Were Used in Battle

How many charioteers there were, how much they cost to maintain, and what their social status was are matters less controversial than how they fought. The strictly military aspects of Bronze Age chariotry have been addressed piecemeal, and the general character of chariot warfare remains unexplored. This chapter will conclude that before the Catastrophe chariots were in all kingdoms used as mobile firing platforms for archers armed with composite bows, but that conclusion is quite unorthodox.

Mycenaean chariots, first of all, are often thought of as having had little utility of any kind on the battlefield. This view is popular especially among archaeologists. Their indifference to the chariot is not entirely surprising: while hundreds of Late Helladic swords and spearheads have been found, and even a number of boar's tusk helmets, no Mycenaean chariot has yet been brought to light, nor are the chances very good that future excavations will produce one. Most archaeological studies of Mycenaean warfare have therefore readily accepted Homer's assurance that the Mycenaeans fought on foot and have assumed that whatever was done with the chariots was of little or no consequence.[42] Mycenologists, on the other hand, have had to confront the Linear B scribes' laborious inventories of chariots and have no

[40] Cf. M. Detienne, "Remarques sur le char en Grèce," in Vernant *Problèmes de la guerre*, 314.

[41] Cf. Kendall, *Warfare*, 128: "The local charioteers seem also to have been a privileged lot. A very great many lived in or around the palace, and their duties often consisted of no more than standing guard as watchmen at the palace portals."

[42] Lorimer's *Homer and the Monuments* devoted pp. 305–28 to the chariot (in comparison, her treatment of infantry weapons fills 173 pages) and dealt primarily with its design and construction. About its use in Mycenaean warfare, she regretted (p. 321) that "we know nothing at all" and did not speculate about it. When Lorimer wrote, of course, Linear B was entirely illegible, and the chariot ideograms on the Knossos tablets were seen by all scholars as dating ca. 1400 B.C. It was therefore possible to believe that although chariots may have been important in LH I and II, by the end of IIIB they were as inconsequential as Homer makes them. In recent scholarship, it is noteworthy that in the exquisitely detailed *Archaeologia Homerica* series the two volumes devoted to *Kriegswesen* do not even include a chapter on the chariot, and Josef Wiesner's *Fahren und Reiten* treats the chariot as primarily a prestige vehicle. In Harding's *Mycenaeans and Europe*, the chapter "Warfare, Weapons and Armour" (pp. 151–87) begins by noting "the use of the light chariot, probably, as in Homer, to transport the warrior to the scene of battle rather than for use as a genuine war chariot" (p. 151), but says nothing more about it.

doubt at all that the chariot was used for military purposes.[43] But the tablets do not say how the chariot was used in warfare, and Mycenologists have not speculated on this matter. A few historians have tried to fill the gap left by our archaeological and documentary evidence, but with varying results. Occasionally the Mycenaean chariot is understood to have been used to propel a thrusting spear.[44] Most often it is seen as nothing more than a battle taxi: the Mycenaean Greeks fought on foot but were transported to and from the battlefield by chariots. The possibility that the Mycenaean chariot was an archer's mobile platform has not, so far as I know, been seriously considered.[45]

Nor is it widely believed that the Hittite chariots were so used. Most scholars who have expressed themselves on the role of the Hittite chariotry have stated that in Hatti the offensive weapon of a chariot warrior was the lance—the thrusting spear—and not the bow. The Hittite chariots, that is, like medieval knights at a joust, made a furious rush at the opponent's vehicles, the chariot warrior attempting to thrust a lance through one of the enemy crewmen.[46] This belief is founded on the Egyptian representations of the Battle of Kadesh: in the reliefs, some of the Hittite chariot crewmen carry lances, but none carries a bow. Several scholars have in fact suggested that the Hittites came up short in the Battle of Kadesh because their chariot lancers were held at a distance by Ramesses' chariot archers.[47]

---

[43] Lejeune, "La civilisation mycénienne et la guerre," devotes most of his discussion to the tablets' references to chariots; so also does Franceschetti, "Armi e guerra in testi micenei."

[44] Greenhalgh, *Early Greek Warfare*, 7–12, argues that "the long thrusting-spear was the main weapon of the Mycenaean chariot-warriors as it was of the Hittites, with whom the Achaeans appear to have been in close touch" (p. 11); cf. also his "The Dendra Charioteer," *Antiquity* 54 (1980): 201–5.

[45] Schachermeyr, "Streitwagen und Streitwagenbild im Alten Orient und bei den mykenischen Griechen," *Anthropos* 46 (1951): 705–53, may have assumed that the Mycenaean chariot warriors were bowmen but did not argue the point and in fact said nothing about how Mycenaean chariots may have been used "im Streit."

[46] For the Hittite chariot warrior's dependence on a thrusting spear see, for example, Yadin, *Warfare*, vol. 1, 80 and 108–9; Schachermeyr, "Streitwagen," 716; F. Stubbings, "Arms and Armour," in Wace and Stubbings, eds., *A Companion to Homer* (London, 1967), 521. The interpretation of Stillman and Tallis, *Armies*, 65, is slightly different: "Against enemy chariotry, the Hittite chariotry would charge into close combat. The Hittites would attempt to get close to their opponents to discharge their spears or thrust with them."

[47] Olaf Höckmann, "Lanzen und Speere der ägäischen Bronzezeit und des Übergangs zur Eisenzeit," in H.-G. Buchholz, *Ägäische Bronzezeit*, 340, describes the Hittite chariot warriors as lancers and then condemns this "aussichtslose Taktik." Similarly, Yadin (*Art of Warfare*, vol. 1, 109) saw Kadesh as an Egyptian victory because chariot lancers were a poor second to chariot archers: "The weakness of the Hittite chariot was immediately evident when the Egyptian chariots armed with the long-range composite bow, went over to the counterattack." It is more likely that the Hittites knew how to use chariots, and got the better of Ramesses at Kadesh.

Even the Egyptian chariot is not always seen as a mobile firing platform: according to an article published by Alan Schulman in 1980, both in Egypt and elsewhere the chariot warrior was indeed an archer, but one who shot his bow from the ground.[48] In this view, the chariot driver drove his horses to a good vantage point, at which the archer would dismount from the chariot, shoot his arrow, remount the chariot, and ride off to another location and another shot.

Schulman's view can be immediately rejected. It arose from two considerations, both of them true: first, in Homeric battles the chariot functions only as a battle taxi;[49] and second, Egyptian evidence shows the chariot warrior as an archer. Instead of seeing the Homeric and the Egyptian evidence as incompatible, and choosing between them, Schulman merged them, producing the taxied archers. But the practice he describes has no support whatever in either literary or archaeological evidence, is unimaginable in practice, and is congruent only with Schulman's own recent argument that chariotry was too inefficient ever to have been of any military importance.[50]

Let us go on to consider the possibility that for the thirteenth-century chariot warrior, especially in Hatti but also in Greece (as Nestor claims at *Iliad* 4.297–309), the offensive weapon was the thrusting spear. Here again we may be categorical: the notion that either Hittite or Mycenaean chariot warriors could have relied upon the lance as their primary offensive weapon is for practical reasons out of the question. Like the chariots of Mycenaean Greece, Nuzi, and Assyria, the Hittite chariot certainly carried a lance. This weapon would have been essential against enemy foot soldiers

---

[48] Schulman, "Chariots, Chariotry, and the Hyksos," *Journal of the Society for the Study of Egyptian Antiquities* 10 (1980), 105–53.

[49] Ibid., 125–28.

[50] Although his earlier contributions are valuable, Schulman's 1980 article rejected not only the consensus but also his own original conclusions about the importance of chariotry in New Kingdom Egypt. In "Chariots, Chariotry, and the Hyksos," Schulman argues that "outside of certain situations where it did have a limited tactical value," the chariot was of little significance in ancient warfare. The article ignores the fact that from the beginning of antiquity to the end the art of warfare went through radical evolutionary and revolutionary changes. In making the argument about the Late Bronze Age, the article relies upon classical sources, such as Arrian's *Tactica*, which claimed that chariots were of little practical value on the battlefield; Schulman's use of such late sources is based on his surprising assumption that "little of the conditions, practice, and weaponry of war had changed between the time of the Hyksos and that of Arrian" (p. 119). Schulman argues that if chariots had little military value to the Greeks and Romans, they would have been just as ineffective in the Late Bronze Age, since Late Bronze Age armies were "as skilled in warfare as were its practitioners in Classical antiquity" (p. 119). While looking to classical authors for an assessment of chariot warfare, Schulman found Late Bronze Age sources suspect: "Although it is true that the Kadesh texts specify that 2500 Hittite chariots, each bearing three men surprised the Egyptian army, we can hardly accept such a figure as other than a gross exaggeration" (p. 132).

or chariot crewmen who had fallen to the ground (a relief from the Old Hittite period shows a warrior in a chariot thrusting his spear toward a prostrate enemy).[51] But that a warrior on a speeding chariot could have thrust a lance against an opposing chariot is quite simply impossible, as Littauer and Crouwel have clearly shown, demonstrating the physical facts with measurements and diagrams.[52] A chariot warrior could not have thrust a spear over the heads of his own horses or out the back of the moving car. That a chariot warrior's offensive assignment was to thrust a spear laterally, as two chariots passed, is also unimaginable.

Finally, we must confront the thesis that in Late Helladic Greece the chariot's military use was confined to transporting infantryman to and from a battle.[53] As we shall see in chapter 11, some of the infantrymen known as "chariot runners" may have ridden with the charioteer and the archer until the enemy came within range, at which point the *apobatai* would have leaped to the ground, and this practice may have been characteristic of Late Helladic chariotries. Furthermore, as Littauer and Crouwel have pointed out,[54] several recently discovered sherds of LH IIIC pottery do portray chariots carrying a driver and an infantryman. It is possible, therefore, that in the middle of the twelfth century B.C. those chariots still to be found in Greece were indeed little more than the personal conveyances of warriors who fought on foot and that Homer reflects this practice. But how chariots were used after the Catastrophe and how they were used before must be regarded as two very different questions. During the century and a half prior to the Catastrophe life in the palace-states seems to have been so secure that Catling described the period as the *pax Mycenaica*.[55] Since it is unlikely that in this period military chariots were often put to the test, we may be dealing more with hypothetical than with actual use.

---

[51] Jeanny Vorys Canby, "Hittite Art," *Bib. Arch.* (1989): 114.

[52] Mary Littauer and J. H. Crouwel, "Chariots in Late Bronze Age Greece," *Antiquity* 57 (1983): 187–92.

[53] This view has prevailed from Homer to the present. For recent arguments that Homer's picture of Mycenaean chariot warfare was essentially correct see Josef Wiesner, *Fahren und Reiten* (Archaeologia Homerica I F [Göttingen, 1968]); Mary Littauer, "The Military Use of the Chariot in the Aegean in the Late Bronze Age," *AJA* 76 (1972): 145–57; Littauer and Crouwel, "Chariots in Late Bronze Age Greece," 187–92; Crouwel, *Chariots*, 126–27. Wiesner, Littauer, and Crouwel supposed that chariots functioned as battle taxis throughout the LH III period. J. K. Anderson argued only that they were so used in the Dark Age, after the great period of chariot warfare had ended. See Anderson's "Homeric, British and Cyrenaic Chariots," *AJA* 69 (1965): 349–52, and "Greek Chariot-Borne and Mounted Infantry," *AJA* 79 (1975): 175–87.

[54] Littauer, "Military Use," 145–46; Littauer and Crouwel, "Chariots in Late Bronze Age Greece," 189–90; the significance of the sherds was first noted by Catling, "A Mycenaean Puzzle from Lefkandi in Euboea," *AJA* 72 (1968): 41–49.

[55] Catling, "A Mycenaean Puzzle," 46, proposed that the period of peace lasted for "about a century and a half" and ended with the disasters ca. 1200.

How, when the palaces were still standing, the Mycenaean palace i̠.̠ *intended* that their chariots should be used in a battle, if a battle were ever to occur, is a question that can not be answered by reading Homer. For the Homeric picture is misleading, as Homer himself was the first to admit. When Nestor gives his advice that the chariots be drawn up in a line, so that they might charge against the Trojans, each warrior thrusting with his spear against the enemy, the old man justifies his advice with the reminiscence (*Iliad* 4.308) that this is how the "men of earlier times" (*proteroi*) did battle. We have already seen that men of earlier times did not—and could not have done—battle in the way Nestor here prescribes, but the reminiscence is nevertheless important because it reveals Homer's own concession that his Achaeans at Troy were not using their chariots in the way that chariots were supposed to be used. In the days when men really did depend on chariots, Homer is here conceding, they did *not* use them merely for transport to and from the battlefield. If we may translate this into our terms perhaps we may propose, along the lines suggested by J. K. Anderson, that the way in which the Greeks of the IIIC period used their chariots was not how the chariot was used, or was meant to be used, in the IIIB period—the generations before the Catastrophe.

The claim that Homer did not know how Mycenaean chariots were meant to be used in battle may be regarded by some as a rash calumny and needs some defense. Although Homer's Achaeans have most often been identified with the occupants of the Mycenaean palaces, there is good reason to believe—as I have argued elsewhere—that the saga originated in the less civilized, more bellicose, and illiterate parts of Achaea (especially the mountainous coast of Thessaly and Phthiotis); and that the Achaeans or "Argives" who sacked Troy (and whose fathers had sacked Thebes) spoke North Greek rather than the South Greek of the Linear B tablets.[56] No one has yet refuted the argument, put forward by Paul Cauer a hundred years ago, that Homer's Achaeans came from the north, and since Ventris's decipherment of the Greek in the Linear B tablets the argument is in fact far stronger than it was in Cauer's day. Evidence also continues to mount that before the Trojan saga circulated among Ionic-speakers it was preserved in the Aeolic dialect of their northern neighbors.[57]

I would suggest, then, that Homer was basically ignorant of chariot warfare because the heroic tradition originated in a society of infantrymen, in which the chariot was indeed nothing more than a prestige vehicle.

[56] Drews, "Argos and Argives in the *Iliad*," *CP* 74 (1979): 111–35. See now H. W. Singor, "Nine against Troy," *Mnemosyne* 44 (1991): 58–59.

[57] Richard Janko, *Homer, Hesiod, and the Hymns: Diachronic Development in Epic Diction* (Cambridge, 1982), 89–92; M. L. West, "The Rise of the Greek Epic," *JHS* 108 (1988): 159–67; Paul Wathelet, "Les datifs analogiques en -εσσι dans la tradition épique," *REG* 104 (1991): 1–14.

Homer's Achaeans were not themselves charioteers or chariot archers but instead were responsible for putting an end to chariot warfare and to the domination of the horse-tamers. They were, that is to say, infantrymen of the new type—fleet of foot, skilled with the javelin or throwing spear, and also carrying long swords—who spelled the doom of the great chariot forces of the Late Bronze Age. Integral to the thesis of this book is the tenet that in Greece chariot warfare virtually disappeared during the Catastrophe and that throughout the Dark Age it was nothing but a vague memory. The LH IIIC period seems in this respect to have been closer to the Dark Age than to the pre-Catastrophic Bronze Age: obviously there were still a number of chariots in the Argolid, on Euboea, and elsewhere in LH IIIC Greece, but the day of chariot warfare was over, and the day of the infantryman had arrived. That Homer knew very little about chariot warfare is precisely, it seems to me, what one should expect of a bard who stands at the end of a tradition that originated in a society of infantrymen.

The thesis that during the palace period Mycenaean chariots served primarily as battle taxis is untenable not because we have evidence to the contrary (we do not) but because it makes no historical sense. The enormously expensive chariot and chariot horses, as Greenhalgh observed, would hardly have been risked by the palace in such a frivolous way, when the wounding of a horse "could easily put the whole apparatus out of action."[58] The rulers of Pylos and Knossos devoted their resources to the maintenance of a chariotry of several hundred vehicles, keeping a large inventory of spare wheels, axles, and boxes and assigning a small bureaucracy to the supervision of the men, horses, and material. It is not reasonable to suppose that the rulers did all this merely to ensure that several hundred of their infantrymen could ride in comfort or dignity to the battlefield. Chariots as status symbols or as convenient means of transportation would have been a private concern: men with ample wealth may have chosen to spend some of it in purchasing a chariot and team and in raising the grain to keep the horses healthy. But a palace would hardly have been so preoccupied with its chariotry if the chariots were nothing more than the personal luxuries of a few hundred foot soldiers. The rulers must have believed that the chariotry they were so diligently maintaining would in a crisis provide the regime and its subjects with protection and security. They must have believed, that is, that the kind of chariot warfare that had once been effective was still effective. In the event, of course, they were wrong. But if the *pax Mycenaica* provided few opportunities for putting the old warfare into practice, the rulers of the Mycenaean palaces can hardly be blamed for imagining that the next war would be fought along the same lines as the last one.

[58] *Early Greek Warfare*, 17.

There is, finally, a decisive argument that before the Catastrophe chariots in Mycenaean Greece were not used, or meant to be used, merely as battle taxis: prior to 1200, chariotry was not merely an adjunct to a Mycenaean king's military forces but the very basis of his army. Here I must anticipate the conclusion of chapter 11. That chapter will show that in the centuries prior to the Catastrophe the armies of eastern Mediterranean kings included no offensive infantry formations: the only offensive foot soldiers in these armies were skirmishers or "runners" who fought in support of the chariot squadron to which they were attached. Our picture of heavily armed infantry units as the bulwark of the Mycenaean palace-states comes not from the archaeological evidence (and certainly not from the Linear B tablets) but from the *Iliad*, and for the period when the Pylos and Knossos palaces were still standing it is demonstrably wrong.

How, then, were war chariots used in the Late Bronze Age kingdoms of the eastern Mediterranean? The answer will be no surprise: as mobile platforms for archers.[59] Throughout this area, when artists depict chariots on the attack, the chariot warrior is regularly shooting his bow from a car traveling at full speed. That is also how the war chariot was used elsewhere. Sanskrit scholars have known all along that the Aryan chariot warriors of India were bowmen, and recently it has become clear that in China too the war chariot carried an archer.[60]

Closer to home, there is no doubt that in Babylonia the chariot warriors of the Kassites depended on the bow.[61] The Nuzi texts are unusually informative, since they detail the issuing of equipment to chariot crews; along with helmets, corslets, a whip, and a sword, bows and a quiver of thirty or forty arrows were standard.[62] From first-millennium Mesopotamia, Assyrian archers in war chariots are familiar from Ashurnasirpal II's Nimrud orthostats, from the bronze doors at Balawat that commemorate Shalmaneser III's victories and from the war reliefs from Sargon II's palace at Chorsabad.[63]

In the Levant, as in Mesopotamia, the war chariot carried an archer. The fact that the bow was the weapon of the chariot warriors who opposed Thutmose III at Megiddo is clear from that king's account, on the Gebel

---

[59] Moorey, "Emergence," 208, likewise concludes that "from the outset archery was fundamental to the role of the light horse-drawn chariot as a war vehicle."

[60] Jacques Gernet, "Note sur le char en Chine," in Vernant, *Problèmes de la guerre*, 310; E. L. Shaughnessy, "Historical Perspectives on the Introduction of the Chariot into China," *Harvard Journal of Asiatic Studies* 48 (1988): 195 and 199. I thank Professor Stuart Piggott for this reference.

[61] Cassin, "Char de guerre," 304.

[62] Kendall, *Warfare*, 210–12; at p. 256 Kendall cites a tablet referring to a lot of twenty thousand arrows (*qanatu*).

[63] Yadin, *Warfare*, vol. 2, 386–87, 402–3, 416–17.

Barkal Stele, of the tribute that his defeated enemies brought him:[64] "All their horses which were with them, their great chariots of gold and silver, as well as those which were plain, all their coats of mail, their bows, their arrows, and all their weapons of warfare. It was these with which they had come from afar to fight against my majesty, and now they were bringing them as tribute to my majesty." In his Karnak annals, Thutmose specifies that he captured 924 chariots and 502 bows from the enemy. Ugaritic texts make frequent mention of bows and arrows, and it will be recalled that the *Tale of Aqhat* revolved about an extraordinary composite bow. One Ugaritic tablet reports that two chariots brought in for repairs "are without quivers," an obvious implication, as Beal notes, "that other chariots did have quivers."[65] Another Ugaritic tablet records the delivery of either harnesses or teams of horses, of armor for men and horses, and of forty bows and a thousand arrows.[66] Although we have few graphic representations of the war chariot from the Levant, an ivory plaque from Megiddo— dating from ca. 1200 B.C.—shows captives marching in front of a Canaanite chariot, the chariot being equipped with quiver and bow case. A ninth-century orthostat from the Neo-Hittite palace at Carchemish shows a chariot archer in the act of shooting, while his chariot rolls over an enemy already brought down by an arrow.[67]

It is well known that Egyptian chariots carried archers. These chariots were outfitted with a bow case and occasionally a quiver attached to the chariot box at a diagonal, the mouth being at a level with the archer's right hand. An Egyptian papyrus notes the departure of a chariot for Syria, the chariot having a quiver stocked with eighty arrows.[68] Egyptian inscriptions rarely go into sufficient detail to clarify what happened in a battle (what happened in the battles at Megiddo and Kadesh will be looked at in detail in the following section), but such references as there are indicate that casualites were normally inflicted by chariot archers. Merneptah's account of his victory over the Libyans in 1208, for example, claims that "the chariot warriors who were upon the chariots of his majesty placed themselves in pursuit of them (*i.e.*, the broken Libyan invaders), they being overthrown by arrows, carried off, and slaughtered."[69] The pharaohs themselves took pride in their skill as chariot archers. Amenhotep II boasted of the rapidity, range, and accuracy of his shooting, claiming that from a speeding chariot he had hit four targets, set thirty-four feet apart,

[64] Wilson's translation, *ANET*, p. 238.

[65] Beal, *Organization*, 578.

[66] Heltzer, *Internal Organization*, 113.

[67] Yadin, *Warfare*, vol. 1, 243; and vol. 2, 366.

[68] Papyrus Koller 1.1–2; cf. Schulman, "Chariots, Chariotry, and the Hyksos," 124n.57.

[69] Merneptah's Karnak Inscription, as translated in Schulman, "Egyptian Chariotry," p. 88. For the full inscription, see Breasted, *AR*, vol. 3, nos. 569ff.

with such force that the arrows went clean through each target's three inches of copper.[70] Egyptian chariot archers in battle appear not only in wall reliefs—as of Seti I's battles, of Ramesses II's battle at Kadesh in 1275, or of Ramesses III's victory over the Libyans in 1182—but also in reliefs etched on the sides of the fifteenth-century chariot found in the tomb of Thutmose IV and on a painted panel of a chest from Tutankhamun's tomb.[71]

The fact that Hittite chariot warriors were bowmen is not generally recognized, but it is nevertheless demonstrable. As noted above, the belief that the lance was the standard weapon of the Hittite chariot warrior derives from Ramesses the Great's reliefs of the Battle of Kadesh.[72] In those reliefs the Egyptian chariots carry archers but none of the Hittite chariots carries an archer, and in fact only the chariot of the Hittite king has a bow case. In each of the other Hittite chariots is a crew of three. One of the three holds the reins, a second man regularly carries a shield, and the third man sometimes holds a lance. The Egyptian sculptor, however, nowhere depicts the Hittite chariots in action (they are either heading toward or retreating from the battlefield). And as Richard Beal points out, as often as not the third man in a Hittite chariot is shown without a weapon of any kind. Since in the inscription Ramesses does mention the archers of the Hittite chariot corps,[73] Beal argues that the reliefs are "clearly a misrepresentation."[74] The Egyptian sculptors have here chosen to portray the enemy armed only with defensive weapons. In battle scenes the pharaoh's artists were careful never to depict an Egyptian corpse or indeed an Egyptian in danger. As portrayed in Egyptian art, only Egyptian troops take the offensive, the obligation of the artist being to propagate the myth of the pharaoh's invincibility.[75] Noting that the relief of the Battle of Kadesh shows one Hittite chariot warrior apparently about to *throw* an arrow at the Egyptians, Beal

[70] See Wilson's translation of Amenhotep's Gizeh stele, *ANET*, 244.

[71] The two volumes of Yadin's *Warfare* provide excellent illustrations of these and other scenes cited; see *Warfare*, vol. 1, 104–5; 192–93, 216–17; 240–41; and vol. 2, 334–37.

[72] It also derives, as Moorey ("Emergence," 203) points out, from such anachronistic sources as Xenophon's *Cyropaedia* and misconceived "analogies drawn from tank warfare."

[73] In the inscription (Gardiner, *Kadesh*, P160–65 and P200–205) a demoralized Hittite proclaims that "one is unable to take up a bow" when one beholds the glorious Ramesses; and Ramesses himself boasts that "whoever shot in my direction, their arrows scattered as they reached me." See also Breasted, *AR*, vol. 3, nos. 337 and 343. The latter is a caption for a scene of a group of prisoners: "List of those countries which his majesty slew, while alone by himself: corpses, horses, and chariots, bows, swords, all the weapons of warfare."

[74] Beal, *Organization*, 575.

[75] Ibid., 617. John Wilson, "The Royal Myth in Ancient Egypt," *Proceedings of the American Philosophical Society* 100 (1956): 439–42. Students of ancient weaponry have also suspected that the Egyptian artists distorted their opponents' weaponry. Stillman and Tallis, *Armies*, 57, note that in the New Kingdom "in many battle scenes only enemies are ever shown dead or wounded and sometimes unarmoured and without weapons."

suggests that for Ramesses' artists an enemy bow may have been "ideologically unportrayable," and concludes that "the evidence seems to show that bows and arrows were the primary weapons of the Hittite chariotry."[76]

The battle reliefs of Ramesses' father, Seti I, confirm this conclusion. When Seti campaigned against the Hittites, he evidently was opposed by Hittite chariot archers, for the Karnak reliefs that celebrate his victory (see plate 1) depict Hittite chariots equipped with bow cases, and in each chariot is a Hittite warrior with a quiver on his back and a bow in his hand.[77] In short, Hittite chariot warriors fought exactly as did their counterparts in Egypt, the Levant, Mesopotamia, and India. In all the Near Eastern kingdoms of the Late Bronze Age, the chariot served as an archer's mobile firing platform.

From Mycenaean Greece, unfortunately, we have no pictorial representations of a chariot battle. For that reason, and perhaps because no composite bow has ever been found in a Mycenaean tomb, Aegean archaeologists have traditionally and stubbornly insisted that the bow had no military importance in the Late Helladic period.[78] That view, however, was invalidated forty years ago. Before the Linear B tablets were read, and when Homer was still taken as a reliable guide to things Mycenaean, it was understandable that scholars imagined the Mycenaeans as contemptuous of the bow. H. L. Lorimer summed up and lent her great authority to the consensus: the composite bow was strictly Oriental and Minoan, and although the Mycenaeans may now and then have seen such a weapon "there is no indication that they learned how to use it." For Lorimer, the composite bows inventoried in Linear B tablets were of course "Minoan" rather than Mycenaean, since she wrote before Ventris's decipherment. On similar grounds she dismissed the importance of the bow in the *Odyssey*: the centrality of Odysseus's great composite bow in the story of his return was "natural when we consider the strong Cretan tinge of much of the poem."[79]

[76] Beal, *Organization*, 578 and 617.

[77] *Reliefs and Inscriptions at Karnak, Volume 4: The Battle Reliefs of King Sety I*, Oriental Institute Publication no. 107 (Chicago, 1986), plates 34 and 35.

[78] The *Kriegswesen* fascicles of *Archaeologia Homerica* thus far published deal with the sword, spear, dagger, and even the club, but not the bow. In their discussions of Mycenaean warfare most archaeological surveys either dismiss the bow in a few sentences or omit it altogether. Not to multiply examples, I cite only Jan Bouzek, *The Aegean, Anatolia, and Europe: Cultural Interrelations in the Second Millennium* B.C. (Göteborg and Prague, 1985). In the very last paragraph of his fifty-page survey of Late Helladic armor and weapons, and after a meticulous analysis of swords, spears, daggers, knives, and axes of the period, Bouzek finally reaches (p. 142) the subject of bows and arrows: "Arrowheads are mentioned only for the sake of completeness. . . . In any case the bow only played a marginal part in warfare during the period in question."

[79] Lorimer, *Homer and the Monuments*, 280 and 289.

PLATE 1. Seti I attacking the chariots of the Hittite king. Line drawing of relief from Amun temple at Karnak

We know now that the tablets from the Knossos "Armoury" contain a primitive form of Greek and so must acknowledge that the Mycenaeans not only had learned how to use a composite bow but knew how to make one, and did so by the hundreds. There is other evidence that the bow was the primary weapon of Mycenaean chariot warriors. Knee-length corslets were evidently provided for chariot crews, and these must have been meant for protection against enemy missiles (in a contest of thrusting spears or rapiers the long corslets would have offered little protection and would have greatly impeded the wearer's movement). Alongside the "chariot tablets" found at Knossos were tablets recording large lots of arrows: 6010 in one batch and 2630 in another, enough for each of two hundred chariot archers to receive forty. Nearby were found stores of bronze arrowheads, which were meant for distribution to Mycenaean rather than (as Evans thought) Minoan warriors. Tablets also refer to bow making and to bowyers (to-ko-so-wo-ko, which "ha un perfetto corrispondente in greco in τοξοϝοϱγοί)."[80] The distribution of in corpore arrowheads from prehistoric Greece also suggests that the bow was far more important from 1600 to 1200 B.C. than it had been in earlier times or would ever be again. Whereas no metal arrowheads have been found in EH or MH contexts, bronze arrowheads of various kinds appear suddenly with the Shaft Graves and continue through the LH IIIB period; then they vanish again, with only a handful attested for the whole of the Dark Age.[81]

Thus there is a great deal of evidence that in the armies of Mycenaean Greece—as of kingdoms everywhere during the Late Bronze Age—the composite bow was the principal offensive weapon. That Homer had some very wrong ideas about how a composite bow was made (cf. especially the description of Pandaros's bow at Iliad 4.105ff.) can no longer mean, as it did for Lorimer, that such a bow was "un-Mycenaean." Rather, it shows how much of Mycenaean warfare had been forgotten in the epic tradition. In a detailed philological study Denys Page concluded that Homer's limited repertory of formulas for bows and arrows is "the disintegrating relic of a much wider and stricter system," and that "the evidence of formular usage is sufficient to carry the bow and arrows back to a remote past."[82]

Although the Mycenaeans may once have sung about the exploits of chariot archers, no written account of chariot warfare has been found at Ugarit, Hattusas, or the Mycenaean palaces. It is something of a paradox

[80] Adele Franceschetti, "Àrmi e guerra in testi micenei," 81; for a perceptive argument that the bow was of much greater military importance in LH III Greece than Homer imagined, and than has generally been assumed, see Renate Tölle-Kastenbein, Pfeil und Bogen im alten Griechenland (Bochum, 1980), 24–26 and 41–42.

[81] Snodgrass, Arms and Armour, 40. For a catalog and typology of the Late Helladic arrowheads see Avila, Lanzen- und Pfeilspitzen.

[82] Page, History and the Homeric Iliad (Berkeley and Los Angeles: 1959), 278–79.

that from the thousands of Late Bronze Age tablets from the Aegean and the Near East, so many of which refer to chariots, one learns so little about how these vehicles were used in battle. Much more can be learned from India. The hymns of the Rig Veda originated in the late centuries of the second millennium, when in India too chariots dominated the battlefield; and here, unlike in Greece, oral tradition kept the world of the chariot warrior alive far into the first millennium, when finally the hymns were written down. One hymn, recited over the chariot crew just before they went into battle, begins by invoking divine blessing upon the warrior's armor:[83] "His face is like a thundercloud, when the armoured warrior goes into the lap of battles. Conquer with an unwounded body; let the power of armour keep you safe." The invocation focuses in turn upon the horses, the chariot, the reins, and the whip but dwells especially upon the bow:

> With the bow let us win cows, with the bow let us win the contest and violent battles with the bow. The bow ruins the enemy's pleasure; with the bow let us conquer all the corners of the world.

> She comes all the way up to your ear like a woman who wishes to say something, embracing her dear friend; humming like a woman, the bowstring stretched tight on the bow carries you safely across in the battle.

> These two who go forward like a woman going to an encounter hold the arrow in their lap as a mother holds a son. Let the two bow-tips, working together, pierce our enemies and scatter our foes.

In the still later *Mahabharata*, chariot archers are again conspicuous. As the Trigarta chariots rolled against the Matsyas, "the sun disappeared behind arrows shot back and forth, but the compact sky was lit up as though by fireflies. The gold-backed bows of the archers, world famous heroes who shot right-handed and left, got tangled when they fell."[84] Virata, hero of the fourth book of the epic, wrought havoc with the Trigartas:

> Virata, having felled five-hundred warriors in the fight, hundreds of horses and five great champions, made his way variously among the chariots, till he encountered Susarman of Trigarta on his golden chariot on the battlefield. The two great-spirited and powerful kings struck out at each other, roaring like two bulls in a cowpen. The chariot fighters circled each other on their chariots, loosing arrows as nimbly as clouds let go their water streams.[85]

[83] Rig Veda 6.75 (*jimutasyeva bhavati pratikam*), translated into English as "To Arms," by Wendy Doniger O'Flaherty, *The Rig Veda: An Anthology* (Harmondsworth, 1981), 236–39.

[84] *Mahabharata* 4 (47) 31.6–7 (trans. J.A.B. van Buitenen).

[85] Ibid., 18–20.

From Hittite, Aegean, and even Egyptian sources there is nothing remotely resembling these vivid pictures of chariot battles in Indian literature.

In summary, whatever evidence we have for chariots in battle indicates that they were used as mobile platforms for archers. This seems to have been true from the beginning of chariot warfare in the seventeenth century until the Catastrophe. Homer did not know how war chariots were used in the LH IIIB period, but that is not surprising since neither did he know anything of the palace regimes that served and were served by the chariotries. In the Near East chariots continued to carry archers, armed with composite bows, down to the eighth century, although by that time chariots played only an ancillary role in battle.

We have only a little information about the organization of chariotries. The smallest tactical unit seems to have been a group of ten chariots (whenever chariots are requested, they are requested in multiples of ten). Schulman assembled evidence that in Egypt, at least, five of these units—or fifty vehicles—normally made up a squadron. The autobiography of Meryptah describes that worthy's service in squadrons named "the Phoenix" and "Manifest in Justice" (among Meryptah's positions were "standard-bearer of the chariot warriors" and "first stablemaster").[86] Each squadron had its own commander, as shown by the Nuzi tablets, and several squadrons together made up a "host of chariots." It may be that the color of the chariot boxes varied from squadron to squadron. Lejeune pointed out that the Linear B scribes consistently (except on one tablet) noted the color of the chariot box—vermillion, purple, red—and suggested that the color was an "élément de signalement."[87] It may also be worthy of note that the Nuzi tablets (as well as occasional tablets from elsewhere) designate vehicles as being either of "the right" or of "the left."[88] The designation is possibly related to the fact that on Egyptian and Assyrian reliefs we see both right-handed and left-handed chariot archers, with the quiver correspondingly mounted on the right or the left side of the chariot box. Although we have no evidence on the matter, we must suppose that all the archers of a given squadron shot their arrows from the same side of the box and that a squadron itself could therefore be described as belonging "to the right" or "to the left." In the *Mahabharata* one of the deadliest heroes is "the valiant Partha, the enemy-killing left-handed archer," who would not turn away even if faced by all the bands of the Maruts.[89]

Finally, we must try to visualize the chariots in battle. Those scholars who have—correctly—imagined chariots as mobile firing platforms (rather than as battle taxis or propellants of thrusting spears) have gener-

[86] On all this see Schulman, "Egyptian Chariotry," 75–84.
[87] Lejeune, "Chars et roues," 29.
[88] Kendall, *Warfare*, 130–31.
[89] *Mahabharata* 4 (47) 37, 10 (trans. J.A.B. van Buitenen).

ally pictured them as participating in the preliminaries and the conclusion to what was essentially an infantry encounter. In T.G.E. Powell's reconstruction, at the outset of a battle chariots provide a thin screen for an infantry formation, the chariots moving *laterally* across the front of their own infantry and the chariot archers shooting—at a right angle—their arrows against the enemy's infantrymen. The chariots then remove themselves while the infantries engage, and after the battle is won the chariots return to pursue the enemy fugitives.[90] Trevor Watkins, on the other hand, suggested that chariots were held in reserve until the infantry battle had reached a decisive stage. At that point the chariots would be committed, in order to tip the scales of the battle.[91] These reconstructions, I am convinced, are quite far from the mark: as will be argued in the next chapter, the assumption that Late Bronze Age battles were essentially infantry contests is without foundation.

Leaving the infantries out of the picture, at least temporarily, we must apparently imagine that opposing chariot forces would hurtle toward each other (chariot warriors are regularly shown shooting over the heads of their horses), the squadrons maintaining an assigned order and the archers

[90] Powell, "Some Implications of Chariotry," in I. Foster and L. Adcock, eds., *Culture and Environment. Essays in Honour of Sir Cyril Fox* (London, 1963), 165–66:

> It is clear that in the opening stages of the battle exchanges of arrows were made from chariots moving up and down their own fronts, but probably at a range which did not seriously endanger the horses. This was the phase for display and intimidation, recognizable again in the *Iliad*, and in Irish epic. Later in the battle, if the opposing side was routed, chariots were again employed for pursuit. To conceive of the likelihood of massed chariots charging an enemy formation, whether also in chariots or on foot, is to ignore practical considerations. Wounds easily to be inflicted on horses would ensure chaos, and certainly allow of no recovery. As was said earlier, the chariot in its Egyptian and Asiatic role provided a mobile vantage point for archery. In the Egyptian reliefs of chariots in action there is no head-on clash, the scene is always that of pursuit, and Egyptian arrows pierce the enemy and his horses from behind. . . . Chariots were never so expendable that one violent collision could have been allowed to risk abandonment on the field.

Powell's description assumes that Late Bronze Age battles were essentially infantry encounters (I shall try to show in chapter 11 that they were not) and ignores the fact that in these battles chariots and horses were indeed lost, by the hundreds. What contribution could have been made by chariots that moved "up and down their own fronts, but probably at a range which did not seriously endanger the horses," is difficult to imagine since, in Powell's view, the two infantries were even farther apart than the two promenading chariotries. It is true that in Egyptian art "there is no head-on clash, the scene is always of pursuit," but that is very likely because in Egyptian ideology enemies regularly flee and Egyptians pursue. The *Iliad*, as indicated above, cannot be used as a guide to the chariot tactics used before the Catastrophe.

[91] So Watkins, "Beginnings of Warfare," 31: "Chariotry was a highly prestigious, hugely expensive and very vulnerable part of any army. It would not be used in battle until the critical moment had arrived; then its task was to launch a drive which would induce a breaking of ranks in the opposing infantry lines. Once the tide of a battle had been turned the chariotry might then also harry and hunt down the dispersed enemy."

beginning to discharge their arrows as soon as the enemy came within range (perhaps at a distance of two hundred meters or more). The archers must have shot ever more rapidly and vigorously as the opposing forces closed the distance between them. Of course many horses were killed or wounded: the whole point of the battle (as Egyptian reliefs show clearly enough) was to bring down as many of the opponent's chariots as possible.

The typical chariot force was probably deployed in a formation broader than it was deep. On a flat plain, only the archers in a front rank of chariots could have had an uninterrupted view of their opponents. And a charioteer driving his horses at the gallop could not have followed too closely upon a chariot in front of him, since he would need to be able to maneuver around any sudden casualty, lest his own team should pile onto a comrade's immobilized vehicle. Perhaps a host of chariots was typically deployed in three or four ranks, ranged behind one another at intervals of twenty or thirty meters, but it is not impossible that on occasion all the chariots were deployed in a single rank. Since (as we shall see in the following section) Thutmose himself rode in the center of the frontline at Megiddo, we must infer that front-line chariots were not conspicuously at risk, and that in turn suggests that the chariot formation was wide and shallow. It probably was important to extend one's line far enough that it could not be outflanked by the enemies' vehicles.

What happened when the opposing chariot forces charged against each other will be imagined in various ways. Horses, unlike men, cannot be driven to charge directly into their opponents, and so we must imagine that in a battle between two more or less equal chariotries the two lines slowed as they closed and then somehow slipped around or through each other (when a large chariotry met a small one, on the other hand, the small force would perhaps either have turned tail long before closing or would have been entirely enveloped, brought to a standstill, and thus destroyed). Perhaps a chariot force may have divided as it approached the enemy, the vehicles on the right pulling farther to the right in order to flank their opponents, while the chariots on the left (all carrying, perhaps, left-handed archers) pulled to the left. Contrarily, the objective may have been to drive wedges into the enemy line, a compact squadron splitting apart the enemy's unbroken line, and the successive ranks funneling into and stretching the gap. It is barely conceivable that all along the line the formation was loose enough that the two opposing lines could completely intermesh and thus pass through each other, but in that case the casualties would have been enormous.

After the surviving teams had made their way past each other, the archers may have faced the rear of their vehicles and fired once or twice at their opponents as they receded. Then the two forces, if they were still cohesive, must have wheeled around and begun their second charge, this time from the opposite direction. Finally, when one of the forces had been heavily depleted or thrown into disorder, the survivors would have made no more return charges but would have tried to escape to a citadel or a guarded position.

THE BATTLES AT MEGIDDO AND KADESH

There are two battles in the Late Bronze Age about which at least a little is known. The Battle of Megiddo was commemorated by the victor, Thutmose III, on the walls of the temple of Amon at Karnak.[92] In his twenty-second year (ca. 1460 B.C.) Thutmose led a great army into the Levant in order to establish his supremacy there and was opposed by a coalition of Canaanite kingdoms under the leadership of the king of Kadesh. On the ninth day after passing the Delta frontier fortress at Sile, Thutmose's army was at Gaza, 150 miles distant; by the standards of antiquity and the Middle Ages, he had moved very quickly.[93] Learning that the Levantine forces were massed at Megiddo, Thutmose's officers worried that if the Egyptian forces proceeded northward in a long column along the central road, the vanguard would be attacked and overwhelmed before the rear elements could catch up and be deployed. Thutmose decided, however, to maintain the single column, and to put himself at the head of it: "[Every man] was made aware of his order of march, horse following horse, while [his majesty] was at the head of his army."

Arriving at the Qina valley, Thutmose spread his force in order to span the entire valley and in early afternoon came within sight of Megiddo and the Canaanite forces. He decided to pitch a camp, however, and to delay the battle until the following day: "Prepare ye! Make your weapons ready, since one will engage in combat with that wretched enemy in the morning." After a night's sleep, Thutmose was advised that "the desert is well" and that all was in readiness. At dawn Thutmose rode forth in his gold-covered chariot. His battle line, according to the inscription, extended from the Qina brook to a point northwest of Megiddo, "while his majesty was in the center, Amon being the protection of his person (in) the melee." Since Thutmose's chariotry must have included more than a thousand vehicles (it routed a Levantine chariotry of at least that size), we may suppose that his battle line was indeed a long one. If the chariots were

---

[92] See Wilson's translation of the inscription, *ANET*, 234–8.

[93] William Murnane, *The Road to Kadesh: A Historical Interpretation of the Battle Reliefs of King Sety I at Karnak* (Chicago, 1985), 145–50 (appendix 2, "Movements of Armies and Timings of Travel in Egypt and the Levant"), notes that the armies of Assyrian kings and of Alexander the Great moved at a rate of between thirteen and fifteen miles a day.

deployed in a single rank, the line would have extended for almost two miles.

The battle then commenced. We have no details about the charge and are told only about its outcome:

> Thereupon his majesty prevailed over them at the head of his army. Then they saw his majesty prevailing over them, and they fled headlong [to] Megiddo with faces of fear. They abandoned their horses and their chariots of gold and silver, so that someone might draw them (up) into this town by *hoisting* on their garments. Now the people had shut this town against them, (but) they [let down] garments to *hoist* them up into this town.

Possibly the Canaanite chariotry did not complete even its initial charge against the Egyptians, turning before the two lines neared each other and fleeing to the city. There the crews leaped from their chariots and began climbing the walls, undoubtedly protected by a covering barrage of arrows shot by bowmen stationed on the walls, and assisted in their climb by ropes and garment-lines let down from the top of the walls. The inscription regrets the fact that at this point Thutmose's men began collecting the enemy's horses and chariots ("an easy prey") instead of pressing on with the attack and killing the enemy as they were being hoisted up the walls of the city. Because of this shortsightedness, a siege of Megiddo was necessary. Thutmose ordered the construction of a fortress to the east of the city, to serve as the Egyptians' base during the siege, and divided the perimeter of the city into sectors, assigning a commander to each. The siege was successful, and the enemy princes eventually came out of the city "to kiss the ground to the glory of his majesty and to beg breath for their nostrils." The booty that Thutmose brought away from the campaign included 1,929 cows, 20,500 sheep, and many costly and beautiful things. More pertinent to our interests are the military personnel and material:

> [List of the booty which his majesty's army carried off from the town of] Megiddo: 340 living prisoners and 83 hands; 2041 horses, 191 foals, 6 stallions, and . . . colts; 1 chariot worked with gold, with a *body* of gold, belonging to that enemy. [1] fine chariot worked with gold belonging to the Prince of [*Megiddo*]. . . and 892 chariots of his wretched army—total: 924; 1 fine bronze coat of mail belonging to that enemy; [1] fine bronze coat of mail belonging to the Prince of Meg[iddo, and] 200 [*leather*] coats of mail belonging to his wretched army; 502 bows; and 7 poles of *meru*-wood, worked with silver, of the tent of that enemy.

The second Late Bronze Age battle about which we know at least a little is the battle that Ramesses II fought against Muwatallis II of Hatti in 1275, when the young Ramesses was in the fifth of his sixty-seven years on the throne. The battle was fought within sight of the city of Kadesh, in northern Syria, and we know about it because Ramesses II assiduously advertised his version of it. He ordered it to be portrayed, with reliefs and inscriptions, not only on his mortuary temple at Thebes (the Ramesseum) but also on temples at Luxor, Abydos, and Abu Simbel.[94] More complete texts of the inscription have also been found on two papyri, one of which runs to eleven pages. As Ramesses recounted the battle, it was a victory and was won almost entirely by his own skill and bravery, his army having panicked and fled. In fact, the battle seems to have been at best—for the Egyptians—a draw, and several units in Ramesses' army made their presence felt.[95]

Great battles were uncommon through most of the thirteenth century B.C. The kings of Assur and Hattusas may have fought in the 1230s, but the matter is quite unclear.[96] In the Aegean, there seems to have been very little military activity from ca. 1375 to ca. 1225. For Egypt, the Kadesh campaign was apparently extraordinary, since we know of nothing remotely similar for the rest of Ramesses' long reign. In his twenty-first year (1259) he and the Hittite king arranged a peace treaty, after which the Levant seems to have been mostly quiet until Ramesses' death in 1212. The Battle of Kadesh may therefore have been by far the greatest battle fought anywhere in the eastern Mediterranean during either the fourteenth or the thirteenth century, and we are fortunate to know something about it.

Ramesses' army spent exactly one month in traveling more than five hundred miles from Avaris, in the eastern Delta, to the vicinity of Kadesh, which was one of Muwatallis's most important vassal states in Syria. We do not know how many chariots and how many infantry Ramesses had assembled, since in describing his force Ramesses' scribes say only that "His Majesty had made ready his infantry and his chariotry, and the Sherden of His Majesty's capturing whom he had brought back by the victory of his strong arm; supplied with all their weapons, and the plan of fighting having been given to them."[97] The army moved in four divisions, named after the gods Amon, Ptah, Re, and Seth, with Ramesses himself in the leading division of Amon. Upon reaching the vicinity of Kadesh, and having been given the false information that the Hittite army was far to the north,

[94] For the reliefs see Wreszinski, *Atlas*, vol. 2, plates 63ff. (Luxor), 82ff. (Ramesseum), and 176ff. (Abu Simbel). For translation of the texts see Alan Gardiner, *The Kadesh Inscriptions of Ramesses II* (Oxford, 1960). Gardiner's translations supersede those of Breasted, *AR*, vol. 3, nos. 306–51.

[95] For reconstructions of the battle see Breasted, *The Battle of Kadesh* (Chicago, 1903); Yadin, *Warfare*, vol. 1, 103–10; Kitchen, *Pharaoh Triumphant*, 53–62. These reconstructions seem to me misleading only in the assumptions that the Hittites failed to achieve a clear-cut victory because their chariot warriors were armed with lances instead of composite bows (Yadin, naturally enough, found this to be the major "weakness" of the Hittite chariotry) and because Muwatallis failed, for one reason or another, to commit his immense infantry.

[96] Itamar Singer, "The Battle of Nihriya and the End of the Hittite Empire," *ZA* 75 (1985): 100–123.

[97] Gardiner's translation, *Kadesh*, P25–30.

Amon division crossed the Orontes and proceeded north to a campsite. When the second division, Re, began fording the river, the Hittite king launched his chariots upon it from a concealed position near the city wall: "But the wretched Chief of Khatti stood in the midst of his army which was with him and did not come out to fight through fear of His Majesty. But he had sent men and horses exceeding many and multitudinous like the sand, and they were three men on a chariot and they were equipped with all weapons of warfare."[98]

In what follows we can deduce that the Re division, caught astride the Orontes, consisted of both chariotry and infantry, neither of which withstood the onslaught. The Hittite chariots "came forth from the south side of Kadesh and broke into (?) the army of Pre' in its midst as they were marching and did not know nor were they prepared to fight. Thereupon the infantry and the chariotry of His Majesty were discomfited before them."[99] With the Hittite chariots in hot pursuit, many of the Re chariots fled toward the Amon division, which was setting up camp under the supervision of Ramesses himself. The enemy chariots "hemmed in the followers of His Majesty who were by his side," but Ramesses quickly "assumed the accoutrements of battle and girded himself with his corslet."[100] After ordering couriers to take a message to the third division (Ptah), commanding it to speed to assistance, Ramesses mounted his chariot and entered the fray, perhaps with little more than his own chariot squadron:

> His Majesty went to look about him and he found 2,500 chariots hemming him in on his outer side, consisting of all the champions of the fallen ones of Khatti. . ., they being three men on a chariot acting as a unit, whereas there was no high officer with me, no charioteer, no soldier of the army, no shield-bearer, my infantry and my chariotry scampering away before them, and not one of them stood firm to fight with them.[101]

Ramesses claimed not only to have rushed into the thick of the Hittite squadrons but to have wheeled about and charged no less than six times:

> Then said His Majesty to his shield-bearer: "Stand firm, steady thy heart, my shield-bearer. I will enter in among them like the pounce of a falcon, killing, slaughtering, and casting to the ground. What careth my heart for these effeminate ones at millions of whom I take no pleasure?" Thereupon His Majesty started forth quickly and entered at a gallop into the midst of the battle for the

[98] Ibid., P65–70.

[99] Ibid., P70–75.

[100] Ibid., B80-B90. For reliefs of the camp scenes and the main chariot battle see Wreszinski, *Atlas*, vol. 2, plates 63, 70, 82, 84, 88, 178.

[101] Gardiner, *Kadesh*, P80–90.

sixth time of entering in amongst them. I was after them like Ba'al at the moment of his power.[102]

Whatever the truth may be about Ramesses' personal heroics, he and his fellow charioteers from Amon division and the fugitives from Re evidently held the field long enough to enable the Ptah chariots to arrive. At that point the Hittite chariots too were reinforced, by a thousand chariots of Muwatallis's allies.

While the battle had been raging, certain of the Hittite chariot crews had dismounted to begin plundering the Amon camp, which apparently had been abandoned by its defenders. But as the Hittites were engaged in looting, warriors whom Ramesses called "the ne'arim from Amor" and whom Yadin described as "Canaanite mercenaries serving in the army of Rameses II" came to save what was left of the camp and fell upon the Hittite crews, killing them all.[103]

How many casualties there were on either side, and whether either side was in fact victorious, we do not know. Ramesses claimed victory, but the Egyptians apparently lost little time in moving south, perhaps to avoid another surprise attack.

The size of the Hittite army can be pieced together from several statements in the inscriptions. Ramesses reports that the chariotry that Muwatallis initially launched against the Re division and that followed up with an attack upon the Amon camp, consisted of twenty-five hundred vehicles, each carrying three men. Late in the battle, perhaps after the Ptah division had arrived on the scene, Muwatallis launched another thousand chariots, these apparently being allied squadrons.[104]

We also have precise figures for the Hittite infantry. Ramesses' reliefs, and the accompanying legends, indicate that Muwatallis had one large body of warriors before him and another behind him. Breasted read the two figures as eight thousand and nine thousand respectively, but Alan Gardiner corrected the reading to eighteen thousand and nineteen thousand.[105] Gardiner's readings are probably to be preferred, although there is not yet a clear consensus among Egyptologists.[106]

Whether numbering seventeen thousand or thirty-seven thousand, the

---

[102] Ibid., P215–225.

[103] Ibid., R11; cf. Yadin, *Art of Warfare*, vol. 2, 267.

[104] Ibid., P150–155.

[105] Ibid., R43 and R44.

[106] For discussion see Beal, *Organization*, 356–57. Beal consulted Murnane on the reading and at n. 1116 quotes from Murnane's response: "I don't think Gardiner is necessarily wrong (and he seems to have been accepted in this by more recent scholars) but I would still say that there is some uncertainty." Murnane's own *The Road to Kadesh* deals with events leading up to Ramesses' campaign, but not with the campaign itself. Kitchen, *Pharaoh Triumphant*, 53, accepts Gardiner's readings.

Hittite infantry at Kadesh was substantial, and it is therefore all the more noteworthy that it took no part in the battle itself, the Hittite king sending only his chariotry (approximately ten thousand, five hundred men) to the attack. Not only do the inscriptions say that Muwatallis sent his chariots into battle, while he stayed at Kadesh with the infantry, but the reliefs tell the same story. The reliefs of the battle on the Ramesseum and the Luxor and Abu Simbel temples portray a massed infantry standing guard near the city of Kadesh, toward which the routed Hittite chariots flee.[107] It would therefore appear that Muwatallis used his massed infantry as a defensive force, forming a cordon around the city gates and the approaches to Kadesh.

The size of Ramesses' army is nowhere stated, but chariotry appears to have been its offensive element. Except for the Amorite *ne'arim*, who probably (as we shall see in chapter 11) were "runners" attached to the Amon division, no footsoldiers under Ramesses' command are known to have engaged the enemy. When the king, with the Amon division, was informed that the Re division had been routed, he seems to have counterattacked with as many of the Amon chariots as could be got ready, charging and turning about to repeat the charge six times. Whatever infantry formation was included in the Amon division was evidently not part of its offensive force and in fact was not even sufficient to defend the camp. One may suppose that in Ramesses' army, as in Muwatallis's army, the chariotry's charge was not coordinated with the charge of an infantry formation.

[107] For the three reliefs see Yadin, *Art of Warfare*, vol. 1, 238.

Chapter Eleven

FOOTSOLDIERS IN THE LATE BRONZE AGE

IT IS SURPRISING to discover how little information survives about Late Bronze Age infantries. No infantryman's archive has been found to compare with the "chariot tablets" from Knossos, the "horse texts" from Ugarit and Hattusas, and the many Nuzi tablets dealing with the chariot corps. As a result, in each of the text-based studies that have been done on things military at Nuzi, Hattusas, Ugarit and Mycenaean Greece, the space devoted to infantry is only a small fraction of that devoted to chariotry.[1] A general study of Late Bronze Age infantry has yet to be made.

In lieu of information, it has been widely assumed that Late Bronze Age infantries were much the same as infantries in other periods of antiquity. More particularly, it has been supposed that in battles all through the Late Bronze Age infantries played the primary role, with the chariotries in support. These assumptions do not seem to be borne out by the meager evidence that we have.

In better-documented periods of antiquity, the infantry was central to an army's attack, and horse troops were peripheral. Horse troops operating independently were useful for reconnaissance, for harassing an enemy line of march (as the Syracusan cavalry harassed the Athenian hoplites on their retreat in 413 B.C.), or for small-scale action, but in a pitched battle horse troops regularly served to support the infantry's attack. Persian, Greek, and Roman battle tactics required that the movement of infantry and horse troops be coordinated, the infantry normally forming the center of a battle formation and the horse troops being posted at the infantry's right and left flanks or being held in reserve for commitment after the infantry battle had begun. Occasionally, as Hannibal did at the Trebia River, a commander might order his cavalry to initiate the battle, in order to draw the enemy infantry into a position of his choosing. But whatever role was assigned to the horse troops was chosen with the infantry battle in mind, since in classical antiquity an army's center of gravity was invariably its infantry.

This "normal" balance has also been assumed for the Late Bronze Age. The thesis that Mycenaean chariots hauled infantrymen to and from a battlefield is based on the assumption (common in archaeological circles)

---

[1] Chapter III of Kendall's *Warfare* is a lexicon of military terms from Nuzi; approximately 80 percent of the terms refer to horses, chariots, and the chariot corps. In Beal's *Organization* there are 36 pages (58–93) on the chariotry and only two (103–4) on the infantry. Lejeune's and Franceschetti's text-based studies of Mycenaean warfare deal primarily with two topics: chariots and the *o-ka* tablets.

that the Mycenaeans fought on foot. Some scholars have in fact supposed that in the Near East as well chariots were militarily useful only as infantry transports. Thus Jacques Gernet, comparing the military chariots of China with those of "les civilisations occidentales," found it noteworthy that in China the chariot was actually used *in battle*: he assumed that in the West it served only as a taxi for footsoldiers, especially those needing a fast getaway from the battlefield.[2] Even Egyptologists have been inclined to see the infantry as basic to New Kingdom warfare. As noted in chapter 10, Schulman recently proposed that in New Kingdom Egypt the chariotry played a marginal role while the infantry bore the brunt of the fighting (he assumed that there were fifty infantrymen for each chariot). In R. O. Faulkner's reconstruction of New Kingdom warfare, chariots are more important but nevertheless function primarily as a screen for a massed infantry: "In a field action it seems to have been the chariotry who took the first shock of battle, the infantry advancing behind them to exploit a tactical success or to stem the enemy's advance if matters went awry, somewhat as in modern warfare the infantry operate behind a screen of armoured vehicles."[3] Similarly, the thesis that Hittite chariot warriors fought with the thrusting spear generally presupposes that the primary objective against which the Hittite chariots delivered their frontal charge was an enemy infantry formation.

The conclusions reached in chapter 10 about the nature of chariot warfare leave little room for the clash of close-order infantry formations. Battles between eastern Mediterranean kingdoms of the Late Bronze Age, like those described in the *Mahabharata*, must have consisted primarily of two chariot forces charging against and past each other and then circling back to charge each other again, the archers all the while shooting against the opposing squadrons. How a mass formation of offensive infantry could have contributed something to such a battle (or even have kept abreast of it) is not self-evident, and that it did cannot be taken for granted.

We have seen that at Kadesh there was no encounter between opposing infantries, nor does there seem to have been one at Megiddo, the only other Late Bronze Age battle about which some details are known. In describing his army's march to Megiddo, Thutmose III noted the presence of an infantry,[4] but he does not mention it in connection with the battle itself, and his booty list implies that there was no infantry engagement (the Egyptians, it will be recalled, slew fewer than a hundred men and captured

<hr />

[2] Gernet, "Note sur le char en Chine," 310: "Les indications qu'on possède pour les civilisations occidentales laissent penser que le char sert normalement au transport des combattants à pied d'oeuvre et leur permet si besoin est de prendre la fuite. Ce n'est pas en char que se déroulent ordinairement les combats. Le combat en char est au contraire de règle en Chine."

[3] Faulkner, "Egyptian Military Organization," *JEA* 39 (1953): 43.

[4] *ANET*, 235 (trans. John Wilson).

only 340, while seizing 924 chariots and 2041 horses). Apparently Thutmose's infantry was not put to work until the seven-month siege of Megiddo began. On the Canaanite side there surely also were infantrymen, but during the battle they may have been stationed at Megiddo itself, serving as defensive bowmen atop the walls and—until they panicked and closed them—before the gates of the city.

References to less famous battles also conspicuously ignore infantry encounters. In the Nuzi texts are such reminiscences as "when the chariots of Hanigalbat gave battle at the town of Lubti" or "when the chariots gave battle in Silliawa."[5] Possibly infantrymen also gave battle at these times and places; but if they did, their contribution was apparently too small to have been appreciated or mentioned. If one is looking for the kind of battle familiar from classical antiquity—heavy infantries fighting hand-to-hand in the center, with horse troops engaged on the wings—one will search in vain the documents and pictorial representations that have come down to us from the Late Bronze Age kingdoms prior to the Catastrophe. The notion that Late Bronze Age chariotries fought in support of massed infantry formations is a misapprehension and an anachronism.

There is no doubt that some Near Eastern kings raised substantial infantries when they went to war. Although we have no figures for New Kingdom Egypt, it is probably safe to assume that on a major campaign the pharaoh took along several thousand infantrymen. Egyptian footsoldiers were either "shooters" (bowmen) or *nakhtu-aa*, a term that literally means "strong-arm boys" and denotes hand-to-hand fighters.[6] The "shooters," perhaps all native Egyptians, were grouped in companies of 200 or 250 men, the companies bearing names such as "Aten Appears for Him" or "Pacifier of Gods."[7]

The Great King of Hatti was often accompanied on campaign by many more men on foot than in chariots. His vassal, the king of Kizzuwatna, brought to his lord a force of one thousand infantrymen and one hundred chariots; even if each of the chariots had a three-man crew, the infantry would have outnumbered the men of the chariotry by more than three to one. A similar ratio is attested in the forces of two kingdoms that fought against the Hittites.[8] And at Kadesh, as we have seen, Muwatallis was accompanied by an infantry formation of at least seventeen thousand and probably thirty-seven thousand men. The Hittite vassals of eastern Syria must have brought thousands of troops to their confrontation with Tukulti-Ninurta I of Assur, since he claims to have captured twenty-eight thousand of them.[9]

[5] Kendall, *Warfare*, 114 and 132.

[6] Stillman and Tallis, *Armies*, 8.

[7] Ibid. See also Faulkner, "Egyptian Military Organization," 45.

[8] Beal, *Organization*, 702.

[9] D. D. Luckenbill, *Ancient Records of Assyria and Babylonia*, vol. 1, nos. 164 and 171.

The crucial question is not how many footsoldiers there were in Egypt or in Hatti but what they did. Hittitologists have recognized that despite its size the infantry seems not to have counted for much in the typical Hittite battle. Oliver Gurney concluded that in most battles the Hittite infantry played only "a subordinate part," and Beal found that "the key part of the Hittite armed forces was the chariotry."[10] The reason why the tablets say so little about the infantry, I believe, is that in the typical battle there was no engagement of massed infantries.

We have evidence for infantries going on the attack in the Late Bronze Age prior to the Catastrophe but not in conjunction with a chariotry. A contrast emerges, it seems, between warfare against civilized enemies and warfare against men from the hinterland, whom I shall call barbarians. The kingdoms, and cities generally, were sited in fertile plains, which could be dominated and defended by chariots. When one king attacked another the confrontation was therefore a chariot battle. Similarly, a kingdom could depend on its chariots against barbarians who raided its perimeter. Thus Egyptian reliefs illustrate battles in which Ramesses the Great led his chariotry against various tribesmen who invaded the kingdom or its dependencies. Reliefs on a temple at Beit-el-Weli show Ramesses in his chariot, shooting his arrows at a crowd of Nubian infantry bowmen.[11] No Egyptian infantrymen are shown in the reliefs or mentioned in the inscriptions, and the relief depicts only Ramesses and two other Egyptian chariot archers, shooting into the crowd of retreating Nubians. A second relief at Beit-el-Weli portrays Ramesses' victory over Shoshu, or Bedouin, tribesmen. The Shoshu warrior typically carries a single spear (evidently a thrusting spear) and a short weapon whose function has not been identified.[12] Like the Nubians, the Shoshu warriors carry no shield and wear no metal armor. Here too, it may be that Ramesses depended in part on offensive infantrymen, but they are not shown or mentioned.

On the other hand, in order to carry the battle to mountainous or rough terrain, where chariots could not go, a king necessarily depended on an infantry. There is one clear case of an Egyptian infantry force confronting a barbarian infantry prior to the Catastrophe, although it is hypothetical rather than real. Our source here is the Papyrus Anastasi, one of the most illuminating pieces of evidence we have for the military situation on the eve of the Catastrophe.[13] This papyrus, dated to the end of the Nineteenth Dynasty, is a letter written by a royal official named Hori to an ambitious

---

[10] Gurney, *The Hittites* (Harmondsworth: 1961), 106; Beal, *Organization*, 698.

[11] Yadin, *Art of Warfare*, vol. 1, 234–35.

[12] For the relief see ibid., 232–33; Yadin suggests that the second weapon of the Shoshu tribesmen may be a sickle sword. One Shosu warrior carries two short spears, presumably javelins.

[13] See Wilson's translation of the papyrus in *ANET*, 475–79.

but inexperienced and untutored young man. In the course of ridiculing his correspondent's ignorance of practical affairs, Hori puts before him a hypothetical military situation, asking him what sort of food supplies he would need were he quartermaster for an army of five thousand men sent to crush a rising of the *ne'arim* in *Djahan* (the significance of this *casus belli* we shall examine in chapter 14). Hori details what this hypothetical expeditionary force would consist of: "The bowmen of the army which is before thee amount to 1900, the Sherden 520, the Qeheq 1600, the Meshwesh (100), and the Nubians 880—TOTAL 5000 in all, not counting their officers." Since food for the horses is not part of the problem, we may assume that the nineteen hundred bowmen are on foot rather than in chariots. And since the other thirty-one hundred troops—all barbarian— are differentiated from the bowmen, they are presumably hand-to-hand warriors.

The Papyrus Anastasi does suggest that at the end of the thirteenth century B.C. the Egyptians could field an infantry force of five thousand men, most of these being professional skirmishers. The papyrus does not, however, suggest a close-order formation (each of the national contingents apparently has its own officers, and the type of battle envisaged must be a *guerrilla* since it will be fought against disorganized tribesmen). And since no chariots accompany the five thousand infantrymen the papyrus certainly does not contradict our thesis that prior to the Catastrophe chariots were not used to support mass formations of offensive infantry. In battles fought close to home, or against another kingdom, a palace could rely entirely upon its chariot force. Only on those occasions when a kingdom fought against barbarian tribesmen in the tribesmen's own habitat would footsoldiers bear most or all of the burden.

Although we may generalize that in the Late Bronze Age men of the cities and kingdoms normally relied on chariotry, an exception may be inferred for the kingdom of Assur, on the northeastern frontier of the civilized world. In the thirteenth century, as was noted in chapter 2, the kings of Assur frequently fought against barbarous enemies on their northern and eastern borders, and here the mountainous terrain must have required the employment of a sizeable Assyrian infantry. When Gutians, from Guti in the Zagros Mountains, came down into the plain to raid Assyrian dependencies, Shalmaneser I (1274–1245) left his infantry behind and swiftly rode out—with only a third of his chariots—to rout the Gutians, "whose numbers are countless as the stars of heaven, and who know how to plunder."[14] But when Tukulti-Ninurta I (1244–1208) boasts of invading Guti itself and of slaughtering "the armies of the Kuti (in their) mountain

[14] Luckenbill, *Ancient Records of Assyria and Babylonia*, vol. 1, no. 117.

fastnesses,"[15] we must assume that this was done by an infantry capable of hand-to-hand fighting. Perhaps the Assyrians' long experience in infantry warfare was not unrelated to the fact that the kingdom of Assur was one of the few to survive the Catastrophe.

In kingdoms other than Assur dependence on an offensive infantry must have been unusual. In the Aegean, the palaces in the plains may have been occasionally raided by mountaineers early in the Late Helladic period; although the plains could be defended by chariots, retaliation would have been undertaken by infantries. The famous "Captain of the Blacks" fresco from Knossos seems to have shown a troop of black spearmen, led by a "Minoan" captain.[16] What remains of the Pylos "Battle Scene" (see plate 2) shows the palace's warriors overcoming a group of savages clad in animal skins.[17] This is not a battle between infantry formations but a *guerrilla* in which each of the palace's men duels with an opponent. Since the Pylians wear boar's-tusk helmets, they are obviously warriors of high status (the tusks of more than seventy boars were required to make a single helmet). But whether the Pylos fresco reflects contemporary life or recalls a legendary event, we do not know—and at any rate it is doubtful that in the *pax Mycenaica* the palaces were often threatened by barbarous opponents. The Hittite kings had more opportunities to use an infantry. From time to time they campaigned against barbarians who fled into hilly or mountainous country, and on such occasions the Hittite king boasts of having pursued the fugitives on foot. It may be that the first phase of such a war featured the Hittite chariotry, and the second phase—in rough terrain— the infantry. Even for the Hittites, however, infantry fighting was unusual. In his study Richard Beal identified the Sumerogram ERÍN.MEŠ GÌR.ḪI.A as the strict equivalent of our word "infantry" (as in the expression "the chariotry and the infantry") but found only seven instances of the term in the Hittite texts.[18] References to infantry in documents from other Late Bronze Age kingdoms seem to be equally scarce.

In any case, what evidence we have suggests that prior to the Catastrophe infantry battles occurred only in places that chariots could not go. In the plains and in "normal" terrain, where the chariot forces were at home,

[15] Ibid., no. 152.

[16] On this fresco see Arthur Evans, *The Palace of Minos at Knossos*, vol. 2, part 2 (London, 1928), 755–57 and the accompanying color plate (plate xiii). The black soldier running behind the Aegean "captain" seems to carry a single spear. The date of the fresco cannot be ascertained (it was found near—but not in—the House of the Frescoes). Evans noted that the fragments "differ in character" from those in the fresco stack and "seem to have belonged to a somewhat later date."

[17] For the fragments in their original state and for Piet de Jong's reconstruction see Mabel Lang, *The Palace of Nestor at Pylos in Western Messenia*, vol. 2: *The Frescoes* (Princeton, 1969), plate M (22 H 64); for Lang's comments see pp. 42–47.

[18] Beal, *Organization*, 103–4.

PLATE 2. Reconstructed "Battle Scene" fresco from Pylos

the chariotries themselves did the fighting. In the Late Bronze Age chariots did not serve—whether as a screen in the front or as pincers on the flanks—to support mass infantry formations.

"Runners": The Role of Infantrymen in Chariot Warfare

On the contrary, before the Catastrophe footsoldiers seem to have supported the chariotry. On the march, footsoldiers can be assumed to have served as an escort for the chariots moving in column and as a guard for the nightly encampment (in which a chariot army, its horses all unyoked and tethered, would have been exceptionally vulnerable). In the aftermath of a victory, infantrymen would probably have pursued fugitives who fled to uneven ground, and it was the infantrymen who would have to besiege a city and finally assault it.

In the chariot battle itself infantrymen rendered important services. In 1275 B.C., as we have seen, each of Ramesses' four chariotry divisions must have been accompanied by a troop of footsoldiers, and Muwatallis may have had as many as thirty-seven thousand. The reliefs show that during the Battle of Kadesh the Hittite infantrymen had a stationary and defensive assignment at the gates of Kadesh. They seem to have provided a cordon or a "resort" to which an individual chariot could retire if one of the crewmen were killed or wounded, or to which the entire chariot host could flee in the event of a rout. Many Egyptian infantrymen in the same battle also had a defensive role: the Ramesseum relief depicting the camp of the Amon division shows the entire camp encircled by Egyptian infantrymen, their oblong shields forming a solid front. With the shields the cordon protected itself against enemy arrows and, with self bows, javelins, or short spears, would have been able to ward off oncoming chariots.

There was, however, an even more crucial service that infantrymen performed for charioteers: the hand-to-hand combat that accompanied a chariot encounter. In describing the forces that he led against the Libyans in 1208, Merneptah makes a distinction between his *mnfyt*, a term that seems to denote infantry conscripts with little training, and "those who bear the hand-to-hand fighting, beautiful in appearance."[19] The role played in chariot battles by the hand-to-hand fighter, whom we may also call a skirmisher, has generally gone unnoticed. Yadin's *Art of Warfare* observed that "chariot runners" accompanied the king's chariot in Iron Age Israel but assumed that these were royal bodyguards, part of the king's entourage but not regular members of a chariot corps.[20] The recent books on chariotry focus, of course, on the vehicle itself, saying little about chariot warfare and nothing about the presence of infantry skirmishers in a chariot battle. Nor has the role of the skirmisher or runner been discussed in the detailed studies of the military forces of Nuzi, Ugarit, Hattusas, and the Mycenaean palaces.

It is in the Egyptian texts and pictorial evidence that the "runner" (*phrr*) appears,[21] and it was Alan Schulman's contribution to have defined the

[19] Breasted, *AR*, vol. 3, no. 578, with footnote; although the literal meaning of the Egyptian term, according to Breasted, is "those who bear the hand-to-hand fighting," in his text he translates it as "the heavy armed troops." In light of what we know about the arms and armor of these skirmishers, "heavy armed troops" is misleading. As for the *mnfyt*, they may have been bowmen, or non-professional infantrymen; see Edgerton and Wilson, *Historical Records of Ramses III*, p. 54, note on 20d.

[20] Yadin, *Art of Warfare*, vol. 2, 284–85.

[21] Cf. a sentence from Ramesses III's inscriptions at Medinet Habu (Edgerton and Wilson, ibid., plate 46 [p. 55]): "The chariotry consisted of runners, of picked men, of every good and capable chariot warrior." In a note on the line, Edgerton and Wilson observe that "the reliefs

runner as a footsoldier who fought in support of an Egyptian chariot crew. Although Schulman did not say much about these runners, he did point out the bits of evidence for them in Egyptian reliefs as well as inscriptions.[22] To Schulman's evidence can be added several references, noted by Richard Beal, to warriors who "ran before" the chariots of the king of Hatti. Perhaps the most helpful exploration to date of the role of chariot runners in Late Bronze Age warfare is to be found in Stillman's and Tallis's *Armies*, a book that unfortunately has received little scholarly attention. Following Schulman's lead, Stillman and Tallis recognized the existence of runners in the chariot armies of New Kingdom Egypt[23] and went on to sketch—more boldly, it must be said, than the evidence warrants—what these runners did:

> As the name suggests, runners were expected to try and keep pace with the chariotry. They could perform several tactical functions such as screening the chariotry, following up a charge to despatch or capture fallen enemy crewmen, clearing and holding any terrain impassable to chariots and rescuing wounded friendly crewmen. A body of runners following some distance behind their chariotry, could also engage enemy chariots who had passed through them and were attempting to rally for a second charge. Enemy chariotry would then be caught between the runners and returning friendly chariotry. Clashes between opposing bodies of runners could also be expected in the vicinity of chariotry engagements.[24]

A runner the *phrr* would certainly have been,[25] simply to keep up with the action in a chariot melee (much of the infantry, as we have seen, was essentially stationary during the battle, serving to cordon off a camp or

---

often show a man running beside the horses. Is this a function of the 'runner'? But the latter is probably a more general term."

[22] Schulman, *Military Rank*, 38–39. See also his remarks in "Egyptian Chariotry," 89–90: "It is generally accepted that *phrr* means 'the runner'; the word, clearly written with the ideogram of the running man, who is sometimes even shown armed with a shield and a javelin, compels us to understand him, in the chariotry, as a soldier who fought on foot. Egyptian footsoldiers are frequently illustrated marching, as individuals, alongside the chariot-horses, and once, in a Sakkara tomb-relief, a squad of four of them are pictured running there. These could have been Egyptian chariotry runners. Their function in battle was probably to protect the horses from the enemy foot and runners." In this very helpful paragraph the only misleading item is the "javelin" that a runner is sometimes shown carrying: if the runner carries only one weapon, it is far more likely to be a thrusting spear than a javelin, since once you have thrown your javelin you have no weapon at all.

[23] *Armies*, 8: "Attached to each chariot was a *peherer*, 'runner,' who fought on foot in support of the chariot."

[24] Ibid., 56.

[25] Corresponding to the noun *phrr* is a verb, identically transliterated, meaning "to run." I thank John Darnell, at the Oriental Institute, for this information.

PLATE 3. A *shardana* skirmisher slaying a Hittite charioteer at Kadesh. Abydos relief

fortification). Possibly on some occasions skirmishers rode into battle on their comrades' chariots (the Greek *apobates* comes to mind here) and dismounted when their vehicles began to close with the enemy. Alternatively, skirmishers may have moved as a troop. In reliefs, squads of four Egyptian infantrymen are sometimes shown marching alongside a chariot as it proceeds toward battle, the four carrying shields and either spears or sickle swords. The Amorite *ne'arim* who saved the Amon camp in 1275 B.C. seem to have reached the camp as a company.

The unusually realistic Abydos reliefs of the Kadesh battle show that Egyptian runners must have worked closely with their chariot squadron, their function being to deal with those of the enemy who were on foot. In a chariot battle, the enemy on foot would have included not only the opposing runners but also casualties from the chariots themselves: skirmishers must thus have been responsible for "finishing off" an enemy chariot crew whose vehicle had been immobilized. We can assume that in any chariot battle a rapidly moving chariot host would leave its casualties in its wake. These might be individual men, wounded or simply fallen from their chariots; or the casualty might be an entire chariot and its crew, one of the horses having been killed or wounded, or perhaps the vehicle itself having been immobilized by a broken wheel or axle. The dispatching of these stranded casualties, it is clear from Egyptian pictorial evidence (see plates 3 and 4), was left to footsoldiers. Armed with a short spear and dirk, the skirmisher was indeed indispensable for all phases of a chariot battle. We might say that whereas in Greek and Roman times horse troops supported the infantry formation, in chariot warfare infantrymen as individuals or in small squads supported the horse troop to which they were attached.

Although very little can be learned about these runners, we can hardly avoid supposing that every chariot corps had them. Although detected in Egypt by Schulman, they have not yet been spotted in the lexicographical fog that envelops military matters at Knossos, Pylos, and other sites with limited pictorial evidence on warfare. It is nevertheless possible that the *aḫu* in fourteenth-century Nuzi was a chariot runner. Literally, the *aḫu* was a "brother," but the designation was in fact used for a certain kind of warrior and most likely for a certain kind of footsoldier attached to the

PLATE 4. A *shardana* skirmisher cutting off the hand of a slain Hittite charioteer at Kadesh. Abydos relief

chariotry. Kendall's analysis shows that these warriors were neither charioteers nor chariot warriors but were attached to chariot units, and that
there were two such brothers for every charioteer.[26]

It is certain that the Hittite kings used chariot runners, but little can be
said about them. Beal's survey turned up several references to troops who
were to "run before" the Hittite king.[27] No Hittite term for "chariot
runner" emerged from the texts, although the *piran huyatalla* ("forerun-
ner") may in several passages have some such meaning.[28] It is also possible
that the *sharikuwa* troops, who seem to have been a *tertium quid* alongside
"infantry" and chariotry, were skirmishers.[29] The importance of runners
in Hittite chariot warfare was after all great enough that Ramesses II
mentioned them immediately after the chariots themselves. The "poetic"
account of the Battle of Kadesh declares that Ramesses "found twenty-five
hundred chariot-teams surrounding him in his road, together with all the
runners belonging to the foes of Hatti and the numerous countries which
were with him."[30] These Hittite runners must be contrasted with the stolid
ranks of infantry that stand motionless, in the reliefs, around the fortress of
Kadesh.

In Linear B tablets no term has yet been interpreted as the equivalent of
skirmisher or *runner*. The professional warriors employed by the Pylos and
Knossos palaces, however, may very well have been intended to serve in
that capacity. There may be a bit of pictorial evidence for Mycenaean
runners (or, more accurately, walkers). On a late thirteenth- or early
twelfth-century krater from Tiryns two warriors, each armed with a short
spear and a small, round shield, proceed on foot in front of a chariot.[31] It is

[26] Kendall, *Warfare*, 78, finds that "the 'brothers' and the charioteers have the same
commanding officers, and that the former are generally twice as numerous as the latter."

[27] Beal, *Organization*, 234–35, 237, 238n.723, and 555.

[28] For references see ibid., 554–59; Beal's own preference is to translate the term as
"leader" or "vanguardsman."

[29] Beal, ibid., 125–27, cites a number of texts that refer to "the infantry, the horse troops,
and the *sharikuwa*," but no text suggests the basis for the differentiation. Cf. Beal's summary: "If the *šarikuwa*- were neither infantry nor horse troops, what were they? . . . On the
basis of present evidence it is impossible to say what sort of troops they were." In private
correspondence Beal welcomes the identification of the *sharikuwa* troops as chariot runners
but regrets that "it cannot be proven one way or another."

[30] Kadesh poem, lines 84–85, as translated by Schulman, "Egyptian Chariotry," 90n.111
(cf. p. 89n.106); the Egyptian term used here is *pḥrr*, accompanied by an ideogram of a
running man armed with shield and spear. In Gardiner's translation (*Kadesh*, P85) the word is
translated not as "runners" but as "champions." In his note on the line Gardiner explains:
"*Pḥrr* means literally 'runner,' but *Wb*. i 541. 14–18 shows that it was a general term for
doughty warriors." On the Hittite runners see also Stillman and Tallis, *Armies*, 41.

[31] Vermeule and Karageorghis, *Mycenaean Pictorial Vase Painting*, 108–9, with plate X.1.
Although the artist did not show the warriors with any other weapons, he may have intended
the spears as throwing-spears or javelins: the shaft is gripped with the fingertips of a cocked
hand. The authors date the vase to the transition between LH IIIB and IIIC.

also possible that the *apobates* known from first-millennium athletic contests was the distant descendant of a second-millennium chariot runner.[32]

Let us summarize what can be deduced about the role of infantrymen in the Late Bronze Age kingdoms of the eastern Mediterranean. Infantry battles of a guerrilla type were evidently fought in barbaria, or in locales impassable for chariots. Kings also required an infantry for such stationary assignments as the siege or defense of a city. When the chariotry was on the march, footsoldiers would have provided an escort and guarded the encampment. During the battle itself footsoldiers were apparently employed in one of two ways. Many of them seem to have served as a cordon, a haven to which worsted chariots could flee. Others served as hand-to-hand skirmishers—or runners—who fought in immediate support of the chariot squadron to which they were attached. These various responsibilities were all important, but they were nevertheless ancillary: infantrymen supplemented the chariotry, rather than the other way around. Prior to the Catastrophe there is no evidence for a clash of close-order infantry formations or for chariot warriors supporting their comrades on foot.

THE RECRUITMENT OF INFANTRYMEN IN THE LATE BRONZE AGE

The recruitment of footsoldiers by the eastern Mediterranean kingdoms is consistent with the secondary role that infantry played in the Late Bronze Age. There is, first of all, no evidence for a general call-up of adult males in these kingdoms: nothing, that is, to parallel the citizen militias of Archaic Greece and Italy or the tribal militias of Israel and Judah in the early Iron Age. Before the Catastrophe, kings depended upon professionals rather than upon mobilized civilians, and many infantrymen were apparently just as professional (even though of relatively low status) as were the chariot crews. Assyria, again, may have been exceptional. Since Assyria was a frontier kingdom, the tradition of a tribal militia may have prevailed there in the second millennium, as it apparently did in the first (although the practice cannot be demonstrated from the few Middle Assyrian documents that survive). At any rate, in those kingdoms for which there is substantial evidence the general population was never mobilized.

Some kings ordered a conscription on occasion, but the number of men called up was small. Levies in Egypt traditionally took one of every ten temple servitors for military service, but Ramesses III prided himself on

---

[32] N. B. Crowther, "The Apobates Reconsidered (Demosthenes lxi 23–9)," *JHS* 111 (1991): 174–76, brings together all the Greek texts referring to this obscure athlete, who leapt from a chariot to accomplish several feats of running and warfare. Crowther (p. 174) notes that fourth-century Athenians imagined that the *apobatai* whom they were watching were replicating the way that "Greeks and barbarians in Homer made war against each other."

having forgone even this modest exaction.[33] For his footsoldiers he will have relied upon the professionals whom he hired. These included both "picked men" of Egypt and barbarians. The Egyptians were apparently not employed as runners, since a Medinet Habu inscription differentiates the two groups.[34]

The Hittite kings depended primarily upon their regular army, the professional infantrymen known as UKU.UŠ and *sharikuwa*. When a serious campaign was planned, this "standing army" was routinely supplemented by troops sent, under treaty, by pacified districts on the frontier, especially to the north of Hatti (where thousands of Kaskans, renowned for their valor, were to be found).[35] Only in emergencies was it necessary for the Great King to levy troops from the civilian population of Hatti itself; and when such levies were held, the recruits were discharged as soon as possible.[36]

In Ugarit, Heltzer found some evidence for conscription,[37] individuals from various villages being issued bows by the palace or being assigned as rowers on the king's ships. But again, their role was marginal, and for the most part the king of Ugarit relied upon his professionals—the *mdrglm*-guards and the *tnnm* (the latter seems to have meant something like "hand-to-hand warriors").[38] The entire military force at Ugarit, according to Heltzer's calculation, was only 2077 men, with one-twelfth—or about 175 men—serving in any given month. Although this figure may be much too low (Heltzer himself notes that the king of Ugarit may have had a thousand chariots), Heltzer's winnowing of the tablets has at least shown that there is no evidence for any massed infantry in that city. The single largest contingent in his list are the *mdrglm*-guards, who account for over half (1050 men) of his total.[39]

In the Mycenaean kingdoms there may have been no conscription at all. At Pylos, where there were several hundred chariots, the chariot crews must have been almost as numerous as the infantry. As indicated above, the estimates for the population ruled by the Pylos palace range from 50,000 to 120,000 people, but nowhere do we hear of thousands of Messenians

---

[33] Breasted, *AR*, vol. 4, no. 354; cf. Gardiner, *Egypt*, 293.

[34] Edgerton and Wilson, *Historical Records of Ramses III*, plate 29: "The army is assembled, and they are the bulls of the land: every picked man [of] all [Egypt] and the runners."

[35] Beal, *Organization*, 220–40.

[36] On Hittite levies see ibid., 133–46.

[37] Heltzer, *Internal Organization*, 108–11.

[38] M. Dietrich and O. Loretz, "Die Schardana in den Texten von Ugarit," in R. Stiehl and G. A. Lehmann, eds., *Antike und Universalgeschichte: Festschrift Hans Erich Stier* (Münster, 1972), 41, suggest "Nahkämpfer" as a translation of *tnnm*, a term that at Ugarit is almost interchangeable with *shardana*.

[39] Heltzer, *Internal Organization*, 105–8.

being called to the colors. The five *o-ka* tablets enumerate 770 *pedijewe*, a word that is probably to be equated with classical Greek *pedieis* and should therefore mean "footsoldiers" (although it must be said that some Mycenologists have recently denied that the *o-ka* tablets have anything to do with military matters).[40] At any rate, the 770 men listed in these tablets would be by far the largest number of men attested for military purposes at Pylos, and the *ethnica* designating them suggest that they were not Messenian natives.[41] That there were no militias in the palace-states of thirteenth-century Greece may seem a heretical view, since the Mycenaean *lawagetas* is usually thought of as being a Homeric "shepherd of the host" and so as marshal of a vast array of infantry formations. But in all of the tablets the only reference to the *lawagetas* in a context that might conceivably be military is an entry mentioning "the charioteer of the *lawagetas*."[42] At Knossos, center of a kingdom ruling well over 100,000 people, the largest numbers of men recorded in the Linear B tablets are 900 and 428. Here too, as Jan Driessen has argued, what few infantrymen are attested are very likely professional and non-Cretan.[43]

One must suspect that in those Near Eastern kingdoms in which conscription was practiced the caliber of the levied troops was not very high. Even in battle the conscript may have been more a civilian than a soldier. In Egypt, as noted, one out of ten temple servitors might be conscripted for military duty, and persons so infrequently levied are not likely to have had prior military experience. Hittite records indicate that the men collected in a royal levy might be assigned to a variety of menial tasks: serving as a footsoldier was one, but alternatively the draftee might be assigned to carry ice or harvest a vineyard.[44] At Nuzi, the typical *sab shepi* ("footsoldier") was apparently a conscript: in one of the few references to such a troop, the

[40] On the *pedijewe* in the *o-ka* tablets see Lejeune, "Civilisation," 31. Alexander Uchitel, "On the 'Military' Character of the *O-KA* Tablets," *Kadmos* 23 (1984): 136–63, argues that the *o-ka* tablets have nothing to do with military matters and instead refer to "some sort of agricultural work, probably ploughing" (p. 163). Uchitel's argument has been strongly endorsed by James T. Hooker, "Titles and Functions in the Pylian State," in Killen, *Studies in Mycenaean and Classical Greek Presented to John Chadwick*, 264–65. If the *o-ka* men were "foreigners," however, as they seem to have been, it is likely that their occupation was something more specialized than working in the fields.

[41] J. M. Driessen and C. Macdonald, "Some Military Aspects of the Aegean in the Late Fifteenth and Early Fourteenth Centuries B.C.," *ABSA* 79 (1984): 49.

[42] Lejeune, "Civilisation," 31 and 49.

[43] Driessen, "Military Aspects," 51–52 and 55–56, finds no evidence for "native" infantrymen in the service of the Knossos palace. If the designations of the several groups of infantrymen mentioned in the tablets are indeed ethnic, the men were very likely of foreign origin, "since these designations cannot be connected with Cretan place-names mentioned in the Knossian archive or later" (p. 52).

[44] Beal, *Organization*, 140–41.

tablet specifies that of seven footsoldiers one was a fuller, two were smiths, and one was a temple official.[45]

How such recruitment might have been conducted in the Late Bronze Age is not indicated, so far as I know, in any of our records. In the Middle Bronze Age, we catch a glimpse of how things might have proceeded at Mari. The officer in charge of recruitment there decided, as Watkins observed,[46] that something must be done "pour encourager les autres" and so sent to King Zimri-Lim a modest proposal: "If my lord will agree, let me execute a criminal in the prison, cut off his head and parade it all around the town. . .to make the men afraid so that they will assemble quickly." How conscripts were used in Late Bronze Age warfare is unclear. At Ugarit, as mentioned, they were sometimes issued bows, and perhaps we may imagine them employed in either assaulting or defending a fixed position. Possibly some of the thirty-seven thousand infantrymen who stood with Muwatallis at the gates of Kadesh were conscripts, although Ramesses' inscription does say that these men were all *thr* warriors, a term that means something like "valiant" and was applied to experienced troops. No text mentions the training of conscripts, and we may suppose that they were assigned duties of a routine nature. There is no reason to think that conscripts were expected—or able—to engage in hand-to-hand combat.

We may turn, then, to the professional footsoldiers, who appear under a variety of designations. In the first centuries of the Late Bronze Age most professional footsoldiers may have been natives of the kingdom in which they fought. In late fifteenth-century Nuzi there is little evidence for foreign infantrymen. In Eighteenth-Dynasty Egypt the infantrymen who supported the chariotry were probably Egyptian *nfrw*, which literally may have meant "young men" but which Schulman translates as "elite troops." On the Konosso stele, Thutmose IV described his forces as he attacked a Nubian prince who had rebelled: "The chariotry was in battle-lines beside him, his infantry was with him, the strong-of-arm consisting of the *nfrw* who were (usually) beside him on both flanks."[47]

Even at the end of the Eighteenth Dynasty the pharaoh's chariot runners were probably still native Egyptians. On a chest from the tomb of Tutankhamun, from the middle of the fourteenth century, is a painting of a battle in the Levant. The pharaoh, acting as both charioteer and chariot warrior, dominates the scene, shooting the enemy's chariot horses. But the work of dispatching the crews of those chariots that have been immobilized is performed by footsoldiers who attack with short thrusting spears; and

---

[45] Kendall, *Warfare*, 148; it is symptomatic that the entire discussion of Nuzi's infantry can be contained on this one page.

[46] Watkins, "Beginnings," 27; for the text see *Archives Royales de Mari*, vol. 2, no. 48.

[47] Translation from Schulman, "Egyptian Chariotry," 76.

from their garb, hair, and weapons one would suppose the men to be native Egyptians.[48]

Among foreign professionals, the lowest level seems to have been that of the *hapiru* (or *'prw*), free-lancers who were hired merely for a season or campaign. Egyptian, Ugaritic, and Hittite texts all make mention of *hapiru*, both as hired troops and as troublesome elements against whom action had to be taken. The "Hebrew" traditions in early Israel indicate that many of the *hapiru* who fought for the pharaoh were hired from the less settled populations in the southern Levant. Etymologically, the word *hapiru* seems to have had no specifically military connotation, meaning something like "vagrants" or "those who have crossed boundaries," and clearly not all *hapiru* were warriors.[49] But in the Late Bronze Age many *hapiru* were associated with mercenary military service, and apparently they were hired for hand-to-hand rather than for long-range combat. The Sumerian ideogram that is often used alongside or in place of the word *hapiru* is *SA.GAZ*, which seems originally to have meant "he who commits aggression," or "one who knocks down," or even "killer."[50] The *hapiru*, or *SA.GAZ*, seem to have fought in conjunction with chariots but were not themselves charioteers or chariot archers.[51]

A preferable source of seasoned infantrymen for temporary service was a vassal state or a province on the frontier. As indicated above, the Hittite kings (who rarely hired *hapiru*) seem to have assembled the considerable infantry needed for a major campaign by requiring every subject district to send to the Great King a certain number of troops. If one were to believe Ramesses the Great's account of the Battle of Kadesh, the kings of Hatti depended very much upon mercenaries. According to Ramesses, Muwatallis stripped his treasury bare in order to hire manpower for the showdown at Kadesh. Although Ramesses provides us with a great list of places that supplied troops to Muwatallis, it is not clear which of these were Hittite vassals and which were simply areas from which volunteers or mercenaries may have come. At any rate, few of Muwatallis's thirty-seven thousand infantrymen were conscripts from Hatti: Ramesses refers to both groups of Muwatallis's infantrymen as "*thr* warriors," a word that may mean "champions" or "valiant men" but that more objectively seems to

[48] For color illustration see Yadin, *Art of Warfare*, vol. 1, 216–17.

[49] Of a score of studies on the *hapiru* the most recent is by Nadav Na'aman, "Hapiru and Hebrews: The Transfer of a Social Term to the Literary Scene," *JNES* 45 (1986): 271–88; see also H. Cazelles, "The Hebrews," in D. Wiseman, ed., *Peoples of Old Testament Times* (Oxford, 1973), 1–28.

[50] Mary Gray, "The Ḥâbirū-Hebrew Problem in the Light of the Source Material Available at Present," *Hebrew Union College Annual* 29 (1958): 137ff.

[51] W. Helck, *Die Beziehungen Ägyptens zu Vorderasien im 3. und 2. Jahrtausend v. Chr.* (Wiesbaden, 1962), 522–31, proposed that the terms *maryannu* and *'prw* stood respectively for chariotry and infantry professionals.

distinguish seasoned veterans from conscript troops.[52] Egyptian kings also depended on frontier vassals for auxiliary troops. The Amorite *ne'arim* who fought for Ramesses II in 1275 B.C. may have been furnished by his vassals in the Levant.

In the thirteenth century, however, many kings preferred to secure the services of valiant barbarians on a permanent basis. In return for a plot of land, and for some other compensation, the warrior would be available for annual campaigns and might perform guard or sentinel duty at other times of the year. The advantages of having such men in one's service were, for a Near Eastern king, considerable. For natives of Egypt and other kingdoms of the Near East life was normally pacific, and consequently they were not such keen hand-to-hand warriors as were men from less settled lands. In the royal reliefs, the native Egyptians engaged in hand-to-hand warfare fight in squads of four, the four standing shoulder to shoulder and so presenting a solid wall of oblong shields. The barbarian skirmisher, on the other hand, fights on his own; with no comrade to right or left, he depends on his own round shield. Mobility rather than solidarity was essential. For offense, the native Egyptian skirmishers wielded either thrusting spears or long metal staves, with which they beat their opponent to the ground. Such weapons were suitable for the compact squad, since a man was not likely to injure his fellows if his weapon was parried or misdirected. The barbarian was a far more efficient skirmisher: ferocious in his horned or feathered helmet, he used his long sword to threaten opponents in a wide perimeter.

Although the Egyptian pharaohs procured many of their professionals from Nubia and Libya, some of the best (and perhaps the most picturesque) skirmishers evidently came from Sardinia. Both in Egypt and at Ugarit a term sometimes applied to foreign professionals skilled at hand-to-hand combat is *shardana*.[53] As I have argued in chapter 4, the word originally must have meant "a man from Sardinia." That phrase, however, although entirely meaningful when spoken by a Sardinian native living in Egypt, would have meant little or nothing to a native Egyptian, who had never seen a sea, an island, or a map. The proper noun therefore may sometimes have been used as a common noun denoting a man's function in society and his physical type. In Egyptian inscriptions the phonetic rendering of the word *shardana* is occasionally illustrated by a determinative: a warrior wearing a horned helmet (between the horns is a small disk) and usually carrying a small round shield and either a sword or a spear.[54] As Helck concluded, whenever we see warriors in horned helmets depicted in

---

[52] On the *thr* warriors see Helck, *Beziehungen*, 531–32; Helck translates the term as "Garde" or "Held."

[53] Dietrich and Loretz, "Die Schardana in den Texten von Ugarit," 39–42; G. A. Lehmann, *Mykenische Welt*, 33–34.

[54] Helck, "Die Seevölker," 9.

Helck concluded, whenever we see warriors in horned helmets depicted in Egyptian reliefs we may reasonably "sie als *Sardin* identifizieren."[55] However, we must also suppose that for a thirteenth-century Egyptian scribe the word *shardana* had a semantic field quite different from that of our word *Sardinian*. So far as the provenance of such warriors was concerned, the Egyptian scribe perhaps knew only that they came from a barbarous place "in the midst of the sea."

The first Sardinians attested in Egypt were raiders who ravaged the Delta in 1279 and were defeated and captured by Ramesses the Great. They had come "in their warships from the midst of the sea, and none were able to stand before them."[56] Once impressed into Ramesses' service, the Sardinians evidently served him very well. They were an important and conspicuous part of the army he took to Kadesh in 1275 B.C.: in the Abydos reliefs (see plates 3, 4, and 5), some Sardinian runners—warriors wearing horned helmets and carrying dirks or short swords—are slaying the fallen Hittite chariot crewmen and cutting off their hands, while others serve as personal bodyguards for Ramesses. By the end of the thirteenth century, as the Papyrus Anastasi suggests, a great many Sardinians (there are 520 in Hori's imaginary force) were employed by the pharaoh. As noted above, in the Medinet Habu reliefs we see warriors in horned helmets doing yeoman service for Ramesses III against the Philistines, and the accompanying inscription divides the pharaoh's army into "the infantry, the chariotry, the troops, the Sherden, and the Nubians."[57] At the same time, some warriors in horned helmets had been recruited by the Philistine side. At least some of these, too, were *shardana* in the narrower rather than the generic sense, since one of the Medinet Habu reliefs identifies as a *shardana* a captured chief who wears a horned helmet.[58] After the eventful battles of his early years, Ramesses III still employed many *shardana* and other barbarians (especially from Libya), since in the Papyrus Harris the dead king addresses "the princes, and leaders of the land, the infantry and chariotry, the Sher-

[55] Helck, "Die Seevölker," 9.

[56] From the Tanis stele, as translated by Gardiner, *Egypt*, 259.

[57] Edgerton and Wilson, *Historical Records of Ramses III*, plate 29.

[58] Sandars, *Sea Peoples*, figs. 68 and 79. There is no reason, however, to suppose that all warriors in horned helmets came from Sardinian stock. Sandars pointed out (ibid., 106–7) that the horned helmet has an ancient pedigree in the Near East, going back to Naram-Sin of Akkad. Perhaps it would be safest to think of the horned helmet as appealing to a variety of European, Mediterranean, and Near Eastern warriors: a professional warrior who wished to look and feel formidable could hardly do better than strapping on his head the horns of a bull. Most if not all Sardinian warriors serving in the eastern Mediterranean may have worn the horned helmet. But Sicilians may also have worn it, since in the Medinet Habu relief of the naval battle in 1179 B.C. the enemy wear horned helmets, and the accompanying inscription identifies *Shekelesh* but not *Shardana* among the enemy. We need not identify as Sardinians the soldiers on the Mycenaean "Warrior Vase," simply because they wear horned helmets, nor the similarly accoutred Ingot God of Cyprus.

PLATE 5. *Shardana* bodyguards of Ramesses II, at Kadesh. Abydos relief

den, the numerous archers, and all the citizens of the land of Egypt."
Further on in the papyrus he boasts that he had "Sherden and Kehek
without number" in his service and that conditions in his kingdom were so
peaceful that "the Sherden and the Kehek in their villages . . . lie at night
full length without any dread."[59] And in the reign of Ramesses V (1149–
45) the Wilbour Papyrus identifies *shardana* as proprietors of land granted
to them by the king.[60]

In the Levant, Sardinians apparently served as mercenaries already in the
Amarna period. In correspondence denouncing Rib-Addi of Byblos, *shardana* are mentioned three times, and they are quite clearly soldiers.[61] In the
Ugarit tablets there are several references to *shardana*, although by ca.
1200 B.C. the term may here too have denoted function rather than provenance. Heltzer regards the *shardana* as "foreigners in the royal service of

[59] Breasted, *AR*, vol. 4, nos. 397, 402, and (as translated in Gardiner, *Egypt*, 293) 410.
[60] Gardiner, *Egypt*, 296–97.
[61] Helck, "Seevölker," 8, concludes "dass sie Soldaten sind. Ob sie im Dienst des Ribaddi
stehen oder zu einer ägyptischen Einheit gehören, ist nicht erkennbar."

Ugarit,[62] and in some sense they undoubtedly were foreigners. Yet one of the few *shardana* mentioned by name is "Amar-Addu, son of Mutba'al." The names of father and son are both Semitic. Another *shardana* seems to have inherited fields at Ugarit,[63] the normal practice being that the *shardana* received land from the king in return for military service. It thus appears that at Ugarit some of the *shardana* may have been fairly well assimilated into the general population. At Ugarit some *shardana* served as *mdrglm*-guards and as *tnnm*; the latter term, as noted above, evidently means "hand-to-hand warriors."[64]

The king of Hatti seems to have recruited much of his standing army— the UKU.UŠ and the *sharikuwa*—from men living near or beyond the frontier and especially along the Pontic range in the north. Here lived the barbarous Kaskans, a source of danger as well as manpower. After subjugating some of the Kaskan lands, Hattusilis III brought back warriors to serve with his UKU.UŠ.[65] The king of Ugarit may also have kept a troop of Kaskans. Liverani at any rate suggested that what seems to be a reference, in a Ugaritic text, to the "capo dei Kaska" can best be explained on the assumption that "si tratta di un gruppo di soldati mercenari."[66]

For the Aegean world, there is little evidence on our topic. What there is, however, suggests that prior to the Catastrophe the Mycenaean palaces might have depended almost entirely on "foreign" professionals for their infantry forces. The "Captain of the Blacks" fresco at Knossos may have portrayed an Aegean captain leading a company of black troops (one thinks of the Nubians who fought for the Egyptian pharaohs). The "Battle Scene" fresco from Pylos (see plate 2) shows three palace warriors who are surely professional but who seem to fight in the same style—and with the same weapons—as their "wild" opponents. The six groups of men named in the *o-ka* tablets from Pylos are likely to be six ethnic designations.[67] Although none of the designations suggests a provenance from outside the Aegean, there is some reason to see these men—if they are indeed soldiers, as they are usually thought to be—as "foreign" professionals. Driessen has argued that at Knossos the designation *kesenuwija* is ancestral to the classical Greek *xenoi*, a word that literally means "strangers" but must often be translated as "mercenaries." Since three or possibly four of the Pylos *o-ka* groups show up in the Knossos archive, Driessen concludes that the Greek rulers of Knossos brought in "foreigners" or mercenaries to

---

[62] "Heltzer, *Internal Organization*, 127.

[63] On both these individuals see Heltzer, *Internal Organization*, 126.

[64] Dietrich and Loretz, "Schardana," 41.

[65] Beal, *Organization*, 122–23, 235, and 237; see also E. Laroche, "Lettre d'un préfet au roi hittite," *Revue hittite et asianique* 67 (1960): 81–86.

[66] Liverani, *Storia di Ugarit*, 154.

[67] Driessen, "Military Aspects," 49.

maintain the kingdom's security.[68] The place-names that can be got out of (or read into) the terms suggest that the *xenoi* came from backward areas of the Aegean.[69] Since the foreigners show up on tablets registering land allotments, it may be "that small groups of foreigners were admitted to the Pylian kingdom and were allotted small fiefs of land for cultivation. In return, they had to contribute a certain amount of flax and render military service in the Pylian army."[70] At Knossos there is no direct evidence for this practice, but Driessen thinks it likely that there too the palace brought in foreigners "who rendered military service in return for fiefs of land."

So far as our limited evidence goes, then, we may suppose that Mycenaean infantrymen were normally professionals and came from the less pacific parts of the Aegean. Elsewhere I have argued that in the Late Helladic period the lower classes in the palace states of Boeotia, the Peloponnese and Crete still spoke the pre-Greek language that had been current throughout the area in Early and Middle Helladic times: most subjects of the palaces, that is, would at best have had only a limited acquaintance with the Greek language spoken by the lords of the palaces and their charioteers. I would therefore here suggest that when the Pylian king, for example, hired professional infantrymen, he hired North-Greek speakers from the mountains beyond Boeotia. It is likely that the mountaineers were more warlike than the Messenian natives, whose relationship to the palace seems to have anticipated that of the helots to their Dorian masters in the Iron Age.

Such indications as we have of numbers suggest that the typical foreign contingent was composed of several hundred (and not several thousand) men. In the Papyrus Anastasi army, the largest foreign contingent we are to imagine is that of the Qeheq, a Libyan tribe, who would account for sixteen hundred of the five thousand–man force. When Ugaritic texts make reference to *shardana*, the references are not to hundreds but to groups of four and five, and Heltzer calculates their total as about sixty.[71] The Linear B tablets are unusually informative on this point. The *o-ka* tablets from Pylos show that two hundred *okara* men formed the largest contingent, the smallest being a group of seventy *urupijajo*.[72] The Pylos palace did not, however, have all two hundred *okara* serving together but broke them up

[68] Ibid., 50–56.

[69] Driessen, ibid., 50, suggests that the *Iwaso* were troops who came from Iasos, that the *Urupijajo* were troops from Olympia, and that all the troops "were originally non-Messenian" (in n. 5 Driessen passes on the suggestion that two of the other contingents may have come from Corcyra and Skyros). I would suggest only that *Urupijajo* is more likely to point to Mt. Olympus than to Peloponnesian Olympia; the latter name seems to be derived from the former, and there is no reason to suppose that it is much older than the sanctuary.

[70] Ibid.

[71] Heltzer, *Internal Organization*, 106–7 and 126.

[72] Lejeune, "Civilisation," 39–40.

into smaller groups and posted them in several locations. In the Knossos archive, tablet B164 refers to at least 368 men, apparently all of them "foreigners."[73]

When Meryre of Libya—about to attack Egypt in 1208 B.C.—supplemented his Libyan force by recruiting warriors from "all the northern lands," he was following a traditional practice. What was not traditional is that the runners whom he secured were not cast in a supporting role to chariotry, since Meryre had no chariotry of any significance. Instead, the skirmishers were themselves assigned the task of destroying the Egyptian chariot army. That battle belongs to the Catastrophe and we shall return to it in our final chapter, but Meryre's scheme and the Catastrophe can only be understood against the background of what infantry forces were available to the Late Bronze Age kingdoms.

To summarize: Insofar as our evidence illuminates such things, it appears that prior to the Catastrophe an eastern Mediterranean king might send infantrymen into the mountainous hinterland to punish barbarians who had misbehaved. Such combat was probably a melee rather than a conflict of close-order formations. When two civilized kingdoms went to war, the hand-to-hand fighting was subordinated to and integrated with the chariot battle. In chariot warfare there was no engagement of mass formations of infantry, and what hand-to-hand fighting was required was the responsibility of professional chariot runners, or skirmishers. In the thirteenth century these men were rarely natives of the kingdoms in which they fought and tended to come from barbarian lands such as Nubia, Libya, and Sardinia or from the more backward parts of Greece and the Levant. Their service as skirmishers was undoubtedly hazardous and demanding and must have required a great deal more stamina, skill, recklessness, and perhaps ferocity than could be found in the typical resident of Ugarit, Messenia, or Memphis.

INFANTRY FORCES IN THE CATASTROPHE

During the Catastrophe, some rulers trying to defend their cities and palaces apparently made significant changes in their armed forces. As we shall see in detail in chapter 14, the aggressors were runners and skirmishers, and they therefore had to be contained and countered by infantrymen. For the first time in four centuries, at least a few battles in the plains and in defense of the palaces themselves seem to have been primarily infantry clashes.

[73] Driessen, "Military Aspects," 51.

In 1208 B.C. Merneptah seems to have relied greatly on his chariotry to defeat the Libyans, but he also celebrated his hand-to-hand warriors and a "militia" (*mnfyt*) of Egyptians.[74] When Ramesses III fights against the Philistines in 1179 not only are his horses like falcons but his infantry are "like bulls ready on the field of battle." And to counter the Libyan infantry in 1176 Ramesses leads forth not only his chariotry but also "the mighty men [whom he had] trained [to] fight."[75] In both battles Ramesses himself was of course a peerless archer in his royal chariot, as New Kingdom pharaohs had always been. But he is also, surprisingly, a footsoldier who fights hand-to-hand. One relief shows Ramesses dismounted from his chariot and overpowering the enemy, and the accompanying text lauds his prowess "on his two feet."[76]

In the land battle against the Philistines, Ramesses' footsoldiers are conspicuous, some of them in traditional Egyptian headdress and others wearing the *shardana* helmet (see plate 6). The latter, as they always had, tend to fight on their own, as individuals, each *shardana* auxiliary taking on one or more of the enemy with his sword or thrusting spear. The Egyptians, on the other hand, fight in their traditional squads. The artist shows them in groups of four, all four men moving and striking in concert. Although the divine Ramesses and other chariot warriors are shown on the right-hand side of the Land Battle Relief, each of the five registers of the relief is primarily a depiction of the valor of Ramesses' hand-to-hand warriors. Egypt probably owed its survival to Ramesses' recruitment or training of thousands of footsoldiers who could take the offensive against the raiders. Although his barbarian professionals could fight in guerrilla fashion, the Egyptians needed to be placed in organized units, each man being thus supported and assisted by his comrades in a close-order formation.

In the sea battle (see plate 7) the main burden fell on native Egyptian infantrymen. In order to catch his opponents before they landed, Ramesses assembled a great many boats and manned them with Egyptian archers (some of these, of course, could have been chariot archers) and hand-to-hand warriors. The latter were Egyptians, armed with the usual shields and staves, and were responsible for dealing with those of the enemy who tried to board the Egyptian boats. In Ramesses' vaunt, his boats were filled from bow to stern with warriors: "The militia (*mnfyt*), consisting of every picked man of Egypt, were like lions roaring upon the mountain tops."[77] How he

---

[74] Breasted, *AR*, vol. 3, no. 578.

[75] Edgerton and Wilson, *Historical Records of Ramses III*, plates 31 and 80–83 (pp. 77–78).

[76] Edgerton and Wilson, ibid., plate 68; cf. Breasted, *AR*, vol. 4, no. 106.

[77] Edgerton and Wilson, *Historical Records of Ramses III*, plate 46, pp. 54–55. In a note on their translation of *mnfyt* as "militia" the authors observe that "*mnfyt* seems to be in contrast to *thr*."

PLATE 6. Land battle of Ramesses III, in Year 8, against Philistine and other aggressors

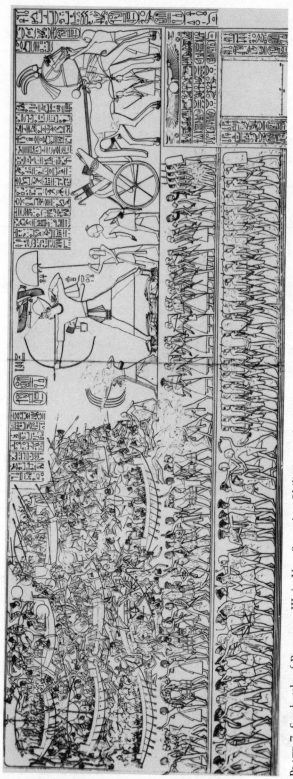

PLATE 7. Sea battle of Ramesses III, in Year 8, against Philistine and other aggressors

recruited these "picked men of Egypt" we cannot know, but it is importa\
to note the unusual effort to augment the professional infantry.

In Greece too, it appears, the communities that came through the early
horrors of the Catastrophe began in the IIIC period to create forces of
footsoldiers. Since we have no written documents from the period, we must
here depend entirely on pictorial evidence. Professional skirmishers, first of
all, seem to have enjoyed an unwonted status in IIIC communities. Individual warriors, relatively well armored, appear on kraters of LH IIIC date at
Tiryns and on pots at Nauplia and Lefkandi. Littauer and Crouwel have
pointed out that these warriors, carried in chariots, are footsoldiers, apparently en route to a battle.[78] As suggested in chapter 10, the Homeric
description of chariots as battle taxis may be a reminiscence of this twelfth-
century development. Possibly in IIIC Greece the horses and vehicles that
survived from the pre-Catastrophe chariot forces became nothing more
than prestige vehicles for the professional warriors who until then had been
runners in the chariot corps. The chariot on these IIIC vases, at any rate,
suggests that its passenger is a footsoldier of unusual status, and we may
suppose that he was an individual skirmisher, capable of holding his own in
a man-to-man encounter with any barbarian raider.

But in addition to the individual skirmishers, who may have been regarded as the *promachoi* or "champions" of their communities, the IIIC
towns may also have fielded forces of nonprofessional footsoldiers. In
order to stand their ground in hand-to-hand combat against the barbarian
raiders, these men would necessarily have been put into a close-order
company. Lines of footsoldiers appear on the Warrior Vase and the Warrior
Stele from Mycenae, both of which date either to the IIIC period or to the
very end of IIIB.[79] On the krater, the "front" panel (see plate 8) shows six
bearded soldiers wearing horned helmets, a sleeved corslet that reaches to
the waist, a fringed leather skirt, and greaves (whether these are to be
understood as being made of bronze or of leather cannot be determined).
Each of the soldiers carries a six-foot spear and a round shield. The five
soldiers of the rear panel brandish shorter spears and wear "hedgehog"
helmets but otherwise resemble their counterparts on the front. On the
Warrior Stele there are again five infantrymen, almost identical to those on
the reverse of the vase, brandishing spears. In both representations the
infantrymen are in close order, marching with spears on their shoulders, or

---

[78] Littauer, "Military Use," 145–46; Littauer and Crouwel, "Chariots in Late Bronze Age
Greece," 189–90; for the representations see Vermeule and Karageorghis, *Mycenaean Pictorial Vase Painting*, nos. XI.1a–b, XI.16, XI.18, XI.28.

[79] The representations are usually dated to the early IIIC period. Vermeule and Karageorghis, ibid., 130–34, with plates XI.42 and XI.43, assign them to their "transitional"
period. For an argument that the representations date to the end of the IIIB period see John
Younger, "The End of Mycenaean Art," in Thomas, *Forschungen*, 63–72.

PLATE 8. "Warrior Vase" from Mycenae, Side A

about to throw their spears in a "ceremonial volley" (the stele is certainly and the vase is probably funerary). It is perhaps possible that the artist intended one of the groups to represent foreigners, since the horned helmets are an exotic element, whereas the "hedgehog" helmet appears on many LH IIIC sherds. But it is more likely that both groups are intended to represent native troops: the warriors in horned helmets pass in front of a woman who is either bidding them farewell or mourning, and either a farewell or a funeral suggests that these are men from the locality in which the vase was cherished.

The scenes suggest that the artist and his patrons were familiar with infantry formations and more particularly with formations of spearmen, all the soldiers being uniformly accoutred and armed and all having an assigned position within the relatively dense formation. These Mycenaean infantrymen were not about to do battle with chariots: they had been organized and equipped—with a hand-to-hand weapon, a shield, and body armor—in order to confront infantrymen in close combat.

Although it has often been committed, it is a methodological sin to present the scenes on the Warrior Vase and Warrior Stele as examples of "typical" Mycenaean practices of the Late Bronze Age. Similarly, the Medinet Habu reliefs of Ramesses III's battle against the Philistines and the Libyans should surely not be used as a guide to Egyptian military practices in the reigns of his Eighteenth- and Nineteenth-Dynasty predecessors. These representations were made after the Catastrophe had run much if not most of its harrowing course, and they must not be torn from that chronological context. The Mycenae vase and stele, whether dated to the end of IIIB or to IIIC, were at any rate made several decades after Troy VI and Thebes had been destroyed, and after Mycenae and Tiryns were fortified and the Isthmus wall was begun. The Medinet Habu reliefs show what the Egyptian army looked like in 1179 B.C., by which time palaces and cities had been destroyed all through Greece, Anatolia, Cyprus, and the Levant, and Egypt seemed about to become the next victim. The representations therefore do not show us the military character of the eastern kingdoms at their zenith but instead reveal how some kingdoms that had thus far survived the Catastrophe were responding to their dire situation. Professional skirmishers were never more valued and perhaps provided much of the defense against their predatory kinsmen. In addition, formations of native infantrymen—so difficult to find in our pre-Catastrophe documentation—were now being armed and trained, as the few centers still flourishing sought to escape the fate that had by that time overtaken so much of the eastern Mediterranean world.

Chapter Twelve

INFANTRY AND HORSE TROOPS

IN THE EARLY IRON AGE

THE LAST two chapters have argued that, from the late seventeenth to the late thirteenth century, for the eastern Mediterranean kingdoms warfare was a contest between opposing chariot forces, and the only offensive infantrymen who participated in battle were the "runners"—the skirmishers who ran among the chariots. The present chapter will review what we know about warfare in the early Iron Age. Although there is distressingly little information for the centuries following the Catastrophe, what there is suggests that all over the eastern Mediterranean the principal role in battle was now borne by offensive infantrymen. Thus chariot warfare, which in the Late Bronze Age had distinguished cities and kingdoms from the barbarous hinterlands (where horses and a chariot were a luxury that few, if any, could afford), did not survive into the Iron Age, and even the wealthiest kings had now to depend primarily upon footsoldiers.

It is generally recognized that the chariot was less important in the Iron Age than in the Late Bronze Age. By the reign of Tiglath-Pileser III (745–27) the light, two-horse chariot rarely appeared on the battlefield,[1] since by that time the tasks hitherto assigned to chariots were normally carried out by cavalry. As a result, the Neo-Assyrian chariot became an enormous and cumbersome vehicle, carrying a variety of passengers and drawn by three or four horses. Such vehicles had little in common with the war chariot of the Bronze Age and seem to have served as prestige conveyances for the king and lesser dignitaries.[2] In classical times (if we except the dreadful but ineffective "scythed" chariots of the Persians) the chariot was associated almost entirely with status, parades, and recreation. We may thus say that in the Iron Age cavalry "replaced" chariotry as an effective military arm.

Prior to the Catastrophe there were, so far as our evidence indicates, no troops of cavalry or camelry. The Egyptian reliefs, however, do include occasional individuals on horseback, and some of these figures are depicted as carrying a bow and quiver. Without saddle or stirrups riding a horse was

---

[1] Littauer and Crouwel, *Wheeled Vehicles*, 130–31.

[2] In reliefs from the last century of Assyrian history these huge chariots are frequently standing still, serving as lofty and well protected (but basically stationary) platforms from which a few privileged archers could shoot their bows. See Littauer and Crouwel, ibid., 131–32.

difficult enough, and the Bronze Age rider was not yet able to control his mount and shoot a bow at the same time. Perhaps, therefore, the bow carried by a Bronze Age rider was meant for self-defense, and the few men on horseback were scouts or messengers rather than mounted archers.[3]

The earliest representations of archers shooting from the backs of galloping horses are ninth-century Assyrian reliefs. These reliefs show the cavalry archers operating in pairs: one cavalryman holds the reins of both his own and his partner's horse, allowing the partner to use his hands for the bow and bowstring. The early cavalry teams thus parallel exactly the charioteer and chariot archer.[4] The cavalry archer was undoubtedly less accurate than his counterpart on a chariot (bouncing on a horse's back was less conducive to a good shot than standing—knees bent—on the leather-strap platform of a chariot). But in other respects the cavalry teams were surely superior. They were able, first of all, to operate in terrain too rough for wheeled vehicles. And their chances for flight, when things went wrong, were much better: when a chariot horse was injured, both crewmen were in immediate danger, but if a cavalryman's horse was killed or injured the cavalryman could immediately leap on the back of his partner's horse and so ride out of harm's way. Yet another advantage of cavalry over chariotry was economic, since the cost of purchasing and maintaining a vehicle was considerable. The Chronicler claims (2 Chronicles 1.17) that in the tenth century the chariot itself cost twice as much as the team that pulled it.

How early in the Iron Age kings began to use cavalries in place of or alongside chariotries cannot be determined, since there is so little documentary and pictorial evidence for the period 1150–900 B.C. By the middle of the ninth century cavalries were obviously well established, since at the Battle of Qarqar Shalmaneser III faced many men on horseback (and some on the backs of camels) and since he himself claimed to have 2,002 chariots and 5,542 cavalrymen.[5] For earlier centuries all we have are Hebrew traditions, and although they are hardly trustworthy it must be noted that they routinely associate cavalries with the kings of the period. Solomon was said to have maintained twelve thousand *parashim*; David was believed to have defeated enormous horse troops consisting of both chariots and cavalrymen; and Saul was reported to have been slain on Mt. Gilboa by Philistine *parashim*.

More reliable Hebrew traditions in fact imply that the substitution of

[3] Beal, *Organization*, 94; Stephanie Dalley, "Foreign Chariotry and Cavalry in the Armies of Tiglath-Pileser III and Sargon II," *Iraq* 47 (1985): 37–38.

[4] Littauer and Crouwel, *Wheeled Vehicles*, 135: "The chariot complement—warrior and driver—is simply transferred to the back of its team, the men's respective functions remaining the same."

[5] M. Elat, "The Campaigns of Shalmaneser III against Aram and Israel," *IEJ* 25 (1975): 27.

y teams for chariots began in the Catastrophe itself. Poetic references
ın Genesis and Exodus to "the horse and his rider" among Israel's enemies
indicate that at least a few kings began to put some of their archers on
horseback as early as the twelfth century. In the "Song of the Sea" the poet
exults that not only "Pharaoh's chariots and his host" but also "the horse
and his rider" have been thrown into the sea (Exodus 15.1 and 21). In the
"Blessing of Jacob" the patriarch promises (Genesis 49.17–18) that the
tribe of Dan "shall be a serpent in the way, a viper by the path, that bites
the horse's heels so that his rider falls backward."[6]

It appears, then, that the use of cavalry began in the twelfth century, that
by the tenth century some kings employed thousands of cavalrymen, and
that the ninth-century Assyrian kings had at least as many horses in their
cavalry as in their chariotry. The final obsolescence of chariotry came with
the discovery, in the eighth century, of new techniques for reining a ridden
horse. The new method, apparent in the reliefs of Tiglath-Pileser III, allowed cavalrymen to operate independently rather than in pairs, each rider
now controlling his own mount.[7] With every rider an archer, the "firepower" on the backs of a hundred cavalry horses was double the firepower
drawn by a hundred chariot horses. Thus by ca. 750 B.C. the replacement
of chariots by cavalry was more or less complete.

But horse troops of any kind, whether chariotry or cavalry, were of much
less importance in the Iron Age than had been their predecessors in the Late
Bronze Age. Whereas before the Catastrophe warfare was the swirl of
chariot squadrons, with drivers charging, wheeling, and then charging
again while the archers sent volleys of arrows against the oncoming enemy
chariots, in the Iron Age the focus of the action was combat between
opposing infantries. Here a horse troop's initial mission was to deal with
the opponent's horse troop, but the ultimate mission was to assist in destroying the enemy infantry, by encircling, flanking, or dividing it. Assyrian
reliefs show that cavalrymen were also used for pursuing and dispatching
individual fugitives after the enemy infantry had been routed, and for this
assignment the lance rather than the bow was the appropriate weapon.

From the twelfth century to the end of antiquity horse troops did not
establish the battle but played a supporting role. On occasion, as at Issus or

[6] It is sometimes said that the lines refer to chariotry, the assumption being that cavalry was
still unknown when the poems were written. See, for example, Gottwald, *Tribes of Yahweh*,
540: "The horse and its rider which Dan attacks . . . refers almost certainly to horse-drawn
chariots. . . . It is now well documented that cavalry units were only introduced effectively
into the Near East by the Assyrians in the eighth-ninth centuries." That cavalry was introduced into the Near East by Assyrians in the ninth century is not documented at all; we know
only that in the middle of the ninth century the Assyrians had an enormous cavalry.

[7] Littauer and Crouwel, *Wheeled Vehicles*, 138; cf. Dalley, "Foreign Chariotry," 37–38,
who refers to J. Spruytte, "La conduite du cheval chez l'archer assyrien," *Plaisirs Equestres*
129 (1983): 66–71.

Adrianople, that supporting role might be decisive, and we even hear of armies (the Parthians at Carrhae) that consisted almost entirely of cavalry. But the normal expectation of Chaldaeans, Persians, Carthaginians, Greeks, and Romans was that a battle was in essence a clash of infantries. Thus chariotry, and then cavalry, made important contributions in Iron Age warfare, but what we see in the Iron Age should not be called "chariot warfare."

The centrality of an offensive infantry is clear when our documentation resumes in the ninth century, with the inscriptions and reliefs of Ashurnasirpal II and Shalmaneser III. Although Shalmaneser's horse troops were impressive, they were evidently secondary to his infantry, which in a major campaign numbered more than 100,000 men. Another inscription of the early ninth century describes an Assyrian army of 1,351 chariots and 50,000 footsoldiers.[8] These enormous infantries were of course levied from the general population in Assyria, where the tradition of militia service seems to have been still flourishing in the ninth century.[9] Although neither reliefs nor inscriptions and literary accounts give us a clear picture of a ninth-century battle, what can be pieced together indicates that in the armies of Assyria, Israel, and Judah an advancing infantry formed the center of a battle line, and horse troops operated on the wings "for pincer movements and efforts to overwhelm and turn the enemy flank."[10] In the ninth century, in other words, infantry units no longer served merely to escort chariotries on the march and, in battle, to provide a haven for chariots in trouble but were now at the center of the offensive action. The Assyrian infantry included companies of archers (protected by defensive armor and armed with composite bows) and of spearmen, and all carried a straight sword as a secondary weapon.

But if we have reasonable documentation for ninth-century warfare, the three centuries from the Catastrophe to Ashurnasirpal's reign are a dark age. Nevertheless, we have just enough evidence to conclude that in this period too, in the immediate aftermath of the Catastrophe, infantries already played the primary offensive role. Egypt, which tells us so much about Late Bronze Age warfare, has almost nothing to offer for the early Iron Age. But although we have no advertisements of victories by the later Ramessids and the weak kings of the Twenty-First Dynasty, papyri from the

---

[8] Elat, "Campaigns of Shalmaneser," 27; Luckenbill, *Ancient Records of Assyria and Babylonia*, vol. 1, no. 658; Stillman and Tallis, *Armies*, 31.

[9] Walther Manitius, "Das stehende Heer der Assyrerkönige und seine Organisation," *ZA* 24 (1910): 104–5, emphasized that the militia was the normal force for ninth-century Assyrian kings and that a standing, professional army was not introduced until the eighth century.

[10] Stillman and Tallis, *Armies*, 60; see also their excellent presentation on Assyrian military organization, pp. 26–31.

reign of Ramesses IX (1137–1120) refer to great numbers of barbarians—especially Libyans and Meshwesh—who were creating disturbances at Thebes.[11] Since Libyans and Meshwesh in Egypt were traditionally offensive infantrymen, perhaps we are justified in assuming that the troublemakers at Thebes were also professional infantrymen, whom the pharaoh had settled in Upper Egypt as a military reserve. Ultimately a Libyan, or more precisely a "chief of the Meshwesh," seized royal power and inaugurated the Twenty-Second Dynasty (ca. 940 B.C.).

Assyria was the one Late Bronze Age kingdom in which an offensive infantry was important, and so it is not surprising to find here a reliance on infantry in the early Iron Age. The only well-documented reign in the twelfth and eleventh centuries is that of Tiglath-Pileser I (1115–1077). When this king marched north into the Elazig region of eastern Anatolia he defeated 20,000 Mushkian tribesmen on "Mount Kashiari, a difficult region,"[12] and for that battle he must have had a formidable infantry. Still further north, he suppressed the Kaskans who had taken over the cities of Hatti, and he captured 4,000 of their men and 120 chariots.[13] To the east, Tiglath-Pileser had to confront the Gutians, a traditional scourge from the Zagros:

> The sons of the [mountains?] devised warfare in their hearts.
> They prepared for battle, they sharpened their weapons.
> The enemies initiated their war.
> All the highland(ers) were assembled clan by clan. . . .
> The Gutian seethed, aflame with terrifying splendor.
> All the armies of the mountains, the Confederation of the Ḫabḫu lands
> came to each other's aid in strength.[14]

Since Tiglath-Pileser carried the battle into the mountaineers' homeland, we must again imagine him relying primarily upon footsoldiers.

Anatolian warfare after the fall of the Hittite kingdom is quite unknown. Virtually all that we have are the Assyrian inscriptions cited above, which indicate that at the end of the twelfth century the Mushkians and Kaskans, at least, had very few chariots and a great many men on foot. This is of course what one would expect from barbarous tribesmen, and in Anatolia after the Catastrophe there evidently was no Great Kingdom (the kings of Carchemish, as already noted, usurped the title "Great King of Hatti" after the fall of Hattusas)—and perhaps no kingdoms at all.

---

[11] Gardiner, *Egypt*, 299.

[12] Luckenbill, *Ancient Records of Assyria and Babylonia*, vol. 1, no. 221.

[13] Ibid., no. 226.

[14] Victor Hurowitz and Joan Westenholz, "LKA 63: A Heroic Poem in Celebration of Tiglath-Pileser I's Muṣru-Qumanu Campaign," *Journal of Cuneiform Studies* 42 (1990): 5.

For Dark Age Greece we have the *in corpore* weapons found in Proto-geometric and Geometric graves, a few figured vases depicting combat, and of course the problematical battle descriptions provided by Homer. All three types of evidence would suggest that the Dark Age Greeks commonly fought on foot (arrowheads, for example, hardly appear at all in Dark Age graves). But that fairly obvious generalization was for a long time obscured by the authority of Aristotle. According to Aristotle,

> Among the Greeks, government from the beginning (after the end of kingship) depended on those who did the fighting in war. The earliest of the polities was based on the *hippeis*, since in war the decisive and overwhelming force was that of the *hippeis*; for without organized formations a hoplite force is useless, and among the ancients there was no experience in tactical matters. It was for that reason that the real strength was in the *hippeis*.[15]

Classicists understood Aristotle to mean that until the perfection of the hoplite phalanx (usually thought to have been attained in the early seventh century) the typical Greek battle featured the clash of a few noble cavalry-men. Since it was also understood that Greeks did not ordinarily use the bow, it was imagined that these early "knights" fought with thrusting spears. This picture, of armored and spear-thrusting knights dominating the battlefield in early Greece, was until the 1970s widely accepted.[16] But it does not stand up under careful scrutiny. P.A.L. Greenhalgh showed that although the Geometric "knights" may have owned horses, they did not fight from horseback; attended by a squire, the *hippeus* would ride to the battlefield and there dismount to fight as an infantryman.[17]

With the mounted lancers out of the way, we can now begin to see what warfare in Dark Age Greece may have looked like. Recent analyses of Homer's battle descriptions suggest that during the Dark Age the typical battle between Greek poleis featured massed infantries that were drawn up in a line, or *phalanx*, of spearmen (a mass, or a company several *phalanges* deep, was called a *stix*). Dueling nobles are essential for the poet's story, but in reality the *promachoi* were much less important than the anonymous multitude in whose front rank they stood.[18] The evidence from graves

---

[15] Aristotle, *Politics* 1297b; cf. 1289b, 1306a.

[16] See, for example, V. Ehrenberg, *The Greek State* (Oxford, 1960): 21: "Single combat which—almost exclusively—ruled the tactics of the age. . . survived in the name of the 'knights,' the *hippeis*." Cf. A. Alföldi, "Die Herrschaft der Reiterei in Griechenland und Rom nach dem Sturz der Könige," *Gestalt und Geschichte: Festschrift K. Schefold* (Berne, 1967): 13–47; J. Bury and R. Meiggs, *A History of Greece*, 4th ed. (London, 1975) 94.

[17] Greenhalgh, *Early Greek Warfare*, 40–61.

[18] For the organized, massed infantries of Homeric warfare see J. Latacz, *Kampfparänese, Kampfdarstellung und Kampfwirklichkeit in der Ilias, bei Kallinos und Tyrtaios* (Munich, 1977); and Hans van Wees, "Leaders of Men? Military Organization in the Iliad," *CQ* 36

suggests that a very small proportion of the adult males in a Dark Age community were able to afford both a sword and a spear, and defensive armor is conspicuously lacking.[19] In the Ionian poleis a relatively well armed *basileus* might therefore have had a sword, a spear, and a leather shield, and perhaps wore a helmet, corslet, and greaves all made of leather. The men under his command would have had no more than spears and shields. The Dorians were perhaps better armed: whether or not their name was derived from the *doru*,[20] these were "spearmen" par excellence and in the Geometric period formed a privileged military caste in Crete, Laconia, the Argolid, and other places where a non-Dorian population was protected and exploited by a Dorian elite. Among the Dorians there was no tradition of either chariotry or cavalry, nor even of wealthy *hippeis* riding to the battlefield.

Greek infantries in the Dark Age were hardly impressive by later standards, but the important point here is that an infantry was a community's principal—and, in most cases, its only—defense. We have seen that the noble cavalrymen, described from Aristotle's time to our own as the bulwark of the nascent polis, are imaginary. Nor was chariotry revived after the Catastrophe. Although a few wealthy individuals must have continued to use chariots for pleasure or prestige in the Dark Age, chariots were no longer used on the battlefield. This is indicated not only by Homer's ignorance of the subject but also by the complete lack of archaeological evidence for chariots in Greece between the twelfth century B.C., when they were represented on LH IIIC pots, and the eighth century, when the chariot reappears both on Geometric pottery and in bronze and terracotta figu-

---

(1986): 285–303. For criticism see Singor, "Nine against Troy," 17–62. On the role of the *basileis* as *promachoi* see Van Wees, "Kings in Combat: Battles and Heroes in the *Iliad*," *CQ* 38 (1988): 1–24.

[19] Snodgrass, *Arms and Armour*, 38.

[20] Classical Greeks derived the name of the Dorians from an eponymous Doros, son of Hellen. Moderns have often supposed that the Dorians got their name from tiny Doris, but the borrowing seems to have been reversed: the Spartans created Doris Metropolis as a counterweight to Athenian influence in the late fifth century. On Doris see now D. Rousset, "Les Doriens de la Metropole, I," *BCH* 113 (1989): 199–239. The derivation of Δωριεύς from δόρυ was accepted by Meyer in the second edition of *Geschichte des Altertums*, vol. 2, 570–71: "Die Dorer. . . sind ein kriegerische Stamm, dessen Name als 'Lanzenkämpfer' zu bezeichnen scheint." Hermann Bengtson, *Griechische Geschichte*, 4th ed. (Munich, 1969): 52, stated without further ado that *Dorieis* is indeed a "Kurzform" of *dorimachoi*. P. Ramat, "Sul nome dei Dori," *Parola del Passato* 16 (1961): 62–65, argued that *doru* was indeed the base of the name, but the *doru* Ramat had in mind was a tree rather than a spear (the tree being something of a totem for the "Dorians"). Singor, "Nine against Troy," 30, has most recently given the etymology lukewarm endorsement.

rines.[21] Thus the infantry militias of Dark Age Greece offer a sharp contrast to the chariot-based armies attested for the Late Helladic kingdoms.

Finally, we must look at the Levant and the dubious evidence that the Old Testament provides on post-Catastrophe warfare. For the first century and a half after the Catastrophe the various tribes of Israel and Judah were scarcely urbanized and had no centralized state. But late in the eleventh century the tribes of Israel appointed Saul as their king, with a residence at Gibeah, and soon thereafter the men of Judah made David king at Hebron. The fusion of these two kingdoms by David resulted in a highly centralized and remarkably wealthy regime, and the trappings of monarchy soon appeared. Along with splendid buildings (palace and temple) in Jerusalem came a magnificent display of horses and chariots. Solomon was known for his horses, and is reputed to have maintained four thousand chariot teams and twelve thousand cavalrymen (*parashim*).[22] If these fabulous figures are

---

[21] See Crouwel, *Chariots*, 143–44; Snodgrass, *Early Greek Armour and Weapons*, pp. 160–63; Greenhalgh, *Early Greek Warfare*, 38. The scenes of chariot combat on eighth-century Geometric kraters in Attica are not reflections of actual chariot warfare. As Snodgrass and Greenhalgh argue, the eighth-century artist was inspired by saga, by reports of chariots in use in the Near East, and by surviving Mycenaean representations of chariots.

[22] 2 Chronicles 9.25. At 1 Kings 4.26 Solomon is said to have had not four thousand but forty thousand *'urwōt* horses and chariots, and twelve thousand *parashim*; in this case the Chronicler's figure is more likely to be "correct" (which is to say that the textual tradition of 2 Chronicles 9.25 is sounder than the textual tradition of 1 Kings 4.26). The meaning of *'urwōt* has been well explained by G. I. Davies, "'*Urwōt* in I Kings 5:6 (Evv. 4:26) and the Assyrian Horse Lists," *Journal of Semitic Studies* 34 (1989): 25–38. Davies calls attention to Assyrian parallels suggesting that *'urwōt* does not mean "stalls" or "stables," as most translators have thought, but "teams." Whether Solomon in truth had four thousand teams of chariot horses and twelve thousand *parashim* is another question; if the figures are not grossly exaggerated, they might account for the resentment that Solomon's subjects harbored against him and his grandeur.

A less persuasive part of Davies's argument does away with Solomon's cavalry, leaving only the chariots. Davies concluded that the original meaning of 1 Kings 4.26 was as follows: "Solomon had 4000 teams of horses for his chariotry, namely 12,000 horses." The figure of four thousand, instead of forty thousand, is justified by the Septuagint reading and by the parallel account at 2 Chronicles 9.25. But that the Chronicler intended *parashim* as "horses" or "chariot horses"—saying, in effect, that the four thousand teams consisted of twelve thousand horses, three to each team—is most unlikely. According to Davies's argument the Chronicler, using so unfamiliar a term as *'urwōt*, accommodated his readers by spelling out for them what this obscure term meant (at p. 36n.35, Davies suggests that the conjunction be understood as an "explicative *waw*" and be translated not as "and" but as "namely"). But if a writer wanted to clarify for his readers that these four thousand *'urwōt* of horses were—in plain Hebrew—twelve thousand horses, he would surely have used the word *susim*. The very worst way to clarify the exotic term *'urwōt* would be to write that Solomon had "four thousand *'urwōt* of horses and twelve thousand *parashim*." The latter word must here mean "cavalrymen," as it does in other passages and as the Septuagint translators assumed it does here.

close to the mark, Solomon acquired the greatest horse troop that the ancient world had ever seen. But Solomon never went to war, and so it is difficult to say how these horsemen might have been deployed in a battle. Certainly there was no enemy in sight against whom such a gargantuan horse troop might have been used.

David, unlike his son, had been a warrior and in the early tenth century had established a kingdom that was perhaps the most powerful in the world. Renowned as a "slayer of myriads," David won his victories with footsoldiers.[23] We are told that when he captured a thousand chariots from Hadadezer of Zobah he "houghed" all but a hundred of the chariot teams.[24] The traditions about him quite consistently present him as making no use of chariots in battle and as fighting under the aegis of the infantryman's god, the Lord of Hosts.

David's infantry consisted of both professional "mighty men" and a levied militia.[25] The former group was relatively small (six hundred Gittites, the same number of Judahites, and the mysterious "Pelethite and Kerethite guards") and constituted his regular army. David's militia was said by the Chronicon to have numbered 288,000 men, but its actual strength is usually estimated at only a half or a third of that figure.[26] The "mighty men" were evidently well armed, whereas the militiamen may have had spears and shields but nothing else.

The farther back one goes in the history of the Israelite monarchy, the greater the role that one finds for the militiamen of the infantry. Saul seems to have had no regular army of professionals, and no horse troops. Traditions about his great victory over the Ammonites, as well as about his defeat at the hands of the Philistines, speak only of infantrymen (the Philistines, on the other hand, surely had horse troops, since Saul was hunted down on Mt. Gilboa by Philistine chariots and *parashim*). Finally, before the creation of the Israelite monarchy the people of Israel, as of Judah,

---

[23] Yadin, *Art of Warfare*, vol. 2, 285; Stillman and Tallis, *Armies*, 37.

[24] 2 Samuel 8.3–4 (cf. 1 Chronicles 18.3–4).

[25] This has been well treated by A. van Selms, "The Armed Forces of Israel under Saul and David," in *Studies on the Books of Samuel: Papers Read at the 3rd Meeting of Die O. T. Werkgemeenskap in Suid-Afrika* (1960): 55–66.

[26] Yadin, *Art of Warfare*, vol. 2, 279–82, argued that the figures from the Chronicler (1 Chronicles 27.1–15) in this instance were derived from an accurate source. The militia figures for the early monarchy in Israel were scaled down drastically by George Mendenhall, "The Census Lists of Numbers 1 and 26," *JBL* 77 (1968): 52–66. Whereas Numbers 1.32, for example, says that the number of those men in Ephraim who were "able to go forth to war" was 40,500, Mendenhall reduced the figure to a mere 500 men, organized in 40 units. But Mendenhall's argument rests on analogies from Mari; like most other scholars, of course, Mendenhall did not reckon with the revolutionary changes in the art of war that occurred between the seventeenth century and the tenth. In fact, the concept of a militia was unknown in seventeenth-century Mari.

depended for security entirely on a militia.[27] It is true that by the late eleventh century this style of fighting was no longer very effective: the league of Philistine cities, with a smaller but well-armed and regular force, soundly defeated the tribal militias rallied by the priests of Yahweh and added insult to injury by seizing the Ark of the Covenant. But in the twelfth century the tribesmen were evidently quite formidable.

Sheer numbers were essential to this early Israelite renown: "The forty thousand of Israel" (Judges 5.8) was probably an optimistic figure, but it suggests that a general mobilization of the tribes living in Israel could and did furnish tens of thousands of warriors. Although untrained and hardly well armed, tribesmen so numerous—especially when stirred to furor by oracles from the Lord of Hosts—must have been a force with which neither the coastal cities of Canaan nor the later Ramessids in Egypt cared to do battle. An index of how drastically warfare had changed in the Catastrophe is that thereafter the militiamen of Israel, without any horse troops at all, were able to maintain complete independence from the last Ramessids and the Twenty-First Dynasty kings of Egypt. Prior to the Catastrophe, the land of Israel had for almost four hundred years chafed under Egyptian hegemony, a condition so unthinkable in post-Catastrophe circumstances that tradition seems eventually to have transformed it into four hundred years of Israelite "bondage" in the land of Egypt.

[27] Yadin, *Art of Warfare*, vol. 2, 284.

Chapter Thirteen

CHANGES IN ARMOR AND WEAPONS
AT THE END OF THE BRONZE AGE

I N A FEW DECADES before and after 1200 B.C. the eastern Mediterranean world underwent a transformation in the tools of war. Aegean archaeologists, as noted in chapter 9, have long been aware that new types of weapons and armor came into use at the end of the LH IIIB period, and some archaeologists have recently emphasized the range and comprehensiveness of the innovations. As Jeremy Rutter pointed out at the Brown Conference, the rapidity with which "virtually all forms of offensive and defensive weaponry" change ca. 1200 stands in sharp contrast to "the conservatism of developments in military gear during the palatial period."[1]

But the findings of archaeologists have not yet been translated into history. Although there has been some suspicion that the innovations apparent from the material record must reflect the advent of a new style of warfare, historians have barely begun to explore what this new style and its significance might have been.[2] In particular, it has not yet been proposed that the new types of armor and weaponry reflect a historic shift from chariot warfare to infantry warfare. That the new arms and armor belonged to footsoldiers has of course been clear all along, but the significance of this fact has been obscured by the assumption that infantries had played the primary role in warfare all through the Late Bronze Age. Having seen, in chapters 10–12, that before the Catastrophe chariot warfare was the norm for the eastern Mediterranean kingdoms and that offensive infantries came to the fore in the early Iron Age, we are now in a position to appreciate the historical significance of the military innovations that archaeologists have documented for the decades of the Catastrophe.

ARMOR

It was, first of all, during the Catastrophe that the infantryman's corslet made its appearance. Prior to ca. 1200, corslets were designed for the chariot crew. The mail-covered, leather *sariam*, a robe reaching to the calf or even the ankle, provided reasonable protection for a man in a chariot,

[1] Rutter, "Cultural Novelties," 67.
[2] For the suggestions of Muhly and Sandars see p. 103.

and for him the fact that it was difficult to run in such a robe was not a serious liability. Apparently some infantrymen in the Late Bronze Age wore a simplified, much less expensive version of the charioteer's corslet: the Luxor relief of the Battle of Kadesh portrays a line of Hittite auxiliaries in full stride, and most of them wear wide-skirted and ankle-length "robes."[3] Possibly the robes were made of leather rather than of linen, but obviously they were not covered with metal scales.

Alternatively, some Late Bronze Age skirmishers went into battle wearing only a helmet and a kilt. A parallel here would be the primitive tribesmen of a century or two ago, who were as naked in battle as in everyday life. The *shardana* in service to the pharaohs are shown with no defensive armor other than a helmet, and the same is true for the Pylian warriors in the "Battle Scene" fresco (they wear boar's tusk helmets, and kilts).

There is no documentary or pictorial evidence at all for "heavily armored" infantrymen in the Late Bronze Age. That footsoldiers in Mycenaean Greece wore bronze armor is sometimes asserted on the basis of an *in corpore* find: a plate-bronze corslet found in 1960, in a chamber tomb at Dendra.[4] The Dendra Corslet, which dates from late in the fifteenth century B.C., has been identified by several scholars as an infantryman's corslet and as an example of the kind of armor that Mycenaean infantrymen would generally have worn in the LH II and LH IIIA period.[5] Such an interpretation, however, cannot be correct. The Dendra Corslet encases the body from the neck almost to the knees, and the girdle of bronze around the thighs must have prevented the wearer not only from running but from even walking at a normal pace. It must therefore have been worn by a man who in battle would be required to step only occasionally, and then in half-strides, and such conditions point necessarily to a chariot crewman. It is also relevant that the Dendra Corslet bears some resemblance to one of the corslets that a Linear B ideogram records as being distributed to chariot crews.[6]

In the Catastrophe, on the other hand, we have pictorial evidence for infantrymen's corslets. The Medinet Habu relief of the sea battle in 1179 shows that not only the Philistine and *Shekelesh* aggressors but also the Egyptian defenders were protected with waist-length corslets and leather skirts. The corslets were apparently strengthened with strips of metal sewn

[3] Wreszinski, *Atlas*, vol. 2, plate 87; cf. Sandars, *Sea Peoples*, fig. 13.

[4] For description see Catling, "Panzer," 96–98. On the tomb see Paul Åström, *The Cuirass Tomb and Other Finds at Dendra* (Göteborg, 1977).

[5] Harding, *Mycenaeans and Europe*, 151 and 174 (see p. 175 for reconstruction drawing, by K. McBarron, of Dendra warrior as an infantryman, with sword and spear); Crouwel, *Chariots*, 127.

[6] Bouzek, *Aegean*, 108.

to the leather.[7] In the Aegean, too, corslets for infantrymen appear only at the end of the IIIB or beginning of the IIIC period. The Mycenaean infantrymen depicted on the Warrior Vase and Warrior Stele wear corslets. In place of metal strips, these corslets seem to have copper or bronze scales.[8] And like their Philistine and Egyptian contemporaries, the Mycenaean warriors wear leather skirts that reach to midthigh. But it is not just at Mycenae, and not only at the transition from IIIB to IIIC that the infantryman's corslet appears in post-Catastrophe Greece. Figured IIIC sherds from several other sites show footsoldiers (although some riding in chariots) wearing hedgehog helmets, waist-length corslets, and leather skirts.[9]

Every reader of Homer knows that the Achaeans who sacked Troy were "well greaved," and specialists are quite aware that metal greaves came suddenly into vogue ca. 1200.[10] Again, however, we must emphasize the obvious: the warriors who used the new armor were infantrymen. This innovation was mostly limited to the Greek world, perhaps because all through the Late Bronze Age men in Greece protected their lower legs with leather "spats" when at work (so, for example, old Laertes wears *knemides* as he digs around his fruit trees at *Odyssey* 24.228–29) or at war (in the Pylos "Battle Scene" fresco [see plate 2], the Pylian warriors are naked above the waist but wear leather spats). And Late Helladic smiths had occasionally made metal greaves: ca. 1400, the Dendra warrior whose corslet we have just discussed wore bronze greaves.[11] With his plate corslet protecting him from collar to knee, and with greaves protecting at least the fronts of his lower legs, the chariot crewman buried at Dendra was armored as completely, although not as comfortably, as a Nuzi charioteer whose *sariam* reached from collar to midcalf. Thus metal greaves may in Mycenaean Greece have been worn now and then by chariot crewmen who for some reason preferred plate armor to scale armor. But it is unlikely that infantrymen before ca. 1200 wore metal greaves.

Thereafter it is quite a different story. In Cyprus, two burials dating from ca. 1200 have produced bronze greaves. Another pair has been found in a chamber tomb at Kallithea in Achaea, dating from the early twelfth cen-

---

[7] For discussion and color illustration see Yadin, *Art of Warfare*, vol. 2, 251 and 340–41; for a detailed discussion of these corslets see Lorimer, *Homer and the Monuments*, 199–200; cf. Catling, "Panzer," 103.

[8] Catling, ibid., 105; Snodgrass, *Arms and Armour*, 31.

[9] Catling, ibid., 105.

[10] N. K. Sandars, "North and South at the End of the Mycenaean Age: Aspects of an Old Problem," *Oxford Journal of Archaeology* 2 (1983): 43–68; Harding, *Mycenaeans and Europe*, 178–80.

[11] On the greaves see Catling, "Beinschienen," in Buchholz and Wiesner, *Kriegswesen*, vol. 1, 153.

tury (the same tomb yielded a Naue Type II sword).[12] Finally, yet another pair, found in 1960 on the southern slope of the Athenian acropolis, seem also to date from the twelfth century B.C.[13] All these twelfth-century Greek and Cypriote greaves were evidently locally made and were perhaps extemporized by local bronzesmiths. Although Goliath was said to have worn bronze greaves, they were never popular in the Near East. Nor do they seem to have been worn in temperate Europe before they appear in Greece. Harding notes that the earliest greaves thus far found in Italy belong to the tenth century, while those from central Europe and the Balkans "appear to start at the same time as the late Mycenaean examples."[14]

After the middle of the twelfth century, greaves disappear from the archaeological record in Greece and do not reappear until the end of the eighth century. Catling assumes that in the Dark Age leather leggings came back into use.[15] Various scholars have noted that Homer knew little about greaves, other than the fact that the Achaeans had them, and his vagueness may indicate that in his time bronze greaves were only a memory. It thus seems that the use of metal greaves in the early twelfth century was a short-lived experiment, restricted mostly to Greece and Cyprus. The obsolescence of the bronze greave after ca. 1150 can most easily be explained as a result of the general poverty, and especially the scarcity of bronze, that Snodgrass has documented in *The Dark Age of Greece*. This would be all the more understandable if, in an age when bronze was very dear, the bronze greave was regarded as not very "cost-effective." The bronze greaves from the early twelfth century are not impressive pieces. The Kallithea specimens were simply hammered out of sheet bronze, and Catling noted that the smith made no effort to model the greaves to the musculature of the leg. And all these early greaves are relatively thin: those from Enkomi are two millimeters thick, but modern experiments have shown that even a thickness of three millimeters can be entirely cut through by a slashing sword.[16]

Perhaps the most important item of defensive armor that comes into use at the end of the thirteenth century is the round shield, with its conical surface running back from the boss to the rim.[17] Held with a center-grip,

[12] Ibid., 152–53; for a full description of the Kallithea tomb and its contents see N. Yalouris, "Mykenische Bronzeschutzwaffen," *MDAI* 75 (1960): 42–67.

[13] The find was originally assigned to the Geometric period but has been redated by Penelope Mountjoy, "The Bronze Greaves from Athens: A Case for a LH IIIC Date," *Opuscula Atheniensia* 15 (1984): 135–46.

[14] Harding, *Mycenaeans and Europe*, 179.

[15] Catling, "Beinschienen," 158.

[16] Ibid., 156–57.

[17] On shields see Heide Borchhardt, "Frühe griechische Schildformen," in Buchholz and Wiesner, *Kriegswesen*, vol. 1, 1–56.

this symmetrical shield ("balanced all-around" is a common Homeric epithet for the *aspis*) made up for its relatively small size by a superior design. Until the introduction of the round shield, footsoldiers of the eastern Mediterranean kingdoms carried large shields of various shapes. The Mycenaeans in the LH I and II periods (and possibly also in LH IIIA and B, although evidence is lacking) favored the huge "figure eight" shield, which enveloped the warrior on three sides from neck to ankles, while providing some freedom of movement for the arms at the indentations. An alternative for the Mycenaeans, in use also in Egypt, was the slightly smaller "half-cylinder" shield, with sides arching back. Although such a shield protected a man from neck to shins, the absence of arm indentations must have severely restricted his wielding of an offensive weapon. The Hittite shield seems to have been rectangular and relatively flat but had scalloped sides or "cutouts" for the arms. The standard Egyptian shield was oblong with a rounded top, thus offering some protection for the neck.[18] All these Late Bronze Age shields, if held frontally and at the proper height, would have covered most of a footsoldier's body, far more in fact than did a round shield. The Homeric *sakos*—the great shield—was evidently used with a long lance (the *enchos*), both items indicating an intention to keep one's distance in dispatching an opponent. The size and design of these pre-Catastrophe shields are quite understandable if they were intended for defense primarily against missiles, and only occasionally against hand-to-hand weapons.

The round shield, on the other hand, was certainly meant for a hand-to-hand fighter. For him, agility and mobility counted for much, and he sacrificed the security of a full-body shield in order to be fast on his feet and to have free use of his offensive arm. The round shields varied in size from less than two to more than three feet in diameter, but even the largest did not cover a man below midthigh. But because it was perfectly balanced, the round shield was unusually maneuverable. That quality, together with its uniformly sloping surfaces, gave the warrior good protection at the spot that he needed it.

With one exception, there are no round shields attested anywhere in the eastern Mediterranean kingdoms before the late thirteenth century.[19] The exception—from ca. 1270—appears in a Luxor relief of the storming of Depur, a Hittite stronghold in the Levant, by troops of Ramesses the Great. Round shields are carried by several of Ramesses' skirmishers in horned

---

[18] On these Late Bronze Age types see Borchhardt, "Schildformen," 6–17 and 25–27, and the foldout following p. 56.

[19] Ibid., 30: "Im gesamten ägäischen Bereich wie im Vorderen Orient ist der runde Schild erst mit dem Ende des 13. Jahrhunderts eindeutig nachzuweisen, nach dem jeweiligen Zerstörungshorizont, der eben mit der Seevölkerbewegung in Zusammenhang gebracht werden kann."

helmets, and the likelihood is fairly strong that the Egyptian artist intended these figures to represent Sardinian auxiliaries.[20] Thus there is reason to believe that the round shield was introduced to the eastern Mediterranean by barbarian skirmishers from the west. Its ultimate provenance is unknown. Although round shields were common in temperate Europe after 1000, Harding found that only one has been assigned (by at least some scholars) a date earlier than the twelfth century.[21]

Although Sardinian runners were using the round shield on Near Eastern battlefields in the early thirteenth century, it evidently remained a specialty of the barbarian skirmisher for another sixty or seventy years. From late in the thirteenth century or early in the twelfth come several representations of the round shield, found at Megiddo: one on a sherd and two more on ivory plaques.[22] The possibility that ca. 1200 the round shield was becoming familiar in the southern Levant is strengthened by the fact that all the aggressors who attacked Ramesses III in 1179 had round shields. In the Medinet Habu reliefs (see plates 6 and 7) it is carried not only by the western Mediterranean warriors in horned helmets—both the *shardana* fighting for Ramesses and the *Shekelesh* fighting against him—but also by the Philistines and *Tjekker*. Ramesses' Egyptian infantrymen, however, carry the traditional Egyptian shield (oblong, with rounded top).

In the Aegean the round shield—the *aspis*—seems to have come into use rather suddenly soon after 1200 and then quickly become standard. The earliest evidence for it in Greece may be the Tiryns Shield-Bearers Krater, dating to the transition from LH IIIB to IIIC.[23] On the Warrior Vase (see plate 8) and Warrior Stele the spearmen of all three lines carry shields that are round except for a scallop on the bottom.[24] These shields, carried by men in close-order formations, are noticeably larger than those carried by the skirmishers. The round shield also appears on LH IIIC sherds from Tiryns and Nauplia, on a vase from Mycenae, on two mirror-handles from Cyprus, and in the hands of the "Ingot God" from Enkomi.[25]

The innovation of the infantryman's corslet, greaves, and the round shield in the armies of the eastern Mediterranean reflects the importance that was suddenly attached, during the Catastrophe, to hand-to-hand fighting. The round shield had long been favored by Sardinian skirmishers but was now in general demand. The infantryman's corslet was perhaps

[20] Ibid., 28.

[21] Harding, *Mycenaeans and Europe*, 177. The single early specimen was found in west Bohemia.

[22] Yadin, *Art of Warfare*, vol. 2, 242, dates them to ca. 1200. Cf. Borchhardt, "Schildformen," 30.

[23] Vermeule and Karageorghis, *Mycenaean Pictorial Vase Painting*, 108–9 and plate X.1.

[24] Ibid., plate XI.42.

[25] Ibid., plates XI.1a and 1b, and XI.28; Borchhardt, "Schildformen," 29 and 31.

improvised by the defenders of the eastern kingdoms, in order to steel themselves for a type of combat that was unfamiliar and unnerving. The use of greaves may have begun among either the sackers or the defenders of the Aegean palaces (Homer associates greaves with the marauders at Troy, while the *in corpore* evidence shows them in use by defenders of the IIIC communities). Altogether, the armored infantryman was in large part a creation of the Catastrophe.

JAVELINS, SPEARS, AND LANCES

In weapons, as in armor, there were major innovations at the end of the Bronze Age. Although the advent of a new type of sword is perhaps the most conspicuous and dramatic of these innovations, there seems to have been another that was equally important but has hardly been noticed. I refer to the proliferation of a small, long-range weapon that we may call a javelin, although it could also be called a large dart. This was not the javelin familiar from modern track-and-field events but a much smaller missile. The weapon that seems to have played an important role in the Catastrophe was perhaps only half or a third the size of today's sporting javelin, which is almost nine feet long and weighs almost two pounds (eight hundred grams). A closer parallel to the Bronze Age weapon would be the Roman *iaculum*, which Polybius (6.22) describes as two cubits long and thick as a finger.

The Medinet Habu relief shows that in 1179 the typical Philistine or *Tjekker* warrior carried two spearlike weapons, slightly over a meter in length and with diameters small enough that two could be tightly grasped in the palm of the hand. In discussing the relief, Yadin reasonably concluded that these weapons were javelins.[26] He did not, however, see their presence as remarkable, and in most subsequent discussions of the arms of "the Sea Peoples" the javelin has not appeared at all.[27] Even highly specialized studies have overlooked the popularity of the javelin in the late second millennium. De Maigret's classification of Near Eastern spears recognized two types of javelin but noted no increase in their use toward the end of the Bronze Age. On the Aegean side, Lorimer made no mention of javelins, and in Avila's *Lanzenspitzen* there is no category for javelins (as a result, in this otherwise very useful typological study javelin heads must be sought among either the spearheads or the arrowheads). In discussing the importance of javelins in thirteenth- and twelfth-century warfare, then, we cannot simply summarize expert opinion but shall have to look at the primary evidence in some detail.

[26] Yadin, *Art of Warfare*, vol. 2, 251–52.

[27] Neither Sandars's *Sea Peoples* nor Strobel's *Seevölkersturm* (both of which discuss the aggressors' weaponry at some length) mentions the javelin.

It is generally recognized that in the Late Bronze Age javelins were used by hunters.[28] One fresco at Tiryns shows a young man who is presumed to be a hunter shouldering two javelins grasped in the left hand; another shows two hunters, each with a pair of javelins in the right hand.[29] A third fresco, at Pylos, shows a hunter about to throw a javelin at a running stag.[30] Since the Homeric word *aiganeé* apparently means, etymologically, something like "goat spear," that weapon may originally have been used for hunting wild goats.[31] The javelin as a hunter's weapon was common in antiquity and among primitive tribes down to our own time.[32] Strabo (4.4.3) described the Gauls' skill in hunting birds with javelins, declaring that the Gallic hunters were able to throw their javelins farther (and apparently with no less accuracy) than they could shoot an arrow.

In classical times the javelin was of little importance on the battlefield: whether hoplites threw javelins at each other before closing is debated, but it is agreed that in either case the "real" fighting did not begin until the thrusting spears were brought into play. In Rome, the *velites* threw their *iacula*, but it was the legionary's *pilum* (a much heavier missile) and sword that determined the outcome of the battle. In primitive societies, on the other hand, the hunter's javelin was also the primary weapon when a tribe was involved in a *guerrilla* with its neighbors. In Herodotus's catalog (7.71–79) of Xerxes' army the javelin is the main weapon of the Libyan, Paphlagonian, Thracian, Mysian, and Marian contingents, and in still another group of auxiliaries each man carried two "wolf-destroying" spears. Thucydides (3.97–98) gives us a vivid picture of the Aetolian javelineers, whom the Athenians suspected of eating raw meat, picking off "the best men of Athens" when Demosthenes led a force of hoplites into the Aetolian mountains. In Arrian's history of Alexander's campaign, some of the most memorable chapters feature the heroics of the thousand Agrianes, javelin men from the mountains of Paeonia. But these exploits of the javelineer were exceptions to the rule that in classical antiquity javelins were of limited military value.[33]

Toward the end of the second millennium, however, this humble weapon seems to have enjoyed a brief prominence. For the "hunting" of chariot horses the javelin must have been ideal: although it would seldom have

[28] See Olaf Höckmann, "Lanze und Speer," in Buchholz, *Kriegswesen*, vol. 2, 289–90.

[29] Höckmann, "Lanze und Speer," figs. 74a and b. The frescoes belong to the earlier and later Tiryns palace respectively.

[30] Lang, *Palace of Nestor*, plate 12 (no. 16 H 43).

[31] Höckmann, "Lanze und Speer," 315.

[32] E. Norman Gardiner, "Throwing the Javelin," *JHS* 27 (1907): 257, noted that the thonged javelin "is essentially the weapon of less highly civilized peoples. It is a weapon of the chase, a weapon of the common people, but it plays little part in the heavily equipped citizen armies of Greece and Rome."

[33] On the lightly armed javelineers of classical Greece see Snodgrass, *Arms and Armour*, 67 and 78–80.

killed the horse that it hit, the javelin would surely have brought it to a stop, thus immobilizing the other horse, the vehicle, and the crew. Composite bows were appropriate for the chariot warrior, but for a runner a far preferable long-range weapon would have been the javelin. Javelins are thrown on the run, whereas an infantry bowman would have to shoot from either a crouching position or a flat-footed stance (in either case offering chariot archers a stationary target). In addition, the javelineer could carry a small shield, whereas the archer had to use both hands to work his bow. That javelins were in fact used against chariots in the Late Bronze Age is clear from Ramesses the Great's account of his valor at Kadesh: in the "poetic" inscription Ramesses boasts that the Hittites were unable either to shoot their bows or to hurl their javelins at him as he charged against them in his chariot.[34]

The Agrianes mentioned above show the efficiency of javelineers against a chariot force. When he learned that Darius had a hundred scythed chariots in the middle of his line at Gaugamela, Alexander responded by placing his Agrianes (as well as Balakros's javelineers) as a screen for his heavy infantry. The mountain men were deadly marksmen, and not one Persian chariot got through the screen.[35] An argument can be made, despite the fact that the evidence is exiguous, that something similar must have happened time and again during the Catastrophe, and that the javelin played a key role in bringing the era of chariot warfare to an end. A horde of javelineers swarming through a chariot host would have destroyed it: at forty or fifty meters a team of horses would even at the gallop have made a far easier target for a javelineer than he—small, running, and protected by his shield—would have made for the chariot archer.

From the centuries before the Catastrophe there are occasional illustrations of what seem to be javelins carried by warriors, although these are somewhat larger than those carried by the Philistines in 1179. A few of the Shoshu tribesmen whom Seti I defeated early in the thirteenth century may have brought javelins to the contest with the Egyptian chariots, since in a relief (see plate 9) one tribesman is depicted grasping two thin spears of moderate length in his right hand.[36] The same was true when Seti's son, Ramesses the Great, campaigned against the tribesmen.[37] In the Aegean, javelins seem to be carried by the captain (but not by his men, who evidently carry thrusting spears) in the "Captain of the Blacks" fresco: lying across his shoulder are two long and thin lines, which may represent the

[34] Gardiner, *Kadesh*, P135–40 and P160–65.

[35] Arrian, *Anab*. 3.13.5.

[36] *Battle Reliefs of King Sety I*, plate 3.

[37] For relief showing a Shoshu warrior grasping two thin and fairly short "spears" in his right hand see Yadin, *Art of Warfare*, vol. 1, 233.

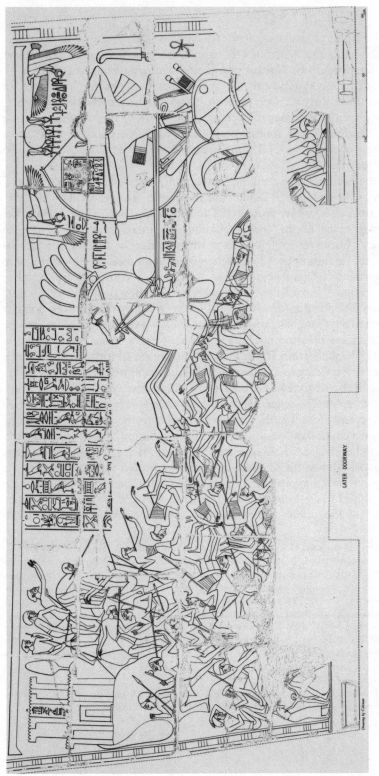

LATER DOORWAY

Drawing by Coleman

PLATE 9. Seti I attacking Shoshu Bedouin in Canaan. Line drawing of relief from Amun temple at Karnak

slender shafts of javelins.[38] If the fresco depicts a squad of skirmishers on their way to a battle, perhaps the captain intended to engage the enemy at long range while his Nubian troops closed in hand-to-hand combat with their thrusting spears. Finally, a few short javelins are portrayed in thirteenth-century warfare: these are tassel-stabilized darts, hardly a meter in length, carried on Egyptian chariots (see plate 1). Bonnet observed that this "Wurfpfeil" first appears on Nineteenth-Dynasty chariots, the crews apparently keeping several of these missiles available for use at a range too close for a bow.[39]

In the twelfth century military javelins are portrayed in greater numbers. There is, first of all, no doubt that the javelin was the weapon that the Philistines and *Tjekker* brought to Djahi in 1179. The Medinet Habu relief portrays many of the enemy holding two small (three- or four-foot) "spears" but never using one for a thrust. Since the fighting is hand-to-hand, the javelins appear to be a useless encumbrance. But it was not only the enemies of Egypt who used javelins in the twelfth century. Another relief shows them in the hands of Ramesses III's own barbarian skir- mishers,[40] evidently for use against enemy infantrymen (this king is not known to have fought against a chariot army). In Greece too we can see the importance of the short javelin as a military weapon in the twelfth century. An LH IIIC sherd from Tiryns shows a warrior armed with javelins.[41] Since the warrior is riding in a chariot, we may identify him as a skirmisher on his way to the battle zone rather than as an infantryman who fought in a close- order company. Another LH IIIC skirmisher is represented on a krater sherd recently found in the *Unterburg* at Tiryns: the warrior in this scene rides on a chariot and carries two javelins in addition to his round shield.[42] Yet another IIIC sherd, this one from Lefkandi, seems to show (the scene is too poorly drawn for us to be certain) an armored warrior holding two javelins.[43] It thus appears that by the early twelfth century javelineers were to be found in the kings' armies as well as among their barbarian oppo- nents. The kingdoms' employment of javelin men probably began before

---

[38] See, for example, Höckmann, "Lanze und Speer," 288–90. Snodgrass, *Early Greek Armour and Weapons*, 115, suggested that the two lines (almost as long as the captain himself) may be outlines of a single spear; but the captain's body is visible between the lines, and if the lines do outline a single spear, it is massive, with a diameter almost as great as the captain's arm. The black man who follows the captain seems to carry a single spear of normal diameter (see Evans, *Palace of Minos*, vol. 2, 2, plate xiii).

[39] Bonnet, *Waffen*, 105–6. For this thirteenth-century innovation see also Yadin, *Art of Warfare*, vol. 1, 88, and his illustration at pp. 240–41.

[40] See Sandars, *Sea Peoples*, fig. 14.

[41] Vermeule and Karageorghis, *Mycenaean Pictorial Vase Painting*, no. XI.18.

[42] Ibid., no. XI.28.

[43] Vermeule and Karageorghis, in ibid., no. XI.61 (p. 136), suggest that the sherd portrays "a sharp-faced soldier in a crested helmet with two light javelins and an oval shield."

the Catastrophe, with runners using javelins to assist in bringing down enemy chariot teams, but the twelfth-century javelineers of Tiryns and Lefkandi presumably threw most often at a human target.

There is a bit of literary evidence that late in the second millennium the javelin was used against footsoldiers. In the *Iliad* there are occasional references to *akontes*, and when Pandaros shoots Menelaus with the bow Menelaus's life is saved by the waistband that he wore as "a barrier against *akontes*" (*Iliad* 4.137). A more surprising source is the story of David and Goliath. Yadin presented an ingenious argument that the story was originally about an Israelite who killed a famous Philistine warrior whose weapon was a javelin.[44] We all know that Goliath carried a spear "like unto a weaver's beam," but that does not help much in a world even less familiar with looms than with spears. Yadin explored the term מנור א׳רגים and found that it has nothing to do with size: it was, instead, a shaft of very slender proportions. What was distinctive about it, however, were the loops that it carried. Yadin concluded that the original Hebrew story described a Philistine warrior who carried a spear equipped with a throwing-thong (the *ankyle* of the classical Greeks, and the *amentum* of the Romans). With a thong spiraled around the shaft, a warrior could rifle a javelin as he threw it, thus adding to its accuracy and its range. Although the story of Goliath and his spear "like unto a weaver's beam" was eventually attached to King David, it was also told of Benaiah of Kabzeel (1 Chronicles 11.22–23) and Elhanan of Bethlehem (2 Samuel 21.19) and may well have originated in a real event.[45] It would appear that the use of the thonged javelin was exceptional in Canaan late in the second millennium and was perhaps limited to a few warriors in Philistia. In Greece the thonged javelin may have been especially distinctive of the north and of Thessaly in particular.[46]

How much *in corpore* evidence we have for the javelin in the second millennium is difficult to say. Many bronze weapon-heads from the period have been found, but in the absence of the shafts one cannot be certain whether the heads were attached to spears, javelins, or arrows. Because the military use of a short, dartlike javelin has scarcely been recognized, however, I believe it likely that many javelin heads from the late second millennium have been erroneously identified as arrowheads.

De Maigret's classification does assign one type of socketed "lance-head" to a javelin, and on this type there should be no argument. Tipo B 7 ("giavellotti a lama triangolare acuta") is large enough—most specimens

---

[44] Yadin, "Goliath's Javelin and the מנור א׳רגים," *PEQ* (1955), 58–69.

[45] On the conflations and contradictions in the story as told in the Masoretic text see Emanuel Tov, "The David and Goliath Saga," *Bible Review* (1986): 34–41.

[46] Euripides' reference (*Bacchae*, 1205) to "Thessalian *ankylomata*" indicates that his audience associated the thonged javelin with Thessaly and assumed its use there in the heroic period.

are about 10 or 12 centimeters long—that it can hardly have come from an arrow; but since the sockets of this type are barely wider than .01m, neither could it have been attached to a thrusting spear. The forty-three specimens of Tipo B 7 heads are almost without exception from the Levant (especially Megiddo) and date from the Middle and the Late Bronze Age.[47] Thus it appears that socketed javelins, with thin (and, one would suppose, short) shafts, were in use in the Levant all through the second millennium.

In the Aegean we also find a number of socketed weapon-heads, most dating from late in the LH III period, which are reasonably identified as javelin heads. Many of these, it is worth pointing out, were found in northwest Greece, just beyond the frontier of the Mycenaean world.[48] Because the "Epirote" specimens have faceted, solid-ring sockets, rather than the split-ring sockets characteristic of Mycenaean spearheads, Avila proposes that they are the southernmost extension of types that originated in the Balkans.[49] We may note that socketed javelin heads have also been found in Italy in contexts dating to the third quarter of the second millennium.[50]

Despite opinion to the contrary, it is also very likely that a somewhat smaller head, this one tanged rather than socketed, came from a javelin. Heads of this type (see figure 2) have an elliptical blade and vary in length from ca. 7 to 13 centimeters (including both tang and blade). They were in use all through the Late Bronze Age[51] but enjoyed their greatest vogue during the twelfth and eleventh centuries B.C. Although found primarily in the Near East, they were also used in Greece. These heads were certainly used in hunting, but there is no doubt that they were also used in battle: one of them was found embedded in the dorsal vertebrae of a man buried at Ugarit.[52] Most often they have been identified as arrowheads, despite the fact that even the shortest is approximately twice the size of the average military arrowhead.[53] In part, I suspect, they have been identified as arrow-

[47] De Maigret, *Lance*, 154–67.

[48] In Avila's *Lanzenspitzen*, nos. 143–60 are all "aus Epeiros," and all measure between 10 and 20 cm. in length, including blade and socket. The dateable specimens come from the LH IIIB or IIIC period. Cf. Snodgrass's Types B and C (*Early Greek Armour and Weapons*, 119–20).

[49] Avila, ibid., 67; Snodgrass, *Early Greek Armour and Weapons*, 119, calls his Type B (found especially in Epirus and Kephallenia) "a well-known Danubian type."

[50] J. M. Coles and A. F. Harding, *The Bronze Age in Europe* (New York, 1979): 179–80. Coles and Harding date these javelin heads from Cascina Ranza, near Milan, to the "earlier Bronze Age" (shortly before 1300).

[51] More than thirty were recovered from the fourteenth-century shipwreck off Ulu Burun; see Cemal Pulak, "The Bronze Age Shipwreck at Ulu Burun, Turkey: 1985 Campaign," *AJA* 92 (1988): 23–24.

[52] The skeleton was found in Grave 75 at Ras Shamra, with pottery from late LH IIIA or early LH IIIB. See Avila, *Lanzenspitzen*, 112–13.

[53] Since we have no catalog of Near Eastern arrowheads, I base my generalization on Avila's findings for the Aegean. Most of the Late Bronze Age arrowheads in his *Lanzen- und*

heads simply because typologists have no classification for a small, dartlike javelin. On the Near Eastern side, de Maigret arbitrarily established a length of 11 centimeters as the minimum for the head of a *giavellotto*; de Maigret duly recognized as javelins the eleven elliptical tanged heads that met this qualification, but he excluded the scores that fell below 11 centimeters, leaving them to be dealt with by an eventual typologist of Near Eastern arrowheads.[54]

More than a dozen heads of the same type have been found in Greece, but these Greek specimens have been classified by Avila as *Pfeilspitzen*.[55] Although these heads would have met de Maigret's length requirement (they average 11 centimeters in length), Avila assumed that "spearheads" must be socketed and that a tanged head could only have come from an arrow. That assumption, which is certainly untenable for the Near East, is probably invalid for Greece too, since a Tiryns fresco seems to portray javelins whose heads are tanged rather than socketed.[56]

What makes the matter especially pertinent for us is that weapons with such a head were clearly instrumental in the Catastrophe. In the destruction level of the central city at Ugarit thirteen such weapon-heads were found, not in a hoard but scattered in the debris.[57] They must therefore

---

Pfeilspitzen have no shaft attachment: the v-base of the blade was simply pressed into the end of the shaft. Looking at all of these Klasse 1 specimens (nos. 163 to 687G), I find that the vast majority are less than 3 cm. long. For example, of the 318 arrowheads from twelfth-century Pylos, the longest is 2.58 cm. and the median 1.84 cm. All tanged heads (nos. 688 through 773) Avila classifies as Klasse 2 arrowheads. These are considerably larger, the median being approximately 4.5 cm. But if my contention is correct that heads over 7 cm. came from javelins, the typical tanged arrowhead would measure a bit less than 4 cm. The sole arrowhead found in Troy VIIa, barbed and tanged, measured 3.9 cm. (a similar specimen from Troy VI measured 3.8 cm.): see Blegen et al, *Troy*, vol. 3: *Settlements VIIa, VIIb, and VIII* (Princeton, 1958): fig. 219. Supporting evidence may be available from a much later date: Mordechai Gichon and Michaela Vitale, "Arrow-Heads from Ḥorvat ʿEqed," *IEJ* 41 (1991): 242–57, report that at this Hellenistic-Roman site forty-three tanged military arrowheads are well enough preserved to be measured. The median length is 3.6 cm., and none of these tanged heads measures over 6.1 cm.

[54] In reference to his Tipo A 7 ii, de Maigret, *Lance*, 90, notes that these javelin heads had morphological parallels to Levantine arrowheads of the Late Bronze Age. The eleven heads in this group come from Hazor (no. 1, undated); Ugarit (nos. 2–4, fourteenth and thirteenth centuries); Alalakh (no. 5, thirteenth or twelfth centuries); Tarsus (no. 6, 700–520 B.C.); Boghazköy (no. 7, fourteenth or thirteenth centuries); and Assur (nos. 8–11, Old or Middle Assyrian). Although no. 2 measures 30 cm. in length, the others range between 11 and 18 cm.

[55] Compare de Maigret's Tipo A 7 ii javelin heads (at *Lance*, 89–91, with fig. 20) and Avila's Klasse 2f arrowheads (*Lanzenspitzen*, 112–13, with plate 28).

[56] Höckmann, "Lanze und Speer," 290: "die Spitzen offenbar mittles eines Schaftdorns in den vorn knaufartig verdickten Holzschaft gesteckt sind."

[57] Marie-José Chavane, "Instruments de bronze," in M. Yon et al., *Ras Shamra—Ougarit III. Le Centre de la ville: 38e–44e Campagnes (1978–1984)*, 357. Chavane, I am happy to note, does not rule out javelins ("treize pointes de flèches ou de javeline").

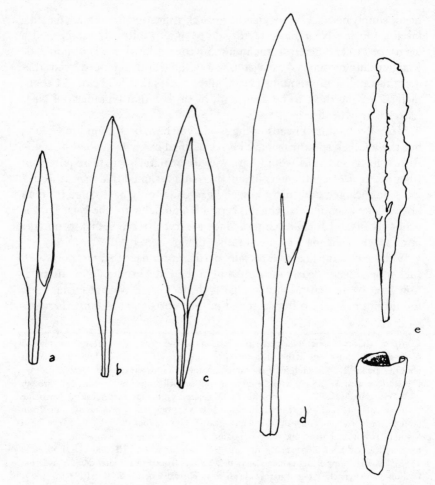

FIGURE 2. Tanged, elliptical weapon-heads of the late second millennium. Scale approx. 5:6

    a and b. From Catastrophe destruction level at Ugarit
    c. From El Khadr, Israel (ca. 1100 B.C.)
    d. From Mycenae (no dated context)
    e. From Hazor (eleventh century B.C.)

have been used by either the aggressors or the defenders in the city's last hours. The three heads from Ugarit thus far published are 7, 8.5 and 8.7 centimeters in length.[58]

If one objects to identifying these and other elliptical, tanged heads of the late second millennium as coming from small javelins, one's only alternative is to argue that at this time archers for one reason or another developed a preference for enormous arrows. But various considerations identify these elliptical, tanged heads as coming from javelins. Many of the specimens that have been found, first of all, are inscribed. This practice, which Frank Cross has called "a fad of the 11th century,"[59] was especially common in the southern Levant but is also attested for Mesopotamia.[60] A hoard of tanged heads came to light at El Khadr, near Bethlehem, in 1953, and five (measuring between 9.2 and 10.5 cm.) are inscribed ḥṣ ʿbdlbʾt, which Cross prudently translated as "dart of ʿAbd-Labiʾt."[61] The Hebrew ḥṣ is normally an arrow, but because these heads seemed too large for an arrow, Cross supposed that the word could also have been used for a small missile that was hurled rather than shot. Since 1953, another eighteen heads have been found bearing what seem to be the names of their owners; still others, from Mesopotamia, are inscribed with royal names. It is less likely that an archer would inscribe all thirty or forty of his arrowheads than that a javelineer might inscribe his few javelin heads.

Not only the size but also the shape of the heads suggests javelins rather than arrows. A military arrowhead was normally barbed, so that the victim could not retract it without tearing his flesh; but these heads are elliptical, designed for easy retraction. The possibility that an archer could or would wish to retrieve a spent arrow is unlikely, but a warrior with only two or three javelins would perhaps have retrieved each of them several times during a skirmish.

[58] M. Yon, Pierre Lombard, and Margo Renisio, "L'organisation de l'habitat: les maisons A, B et E," in Yon, Le centre de la ville, 46–48, with figs. 27 and 28 (objects nos. 80/270, 80/99, and 80/70). Chavane, "Les instruments de bronze," 357, announces that publication of the thirteen heads, along with other bronze pieces, is forthcoming.

[59] Cross, "On Dating Phoenician Inscriptions in Sardinia and the Mediterranean," AJA 94 (1990): 340.

[60] See, most recently, Benjamin Sass, "Inscribed Babylonian Arrowheads of the Turn of the Second Millennium and Their Phoenician Counterparts," UF 21 (1989): 349–56; and J.-M. de Tarragon, "La pointe de flèche inscrite des Pères Blancs de Jérusalem," Rev. Bib. 98 (1991): 244–51. These "arrowheads" are undoubtedly from short javelins (the Jerusalem specimen measures 8.2 cm.).

[61] J. T. Milik and Frank Cross, "Inscribed Javelin-Heads from the Period of the Judges: A Recent Discovery in Palestine," BASOR 134 (1954): 5–15. Two more heads from the same hoard, dated paleographically to ca. 1100, have since surfaced: see Cross, "Newly Found Inscriptions in Old Canaanite and Early Phoenician Scripts," BASOR 238 (1980): 4–7. Unfortunately, between 1954 and 1980 Cross downgraded the El Khadr heads from javelin heads to arrowheads.

Finally, there is the evidence from a votive jar found in Stratum XI (late eleventh century) at Hazor. The jar contained (see figure 2e) not only tanged bronze heads very similar to those from El Khadr, but also shaft butts (the diameters of these butts are 1.6 cm. and 2 cm.).[62] Since it is virtually certain that the shaft butts and weapon heads came from the same weapons, the Hazor weapons must be identified as javelins and not as arrows. Neither of the two Hazor heads exceeds 10 centimeters in length.[63] To say that all tanged heads less than 11 centimeters long are arrowheads is therefore to ignore the only sure evidence we have for the size of tanged javelin heads at the end of the second millennium.

And these small javelins were used in Greece as well as in the Near East. Since the Aegean heads that Avila classified as Klasse 2 *Pfeilspitzen* are morphologically identical to (and, indeed, slightly larger than) the five inscribed El Khadr heads, we must suppose that these too are javelin heads.[64] The one securely dated specimen comes from a LH IIIB chamber tomb near Thebes.[65] That a single such head would be interred with a warrior again indicates that we are dealing here with a javelin rather than an arrow. There is little doubt that toward the end of the Late Bronze Age short javelins of a Levantine type were used as military weapons in Greece.[66]

Both the pictorial and the *in corpore* evidence shows that Late Bronze Age javelins had slender shafts and small heads, and undoubtedly these javelins would have inflicted much less trauma than six- or seven-foot spears. But as missiles for wounding chariot horses or lightly armored men, these humble weapons were perhaps as important as any in the arsenal of the barbarian raiders. In the conventional view that Late Bronze Age warfare was characterized by dense formations of heavy infantry, the utility and the importance of the barbarians' javelins would be difficult to see. But

[62] Cf. Y. Yadin, Y. Aharoni et al., *Hazor: An Account of the Third and Fourth Seasons of Excavations, 1957–1958* (Jerusalem, 1961): plate CCV, nos. 6, 7, 10, and 11 for drawing; for a photograph (to approximately 1:1 scale) see plate CCCXLVII. For illustration of the Hazor votive deposit see Yadin, *Warfare*, vol. 2, 352, and note his comment there: "The fact that the butts were found in the vessel strengthens the theory that the heads were for javelins and not for arrows."

[63] The blade of no. 10 is bent; if straightened, the length of the piece would revert from its current 8.5 cm. to 10 cm. The other head (no. 11) is broken; its preserved length (7.5 cm.) can be assumed to represent at least three-fourths of the original.

[64] I refer to the four heads in Avila's Klasse 2f (nos. 766–69): which average 11 cm. in length. Of the fourteen specimens Avila catalogs as *Pfeilspitzen* 770A–770M and describes as "nicht näher bestimmbare Pfeilspitzen der Grundform 2," at least ten would be reasonably identified as javelin heads on the basis of both size and form.

[65] Avila, *Lanzenspitzen*, no. 767 (p. 112).

[66] Ibid., 112, unequivocally assigns this type of head a Near Eastern origin: "Stielspitzen der Klasse 2f sind nicht griechischen Ursprungs: ihr Hauptverbreitungsgebiet liegt im Vorderen Orient und erstreckt sich von Anatolien und Zypern bis zum heutigen Gazastreifen."

if it is conceded that prior to the Catastrophe the eastern kings depended for offense on their chariotries, one can imagine how much the javelin may have contributed to the raiders' success. And on this matter, as on so many others in ancient military history, imagination is our only resource, since we have no relief, painting, or text that presents the raiders throwing javelins at chariot horses.

Offensive weapons other than the javelin have been the subjects of specialized study, and so we may more briefly review their development at the end of the Bronze Age. Not surprisingly, the spear ("spear" here represents a weapon wielded with one hand, and "lance" represents a weapon so large that it was normally thrust with both hands) in twelfth-century representations is roughly what it had always been: a sharpened head attached to a shaft approximately as long as its wielder is tall.[67] The *in corpore* evidence indicates one change in the manufacture of Aegean spears: the twelfth-century spearheads had solid-ring sockets, whereas earlier sockets had split rings. That difference resulted from a change in the technology of bronze working: instead of forging the spearheads in smithies, twelfth-century bronzeworkers cast them in foundries. The solid-ring socket seems to have had no military significance, although the development of foundries does suggest that mass production of bronze artifacts was suddenly important in the Aegean. In the eleventh and tenth centuries, iron spearheads appeared alongside bronze, both in the Near East and in the Aegean, and that change too may have resulted in part from the need to produce more spearheads than could be had from the limited supply of bronze.

On the Warrior Vase a spear is the only offensive weapon the warriors carry and so must have been used only for a thrust. Homer called the spear an αἰχμή or a δόρυ, and since αἰχμητής was for him a virtual synonym for "warrior" we must suppose that in the Dark Age the Greeks depended primarily upon their spears in combat. Before the Catastrophe, the spear had been less important. The word δόρυ does not appear in the Linear B tablets. Of course the Mycenaeans had spears, but they seem to have had a single word—*enchos*—for both the lance and the spear.[68] It is possible that the word δόρυ was popularized by North-Greek speakers who came south in the Iron Age (in chapter 4 it was suggested that a Δωριεύς was, etymologically, a "spearman").[69] Homeric warriors occasionally carry two *dourata*, throwing one and thrusting the other, but whether that prac-

[67] For a discussion of thirteenth- and twelfth-century spears in Greece see Höckmann, "Lanzen und Speere." For individual types see Snodgrass, *Early Greek Armour and Weapons*, 115–39, and Avila, *Lanzenspitzen*. At pp. 128–29 Avila notes the popularity of "die manneslange Lanze" from LH II through IIIC.

[68] Höckmann, "Lanzen und Speere," 334–35.

[69] For agent nouns terminating in -ευς see Eduard Schwyzer, *Griechische Grammatik*, vol. 1, (Munich, 1939): 476–77.

tice obtained in the real world we do not know.[70] In Israel the spear seems to have been the militiaman's primary weapon during the period of "the Judges." What the role of the spear was in twelfth-century Assyria is unknown, but in the ninth century an Assyrian infantryman carried either a bow or a single spear as his primary weapon.

It is undoubtedly safe to say that in the early Iron Age hand-to-hand fighting throughout the eastern Mediterranean was a contest of thrusting spears. This weapon was appropriate especially for infantrymen in close order formations, whether in Homeric *phalanges* and *stiches*, in Doric *phylai* and phratries,[71] or in the "tens, hundreds, and thousands" of the Near East. A spear not only had a much greater range than a sword but was less apt to injure comrades immediately to one's right and left.

In contrast to the spear, the lance seems to have become a rarity after the Bronze Age, at least in Greece. The lance—the *enchos* of both Homer and the Linear B tablets—must have been used especially for defense of the chariot against runners (as noted in chapter 10, it is so depicted on a Hittite stele)[72] and in Greece may have lost its utility when the chariot became a prestige vehicle. How long these lances were is difficult to say, since the heads (and they are enormous), but not the shafts, have been preserved. At *Iliad* 6.318 and 8.494, however, the poet describes Hector's *enchos* as eleven ells (5.08 meters) long. Philologists have noted that in Homer the *enchos* is usually paired with the great shield, the *sakos*, and seems to reflect an older usage; the younger pair is the *doru* and the *aspis*.[73]

SWORDS

We come finally to the sword, in which the changes ca. 1200—throughout the eastern Mediterranean—are nothing less than revolutionary. Both archaeologists and typologists of weapons have noted that it is at this time that a new type of sword, the Naue Type II, arrived in the eastern Mediterranean, and it has also been pointed out that this is the first true slashing

[70] One would suppose that a warrior who wished to throw a missile at an opponent, before having to engage him with a thrusting spear, would bring to the battle two quite different weapons. At *Early Greek Armour and Warfare*, 136–37, Snodgrass notes that a few graves from the Dark Age yielded one large and one small spearhead, and makes the good suggestion that the smaller head was from a missile.

[71] S. R. Todd, "Citizenry Divisions in Ancient Greek Poleis: Military Aspects of Their Origin and Development" (Ph.D. dissertation, Vanderbilt University, 1991), presents an argument that *phylai* began as the primary divisions—and phratries as subdivisions—of a militia, and that the military organization preferred by the Dorians was tripartite.

[72] Canby, "Hittite Art," 114.

[73] For discussion and bibliography see Höckmann, "Lanzen und Speere," 329–33.

sword that the area knew. But the revolution in swords and swordsmanship in the eastern Mediterranean actually goes deeper than that. Although not literally correct, there is much to be said for Trevor Watkins's generalization that the sword as such was foreign to men of the eastern Mediterranean until "the Peoples of the Sea" brought it forcefully to their attention.[74] Before 1200 B.C., what swordsmanship there was in the eastern kingdoms was a monopoly of skirmishers whom the kings had brought in from barbaria.

In a useful essay on ancient swordsmanship Col. D. H. Gordon provided a technical terminology that can clarify discussion of the weapons of the thirteenth and twelfth centuries.[75] Stabbing weapons shorter than fourteen inches (35 cm.) are knives and daggers. A "sword" between fourteen and twenty inches long (35 to 50 cm.) is more correctly called a dirk, a "short sword" falls between twenty and twenty-eight inches (50 to 70 cm.), and a long sword has a length of at least twenty-eight inches. Although in a pinch a dirk or even a dagger could be used with a slashing (cutting) motion, these weapons were of course designed primarily for thrusting. Proper swords could be serviceable for either function, and the shape of the blade is the best indication of how one was in fact used. Blades that tapered continuously from hilt to tip were generally meant to be thrust. Contrarily, a blade whose edges ran roughly parallel—and that was at least an inch (26 cm.) wide—for most of its length was undoubtedly designed to keep from bending even when brought down in a hard slash.[76] Thus "a cut-and-thrust sword is one that can be used as effectively as its form permits both for cutting and thrusting."[77]

Ca. 1200 B.C. there appeared in the eastern Mediterranean the thoroughly efficient cut-and-thrust sword known to specialists as the Naue Type II,[78] or the *Griffzungenschwert*. Let us take a close look at it (see figures 4a and d) to see what a truly "good" sword was, and what it could do.[79] The Naue Type II was a long (most of them ca. 70 cm. from pommel to tip) bronze weapon. The blade's edges were virtually parallel for much of its length, or even swelling very slightly to a maximum at approximately twenty centimeters from the tip, before tapering to a sharp point (such a blade is therefore called "leaf-shaped"). The blade and hilt were cast as a single piece of metal. The hilt was a flat tang, a little over half as wide as the

[74] Watkins, "Beginnings of Warfare," 25.

[75] D. H. Gordon, "Swords, Rapiers, and Horse-riders," *Antiquity* 27 (1953): 67–78.

[76] Ibid., 70.

[77] Ibid., 71.

[78] The classification derives from Julius Naue, *Die vorrömischen Schwerter aus Kupfer, Bronze und Eisen* (Munich, 1903).

[79] For a detailed typological study see Catling, "Bronze Cut-and-Thrust Swords in the Eastern Mediterranean," *PPS* 22 (1956): 102–25.

blade, from the edges of which curled four flanges. Hilt-pieces of bone or wood were seated within the flanges and attached through the tang by rivets. With such a hilt the warrior could be confident that his blade would not bend from the tang, nor his hilt-pieces loosen, no matter how jarring a slash he struck. The Naue Type II could be used as a thrusting weapon, since the extremity of the blade was tapered and on both sides two shallow "blood channels" ran the entire length of the blade. But obviously this sword was designed primarily for cutting (slashing). In swords whose primary design was for thrusting, the center of gravity was just below the hilt. On the Naue Type II the center of gravity was much farther down the blade (this was especially so for the leaf-shaped blade). In a thrusting sword that would have been a serious drawback, but it added greatly to the force and velocity of a slashing sword. With such a slashing sword a warrior could cut off an opponent's head, leg or arm, or cut him in two: so Diomedes (*Iliad* 5.144) severs Hypeiron's shoulder from his neck and back. The Naue Type II could also, of course, be used with a thrust, and a warrior who had already severed an opponent's limb with a slash would thereupon proceed to run him through with a thrust.

After its introduction ca. 1200, the Naue Type II quickly established itself. By the eleventh century it was virtually the only sword in use in the Aegean, and excavated specimens show that it was also the standard sword in the Near East in the early Iron Age. The only improvement required in the half-millennium that followed its introduction was the substitution of iron for bronze, after ironworking had been developed to the degree that iron could provide a sharper, stronger, and more durable blade. By ca. 900 B.C. swords were regularly made of iron, but the design remained that of the thirteenth-century bronze Griffzungenschwert.[80] The geographical and temporal extent of this weapon's popularity attests to its efficiency. In the Near East, the Aegean, and Europe from Italy and the Balkans to Britain and Scandinavia, the Naue Type II remained the standard sword until at least the seventh century.

Today it is generally agreed that the Naue Type II sword had been in use in central and northern Europe well before it appeared in the eastern Mediterranean.[81] In northeast Italy too, as Stefan Foltiny pointed out, it is

[80] On Greece, for the entire period 1200–600, see Snodgrass, *Early Greek Armour and Weapons*, 106: "It is remarkable that the period should be so thoroughly dominated, from beginning to end, by one type." The Griffzungenschwert was virtually the only kind of sword known in the Protogeometric period and remained standard until the seventh century, when hoplite tactics made a short sword more serviceable. See also Snodgrass, *Arms and Armour*, 36–37, 58, and 97.

[81] Widely believed since the turn of the century, but argued exhaustively (and, for the most part, convincingly) by J. D. Cowen, "Eine Einführung in die Geschichte der bronzenen Griffzungenschwerter in Süddeutschland und der angrenzenden Gebieten," *Bericht der Römisch Germanischen Kommission* 36 (1955): 52ff. See also Cowen's "The Flange-Hilted

quite well represented at an early date.[82] It seems to have originated in the area from the eastern Alps to the Carpathians: in Austria and Hungary specimens belonging to the subtype known as Sprockhoff Ia have been found dating at least as early as 1450.[83] Like all northern swords, these were not forged in smithies (forging was an eastern Mediterranean art) but cast in foundries, a technique that encouraged proliferation: with a mold doing most of his work for him, a founder was able to produce a finished sword in a relatively short time. From the eastern Alps and Carpathians use of the Naue Type II spread northward and westward over most of temperate Europe, and by the fourteenth century swords of this type were in use from the Rhône to Scandinavia (in fact, the Sprockhoff Ia is attested especially in Denmark).[84] Quite remarkably, however, nothing comparable was at that time to be found in Greece and the Near East. By the thirteenth century, the Sprockhoff Ia had evolved into the fully mature Naue Type II, the evolution again having taken place entirely in barbaria.

For contrast, let us now review the arsenal of the eastern Mediterranean kingdoms before the arrival of the Naue Type II. There were "swords" in these kingdoms during all of the Late Bronze Age, but according to the standards of a Roman legionary they would have left much to be desired.[85] One Egyptian weapon that in reliefs may at first glance appear to be a slashing sword was in fact a bronze rod and would have been more appropriate for a Roman lictor than for a legionary. With one of these weapons

---

Cutting Sword of Bronze: Was It First Developed in Central Europe, or in the Aegean Area?" *Bericht über den V. Internationalen Kongress für Vor- und Frühgeschichte* (Berlin, 1961): 207–14. Catling, who in 1956 argued in favor of an Aegean origin, five years later agreed with Cowen that the evidence pointed to temperate Europe: see Catling, "A New Bronze Sword from Cyprus," *Antiquity* 35 (1961): 115–22. For the conclusions of Nancy Sandars, expert on the weapons of both the eastern Mediterranean and temperate Europe, see her *Sea Peoples*, 91–94.

[82] The Italian specimens of the Naue Type II were largely ignored until assembled and published by Foltiny, "Flange-Hilted Cutting Swords of Bronze in Central Europe, Northeast Italy, and Greece," *AJA* 68 (1964): 247–58. The definitive catalog of prehistoric Italian swords is now V. Bianco Peroni, *Die Schwerter/Le Spade*; this catalog does not include Sicily and Sardinia.

[83] Cowen, "Flange-Hilted Cutting Sword," 208–09.

[84] Ibid., 212, fig. 5.

[85] This has not been stated clearly enough by our standard authorities. In his chapter on the weapons of the Near East during the Late Bronze Age, Yadin (*Art of Warfare*, vol. 1, 76–114) described very well what was there but did not call attention to what was not; he therefore did not mention the absence of the straight slashing sword (or its arrival at the end of the Bronze Age). Rachel Maxwell-Hyslop, "Daggers and Swords," provided a full catalog of the weapons from the Near East but did not place them in a larger context. Of the fifty-six types in her catalog, the overwhelming majority (fifty-two or fifty-three of the fifty-six) are daggers or dirks (weapons that Col. Gordon defined as dirks are in Maxwell-Hyslop's terminology either daggers or short swords). In addition to Type 34 (the sickle sword), only Types 48, 49, and 52 are swords, and none of these appear before the last decades of the Bronze Age.

(which Yadin describes as "a long metal scourge or a long baton")[86] a warrior neither cut nor stabbed his opponent but broke his bones and beat him to death. The rod was evidently more than a meter in length and had a diameter of two or three centimeters.[87] Although a standard weapon of native Egyptian infantrymen, it apparently found no favor elsewhere in the eastern Mediterranean. The Egyptian infantryman used the rod with a smiting or clubbing motion, beating his opponent while protecting himself with an oblong shield held in his left hand. The motion required in wielding the rod was therefore somewhat similar to that required with the slashing sword. But whereas the slashing sword could cut an opponent in half, the rod could only knock him to the ground.

Before the arrival of the Naue Type II sword, the only slashing weapon used by men of the eastern kingdoms was the "sickle sword" (see figure 3a), found all over the Near East but not in the Aegean.[88] This "sword," which bears some resemblance to an American farmer's corn knife, evolved from an axelike weapon of the Middle Bronze Age whose edge seldom exceeded 25 centimeters in length. In the Late Bronze Age the sickle sword sported a somewhat longer edge but still provided a slash within a very narrow range. The entire weapon was seldom more than half a meter long, with the handle accounting for almost half of that length. One must imagine it slicing into an opponent's flesh rather than breaking or cleaving his bones. Although it undoubtedly served very well for cutting off an opponent's penis or hand during the collection of trophies, it was evidently too small to cut off his limbs while the battle still raged. Nor did the sickle sword have much else to recommend it. Because of its shape it could not be used at all as a thrusting weapon, nor could it be sheathed: a soldier carrying it would never have both hands free. Despite its ubiquity from Hattusas to Egypt, it was not an impressive weapon.

Thrusting, or stabbing, weapons of the Late Bronze Age come closer to our notion of what an ancient sword "should" have been. In many of the eastern Mediterranean kingdoms a warrior might wear a dagger, dirk, short sword, or occasionally even a long rapier in a scabbard, as a personal weapon or a weapon of last resort. The *in corpore* finds indicate that daggers, dirks, and a very few short stabbing swords were the only swordlike weapons in use in thirteenth-century Greece.[89] Sir Arthur Evans thought that the Linear B tablets from Knossos inventoried Naue Type II swords, but that idea has long been abandoned, and Boardman suggests

---

[86] *Art of Warfare*, vol. 2, 249.

[87] According to Wolf, *Bewaffnung*, 79, the single specimen preserved intact measures 1.26 meters.

[88] On the sickle sword see ibid., 66–68; Maxwell-Hyslop, "Daggers and Swords," 41–44; and Yadin, *Art of Warfare*, vol. 1, 206–7, and, vol. 2, 475.

[89] Sandars, "Later Aegean Bronze Swords," 130.

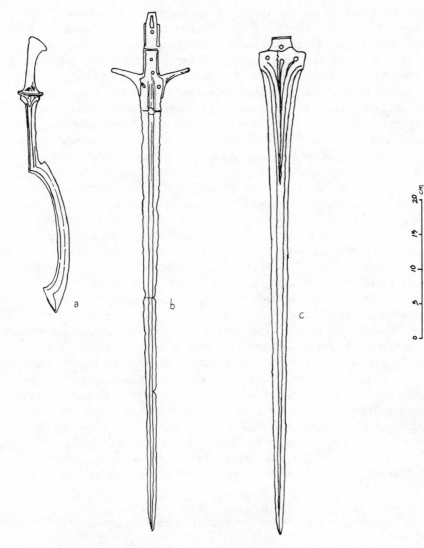

FIGURE 3. Eastern Mediterranean swords of the Late Bronze Age
   a. Sickle sword from tomb of Tutankhamun
   b. LH II rapier from Plovdiv, Bulgaria
   c. Anatolian rapier found near Boghazköy (ca. 1400 B.C.)

that the *phasgana* (*pa-ka-na*) were in fact daggers.[90] In the Pylos "Battle Scene" fresco, while one of the palace's men thrusts his spear into a savage, two other Pylians attack with daggers or short dirks.

A much longer thrusting weapon (see figure 3b) was evidently carried for self-defense by early Mycenaean charioteers. In the sixteenth and fifteenth centuries B.C. many rapiers (some over a meter in length) were elegantly made, but the costly hilting was so precarious that it is doubtful they were meant for serious fighting.[91] From the LH IIIA and IIIB periods *in corpore* rapiers have not been found in Greece, but vases continue to portray char-ioteers carrying such weapons in tasseled scabbards suspended from the shoulder. For the Near East we have less evidence for the long rapier in the Late Bronze Age.[92] A fine specimen, however, was found in 1991 by road workers near Boghazköy.[93] Measuring 79 centimeters in length, the Boghazköy rapier (see figure 3c) has a narrow blade that tapers sharply from 7.5 centimeters at the hilt to 3 centimeters at a quarter's length and 2 centimeters at the midpoint. An Akkadian inscription proclaims that King Tudhaliyas (Tudhaliyas II, ca. 1400 B.C.) dedicated "these swords" to the Storm God after conquering the land of Assuwa (probably "Asia," in western Asia Minor). The dedication suggests that these rapiers too were costly pieces as well as useful weapons.

The traditional weapons of the eastern Mediterranean kingdoms contin-ued in use until the twelfth century. A relief of Ramesses III on the north wall at Medinet Habu shows twenty native Egyptians, all hand-to-hand warriors, guarding a line of captives. Each Egyptian carries a spear in his right hand and another weapon in his left. Of the weapons in the left hand, six are dirks, six are rods, and seven are sickle swords.[94] Not one of the Egyptian infantrymen carries a long sword.

A few men did use a long sword in Late Bronze Age battles in the eastern Mediterranean, but these were *shardana* skirmishers in the Egyptian char-iot corps. Many of the *shardana* carried (often in a scabbard across the

---

[90] John Boardman, *The Date of the Knossos Tablets* (Oxford, 1963): 78–80.

[91] Sandars, "Later Aegean Bronze Swords," 117; Sandars argues persuasively (127–29) that even in the later fifteenth century, by which time the hilting problems had been overcome, the elaborate thrusting swords from the Warrior Graves at Knossos were essentially status symbols.

[92] Under her Type 48, Maxwell-Hyslop ("Daggers and Swords" 54–55) included only two entries dating from before 1200, both from Asia Minor.

[93] I thank Richard Beal for calling to my attention the preliminary publication by Ahmet Ünal et al., "The Hittite Sword from Boğazköy-Hattusa," *Müze* (*Museum*) 4 (1990–91): 50–52. The commentary on the sword misleads only in stating (p. 52) that "as a cut-and-thrust weapon the sword is evidently important as the basic weapon of the Hittite army." The Boghazköy sword has too narrow a blade to have served as a cut-and-thrust weapon; and there is no evidence for its use in the Hittite army.

[94] Yadin, *Art of Warfare*, vol. 2, 252–53; Sandars, *Sea Peoples*, 127, fig. 80.

breast) a dirk or short thrusting sword. The Abydos reliefs (see plate 5) show warriors with horned helmets, quite certainly Sardinians, serving as bodyguards for Ramesses the Great before the Battle of Kadesh in 1275, and each of them holds a dirk or short sword in his hand.[95] Another relief of Ramesses the Great, however, this one depicting the storming of a city in Syria, depicts *shardana* brandishing long swords.[96] In the following century, some of Ramesses III's barbarian skirmishers (see plates 6 and 10) are likewise armed with the long sword, some of them almost a meter in length. The Egyptian reliefs suggest that these long swords of the skirmishers were rapiers rather than slashing swords. The artists portray an occasional skirmisher running his sword through an opponent, but no skirmisher slashing off an opponent's head or arm. Although it is possible that the reliefs are misleading and that the long swords of the skirmishers were indeed used for cutting as well as for thrusting, it is safer to suppose that the *shardana* normally used their weapons—whether dirks or long swords—with a thrust. There is no independent evidence on Sardinian long swords of the second millennium, although a series of statue-menhirs from Corsica indicates that the long swords then in use on the latter island were cut-and-thrust swords rather than rapiers.[97]

A preserved long sword with a continuous taper was found at Bêt Dagin, near Gaza, in 1910, and is now in the British Museum. Although originally thought to be a great spearhead, it was identified as "a broadsword," and more particularly as "a Philistine sword of 'Shardana' type" by H. R. Hall.[98] Subsequently it has come to be called simply "the Shardana sword," and on the basis of this association has conventionally been dated to ca. 1200 or the early twelfth century. That dating, however, is apparently incorrect. A spokesman for the British Museum notifies me that "recent analytical work undertaken on this piece has demonstrated that it is in fact to be dated to the third millennium BC."[99] We therefore have no *in corpore* specimen of the kind of sword that Egyptian artists portray in the hands of Sardinian skirmishers in the thirteenth century.

There is one representation of a native Egyptian wielding a long sword in the Late Bronze Age, and it dates to the eve of the Catastrophe. A relief at Karnak, depicting the siege of Ashkelon, shows an Egyptian soldier (in

[95] Sandars, ibid., fig. 66.
[96] Ibid., fig. 12.
[97] Trump, *Prehistory of the Mediterranean*, 201, 219, and fig. 45.
[98] Hall, *Aegean Archaeology* (London, 1915): 247n.1. Maxwell-Hyslop, "Daggers and Swords," 59, lists the Gaza sword as the first example of her Type 52. For a good illustration of the sword see Yadin, *Art of Warfare*, vol. 2, 344. On analogy with the Egyptian reliefs, Maxwell-Hyslop dated the Gaza sword to 1200–1150.
[99] Personal correspondence (10 July 92) from Mr. Jonathan N. Tubb, in the British Museum's Department of Western Asiatic Antiquities.

PLATE 10. Battle of Ramesses III against Libyans. Line drawing of relief from Medinet Habu

traditional Egyptian headdress, he is apparently a professional infantry-man but not of barbarian extraction) climbing a ladder, and he is armed with a long sword, broad at the base and tapering straight to the point.[100] Since it flanks the text of Ramesses II's peace treaty with the Hittites, the relief has regularly been assigned to Ramesses II. That attribution would suggest that as early as ca. 1270 the use of long swords had been extended from the barbarian auxiliaries to professional infantrymen of the native Egyptian population. Now, however, it appears that the conventional date for this relief is too high. As was noted in chapter 2, Frank Yurco's inspection of the monument revealed that the Karnak relief was cut not for Ramesses II but for his son, Merneptah, whose storming of Ashkelon is recorded on his famous "Israel Stele."[101] That Merneptah did make an

[100] Yadin, *Art of Warfare*, vol. 1, 228.
[101] See p. 20.

effort to secure long swords for his hand-to-hand fighters is also indicated, we shall see, by the "Merneptah sword" discovered at Ugarit.

A long sword, evidently once again a rapier rather than a slashing sword, was the weapon upon which many of the aggressors in the Catastrophe relied in their hand-to-hand fighting. In the Medinet Habu relief (see plate 6) of the land battle in 1179 most of the Philistine warriors are shown with dirks or short thrusting swords. The relief of the naval battle, however, shows the aggressors with long swords. Although in this relief the Philistine and *Shekelesh* opponents are in utter disarray, many still have weapons in their right hands. One has a spear while, according to my count, seventeen have long swords. These are huge weapons. The blade, which tapers continuously, is considerably wider at the base than the hand that clenches the hilt. The hilt and blade together are longer than a man's arm. Similarly, when the Libyans attacked Ramesses III in 1182 and 1176 they depended on the long sword. Another Medinet Habu relief (see plate 10) shows a few Libyans using the bow, while the majority are armed with long swords—longer in fact than those shown in the relief of the sea battle against the Philistines.[102]

As in the last years of the Catastrophe, so in its first years the hand-to-hand weapon preferred by the aggressors was evidently the sword. When the Libyans attacked Merneptah in 1208, that king reported seizing as booty only twelve chariots but 9111 swords.[103] Since that figure almost matches the number (9724) of penises and hands that Merneptah's men gathered as trophies, we must suppose that for the overwhelming majority of the Libyan king's warriors (whether coming from Libya or from one of "the northern lands") the sword was the principal weapon.

It was apparently to trump the raiders' thrusting swords that some men in the eastern Mediterranean began, ca. 1200, to acquire cut-and-thrust swords, and above all the superb Naue Type II. A fair number of later iron specimens of the Naue Type II have been found in the Near East,[104] but very few in bronze (it must of course be said that because few tomb deposits from the period have been found, few twelfth-century swords of any kind have been found in the Near East). Catling counted five in Cyprus (to this relatively high figure from Cyprus must be added four more, found at

[102] For drawing of part of the relief see Yadin, *Art of Warfare*, vol. 2, 334–35. In the relief the artists depict seventeen long swords in a booty pile, and others in the hands of Libyan or Meshwesh warriors. For a sketch of the swords in the pile see Lorna G. Hayward, "The Origin of Raw Elephant Ivory in Late Bronze Age Greece and the Aegean," *Antiquity* 64 (1990): 106, fig. 1.

[103] Breasted, *AR*, vol. 3, no. 589.

[104] Catling, "Bronze Cut-and-Thrust Swords," 117, notes that at Hama "a substantial number of Naue II swords was found with the cremations of which the majority is of iron." None of these iron swords is earlier than ca. 1100.

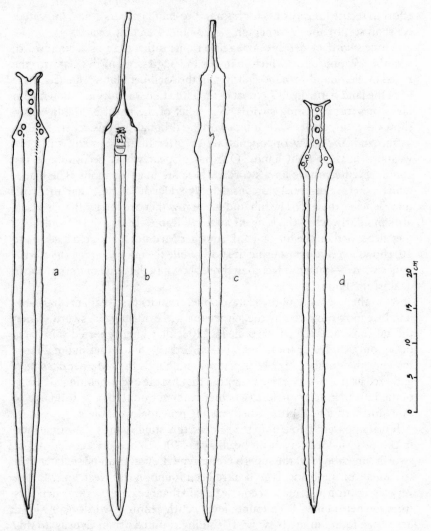

FIGURE 4. Cut-and-thrust swords from the period of the Catastrophe
   a. Naue Type II from Aranyos, Hungary
   b. "Merneptah Sword" from Ugarit
   c. Sword from "la maison du Grand-prêtre d'Ugarit"
   d. Naue Type II from Mycenae

Enkomi in 1967),[105] but only eight in the rest of the Near East.[106] Of these eight, four are undated and three date from the period 1100–900. The eighth, and earliest, is said to have been found in the Egyptian Delta and bears the cartouche of Seti II.[107] The six-year reign of this pharaoh is dated 1202–1196 on the low chronology.

From the Greek world, on the other hand, the number of *in corpore* Naue Type II swords is impressive. As Snodgrass has shown, in the Protogeometric period the Naue Type II was the only kind of sword used in the Aegean.[108] The Protogeometric and Geometric specimens, however, were of iron. The bronze specimens are earlier and fewer in number, but the number is nevertheless extraordinary when we remember that from the two hundred years prior to the arrival of the Naue Type II virtually no Aegean long swords have been found. In his 1968 survey Catling counted twenty-seven bronze Naue Type II swords in Greece and the islands of the Aegean (including Crete).[109] Subsequently another specimen, very well preserved, was found in an LH IIIC Arcadian tomb, and still another in an LM IIIC tomb in the North Cemetery at Knossos.[110] To these twenty-nine we may also add the nine found in Cyprus, for a quite remarkable total of thirty-eight from what can vaguely be called the "Greek world." Perhaps it is not surprising that scholars early in this century referred to the Naue

[105] J. Lagarce, "Quatre épées de bronze provenant d'une cachette d'armurier à Enkomi-Alasia (Chypre)," *Ugaritica VI* (Paris, 1969): 349–68. The four were found, along with the head of a javelin, in a pit deposit dating from the early twelfth century. In Catling, "Bronze Cut-and-Thrust Swords," nos. 16 through 19 come from Cyprus, 20 through 26 from the rest of the Near East. Catling's later survey, "Late Minoan Vases and Bronzes in Oxford," *ABSA* 63 (1968): 101–04, includes one addition from Cyprus and another from the Levant.

[106] In Catling, "Bronze Cut-and-Thrust Swords," nos. 16–19 come from Cyprus, 20–26 from the rest of the Near East. Catling's later survey, "Late Minoan Vases and Bronzes in Oxford," *ABSA* 63 (1968): 101–4, includes one addition from Cyprus and another from the Levant.

[107] Catling, "Bronze Cut-and-Thrust Swords," 116. Cf. Wolf, *Bewaffnung*, 103. Evidently this Naue Type II was somewhat shorter than most of the Aegean specimens, since its original length (both the hilt and the tip of the blade are missing) is estimated at ca. 60 cm.

[108] *Arms and Armour*, 37; cf. *Early Greek Armour and Weapons*, 106.

[109] At p. 103 of "Late Minoan Vases," Catling's chart shows fifty bronze Naue Type II swords. Of these, ten come from "north Greece" (Illyria, Epirus, and Macedonia), and forty from "rest of Greek world." However, as his categories on p. 102 indicate, the rubric "rest of Greek world" includes not only Cyprus but also Egypt and the Levant. If we exclude his thirteen Cypriote and Near Eastern specimens (as well as the ten from "north Greece"), we narrow his list to 27 specimens from the Aegean. Note that to his Cypriote specimens must be added the four found at Enkomi in 1967: Jacques Lagarce, "Quatre épées," 349ff.

[110] On the Arcadian sword see K. Demakopoulou, *Archaiologika Analekta Athenôn* (1969): 226ff.; see also H.-G. Buchholz, "Schlussbemerkungen," in H.-G. Buchholz, ed., *Ägäische Bronzezeit*, 502–3, and abb. 123. For the Knossos sword see Catling, "Knossos, 1978," *AR* (1978–79): 46.

Type II as the "Mycenaean sword." But of course the Mycenaeans were relatively late in adopting it, and it is much better attested to the north and the west. Over 100 bronze swords of this type are known from Italy (the majority from the Po Valley), and over 130 from Yugoslavia.[111]

What is most noteworthy for the present argument is the suddenness with which the Naue Type II established itself in the Aegean. Of the more than thirty bronze swords in the Greek world a few are late, dating from after 1100. All the others "belong exclusively to the late thirteenth and twelfth centuries B.C."[112] Catling's first survey concluded that the earliest swords which come from reliably dateable contexts "can be put with some confidence at *c.* 1200 B.C."[113] Sandars's conclusion was the same: the appearance of the Naue Type II in the Aegean can be dated "at the end of the thirteenth century (probably very little if at all before 1200)."[114] These dates, calculated on the basis of the middle chronology for the Egyptian kings, can on our low chronology be brought down to the first decades of the twelfth century. They therefore arrive in the Aegean during the darkest years of the Catastrophe.

Let us state this baldly and succinctly: for the thirteenth century we have no long swords at all from the Greek world, whereas for the twelfth we have at least thirty of a single type. The archaeological evidence indicates as clearly as one could ask that ca. 1200 warfare in the Greek world changed drastically. The sword, and the ability to use it, had suddenly become immensely important in the Aegean and in Cyprus. That a similar revolution occurred in Egypt and the rest of the Near East is not so clear, since little has there been learned from tombs in this period. We have already noticed, however, the Naue Type II sword with the cartouche of Seti II. And as will be shown below, the French excavations at Ugarit have produced five more long swords—none of them quite Naue Type II, but all designed for both cutting and thrusting—that were made shortly before Ugarit's destruction. These specimens suggest very strongly that between the accession of Merneptah and 1185 the sword had become a weapon of paramount importance in the Near East also.

Since most of the Naue Type II swords from the Aegean were found in "Greek" tombs it is likely that "Greeks" had acquired them. That the swords were made in Greece is less likely, and at any rate they owed much to non-Greek swordsmiths. Harding has pointed out the striking similarities between the earliest Aegean swords of this type and those from

---

[111] Cf. Harding, *Mycenaeans and Europe*, 163; for the Italian swords see Bianco Peroni, *Schwerter/Spade*, nos. 89–189 (nos. 194–271 date from the first millennium).

[112] Catling, "Late Minoan Vases," 101.

[113] "Bronze Cut-and-Thrust Swords," 106.

[114] "Later Aegean Bronze Swords," 142.

northern Italy, and he concluded that "Italy seems to have played an important part in the production and diffusion of the Greek weapons."[115]

Nevertheless, bronzesmiths of the eastern Mediterranean can also be seen at work in the weaponry revolution. The five swords from Ugarit, along with several made in Greece, show that at the end of the thirteenth and beginning of the twelfth century eastern smiths suddenly found themelves obliged to begin producing a weapon with which they were not very familiar. For their models they certainly turned to the Naue Type II, perhaps—as Harding's analysis suggests—especially the specimens brought from northern Italy. The results did not quite match the Naue Type II, but in themselves they are eloquent testimony to the urgency of the demands placed upon the swordsmiths.

Exhibit A on this matter is the so-called Merneptah sword (see figure 4b), which Schaeffer found at Ugarit in 1953. The sword and several other bronze objects, along with a clay figurine of a goddess, were found "buried in a corner of the inner court" of a house to the east of the royal palace.[116] The sword was "in mint condition," with its edges unsharpened. Schaeffer speculated that perhaps Merneptah "had ordered from Ugarit swords of this type, marked with his cartouche, to arm the auxiliary troops."[117] The Merneptah sword was almost certainly meant to serve not only for thrusting but also for slashing. As such, it may be the earliest preserved Near Eastern sword *intended* for slashing. Measuring 74 centimeters, and with a wide blade (5 cm. at the hilt and 4 cm. at midpoint) whose edges are almost parallel for most of its length, the Merneptah sword has been likened to the Naue Type II. Its hilting, however, consisted of a very long and slender tang, so wispy in fact that it is bent vertically and horizontally.[118] The bending of the tang probably occurred during or soon after the sword's manufacture and may well be the reason why the sword's blades were never sharpened. Although no good as a weapon, it was a handsome artifact, especially since

[115] Harding, *Mycenaeans and Europe*, 165; for the distribution of the Italian specimens see Bianco Peroni, *Schwerter/Spade*, tables 69 and 70A.

[116] Schaeffer, "A Bronze Sword from Ugarit with Cartouche of Mineptah (Ras Shamra, Syria)," *Antiquity* 29 (1955): 226–29; for essentially the same presentation, with a few additions, see Schaeffer's report in *Ugaritica III* (*Mission de Ras Shamra*, vol. 8. Paris, 1956): 169–77.

[117] Schaeffer, "A Bronze Sword," 227. Cf. also p. 226: "The sword is not of an Egyptian type. It is known that these big swords did not form part of the armament of Egyptian soldiers till the 13th century when Ramses II and especially his thirteenth son and successor, Mineptah, began enlisting quite important bands of foreign mercenaries."

[118] Schaeffer gives the length of the tang as 15 cm., but does not indicate its width. The width of the blade at the hilt end is 5 cm., and the photographs suggest that the width of the tang is less than a centimeter. The extent of the bending is clear from the photographs and drawings and does not resemble the deliberate bend in "killed" swords ceremonially deposited.

it bore a royal Egyptian cartouche. I assume that because it was one of his most treasured possessions the householder buried it in his courtyard along with the idol and the other bronze objects, in expectations of recovering the hoard after the danger had passed. At any rate, the Merneptah sword has aspirations to be a Griffzungenschwert but has nothing like the *Griffzung* of the Naue Type II.

In the Aegean too we find that early in the twelfth century the first attempts were made to produce a slashing sword. From the very end of the LH IIIB and from the IIIC period come four of Sandars's Class F and G weapons that were intended as slashing, or cut-and-thrust, swords. These are clumsy specimens and show only that ca. 1200 a few Greek swordsmiths began trying to forge a new kind of weapon. A twelfth-century Class G sword from Perati, in Attica, is reminiscent of a butcher's cleaver: "the blade is unique, being truly leaf-shaped with the greatest width in its lower third."[119] Two Class F specimens (one complete, the other fragmentary), found at Mouliana in Crete and dating to the twelfth century, are also slashing swords. A fourth slashing sword, dating from ca. 1200 and coming from Mycenae, is 62 centimeters long but is also badly designed. Sandars observes that it is "most unwieldy and eccentric, more so than the Perati sword, and may be grouped with it and with the Mouliana F sword as examples of inexpert experimentation."[120]

How eastern Mediterranean smiths worked to produce slashing swords during the Catastrophe is most vividly illustrated by a group of four such swords found at Ugarit in 1929 (although not finally published until 1956, by which time, unfortunately, the man who dug them up—Georges Chenet—had died).[121] The four are superior to the "Merneptah sword" from the same city, since their tangs are suitably broad and strong (see figure 4c). Because their tangs are not flanged, the Ugarit swords are not true Griffzungenschwerter, but in other respects they are on a par with the Naue Type II. In length they range from 63 to 73 centimeters. Their tangs are flat but extend through to a pommel spike, and are all more than 2 centimeters wide (that is, two or three times the width of the Merneptah sword). The blades have parallel edges for most of their length, ending in a taper. The four blades vary considerably in width: measured at the midpoint, they are respectively 2.5, 3, 3.3, and 4 centimeters wide. There is no doubt that these are cut-and-thrust swords.[122]

[119] Sandars, "Later Aegean Bronze Swords," 139.

[120] Ibid., 140.

[121] These swords are described by Schaeffer in *Ugaritica III*, 256–59. For their initial announcement, see Schaeffer, "Les fouilles de Minet-el-Beida et de Ras Shamra (campagne du printemps 1929)," *Syria* 10 (1929): 295 and plate LX, fig. 3.

[122] Cf. Catling, "Bronze Cut-and-Thrust Swords," 121; Snodgrass, *Early Greek Armour and Weapons*, 207.

They were never used, however. Cast rather than forged, they are fresh from their molds and are unfinished in that their points and blades were never sharpened, and their tangs are without rivet holes. They are part of a collection of seventy-four bronze objects found underneath "la maison du Grand-prêtre d'Ugarit." Specifically, the excavators found the deposit in a hollow directly beneath the spot once occupied by the threshold of an interior doorway (by 1929 the threshold itself had disappeared, perhaps because it was made of wood).[123]

The swords are usually dated to the fourteenth century. That was Claude Schaeffer's interpretation, based on the sherds found in the fill into which the pit was dug.[124] Schaeffer's assumption was that the bronze objects were a foundation deposit, dedicated when the high-priest's house was built. There is, however, a much better possibility: the objects constitute a hoard buried during the final emergency of Ugarit, ca. 1185, in hopes that after the attackers were gone the objects could be retrieved from their hiding place.

The fourteenth-century sherds in the surrounding fill can be dismissed as a criterion for dating the deposit, since on any reconstruction the pit must have been dug into a preexisting stratum. The question is, When was the pit dug? Schaeffer proposed that it was dug at the time of the house's construction, for a foundation deposit, but this is unlikely. Although foundation deposits under thresholds are known, they tend to contain a sacrificial victim along with a few vases and figurines (a "lamp and bowl" combination was common in the Late Bronze Age).[125] That seventy-four bronze artifacts were buried as a foundation deposit defies belief. In 1929 the ubiquity of hoards at Ugarit was not yet recognized; but in the course of his forty years at the site Schaeffer himself was to find that almost all of the bronze articles discovered there had been squirreled away by the occupants in wall cavities or in hollows under the floors.[126]

A typological argument puts the hoard at least a century later than the date proposed by Schaeffer. Among the seventy-four artifacts is a tripod with pomegranate pendants. Catling noted that the tripod corresponds closely to many such specimens found on Cyprus, all in contexts dateable to the period after 1250. Himself an expert on Cypriote bronzework of the period, Catling concluded that the Ugarit tripod represents an advanced

---

[123] Schaeffer, *Ugaritica III*, 253.

[124] Lagarce, "Quatre épées," 364n.27, reveals that in private conversation Schaeffer eventually conceded that his original date was a bit too early, and that the foundation deposit may have been made "au début du xiiie siècle."

[125] Some thirty-five of these are characterized by Shlomo Bunimovitz and Orna Zimhoni, " 'Lamp and Bowl' Foundation Deposits from the End of the Late Bronze Age—Beginning of the Iron Age in Eretz-Israel," *Eretz Israel* 21 (1990): 102.

[126] Schaeffer, "Commentaires," 763: "très nombreuses cachettes d'objets précieux établies par des particuliers dans des murs ou sous les planchers de leurs habitations."

stage of the type and could hardly have been made much earlier than the end of the thirteenth century.[127]

Finally, the swords themselves argue for a date during the Catastrophe. All four are excellent pieces. From all of the Near East the only known sword that matches these is the Naue Type II, bearing the cartouche of Seti II and so dating no earlier than 1202. Enough is now known about swords at Ugarit, and throughout the eastern Mediterranean, for us to state categorically that in the fourteenth century swordsmiths at Ugarit were not yet casting cut-and-thrust swords of any kind, much less swords so typologically advanced as these. We may conclude that the four Ugarit swords, like the four recently found at Enkomi, were hoarded in the early twelfth century "dans l'espoir d'un retour prochain."[128]

It was the misdating of the four Ugarit swords that for a long time obscured how deficient Late Bronze Age swords in the eastern Mediterranean were in comparison with those of temperate Europe. Until Catling objected, scholars interested in ancient weaponry accepted Schaeffer's interpretation as fact. To Lorimer the four swords demonstrated the presence in fourteenth-century Ugarit of Mycenaean immigrants, some of whom had evidently set up a sword factory.[129] For V. Gordon Childe, C.F.C. Hawkes, Col. Gordon, and others, the Ugarit swords suggested that cut-and-thrust swords were pioneered in the eastern Mediterranean and not in temperate Europe.[130] Even Snodgrass, who found Catling's argument tempting, still presented the four swords as evidence for "a parallel and contemporary evolution" of cut-and-thrust swords in the eastern Mediterranean and in central Europe.[131]

Once the hoard swords from Ugarit are correctly dated, it is plain to see that changes in eastern Mediterranean swords at the end of the Bronze Age were revolutionary rather than evolutionary. The first Naue Type II specimens (in Greece, Cyprus, and Egypt) appear almost simultaneously ca. 1200, and a variety of local experiments attempted to produce a slashing sword of similar efficiency. Some of the experiments resulted in unusable swords, but by ca. 1185 swordsmiths at Ugarit had all but perfected their product. Unfortunately for Ugarit, the time for producing these swords, and for training men to wield them, had run out.

[127] Catling, "Bronze Cut-and-Thrust Swords," 121: "The Ras Shamra stand is typologically very advanced in the series and, in isolation, would almost certainly be dated a good deal later than 1250."

[128] Lagarce, "Quatre épées," 367–68.

[129] Lorimer, Homer and the Monuments, 21 and 33.

[130] Childe, "The Final Bronze Age in the Near East and Temperate Europe," PPS 14 (1948): 183ff.; Hawkes, "From Bronze Age to Iron Age: Middle Europe, Italy, and the North and West," ibid., 198ff.; and Gordon, "Swords, Rapiers and Horse-Riders," 72.

[131] Early Greek Armour and Weapons, 207.

Chapter Fourteen

THE END OF CHARIOT WARFARE

IN THE CATASTROPHE

CHAPTERS 10–12 presented an argument that warfare in the Late Bronze Age was very different from what it was in the early Iron Age (or, for that matter, in any other period of antiquity). Before the Catastrophe, a king might send infantrymen against barbarians in the hills; but combat between two kingdoms was chariot warfare, in which the only infantrymen who played an offensive role were the chariot runners or skirmishers. In the Iron Age, on the other hand, warfare was synonymous with infantry encounters: if horse troops took part in the battle, they were ancillary to the footsoldiers.

The archaeological evidence for armor and weapons, reviewed in chapter 13, locates the period of transition from chariot to infantry warfare precisely in the decades of the Catastrophe. This was evidently the time when, after chariot armies had been supreme for more than four hundred years, infantrymen once again took back the field. Although the forms of some weapons—bows, lances, spears, and javelins—are not known to have changed much in the late thirteenth and early twelfth centuries, their relative importance evidently did. Bows and lances, the weapons of the chariot crew, were far more numerous before the Catastrophe than after. Javelins, on the other hand, thrown on the run by skirmishers, seem to have proliferated at the end of the Bronze Age, and in the Near East remained important through the twelfth and eleventh centuries. The spear, the weapon par excellence of the close-order infantryman, is well attested for the early Iron Age. In Dark Age Greece a single spear normally accompanied a dead man to the afterlife.

Other items of infantrymen's equipment are even more telling. Corslets and greaves for infantrymen were apparently an innovation in the Catastrophe. Round shields had been used by barbarian runners in the thirteenth century but came into general use early in the twelfth. The evidence for swords is most dramatic: the material record shows that a revolution in swordsmanship began in the Aegean, in Egypt, and at Ugarit ca. 1200 B.C. There was suddenly a demand for long slashing swords, whether for the Naue Type II swords brought from northern Italy or the Balkans or for more experimental specimens produced in the eastern kingdoms themselves. In short, the archaeological record of changes in armor and

weaponry presents a decisive argument that it was in the decades immediately before and after 1200 that there began the infantry dominance that
was to continue to the end of antiquity.

On the basis of the circumstantial evidence we may therefore conclude
that chariot warfare ended in the Catastrophe, the raiders and city-sackers
having found a way to defeat the greatest chariot armies of the time. But of
course there is also direct evidence that this is what the Catastrophe was
about. The reliefs at Medinet Habu show clearly enough that the aggressors against Ramesses III—the Libyans, the Philistines and *Tjekker*, and
the northerners who joined in the attack—were infantrymen, supported
by a very few chariots. They also show that Ramesses was able to win his
victories over the marauders by assembling a great number of footsoldiers,
drawn both from barbaria and from Egypt itself. That the aggressors were
infantrymen has generally gone unremarked because it has been assumed
that ancient land battles had *always* been fought primarily by footsoldiers.
Only when one recognizes that in the Late Bronze Age that was not the case
can one appreciate the significance of what is shown in the Medinet Habu
reliefs.

From the reliefs we can also infer that the Libyans and Philistines fought
as skirmishers, perhaps as they had traditionally done in their tribal *guer-
rillas*, rather than as disciplined troops in organized formations. The Medinet Habu relief suggests that the Philistines and *Tjekker* swarmed, as individuals or in small groups, over the field. With a long sword as his primary
weapon for hand-to-hand warfare, the raider required an "open" space, in
which his agility and fleetness could be exploited. But before the hand-to-
hand fighting began, the chariots had to be overcome, and it was surely for
this purpose that the raiders brought their javelins. Again, the javelins
suggest a swarming tactic, the javelineer running forward and then hurling
his weapon at a team of chariot horses. At Djahi in 1179 Ramesses wisely
kept his chariots in the background and relied on the footsoldiers he recruited. But in other battles the raiders must have used javelins to good
effect, destroying the chariot armies and ending the era of chariot warfare.

The fact that the marauders were "runners," and therefore dangerous
for a chariotry, can be inferred from the reliefs but is explicit in the inscriptions. The Great Karnak Inscription, after enumerating the various lands
from which Meryre's auxiliaries had come for the attack in 1208, states
that the wretched Libyan chief had "taken the best of every warrior and
every *phrr* of his country."[1] Thirty years later, Ramesses likewise referred
to both his Libyan and his Philistine enemies as "runners." After beating
back the assault by the Libyans he boasted, "I have cast down the violators
of my frontier, prostrate in their places, their runners pinioned and slain in

---

[1] Breasted, *AR*, vol. 3, no. 579.

my grasp." And of the Philistines and their associates who attacked in 1179 he said, "I have carried away their runners, pinioned in my grasp, to present them to thy ka."[2]

Although the barbarians were able to defeat the chariotries of the eastern kingdoms because their weapons and tactics were suited exactly to the task, the documents also show that they owed their success to overwhelming numbers. When the Libyans and their northern auxiliaries attacked Merneptah in 1208, he boasted of having slain almost ten thousand of them. A generation later, Ramesses claimed to have killed no fewer than 12,235 Libyans. Even after allowing for pharaonic exaggeration, one would suppose that on each occasion the attacking army must have consisted of at least twenty thousand men, all of them skirmishers armed with either javelins or long swords, or both. In legend, "the forty thousand of Israel" confronted the kings of Canaan and at least that many Achaeans descended upon Troy. As the Catastrophe spread and mushroomed, and as the limitations of the chariot armies were everywhere revealed, barbarians all over the Mediterranean world must have been attracted by the prospects of an easy victory and rich booty. Small successes begat great successes, until even Mycenae and Hattusas fell. Against throngs of raiders no kingdom (with the possible exception of Assyria) could have felt secure. Even the Great Kingdoms had traditionally employed only a few thousand skirmishers, and in a small kingdom, such as Pylos or Ugarit, hand-to-hand fighters were counted in the hundreds. When the scribes of Hattusas and Emar speak of these cities being attacked by "hordes" we can understand their peril only when we recall that for defense the kingdoms had traditionally relied on a small number of professional military men.

Finally, we have a few pieces of literary evidence that the Catastrophe resulted from the victory of barbarian footsoldiers over the chariotries of the eastern Mediterranean kingdoms. In the *Iliad* the Trojan War is obviously not described as a conflict between Achaean infantry skirmishers and Trojan charioteers, but vestiges of such a conflict may survive in the tradition. Stories about the Amazons and the Phrygians with their fast horses, about Paris slaying Achilles with a bow shot, and even about the capture of Troy through the ruse of a wooden horse (this story, portrayed on an eighth-century vase from Mykonos, was evidently current long before our *Odyssey* was composed)[3] may have arisen when the horses and chariots of Troy were still remembered. The description of Achilles as "fleet-footed" is especially appropriate for the *arete* of a runner. And the adjective "horse-taming," the conventional epithet both for Hector and for all the Trojans,

---

[2] Edgerton and Wilson, *Historical Records of Ramses III*, plates 26 and 44.

[3] *Odyssey*. 4.271–89 and 8.492–520 assume that the audience knew the story. For the vase see Wood, *Trojan War*, 80.

presumably derives from a real renown of the Trojan charioteers and chariot warriors.

A far more explicit tradition of infantrymen besting chariot armies was
preserved in Israel. Much had been lost and other things added by the tenth
century, when the traditions were first written down, but there was nevertheless a persistent recollection that "the Conquest of Canaan" had been
effected by Israelite footsoldiers against the chariots of the Canaanite cities.
In our texts of Joshua and Judges, the hill-dwellers of Manasseh are for a
time unable to take over the plains of Beth-Shan and Esdraelon because the
Canaanites have "chariots of iron"; and in Judah too the hill men are
temporarily prevented by "chariots of iron" from seizing the plains. Although the expression seems to be the misconception of a writer in the
Persian period,[4] the imagery does reflect the tradition that the conquest of
the most fertile plains in Canaan was costly because of the chariot armies
that guarded them.

Two of the oldest pieces of Hebrew poetry that have come down to us
commemorate victories of Yahweh over great chariot armies. The "Song of
the Sea" (Exodus 15), attributed variously to Moses or his sister Miriam,[5]
celebrates Yahweh's drowning of an Egyptian chariot host:

> I will sing to the Lord, for he has triumphed gloriously;
>   the horse and his rider he has thrown into the sea. . . .
> Pharaoh's chariots and his host he cast into the sea;
>   and his picked officers are sunk in the *yam suph*.
> The floods cover them;
>   they went down into the depths like a stone.
> Thy right hand, O Lord, glorious in power,
>   thy right hand, O Lord, shatters the enemy. . . .
> Thou didst blow with thy wind, the sea covered them;
>   they sank as lead in the mighty waters.

In the prose account that eventually gave the song a setting, six hundred
Egyptian chariots pursue five million Israelites "fleeing" from Egypt.
When the Israelites reach the Red Sea (*yam suph*),[6] Yahweh divides the
waters—allowing his people to march through on dry land—and then
rolls the water back to cover the pursuing Egyptian chariots. On the other

---

[4] Drews, "The 'Chariots of Iron' of Joshua and Judges," *JSOT* 45 (1989): 15–23.

[5] Frank Cross and David Freedman, "The Song of Miriam," *JNES* 14 (1955): 237–50.

[6] The *yam suph* was translated in the Septuagint as *Erythra Thalassa*, and in the Vulgate as
Mare Rubrum, but the translation seems to have been deduced from the P writer's routing of
"the Exodus" through the Red Sea. Many biblical scholars, noting that in several O.T.
passages *suph* means "papyrus reed," believe that the name *yam suph* originally was applied
to a "Reed Sea" somewhere in the eastern Delta. Difficulties with this view are pointed out by
B. F. Batto, "The Reed Sea: *Requiescat in Pace*," *JBL* 102 (1983): 27–35. Batto's own
conclusion is that *yam suph* originally meant "Sea of End/Extinction."

hand, the song itself, which must commemorate a real rather than a mythical event, speaks repeatedly of Yahweh throwing the horse and rider into the sea, the horses and chariots sinking into the water like a stone or a leaden weight. Thus the song seems to exult in the capsizing of ships in a storm, perhaps horse transports making their way toward Canaan through coastal waters. The only period in which "Israel" may have been the objective of chariot armies dispatched from Egypt would be the decades from Merneptah to Ramesses IV, after whose reign the Egyptians seem to have abandoned their claims to hegemony in Canaan.

The second poem is the "Song of Deborah" (Judges 5), which commemorates a great victory over the chariots of Jabin, king of Hazor. The song announces itself as a favorite of those

who ride on tawny asses,
    who sit on rich carpets
    and you who walk by the way.
To the sound of musicians at the watering places,
    there they repeat the triumphs of the Lord.

Since the poem itself is celebratory and exclamatory, the narrative is provided in a prose prologue (Judges 4) that includes some details that are not found in the poem but that are consistent with it. According to the prologue, Jabin, king of Hazor, had for twenty years sorely oppressed the Israelites. The instrument of his oppression was his commander, Sisera, who had nine hundred chariots of iron. At last, the men of Zebulon and Naphtali, north of the valley of Esdraelon and in the immediate hinterland of Hazor, threw off the yoke. Led by Barak, son of Abinoam, and on the strength of an oracle by the prophetess Deborah, ten thousand Zebulonites and Naphtalites occupied Mt. Tabor (some thirty miles to the southwest of Hazor). When Sisera learned of this, he came with his nine hundred chariots to the Valley of Jezreel, a part of Esdraelon below Mt. Tabor. Undaunted, Deborah prophesied to Barak that Yahweh would that day (or possibly that night, since the song suggests a night attack) give him a great victory. "So Barak came charging down from Mt. Tabor with ten thousand men at his back. The Lord put Sisera to rout with all his chariots and his army before Barak's onslaught."[7] All Sisera's men perished; not a man was left alive. Sisera himself fled on foot and sought shelter in the tent of Heber the Kenite. There he was killed as he lay under a rug, hiding from his pursuers: it was Jael, Heber's wife, who killed him, driving a tent peg through his temples.

The prose account is followed by the song itself, which hails as Barak's warriors men of Issachar and several other northern districts alongside

[7] Judges 4.14–15 (NEB translation).

those from Zebulon and Naphtali. All of these swept down, following their marshals clan by clan, into the valley: Yahweh's peasantry (*hupshu*) against "the mighty" of Canaan:

> Kings came, they fought;
>> then fought the kings of Canaan,
> at Taanach by the waters of Megiddo;
>> no plunder of silver did they take.
> The stars fought from heaven,
>> the stars in their courses fought against Sisera.
> The Torrent of Kishon swept him away,
>> the Torrent barred his flight; the Torrent of Kishon;
>> march on in might, my soul!
> Then hammered the hooves of his horses,
>> his chargers galloped, galloped away.[8]

The poem then lauds Jael, who "stretched out her hand for the tent peg, her right hand to hammer the weary," and rejoices at the death of Sisera and at the anxiety of his mother, who peers through the lattice looking for the chariots that never returned. "So perish all thine enemies, O Lord!"

Joshua 11.1–11 presents a southern (Ephraimite or Benjaminite) version of the same event.[9] Here the battle is fought not along the Kishon but at "the waters of Merom." It is not just the tribes north of Esdraelon, but all of Israel that defeats Jabin of Hazor. It is not Barak but the southern hero, Joshua, who is the victorious commander, and Deborah is not mentioned at all. After defeating Jabin's army, Joshua hamstrings all the horses and burns the chariots. He then proceeds to Hazor, massacres all the inhabitants, and burns the city to the ground. On this point the oral tradition was apparently correct, since Yadin's excavations demonstrated that Hazor was indeed destroyed ca. 1200.

The few and precious poems that survive from the early Iron Age therefore support the conclusion inferred from the archaeological evidence and from Egyptian reliefs and inscriptions: in the Catastrophe, thousands of barbarian skirmishers descended upon the plains that they had hitherto eschewed, destroyed the chariot armies on which the defense of the plains depended, and then sacked and burned the cities. From our vantage point we can see that all through the Late Bronze Age the eastern Mediterranean kingdoms had been vulnerable to a concerted attack by barbarian neighbors. But for most of the period this *arcanum imperii* was not perceived, either by the kings at risk or by the barbarians themselves. Only toward the

---

[8] Ibid., 5.19–22.
[9] On the two accounts see Gottwald, *Tribes of Yahweh*, 153–54.

end of the thirteenth century did the latter begin to sense their opportunity and to seize it.

We may close by speculating on the course of history in the eastern Mediterranean in the late thirteenth and early twelfth centuries B.C. For fifty or sixty years after the Battle of Kadesh (1275) the eastern Mediterranean seems to have been a relatively peaceful place. In the Aegean the several palaces, necessarily including one on Crete, supervised their populations with little fear for the future. Neither Knossos nor Pylos was fortified, their rulers evidently trusting in the habit of peace that has aptly been called the *pax Mycenaica*. In Anatolia and the Levant the Great Kingdoms of Hatti and Egypt provided stability, each Great King supporting and supported by networks of vassal kingdoms. After his peace treaty with Hattusilis III, Ramesses the Great's hegemony perhaps extended as far as the mountains of Lebanon. More of an innovation was Ramesses' initiative toward Libya: apparently he established Egyptian strongholds along the Mediterranean coast well beyond El Alamein.[10] The westward expansion of Egyptian authority would have repercussions, although not in Ramesses' own long reign.

The Catastrophe of the eastern Mediterranean kingdoms seems to have begun along the northwest frontier (see figure 1). Here a century and a half of peace must have ended dramatically when Boeotian Thebes and the great city known as Troy VI were captured and sacked. In Greek legend, the Seven who first tried to take Thebes failed to do so, and it was their sons, the *epigoni*, who succeeded: what the generation of Tydeus attempted the generation of Diomedes achieved. From the legends we may extract the probability that "Achaean" warriors (who these "Achaeans" were I shall suggest presently) made an early and unsuccessful assault upon Thebes and that some years later other Achaeans returned, this time taking the city. The same generation of warriors sacked Troy. The LH IIIB pottery found at the two sites permits the conclusion that the destruction of both Thebes and Troy VI occurred toward the end of the long reign of Ramesses the Great. In the event, the fate of these two kingdoms was a harbinger of what could and would happen everywhere in the eastern Mediterranean.

The Catastrophe burst upon Egypt in 1208, the fifth year of Merneptah's reign, when a Libyan chieftain, Meryre, son of Did, ventured to invade the western Delta. We do not know what motivated Meryre's presumptuous act. Ramesses' encroachment on Libya may have provoked him, or perhaps a drought inspired Meryre to seize some of the irrigated lands of the Delta,

---

[10] Gardiner, *Egypt*, 270, noted that stelae of Ramesses II have been found west of El Alamein. Hayward, "Elephant Ivory," 105, reports that "a fortress was built at Zawiyat Umm ar Rakham, about 20 km to the west (of Bates's Island, near Marsa Matruh) during the reign of Ramesses II." On the probable role of Bates's Island in Ramesses' frontier policy cf. Donald White, "The Third Season at Marsa Matruh," *AJA* 94 (1990): 330.

or Meryre may simply have calculated that Merneptah was too weak a king to resist a determined aggressor. But whatever his motivation, it is very likely that Meryre was encouraged in his undertaking by reports of what had happened in the Aegean. For we see in the description of the battle and its results that Meryre did not field much of a chariotry but made up for his deficiencies in that area by assembling tens of thousands of infantrymen. Most of these men came from Libya itself, but his recruitment efforts extended throughout "the northern lands" as well. That a Libyan king could communicate with much of the Mediterranean is no longer surprising, since the recent excavations on Bates's Island, near Marsa Matruh, have produced Mycenaean and Levantine pottery and suggest that the island was something of an exchange center for the eastern Libyans.

According to the Great Karnak Inscription, Meryre sought out runners from all the northern lands, men who could fight as skirmishers in hand-to-hand combat. Evidently his appeal for mercenaries fell on fertile ground in Sardinia, Sicily, southern or western Italy, Lycia, and especially northern Greece. All these lands were in contact with the civilized kingdoms of the eastern Mediterranean but were not themselves civilized. Instead, they were barbarous places, in which opportunities for the better things in life were severely limited. In Pamphylia, Lycaonia, and Lycia, the rugged tract of mountains along Anatolia's southern coast, there seems to have been nothing resembling a city in the Late Bronze Age. While Mycenaean pottery, and the perfumed oil contained in the pots, was shipped in great quantities to the cities of the Levant and the Cilician plain, the only ships that stopped along the Lycian coast were those that sank.[11] It is hardly surprising that as early as the Amarna Age men from the Lycian mountains tried their hand at piracy, raiding the comparatively wealthy coasts of Cyprus.

The Achaeans who joined Meryre's campaign are likely to have been North-Greek speakers.[12] The mountains west and north of Boeotia were

[11] See figure 53 in Harding, *Mycenaeans and Europe*, for the contrast between Mycenaean pottery finds in the Levant and in southern Asia Minor (aside from the Cilician plain).

[12] Hittitologists are generally convinced that the place-name "Ahhiya" (or, later, "Ahhiyawa") of the tablets refers to the Greek mainland. See Hans Güterbock, "The Hittites and the Aegean World, 1: The Ahhiyawa Problem Reconsidered," *AJA* 87 (1983): 133–38; and Trevor Bryce, "Ahhiyawans and Mycenaeans—An Anatolian Viewpoint," *Oxford Journal of Archaeology* 8 (1989): 297–310. But since the "Greek mainland" was not conceptualized until modern times, the Hittite term must have denoted something slightly different. It was, I would suggest, the name used in Asia Minor for the north-south land mass that Asian sailors encountered when sailing west from the Dardanelles. After coasting along Thrace for two days, and rounding the Chalcidice, one reaches the Vardar (Axios) River, where the coastline turns sharply and decisively southward. This is perhaps where *Ahhiya* began, and it ran to the tip of the Peloponnese. In book 2 of the *Iliad*, the land east of the Axios is not Achaea: the Paionians, who come "from the wide river Axios, the Axios, whose water is

far more primitive than the palace-states. Whereas the latter were civilized and Minoanized (South Greek may in fact have differentiated itself from North Greek because of "Minoan" influences), most of the north was an illiterate hinterland, in which the dialect of the Greek-speakers was the conservative North Greek. Troy, Iolkos, Thebes, and Orchomenos were outposts on the northwestern frontier of the civilized world, and beyond these centers there was little discernible prosperity in the LH IIIB period. The two dialects—South Greek and North Greek—thus seem to reflect two rather distinct cultural zones, and when reference is made to "the Achaeans" we must specify which of the two zones is meant. As I have protested betimes,[13] the evidence is considerable that the particular Achaeans who sacked Troy came from the north.

We may imagine, then, that late in the reign of Ramesses II hordes of these northern Achaean footsoldiers had attacked both Troy VI and Thebes and succeeded in taking and sacking both places.[14] The Achaeans attacked Thebes, according to Hesiod,[15] "for the flocks of Oedipus." Prior to their attacks on these kingdoms, the northern Achaeans are likely to have served the kingdoms as skirmishers, and we may imagine that it was during that service that the northerners began to perceive how vulnerable the royal chariotries were. Toward the end of the thirteenth century the rulers of the Argolid began building a fortification wall at the Corinthian isthmus (having already encircled their palaces with stout walls), indicating some alarm about what was happening in the north. It was perhaps among these northern Achaeans that Meryre of Libya was most successful in his solicitation of skirmishers. In the casualty lists, after the Libyans themselves it was the *Ekwesh* who lost the most men (over two thousand).

Ever since Maspero transmogrified them into migratory nations, the *Shekelesh*, *Shardana*, and *Tursha* who joined Meryre's enterprise have received the most attention from scholars interested in the Catastrophe. Numerically, however, they were not very important, since Meryre recruited from Sicily, Tyrsenia, and Sardinia together fewer men than Achaea

---

fairest of all" (*Iliad* 2.849–50), are the Trojans' westernmost allies, while the Achaeans all come from beyond the Axios.

Hittite tablets refer to a Great Kingdom in Ahhiya, and this was probably centered at Mycenae, with vassal kingdoms as far north as Attica and Boeotia, if not Iolkos. But the more primitive people who lived between the kingdoms and the Axios were also "Achaeans." There is good reason to believe that these northern Achaeans were the perpetrators of the Catastrophe, while the Achaeans of the kingdoms were its victims.

[13] "Argos and Argives," 111–15; *Coming of the Greeks*, 222–24; see above, pp. 117–18.

[14] As I have argued at "Argos and Argives," 132–33, the "Argives" led by the Seven against Thebes came from the Pelasgic Argos and not from the Peloponnese. *Iliad* 4.370–99 and 6.223 recall that Thebes was sacked by "Achaeans" but that the kingdom of Mycenae did not participate in the adventure.

[15] *Works and Days*, 161–63.

supplied to him all by itself (it is not impossible that even the Lycians outnumbered the westerners in Meryre's army). But prospectors for mercenaries would undoubtedly have found the lands of the central Mediterranean a promising vein. Sicily was almost entirely barbarous, but for a few Sicilians of the southeast coast a window on the wider world had been opened: on the promontory of Thapsos, jutting out from the shore a few kilometers north of the Syracusan bay, traders from the eastern Mediterranean, and perhaps specifically from Cyprus, had built a town for themselves by 1300, and the town continued through the thirteenth century. Here were spacious and rectilinear buildings, and the residents of the town lived the good life, with eastern artifacts and luxury items.[16] On the coasts of Italy, which was equally primitive, Mycenaeans had established emporia at Scoglio del Tonno, on the Gulf of Taranto, and at Luni sul Mignone, in Etruria. For those "Tyrsenians" who lived nearby, these emporia must have advertised the possibilities that the lands to the east had to offer. The contact between the eastern Mediterranean and Sardinia, and the easterners' exploitation of Sardinian copper, has only recently been appreciated. But it now seems likely that in the thirteenth century most Sardinians who lived within a day's walk of the Golfo di Cagliari would have seen the visitors' ships, if not the visitors themselves, and would have been well aware of the discrepancy between their own condition and that of these people from the east.[17]

To be a warrior, then, was in these barbarous lands no bad thing, since skill as a skirmisher might transport a man to a better life in a better place. Men from southern Sardinia went off to Byblos and Ugarit, and eventually to Egypt, and it is unlikely that many of them returned home or wished to do so. In the eastern kingdoms they could enjoy the pleasures of urban life and at the same time be men of status and property, with lands assigned them by their king; in return, they were obliged only to guard the palace during peacetime and to run in support of the fabled chariot forces on those

[16] Holloway, *Italy and the Aegean*, 87: "It required men and ideas to transform a Sicilian village into an emporium with some urban configuration, and this appears to have been the work of Cypriote residents in the 14th and 13th centuries." See also Holloway, "Italy and the Central Mediterranean in the Crisis Years," in Ward and Joukowsky, *Crisis Years*, 41.

[17] In the twelfth century Cypriotes were probably working metal on the southern coast of Sardinia (see D. Ridgway, "Archaeology in Sardinia and South Italy, 1983–88," p. 134). But the discovery of LH IIIB ware near Cagliari now shows that already in the thirteenth century easterners were resident there, perhaps "casting copper for export in the ingot shape long used in the east." See Holloway, "Italy and the Central Mediterranean," 41. Contact with the interior is difficult to estimate. For a much later period Ferrucio Barreca, "The Phoenician and Punic Civilization in Sardinia," in Miriam Balmuth, ed., *Studies in Sardinian Archaeology*, vol. 2, 145, has shown that from Nora and other sites on the Cagliari bay "settlements began to spread towards the Sardinian hinterland with an average penetration of about twenty kilometers from the coasts."

rare occasions when the chariots gave battle. It is not surprising that young men in Sardinia and elsewhere aspired to serve as skirmishers in the chariot corps of a wealthy king. All that one needed was courage, speed, strength, and an initial investment in the necessary equipment: a sword or spear, a shield, and an intimidating helmet.

When Meryre advertised for skirmishers in Merneptah's early years, those who responded had undoubtedly long hoped to be professional warriors, whether in Egypt itself or in one of the other kingdoms that traditionally hired mercenaries. What was new in 1208 was the mercenaries' enlistment in an army in which they were not to play second fiddle to a chariot corps. As noted above, Meryre had very few chariots—a deficiency that a decade or two earlier would have prevented him from even considering a war with Merneptah. But by 1208 Meryre thought it possible that with a huge force of skirmishers he could defeat the largest chariot army in the world. For the hand-to-hand fighting his men were certainly armed with long swords, since the Karnak Inscription records that over nine thousand of these bronze swords were retrieved as booty. For use against the Egyptian chariots Meryre must have had men expert with long-range weapons of some sort, and there is good reason to think that these were javelins rather than bows. In the primitive lands from which his auxiliaries came there would have been many men who were skilled with the hunting javelin but who had never imagined that their skill might one day be in demand.

Meryre's infantry was defeated, and it was another generation before another Libyan force attacked the Delta. But Meryre's failure, like the Achaeans' successes at Troy and Thebes, seems to have publicized the possibilities of the new kind of warfare. On the eastern side of the Delta, there was trouble in Canaan at about the same time that the Libyans attacked on the western side. Hori, the author of the Papyrus Anastasi, asks his youthful correspondent to imagine himself in charge of supplies for an army sent to Djahan (or, possibly, Djahi) "to crush those rebels called Nearin."[18] The ne'arim of Canaan were hand-to-hand warriors and had distinguished themselves at the Battle of Kadesh in the service of Ramesses the Great. Now, however, at the end of the Nineteenth Dynasty, they have evidently become a problem, and in the scenario drawn by Hori an army consisting entirely of infantrymen, most of whom are barbarian skirmishers, is sent out to deal with them. In this connection we must note the recently discovered evidence that Merneptah did in fact campaign in the Levant and that among his opponents were warriors from Israel. The men of Israel will certainly have fought on foot.

The "rebellious ne'arim" of the southern Levant did not yet pose a threat

---

[18] Trans. Wilson, ANET, 476.

to Egypt itself. There was no king here who organized the tribesmen of Canaan for a campaign on the scale that Meryre managed in Libya. In Hori's imaginary army there are only five thousand men, suggesting that the Levantine warriors against whom they are sent also number in the low thousands. But although not yet a danger to Egypt, the warriors of Philistia and Israel were certainly capable of defeating the vassal cities that were allied with Egypt. Although Merneptah may have maintained Egypt's traditional hegemony over the southern Levant, it is doubtful that his feeble successors were able to do so. Seti II had trouble enough asserting himself in Egypt, having apparently to deal with a usurpation by Amenmesse. At Seti's death, the throne devolved first upon his son Siptah—still a child—and then upon Twosret, Seti's widow. Neither could have intervened in Canaan, and it was evidently in Twosret's reign that the sacking of the great cities of southern Canaan began.

Although we cannot be certain who sacked the cities on the Via Maris—Ashkelon, Ashdod, Akko, and others—there is no reason to look for the culprits in some distant place when there are obvious suspects close by. Undoubtedly the sackers were "Philistines," but that term ought to stand for the population that had traditionally lived in the hinterland of the pentapolis. Armed with the javelins and long swords shown in the Medinet Habu reliefs, the Palestinian tribesmen must have made short work of the chariot armies by which the pentapolis was defended. Further north along the coast, the *Tjekker* must have closed in on and eventually taken the city of Dor. And the warriors of Dan seem to have made a name for themselves by their success, probably with long swords, against both chariots and cavalry.

In the interior, centers such as Deir 'Alla (Succoth), Lachish, and Hazor were most likely sacked by "Israelites," seminomadic tribesmen who for generations had scraped out an existence in the hill country flanking the valleys of the Jordan and its tributaries, and in the desert fringe to the east. Until the Catastrophe, the best that either Philistines or Israelites could hope for was service as *ne'arim* or *hapiru* in the employ of a petty king. But now they were in a position to kill the king, loot his palace and his city, and burn them to the ground. Not all the Canaanite cities between the Jordan and the Mediterranean were razed. Shechem was spared by the Israelite tribesmen, the Israelites foreswearing hostilities against the city, and the Shechemites granting to those Israelites who submitted to circumcision the rights of *connubium* and of participation in the venerable cult on Mt. Gerizim. Gibeon was also spared, having come to terms with the invaders: in return for their lives, the Gibeonites were said to have pledged themselves and their descendants to serve their conquerors as hewers of wood and drawers of water. According to Israelite legend, when the other Canaanite kings took umbrage at the Gibeonites' accommodation and attacked the city, Gibeon's Israelite champions came to its rescue and slaughtere$\cdot$ the Canaanite force, while the sun stood still over Gibeon and the moon halted in the vale of Aijalon. It must have been a long and terrible day in Canaan.

The successes that skirmishers armed with swords and javelins achieved over chariot armies, and the consequent sacking of famous cities, must have generated excitement wherever service as a mercenary footsoldier had once seemed attractive. The motivation for the sacking of a city is not likely to have been anything so rarefied as religious fanaticism, ethnic hatred, or a class struggle. The perpetrators of the Catastrophe had more material objectives: cattle, gold, women, and whatever else caught the eye. The precious objects squirreled away in pits or wall-caches at Ugarit, Mycenae, Kokkinokremos, and other places testify that what the residents of these places feared was an attack by looters. And since at none of the razed cities have archaeologists found "in the open" anything of material value, we may conclude that what the residents feared would happen did happen.

Just as the cities of southern Canaan are likely to have been plundered and razed by warriors from the countryside of Philistia and Israel, so it is likely that some cities in other regions were sacked by raiders who came from a hinterland not too far away. In eastern Syria Emar, possibly along with Carchemish, was sacked by "hordes," and in that part of the world in the early twelfth century such nameless hordes must have been Aramaic-speaking tribesmen. In Boeotia, as suggested above, Thebes had been sacked by raiders from its hinterland. On the Anatolian plateau, Hattusas evidently fell to Kaskans from the Pontic mountains.

In some areas there was no warlike population of barbarians within striking distance. In western Syria, so far as the tablets from Alalakh and Ugarit indicate, there were only peaceful and unarmed villagers. The danger here was posed by raiders who came from the sea, among whom may have been freebooters from Lycia, the northern Aegean, Italy, Sicily, Sardinia, and other maritime regions of barbaria. The tablets from Ugarit warn of the peril posed by marauders who came in ships, and the tablets "from the oven" suggest that Ugarit itself fell to raiders who appeared with little warning. A force of several thousand skirmishers, possibly crammed into no more than thirty or forty boats, would have been sufficient to defeat whatever chariot force sallied out against them from the gates of Ugarit. At any rate, Ugarit, along with all the great cities on the Orontes—Alalakh, Hamath, Qatna, and Kadesh—was sacked and burned.

In the civilized regions of southern Greece there likewise was little to fear from people who lived close by. Within the large palace states administered from Pylos or Knossos there were no warrior populations, the subjects there being pacific and helotized descendants of the pre-Greek inhabitants. Although the palaces in Boeotia may have fallen to raiders from Locris,

Phocis, and inland Thessaly, who came on foot, more sites in the Aegean are likely to have been attacked by raiders who came by sea, many of them undoubtedly from coastal Thessaly and Achaea Phthiotis. From the citadel of Koukounaries, on Paros, one looks down a steep decline to Naoussa Bay. Fifteen minutes after wading ashore, veteran sackers of cities would have been atop the citadel. The huddled skeletons found there in recent excavations indicate that the population had little warning and no chance to escape. Pylos and Knossos, without walls, were entirely vulnerable, and we may imagine that the inhabitants fled at the first alarm. At Troy, Tiryns and other places some sort of siege may have been conducted, but in the end the citadels were taken. Mycenae is not likely to have been surprised, since the citadel is a two-hour walk from Argos Bay, but against several thousand raiders there would have been no real protection. Even if the attack came in broad daylight, and even if the rulers of Mycenae were able to mobilize several hundred chariots, the swarming javelineers would have been elusive targets and deadly marksmen against the chariot horses. After storming a city or a citadel, killing or enslaving those inhabitants who had not been able to flee, and ransacking the buildings for every bit of precious metal, elegant cloth, and usable artifacts, the raiders would have prepared the place for burning and then set fire to it. Such must have been the fate of dozens of the wealthiest cities and palaces in the eastern Mediterranean.

After most of the great palaces had fallen, attempts were made once again upon Egypt. Ramesses III had to face incursions by Libyans, now grown persistent, in 1182 and 1176. These were certainly massive assaults, since Ramesses claims that in the first of these two wars his troops killed 12,535 of the invaders. And by this time the Philistine and *Tjekker* warriors, even without a king to mastermind and finance the venture, posed a threat to Egypt itself. In his eighth year (1179) Ramesses dealt with this threat on his eastern border. His inscription would have us believe that the enemies whom he defeated in that campaign were a vast coalition, a conspiracy of all lands, that had been responsible for devastating the entire Near East from Hatti to Canaan and from Cyprus to Carchemish. Such claims greatly enhanced his own victory and need not be taken literally: from their letters we know that the rulers of Hattusas, Emar, and Ugarit were themselves uncertain about the identity of the hordes intent on sacking their cities, and it is unlikely that Ramesses had any better information on the subject. What Ramesses undoubtedly did know is that the kind of destruction that the Philistines and *Tjekker* had wrought in the southern Levant, and the kind of warfare that these tribesmen practiced, had already come to most of the great cities and palaces farther north.

The Levantine aggressors in 1179 were armed with javelins and long swords, wore helmets and corslets, and carried round shields. In order to defeat them Ramesses had to improvise, and his battle plans seem to have relegated his chariotry to a subordinate role. Ramesses assembled a considerable number of hand-to-hand fighters, both barbarian skirmishers (*shardana*) and native Egyptians. The latter stood shoulder-to-shoulder in close-order formations, carried oblong shields, were armed with the traditional rods or sickle swords, and were hardly as effective as their foreign auxiliaries who fought as free-lancers. But infantrymen of both kinds, helped out by the archers in the chariot corps, were sufficient to win the battle at Djahi.

Whether on that same occasion or soon thereafter, Ramesses destroyed a great force of Philistine, *Tjekker*, and Sicilian skirmishers who were caught on their boats a short distance offshore. The skirmishers had not expected a battle while still in their ships and were virtually annihilated. With remarkable foresight Ramesses had assembled a fleet and assigned to each ship a detachment of archers (most likely the archers who in other circumstances and other times would have shot from chariots) and hand-to-hand warriors. The Egyptian ships were able to cut off the enemy, who had no usable long-range weapons. The Philistine and Sicilian warriors would have had javelins, but javelins on these crowded ships were of no value at all, since a javelin must be thrown on the run. The Egyptian archers, on the contrary, were able to shoot their bows far more effectively from the deck of a ship than from the platform of a bouncing chariot. Even worse for the aggressors, while the Egyptian archers could leave the rowing to the oarsmen whom Ramesses had impressed into service, the Philistine and Sicilian warriors had to do their own rowing. Perhaps the Medinet Habu relief does not exaggerate the extent of Ramesses' victory at sea in 1179.

Even Ramesses' victories, however, illustrated how drastically warfare had changed in the three or four decades of the Catastrophe. The Egyptians' salvation owed little to their chariotry. Most important were the hand-to-hand warriors, whether Egyptian or barbarian, that Ramesses had assembled at Djahi. The archers who had been positioned on the decks of Ramesses' ships had also taken their toll, but the "naval battle" may have been something of a fluke, contingent on timing and luck. The future belonged to men who could stand their ground in hand-to-hand combat.

Those who survived the Catastrophe resorted to new strategies against the probability that the raiders would return. On Crete the small and low-lying settlements were abandoned for "cities of refuge" in the mountains. The Arcado-Cypriote dialect suggests that many South-Greek speakers from the Peloponnese and central Greece fled in two directions, some to the mountains of Arcadia and others to the island of Cyprus. The flight to Ionia, on the other hand, seems to have occurred several generations after the Catastrophe ended.

If towns built in the twelfth century were not in the mountains, they were on the seacoast. On Cyprus, as well as in Phoenicia and Greece, large

coastal towns were built and fortified, and the coastal cities of the Via
Maris were rebuilt and strengthened (with refugees from Crete probably
seeking asylum there). The size of the twelfth-century towns indicates a
belief that there was safety in numbers. The coastal location may have been
preferred for several reasons. It provided, first of all, the optimum vantage
point for spotting hostile ships long before they reached the shore. A city on
the coast, even if it housed few hand-to-hand fighters, was also able to take
some effective offensive measures against raiders who came by sea. As
Ramesses' sea victory had shown, one very good way to confront a seaborne horde of hand-to-hand skirmishers was to keep them from reaching
land. On board their ships the skirmishers were vulnerable, since they had
no bows (the man fortunate enough to own a composite bow would have
found it warped and deteriorated after several days in an open boat). It is
therefore possible that a few of the coastal towns continued to count on
archers, now shooting from coast-guard ships instead of from chariots. It is
more likely, however, that coastal locations were chosen for defensive reasons: a city on the coast might be able to withstand a siege, while a city in
the interior could be entirely cut off.

But no civilized society could defend itself without putting into the field
infantrymen equipped for hand-to-hand combat. Against the new peril
new weapons were required, and new pieces of armor. In Greece especially
we can see that the Catastrophe created the armored footsoldier, protected
by a helmet, corslet, greaves, and a round shield. A short thrusting spear
was most important as the weapon of men who took their position in close-
order infantry formations. For professional skirmishers, who might confront the enemy in man-to-man combat, a long sword was required against
the long swords of the predators. The manufacture of cut-and-thrust
swords began in Merneptah's time, as the unusable "Merneptah sword"
from Ugarit shows. The Aegean productions found at Mouliana, Mycenae,
and Perati are clumsy experiments, but better designs were soon found.
Had there been time to hilt them and edge their blades, the four unfinished
swords from the high-priest's house in Ugarit would have been formidable
weapons. In the IIIC Aegean, however, what those who could afford it
wanted was the terrible Griffzungenschwert that had long been traditional
in northeast Italy and the Balkans. The cartouche of Seti II on a specimen
found in Egypt shows that there too some of the pharaoh's warriors acquired the very best slashing sword that could be found.

Although weapons and armor were important, even more important
were men who could use them, and on this matter the Catastrophe introduced profound changes. In the Late Bronze Age kingdoms warfare had
been a specialist's concern. Civilian conscripts were apparently used only
for defense, and massed offensive infantries were conspicuously absent
when Late Bronze Age kingdoms (except, perhaps, for Assyria) went to

war. After the Catastrophe, political power belonged to those societies in which warfare was every man's concern, the adult males of a community serving as its militia. The Warrior Vase from Mycenae suggests that in the twelfth century at least some men of Mycenae were learning how to march and fight in close-order formations, depending on the thrusting spear and on the new elements of defensive armor. But neither at Mycenae nor in most other civilized communities could a "warrior ethos" have developed in the immediate aftermath of the Catastrophe, and military prowess tended to be associated with the less civilized frontier societies. It is likely that the "Dorians" were North-Greek speakers who became proficient as close-order spearmen. In the Iron Age Levant, communities such as Philistia, Israel, Moab, Ammon, and Aram (in eastern Syria) depended on mass infantries. We need not believe, with the biblical author, that in David's kingdom there were 1,300,000 "able-bodied men, capable of bearing arms." But the militia was apparently counted in six figures, and we can perhaps take the author's word for it that when David wished to curse Joab, the best he could think of was "may the house of Joab never be free from running sore or foul disease, or lack a son fit only to ply the distaff."[19] Typically these frontier societies coalesced into "nations," the nation being a coalition cohesive enough and large enough to defend itself against any foreseeable aggression.[20]

The solidarity of an Iron Age community, whether of a polis or of a nation, stemmed from the recognition that in war the fortunes of the community would depend on every man playing his part. Against mass formations of close-order infantry, the formations being controlled by an efficient chain of command, disorganized hordes of running skirmishers would have been outmatched. The kind of solidarity required in the Iron Age was, with rare exceptions, unnecessary and therefore unknown in the Late Bronze Age, since prior to the Catastrophe a king's subjects were amply protected by the king's chariots and chariot runners. The military revolution that occurred in the Catastrophe was thus a prerequisite for the social and political changes that made the world of the Iron Age so different from that of the Late Bronze Age.

[19] 2 Samuel 24.9; 2 Samuel 3.29.

[20] On nationalism in the early Iron Age see Liverani's discussion of "il fattore gentilizio e lo Stato 'nazionale,'" in his *Antico Oriente*, 654–60.

BIBLIOGRAPHY

Akurgal, Ekrem. "Das Dunkle Zeitalter Kleinasiens." In *Griechenland, die Ägäis und die Levante während der "Dark Ages,"* ed. Sigrid Deger-Jalkotzy, 67–78. Vienna: Österreichische Akademie der Wissenschaft, 1978.

Alföldi, Andreas. "Die Herrschaft der Reiterei in Griechenland und Rom nach dem Sturz der Könige." In *Gestalt und Geschichte: Festschrift K. Schefold*, 13–47. Bern: Francke, 1967.

Anderson, J. K. "Greek Chariot-Borne and Mounted Infantry." *AJA* 79 (1975): 175–87.

———. "Homeric, British, and Cyrenaic Chariots." *AJA* 69 (1965): 349–52.

Arnaud, Daniel. "Les textes d'Emar et la chronologie de la fin du Bronze Récent." *Syria* 52 (1975): 87–92.

Astour, Michael. "New Evidence on the Last Days of Ugarit." *AJA* 69 (1965): 253–58.

Åström, Paul. "Die Akropolis von Midea um 1200 v. Chr." In *Forschungen zur aegaeischen Vorgeschichte. Das Ende der mykenischen Welt*, ed. Eberhard Thomas, 7–11. Cologne: n.p. ("herausgegaben von Eberhard Thomas"), 1987.

———. *The Cuirass Tomb and Other Finds at Dendra*. Göteborg: Åström, 1977.

———. "The Sea Peoples in the Light of New Excavations." *Centre d'Etudes chypriotes* 3 (1985): 3–17.

———, ed. *High, Middle, or Low? Acts of an International Colloquium on Absolute Chronology Held at the University of Gothenburg 20th-22nd August 1987*. Göteborg: Åström, 1987.

———, and Katie Demakopoulou. "New Excavations in the Citadel of Midea 1983–1984." *OA* 16 (1986): 19–25.

———, R. Maddin, J. D. Muhly, and T. Stech. "Iron Artifacts from Swedish Excavations in Cyprus." *OA* 16 (1986): 27–41.

Avila, Robert. *Bronzene Lanzen- und Pfeilspitzen der griechischen Spätbronzezeit* (Prähistorische Bronzefunde, Abt. V, 1). Munich: Beck, 1983.

Balmuth, Miriam, ed. *Studies in Sardinian Archaeology*, vol. 2. Ann Arbor: University of Michigan Press, 1986.

———, ed. *Studies in Sardinian Archaeology*, vol. 3: *Nuragic Sardinia and the Mycenaean World* (B.A.R. International Series 387). Oxford: British Archaeological Reports, 1987.

Barnett, R. D. "The Sea Peoples." *CAH*, vol. 2, part 2: 359–78.

Barreca, Ferrucio. "The Phoenician and Punic Civilization in Sardinia." In *Studies in Sardinian Archaeology*, vol. 2, ed. Miriam Balmuth, 145–70. Ann Arbor: University of Michigan Press, 1986.

The Battle Reliefs of King Seti I. The Epigraphic Survey, University of Chicago, Oriental Institute Publications, vol. 107. Chicago: Oriental Institute of the University of Chicago, 1986.

Batto, B. F. "The Reed Sea: *Requiescat in Pace*." *JBL* 102 (1983): 27–35.

Beal, Richard. "The Organization of the Hittite Military." Ph.D. dissertation, University of Chicago, 1986.

Bengtson, Hermann. *Griechische Geschichte*. 4th ed. Munich: Beck, 1969.

Betancourt, Philip. "The End of the Greek Bronze Age." *Antiquity* 50 (1976): 40–47.

———. *The History of Minoan Pottery*. Princeton: Princeton University Press, 1985.

Bianco Peroni, Vera. *Die Schwerter in Italien/Le Spade nell'Italia continentale* (Prähistorische Bronzefunde, Abt. IV, 1). Munich: Beck, 1970.

Bierbrier, M. "The Date of the Destruction of Emar and Egyptian Chronology." *JEA* 64 (1978): 136–37.

Bimson, J. J. "Merenptah's Israel and Recent Theories of Israelite Origins." *JSOT* 49 (1991): 3–29.

Bittel, Kurt. "Die archaeologische Situation in Kleinasien um 1200 v. Chr. und während der nachfolgenden vier Jahrhunderte." In *Griechenland, die Ägäis und die Levante während der "Dark Ages,"* ed. Sigrid Deger-Jalkotzy, 25–47. Vienna: Österreichische Akademie der Wissenschaft, 1983.

———. *Grundzüge der Vor-und Frühgeschichte Kleinasiens*. 2d ed. Tübingen: Wasmuth, 1950.

Blegen, Carl, et al. *Troy: Excavations Conducted by the University of Cincinnati*, vols. 1–4. Princeton: Princeton University Press, 1950–58.

Boardman, John. *The Date of the Knossos Tablets*. Oxford: Clarendon, 1963.

Bolt, B. A. *Earthquakes*. New York: Freeman, 1988.

Bonfante, Giuliano and Larissa. *The Etruscan Language: An Introduction*. New York: New York University Press, 1983.

Bonnet, Hans. *Die Waffen der Völker des alten Orients*. Leipzig: Hinrichs, 1926.

Borchhardt, Heide. "Frühe griechische Schildformen." In *Kriegswesen*, vol. 1: *Schutzwaffen und Wehrbauten*, ed. H.-G. Buchholz and Josef Wiesner, 1–56. Göttingen: Vandenhoeck and Ruprecht, 1977.

Bouzek, Jan. *The Aegean, Anatolia, and Europe: Cultural Inter-relations in the Second Millennium B.C.* (Studies in Mediterranean Archaeology, 29). Göteborg and Prague: Åström and Academia, 1985.

Braudel, Fernand. "L'Aube." In Fernand Braudel, ed., *La Méditerranée: l'espace et l'histoire*, 65–102. Paris: Arts et métiers graphiques, 1977.

Breasted, James. *Ancient Records of Egypt*, vols. 3 and 4. 3d ed. Chicago: University of Chicago Press, 1927.

———. *The Battle of Kadesh*. Chicago: University of Chicago Press, 1903.

Brinkman, J. A. "Notes on Mesopotamian History in the Thirteenth Century B.C." *Bibliotheca Orientalis* 27 (1970): 301–14.

Briquel, Dominique. *Les Pélasges en Italie. Recherches sur l' histoire de la légende*. Rome: Ecole Française, 1984.

Brug, John F. *A Literary and Archaeological Study of the Philistines* (B.A.R. International Series 265). Oxford: British Archaeological Reports, 1985.

Bryce, Trevor. "Ahhiyawans and Mycenaeans—An Anatolian Perspective." *Oxford Journal of Archaeology* 8 (1989): 127–34.

———. "Lukka Revisited." *JNES* 51 (1992): 121–30.

Bryson, R. A., H. H. Lamb, and D. R. Donley. "Drought and the Decline of Mycenae." *Antiquity* 48 (1974): 46–50.

Buchholz, H.-G. "Schlussbemerkungen." In *Ägäische Bronzezeit*, ed. Buchholz, 499–534. Darmstadt: Wissenschaftliche Buchgesellschaft, 1987.

———, and V. Karageorghis. *Prehistoric Greece and Cyprus*. London: Phaidon, 1973.

———, ed. *Ägäische Bronzezeit*. Darmstadt: Wissenschaftliche Buchgesellschaft, 1987.

———, ed. *Kriegswesen*, vol. 2: *Angriffswaffen* (Archaeologia Homerica Bd. I, Kap. E, Teil 2). Göttingen: Vandenhoeck and Ruprecht, 1980.

———, and Josef Wiesner, eds. *Kriegswesen*, vol. 1: *Schutzwaffen und Wehrbauten* (Archaeologia Homerica Bd. I, Kap. E, Teil 1). Göttingen: Vandenhoeck and Ruprecht, 1977.

Buitenen, J.A.B. van, trans. *The Mahabharata*. 3 vols. Chicago: University of Chicago Press, 1978.

Bunimovitz, Shlomo, and Orna Zimhoni. " 'Lamp and Bowl' Foundation Deposits from the End of the Late Bronze Age." *Eretz-Israel* 21 (1990): 102.

Bury, J. B., and Russell Meiggs. *A History of Greece*. 4th ed. London: St. Martins, 1975.

Cadogan, Gerald. "Maroni and the Late Bronze Age of Cyprus." In *Cyprus at the Close of the Late Bronze Age*, ed. Vassos Karageorghis and J. D. Muhly, 1–10. Nicosia: Zavallis, 1984.

Canby, Jeanny V. "Hittite Art." *Bib. Arch.* (1989): 109–30.

Capelle, W. "Erdbebenforschung." *RE* Supplementbd. IV (1924), cols. 344–74.

Carpenter, Rhys. *Discontinuity in Greek Civilization*. New York: Norton, 1968.

Cassin, Elena. "A propos du char de guerre en Mésopotamie," In *Problèmes de la guerre en Grèce ancienne*, ed. J. P. Vernant, 297–308. Paris: Mouton, 1968.

Casson, Lionel. *The Ancient Mariners: Seafarers and Sea Fighters in the Mediterranean in Ancient Times*. New York: Macmillan, 1959.

Catling, H. W. "Archaeology in Greece." Annually from 1978–79 through 1988–89 in *Archaeological Reports* (published by the Society for the Promotion of Hellenic Studies and by the British School at Athens).

———. "Archaeology in Greece, 1978–79." *AR* (1978–79): 3–42.

———. "Archaeology in Greece, 1980–81." *AR* (1980–81): 3–48.

———. "Archaeology in Greece, 1982–83." *AR* (1982–83): 3–62.

———. "Archaeology in Greece, 1986–87." *AR* (1986–87): 3–61.

———. "Archaeology in Greece, 1988–89." *AR* (1988–89): 3–116.

———. "Beinschienen." In *Kriegswesen*, vol. 1: *Schutzwaffen und Wehrbauten*, ed. H.-G. Buchholz and Josef Wiesner, 143–61. Göttingen: Vandenhoeck and Ruprecht, 1977.

———. "Bronze Cut-and-Thrust Swords in the Eastern Mediterranean." *PPS* 22 (1956): 102–25.

———. "Late Minoan Vases and Bronzes in Oxford." *ABSA* 63 (1968): 89–131.

———. "A Mycenaean Puzzle from Lefkandi in Euboea." *AJA* 72 (1968): 41–49.

———. "A New Bronze Sword from Cyprus," *Antiquity* 35 (1961): 115–22.

———. "Panzer." In *Kriegswesen*, vol. 1: *Schutzwaffen und Wehrbauten*, ed. H.-G. Buchholz and Josef Wiesner, 74–118. Göttingen: Vandenhoeck and Ruprecht, 1977.

Caubet, Annie. "Reoccupation of the Syrian Coast after the Destruction of the 'Crisis Years.'" In *The Crisis Years: The 12th Century B.C.*, ed. Wm. A. Ward and Martha Joukowsky, 123–31. Dubuque: Kendall/Hunt, 1992.

Cazelles, H. "The Hebrews." In *Peoples of Old Testament Times*, ed. D. J. Wiseman, 1–28. Oxford: Clarendon, 1973.

Chabas, F. *Etudes sur l'Antiquité historique d'après les sources égyptiennes et les monuments réputés préhistoriques.* Paris: Maisonneuve, 1872.

Chadwick, John. "I Dori e la creazione dei dialetti greci." In *Le Origini dei Greci: Dori e mondo egeo*, ed. Domenico Musti, 3–12. Rome: Laterza, 1990.

———. "The Organization of the Mycenaean Archives." In *Studia Mycenaea. Proceedings of the Mycenaean Symposium, Brno, April 1966*, ed. A. Bartoněk, 11–21. Brno, 1968.

———. "Who Were the Dorians?" *La Parola del Passato* 31 (1976): 103–17.

Chavane, Marie-José. "Instruments de bronze." In *Ras Shamra—Ougarit III. Le Centre de la ville: 38e–44e Campagnes (1978–1984)*, ed. Marguerite Yon et al., 357. Paris, 1987.

Childe, V. G. *The Danube in Prehistory*. Oxford: Clarendon, 1929.

———. "The Final Bronze Age in the Near East and Temperate Europe." *PPS* 14 (1948): 177–95.

———. *Prehistoric Migrations in Europe*. Oslo: Inst. for Sammenlignende Kulturforskning, 1950.

———. *What Happened in History*. Harmondsworth: Penguin, 1942.

Coles, J. M., and A. F. Harding. *The Bronze Age in Europe*. New York: St. Martin's, 1979.

Cousin, G, and F. Durrbach. "Bas-relief de Lemnos avec inscriptions." *BCH* 10 (1886): 1–6.

Cowen, J. D. "Eine Einführung in die Geschichte der bronzenen Griffzungenschwerter in Süddeutschland und der angrenzenden Gebieten." *Bericht der Römisch Germanischen Kommission* 36 (1965): 52–155.

———. "The Flange-Hilted Cutting Sword of Bronze: Was It First Developed in Central Europe, or in the Aegean Area?" *Bericht über den V. Internationalen Kongress für Vor- und Frühgeschichte* (Berlin, 1961): 207–14.

———. "The Origins of the Flange-Hilted Sword of Bronze in Continental Europe." *PPS* 32 (1966): 292–312.

Cross, Frank. "Newly Found Inscriptions in Old Canaanite and Early Phoenician Script." *BASOR* 238 (1980): 4–7.

———. "On Dating Phoenician Inscriptions in Sardinia and the Mediterranean." *AJA* 94 (1990): 340.

———. "Phoenicians in the West: The Early Epigraphic Evidence." In *Studies in Sardinian Archaeology* vol. 2, ed. Miriam Balmuth, 117–30. Ann Arbor: University of Michigan Press, 1986.

———, ed. *Symposia Celebrating the Seventy-Fifth Anniversary of the Founding of the American Schools of Oriental Research (1900–1975)*. Cambridge, Mass.: American Schools of Oriental Research, 1979.

———, and David Freedman. "The Song of Miriam." *JNES* 14 (1955): 237–50.

Crouwel, J. H. *Chariots and Other Means of Land Transport in Bronze Age Greece*. Amsterdam: Allard Pierson Museum, 1981.

Crowther, N. B. "The Apobates Reconsidered (Demosthenes lxi 23–9)." *JHS* 111 (1991): 174–76.

Cutler, B., and J. Macdonald. "Identification of the *naʿar* in the Ugaritic Texts." *UF* 8 (1976): 27–35.

Dalley, Stephanie. "Foreign Chariotry and Cavalry in the Armies of Tiglath-Pileser III and Sargon II." *Iraq* 47 (1985): 31–48.

Davies, G. I. "'*Urwōt* in I Kings 5:6 (Evv. 4:26) and the Assyrian Horse Lists." *Journal of Semitic Studies* 34 (1989): 25–38.

Deger-Jalkotzy, Sigrid. *E-qe-ta. Zur Rolle des Gefolgschaftswesen in der Sozialstruktur mykenischer Reiche.* Vienna: Österreichische Akademie der Wissenschaft, 1978.

———. "Das Problem der 'Handmade Burnished Ware.'" In *Griechenland, die Ägäis und die Levante während der "Dark Ages,"* ed. Sigrid Deger-Jalkotzy, 161–68. Vienna: Österreichische Akademie der Wissenschaft, 1983.

———, ed. *Griechenland, die Ägäis und die Levante während der "Dark Ages."* Vienna: Österreichische Akademie der Wissenschaft, 1983.

Delbrück, Hans. *Geschichte der Kriegskunst im Rahmen der politischen Geschichte,* vol. 1: *Das Altertum.* Berlin: G. Stilke, 1900.

Delpino, M. A. Fugazzola. "The Proto-Villanovans: A Survey." In *Italy before the Romans: The Iron Age, Orientalizing, and Etruscan Periods,* ed. D. and F. Ridgway, 31–51. London: Academic Press, 1979.

Desborough, Vincent. *The Greek Dark Ages.* New York: St. Martin's, 1972.

———. *The Last Mycenaeans and Their Successors: An Archaeological Survey ca. 1200–1000 B.C.* Oxford: Oxford University Press, 1964.

Detienne, Marcel. "Remarques sur le char en Grèce." In *Problèmes de la guerre en Grèce ancienne,* ed. J.-P. Vernant, 313–18. Paris: Mouton, 1968.

Dever, Wm. "The Late Bronze—Early Iron I Horizon in Syria-Palestine: Egyptians, Canaanites, 'Sea Peoples,' and Proto-Israelites." In *The Crisis Years: The 12th Century B.C.,* ed. Wm. A. Ward and Martha Joukowsky, 99–110. Dubuque: Kendall/Hunt, 1992.

Dickinson, O.T.P.K. "Drought and the Decline of Mycenae: Some Comments." *Antiquity* 48 (1974): 228–29.

Dietrich, M., and O. Loretz. "Die Schardana in den Texten von Ugarit." In *Antike und Universalgeschichte: Festschrift Hans Erich Stier,* ed. R. Stiehl and G. A. Lehmann, 39–42. Münster: Aschendorff, 1972.

Dobesch, Gerhard. "Historische Fragestellungen in der Urgeschichte." In *Griechenland, die Ägäis und die Levante während der "Dark Ages,"* ed. Sigrid Deger-Jalkotzy, 179–230. Vienna: Österreichische Akademie der Wissenschaft, 1983.

Dothan, Moshe. "Ashdod at the End of the Late Bronze Age and the Beginning of the Iron Age," In *Symposia Celebrating the Seventy-Fifth Anniversary of the American Schools of Oriental Research (1900–1975),* ed. Frank Cross, 125–134. Cambridge, Mass.: American Schools of Oriental Research, 1979.

———. "Sardina at Akko?" In *Studies in Sardinian Archaeology,* vol. 2, ed. Miriam Balmuth, 105–15. Ann Arbor: University of Michigan Press, 1986.

Dothan, Trude. "Anthropoid Clay Coffins from a Late Bronze Age Cemetery near Deir el-Balaḥ." *IEJ* 23 (1973): 129–46.

——. *The Philistines and Their Material Culture*. 4th ed. New Haven: Yale University Press, 1982.

——. "Some Aspects of the Appearance of the Sea Peoples and Philistines in Canaan." In *Griechenland, die Ägäis und die Levante während der "Dark Ages,"* ed. Sigrid Deger-Jalkotzy, 99–117. Vienna: Österreichische Akademie der Wissenschaft, 1978.

Driessen, J. M., and C. Macdonald. "Some Military Aspects of the Aegean in the Late Fifteenth and Early Fourteenth Centuries B.C." *ABSA* 79 (1984): 49–74.

Drews, Robert. "Argos and Argives in the *Iliad*." *CP* 74 (1979): 111–35.

——. "The 'Chariots of Iron' of Joshua and Judges." *JSOT* 45 (1989): 15–23.

——. *The Coming of the Greeks: Indo-European Conquests in the Aegean and the Near East*. Princeton: Princeton University Press, 1988.

——. *The Greek Accounts of Eastern History*. Washington, D.C.: Center for Hellenic Studies, 1973.

——. "Herodotus 1.94, the Drought ca. 1200 BC, and the Origin of the Etruscans." *Historia* 41 (1992): 14–39.

——. "Myths of Midas and the Phrygian Migration from Europe." *Klio* (forthcoming).

Easton, D. F. "Has the Trojan War Been Found?" *Antiquity* 59 (1985): 188–95.

Edgerton, Wm. F., and John Wilson. *Historical Records of Ramses III: The Texts in "Medinet Habu," Volumes I and II Translated with Explanatory Notes*. Chicago: University of Chicago Press, 1936.

Ehrenberg, Victor. *The Greek State*. Oxford: Blackwell, 1960.

Elat, M. "The Campaigns of Shalmaneser III against Aram and Israel." *IEJ* 25 (1975): 25–35.

Erard-Cerceau, Isabelle. "Documents sur l'agriculture mycénienne: peut-on concilier archéologie et épigraphie?" *Minos* 23 (1988): 183–90.

Evans, Sir Arthur. *The Palace of Minos at Knossos*, vols. 1–5. London: MacMillan, 1921–35.

Faulkner, R. O. "Egyptian Military Organization." *JEA* 39 (1953): 32–47.

Fidio, Pia de. "Fattori di crisi nella Messenia della Tarda Età del Bronzo." In *Studies in Mycenaean and Classical Greek Presented to John Chadwick*, ed. John T. Killen et al., 127–36. Salamanca, 1987.

Foltiny, Stephan. "Flange-Hilted Cutting Swords of Bronze in Central Europe, Northeast Italy, and Greece." *AJA* 68 (1964): 247–58.

Franceschetti, Adele. "Armi e guerra in testi micenei." *Rendiconti dell'Accad. di Archeologia, Lettere e Belle Arti di Napoli* 53 (1978): 67–90.

Franken, H. J. "The Excavations at Deir 'Alla, Jordan." *VT* 11 (1961): 361–72.

French, Elizabeth. "Archaeology in Greece, 1989–90." *AR* (1989–90): 3–82.

——, and Jeremy Rutter. "The Handmade Burnished Ware of the Late Helladic IIIC Period: Its Historical Context." *AJA* 81 (1977): 111–12.

Freu, Jacques. "La tablette RS 86.2230 et la phase finale du royaume d'Ugarit." *Syria* 65 (1988): 395–98.

Gardiner, Alan. *Egypt of the Pharaohs*. Oxford: Oxford University Press, 1961.

——. *The Kadesh Inscriptions of Ramesses II*. Oxford: Griffith Institute, 1960.

——. "Only One King Siptah and Twosre Not His Wife." *JEA* 44 (1958): 12–22.

Gardiner, E. Norman. "Throwing the Javelin." *JHS* 27 (1907): 249–73.

Garlan, Y. *War in the Ancient World. A Social History.* London: Chatto and Windus, 1975.

Garnsey, Peter. *Famine and Food Supply in the Graeco-Roman World.* Cambridge: Cambridge University Press, 1988.

Gernet, Jacques. "Note sur le char en Chine." In *Problèmes de la guerre en Grèce ancienne,* ed. J. P. Vernant, 309–12. Paris: Mouton, 1968.

Gesell, G. C., L. P. Day, and W. D. Coulsen. "The 1991 Season at Kavousi, Crete." *AJA* 96 (1992): 353.

Gichon, Mordechai, and Michaela Vitale. "Arrow-Heads from Ḥorvat ʿEqed." *IEJ* 41 (1991): 242–57.

Glock, Albert. "Warfare in Mari and Early Israel." Ph.D. dissertation, University of Michigan, 1968.

Godart, Louis. "La caduta dei regni micenei a Creta e l'invasione dorica." In *Le Origini dei Greci: Dori e mondo egeo,* ed. Domenico Musti, 173–200. Rome: Laterza, 1990.

Godart, L., and Y. Tzedakis. "Les nouveaux textes en Linéaire B de la Canée." *RFIC* 119 (1991): 129–49.

Gordon, Col. D. H. "Fire and Sword: The Technique of Destruction." *Antiquity* 27 (1953): 149–52.

———. "Swords, Rapiers, and Horse-Riders." *Antiquity* 27 (1953): 67–78.

Gorny, R. L. "Environment, Archaeology, and History in Hittite Anatolia," *Bib. Arch.* (1989): 78–94.

Gottwald, Norman. *The Tribes of Yahweh: A Sociology of the Tribes of Liberated Israel, 1250–1050 B.C.E.* Maryknoll, N.Y.: Orbis, 1979.

Gray, Mary. "The Ḫābirū-Hebrew Problem in the Light of the Source Material Available at Present." *Hebrew Union College Annual* 29 (1958): 135–202.

Greenhalgh, P.A.L. "The Dendra Charioteer." *Antiquity* 54 (1980): 201–5.

———. *Early Greek Warfare: Horsemen and Chariots in the Homeric and Archaic Ages.* Cambridge: Cambridge University Press, 1973.

Gurney, O. *The Hittites.* 2d ed. Harmondsworth: Penguin, 1961.

Gutenberg, B., and C. F. Richter. *Seismicity of the Earth and Associated Phenomena.* Princeton: Princeton University Press, 1954.

Güterbock, Hans. "The Hittites and the Aegean World, 1: The Ahhiyawa Problem Reconsidered." *AJA* 87 (1983): 133–38.

Hackett, General Sir John. *Warfare in the Ancient World.* London: Sidgwick and Jackson, 1989.

Haggis, Donald. "Survey at Kavousi, Crete: The Iron Age Settlements." *AJA* 95 (1991): 291.

Hall, H. R. *Aegean Archaeology.* London: Warner, 1915.

———. "Keftiu and the Peoples of the Sea." *ABSA* 8 (1901–2): 157–89.

Halpern, Baruch. *The Emergence of Israel in Canaan.* Chico, Calif.: Scholars Press, 1983.

Harding, Anthony. *The Mycenaeans and Europe.* London: Academic Press, 1984.

Harmand, J. *La guerre antique, de Sumer à Rome.* Paris: Presses Universitaires de France, 1973.

Hawkes, C.F.C. "From Bronze Age to Iron Age: Middle Europe, Italy, and the North and West." *PPS* 14 (1948): 196–218.

Hawkins, J. D. "Kuzi-Tešub and the 'Great Kings' of Karkamiš." *AS* 38 (1988): 99–108.

Hayward, Lorna. "The Origin of Raw Elephant Ivory in Late Bronze Age Greece and the Aegean." *Antiquity* 64 (1990): 103–9.

Helck, W. *Die Beziehungen Aegyptens zu Vorderasien im 3. und 2. Jahrtausend v. Chr.* 2d ed. Wiesbaden: Harrassowitz, 1971.

———. "Die Seevölker in den ägyptischen Quellen." In *Geschichte des 13 und 12 Jahrhundert v. Chr. Frankfurt Colloquium, February 1976*, ed. H. Müller-Karpe, 7–21. Munich, 1977.

Heltzer, Michael. *The Internal Organization of the Kingdom of Ugarit.* Wiesbaden: Dr. Ludwig Reichert Verlag, 1982.

Herzog, Chaim, and Mordecai Gichon. *Battles of the Bible.* New York: Random House, 1978.

Höckmann, Olaf. "Lanze und Speer." In *Kriegswesen*, vol. 2: *Angriffswaffen*, ed. H.-G. Buchholz, 275–319. Göttingen: Vandenhoeck and Ruprecht, 1980.

———. "Lanzen und Speere der ägäischen Bronzezeit und des Übergangs zur Eisenzeit." In *Ägäische Bronzezeit*, ed. H.-G. Buchholz, 329–358. Darmstadt: Wissenschaftliche Buchgesellschaft, 1987.

Hölbl, G. "Die historischen Aussagen der ägyptischen Seevölkerinschriften." In *Griechenland, die Ägäis und die Levante während der "Dark Ages,"* ed. Sigrid Deger-Jalkotzy, 121–43. Vienna: Österreichische Akademie der Wissenschaft, 1983.

Holloway, R. Ross. *Italy and the Aegean 3000–700 B.C.* Louvain-la-Nueve: Collège Erasme, 1981.

———. "Italy and the Central Mediterranean in the Crisis Years." In *The Crisis Years: The 12th Century B.C.*, ed. Wm. A. Ward and Martha Joukowsky, 40–45. Dubuque: Kendall/Hunt, 1992.

Hooker, James T. "Titles and Functions in the Pylian State." In *Studies in Mycenaean and Classical Greek Presented to John Chadwick*, ed. John T. Killen, 257–67. Salamanca, 1987.

Hope Simpson, R., and O.T.P.K. Dickinson. *A Gazetteer of Aegean Civilization in the Bronze Age*, vol. 1: *The Mainland and Islands.* Göteborg: Åström, 1979.

Houwink ten Cate, Philo. "The History of Warfare According to Hittite Sources: The Annals of Hattusilis I." *Anatolica* 10 (1983): 91–110; and *Anatolica* 11 (1984): 47–83.

Hurowitz, Victor, and Joan Westenholz. "LKA 63: A Heroic Poem in Celebration of Tiglath-pileser I's Muṣru-Qumanu Campaign." *Journal of Cuneiform Studies* 42 (1990): 1–49.

Iakovides, Sp. "Perati, eine Nekropole der ausklingenden Bronzezeit in Attika." In *Ägäische Bronzezeit*, ed. H.-G. Buchholz, 437–77. Darmstadt: Wissenschaftliche Buchgesallschaft, 1987.

———. "The Present State of Research at the Citadel of Mycenae." *BIAL* 14 (1977): 99–141.

Janko, Richard. *Homer, Hesiod, and the Hymns: Diachronic Development in Epic Diction.* Cambridge: Cambridge University Press 1982.

Kanta, A. *The Late Minoan III Period in Crete. A Survey of Sites, Pottery, and Their Distribution* (=*SIMA* 58). Göteborg: Åström, 1980.

Karageorghis, Vassos. "The Crisis Years: Cyprus." In *The Crisis Years: The 12th Century B.C.*, ed. Wm. A. Ward and Martha Joukowsky, 79–86. Dubuque: Kendall/Hunt, 1992.

———. *The End of the Late Bronze Age in Cyprus*. Nicosia: Zavallis, 1990.

———. "New Light on Late Bronze Age Cyprus," In *Cyprus at the Close of the Late Bronze Age*, ed. Vassos Karageorghis and J. D. Muhly, 19–22. Nicosia: Zavallis, 1984.

———, and J. D. Muhly, eds. *Cyprus at the Close of the Late Bronze Age*. Nicosia: Zavallis, 1984.

Kendall, Timothy. "Warfare and Military Matters in the Nuzi Tablets." Ph.D. dissertation, Brandeis University, 1975.

Kilian, Klaus. "Ausgrabungen in Tiryns 1982/3." *Arch. Anz.* 1988: 105–51.

———. "La caduta dei palazzi micenei continentali: aspetti archeologici." In *Le Origini dei Greci: Dori e mondo egeo*, ed. Domenico Musti, 73–116. Rome: Laterza, 1990.

———. "Zum Ende der mykenischen Epoche in der Argolis." *Jahrbuch des Römisch-Germanischen Zentral-Museums Mainz* 27 (1980): 166–95.

Killen, John T., et al., eds. *Studies in Mycenaean and Classical Greek Presented to John Chadwick* (vols. 20–22 of *Minos*). Salamanca, 1987

Kitchen, K. A. "The Basics of Egyptian Chronology in Relation to the Bronze Age." In *High, Middle, or Low?* ed. Paul Åström, 37–55. Göteborg:Åström, 1987.

———. *Pharaoh Triumphant: The Life and Times of Ramesses II*. Warminster: Aris and Phillips, 1982.

Knapp, A. B. *Copper Production and Divine Protection: Archaeology, Ideology, and Social Complexity on Bronze Age Cyprus*. Göteborg: Åström, 1986.

Korfmann, Manfred. "Altes und Neues aus Troia." *Das Altertum* 36 (1990): 230–40.

Kromayer, Johannes, and Georg Veith. *Antike Schlachtfelder*, vols. 1–4. Berlin: Weidman, 1903–31.

———. *Heerwesen und Kriegsführung der Griechen und Römer*. Munich: Beck, 1928.

Kuniholm, P. I. "Dendrochronology at Gordion and on the Anatolian Plateau." In *Summaries of Papers, 76th General Meeting, Archaeological Institute of America*, 66. New York: Archaeological Institute of America, 1974.

Lagarce, Jacques. "Quatre épées de bronze provenant d'une cachette d'armurier à Enkomi-Alasia (Chypre)." In *Ugaritica VI*, 349–68. (Paris: Geuthner, 1969).

Lang, Mabel. *The Palace of Nestor at Pylos in Western Messenia*, vol. 2, *The Frescoes*. Princeton: Princeton University Press, 1969.

Lapp, Paul. "The Conquest of Canaan in the Light of Archaeology." *Concordia Theological Monthly* 38 (1967): 283–300.

Laroche, E. "Lettre d'un préfet au roi hittite." *Revue hittite et asianique* 67 (1960): 81–86.

Latacz, J. *Kampfparänesen, Kampfdarstellung und Kampfwirklichkeit in der Ilias, bei Kallinos und Tyrtaios*. Munich: Beck, 1977.

Lehmann, G. A. "Zum Auftreten von 'Seevölker'-Gruppen im östlichen Mittelmeerraum—eine Zwischenbilanz." In *Griechenland, die Ägäis und die*

Levante Während der "Dark Ages," ed. Sigrid Deger-Jalkotzy, 79–97. Vienna: Österreichische Akademie der Wissenschaft, 1978.

Lehmann, G. A. *Die mykenisch-frühgriechische Welt und der östliche Mittelmeerraum in der Zeit der 'Seevölker'-Invasionen um 1200 v. Chr.* Opladen: Westdeutscher Verlag, 1985.

———. "Der Untergang des hethitischen Grossreichs und die neuen Texte aus Ugarit." *UF* 2 (1970): 39–73.

Lejeune, Michel. "Chars et roues a Cnossos: Structure d'un inventaire." *Minos* 9 (1968): 9–61.

———. "La civilisation mycénienne et la guerre." In *Problèmes de la guerre en Grèce ancienne,* ed. J.-P. Vernant, 31–51. Paris: Mouton, 1968.

Lepsius, Richard. *Denkmäler aus Ägypten und Äthiopien.* 6 vols. Berlin, 1849–58.

Lesko, Leonard. "Egypt in the 12th Century B.C." In *The Crisis Years: The 12th Century B.C.,* ed. Wm. A. Ward and Martha Joukowsky, 151–56. Dubuque: Kendall/Hunt, 1992.

Lilliu, Giovanni. *La civiltà nuragica.* Sassari: Carlo Delfino Editore, 1982.

Littauer, Mary. "The Military Use of the Chariot in the Aegean in the Late Bronze Age." *AJA* 76 (1972): 145–57.

———, and J. H. Crouwel. "Chariots in Late Bronze Age Greece." *Antiquity* 57 (1983): 187–92.

———. *Wheeled Vehicles and Ridden Animals in the Ancient Near East.* Leiden: Brill, 1979.

Liverani, Mario. *Antico Oriente.* Rome: Laterza, 1988.

———. "The Collapse of the Near Eastern Regional System at the End of the Bronze Age: The Case of Syria." In *Centre and Periphery in the Ancient World,* ed. M. Rowlands, M. Larsen and K. Kristiansen, 67–73. Cambridge: Cambridge University Press, 1987.

———. *Storia di Ugarit nell' età degli archivi politici.* Rome: Centro di Studi Semitici, 1962.

———. "Variazioni climatiche e fluttuazioni demografiche nella storia siriana." *Or. Ant.* 7 (1968): 77–89.

Lorimer, H. L. *Homer and the Monuments.* London: Macmillan, 1950.

Luckenbill, D. D. *Ancient Records of Assyria and Babylonia,* vols. 1 and 2. Chicago: University of Chicago Press, 1926.

Macalister, R. A. *The Philistines: Their History and Civilization.* London: Oxford University Press, 1914.

Macdonald, Colin. "Problems of the Twelfth Century BC in the Dodecanese." *ABSA* 81 (1986): 125–52.

Maigret, Alessandro de. *Le lance nell'Asia anteriore nell'Età del Bronzo* (Studi Semitici, 47). Rome: Istituto di Studi del Vicino Oriente, 1976.

Manitius, Walther. "Das stehende Heer der Assyrerkönige und seine Organisation." *ZA* 24 (1910): 97–149.

Maspero, Gaston. Review of F. Chabas's *Etudes.* In *Revue Critique d' Histoire et de Littérature* (1873), 81–86.

———. Review of E. de Rougé's *Inscriptions hiéroglyphiques.* In *Rev. Crit.* (1878), 317–21.

———. *The Struggle of the Nations.* Ed. A. H. Sayce. Trans. from the French by M. L. McClure. New York: Appleton, 1896.

Maxwell-Hyslop, Rachel. "Bronze Lugged Axe- or Adze-Blades from Asia." *Iraq* 15 (1953): 69–87.

———. "Daggers and Swords in Western Asia." *Iraq* 8 (1946): 1–65.

———. "Western Asiatic Shaft-Hole Axes." *Iraq* 11 (1949): 90–129.

McLeod, Wallace. "An Unpublished Egyptian Composite Bow in the Brooklyn Museum." *AJA* 62 (1958): 397–401.

Mendenhall, George. "The Census Lists of Numbers 1 and 26." *JBL* 77 (1968): 52–66.

———. *The Tenth Generation: The Origins of Biblical Tradition.* Baltimore: Johns Hopkins University Press, 1973.

Merrillees, R. S. "The Crisis Years: Cyprus. A Rejoinder." In *The Crisis Years: The 12th Century B.C.,* ed. Wm. A. Ward and Martha Joukowsky, 28–30. Dubuque: Kendall/Hunt, 1982.

Meyer, Eduard. *Geschichte des Alterthums,* vol. 2. Stuttgart: Cotta, 1893.

———. *Geschichte des Altertums.* 2d ed. Vol. 2, part 1. Stuttgart and Berlin: Cotta, 1928.

———. "Die Pelasger in Attika und auf Lemnos." In Eduard Meyer, *Forschungen zur alten Geschichte,* vol. 1, 5–124. Halle, 1892.

Milik, J. T., and Frank Cross. "Inscribed Javelin-Heads from the Period of the Judges: A Recent Discovery in Palestine." *BASOR* 134 (1954): 5–15.

Möller, G. "Die Aegypter und ihre libyschen Nachbarn." *ZDMG* 78 (1924): 36–51.

Moorey, P. S. "The Emergence of the Light, Horse-Drawn Chariot in the Near East c. 2000–1500 B.C." *World Archaeology* 18 (1986): 196–215.

Mountjoy, Penelope. "The Bronze Greaves from Athens: A Case for a LH IIIC Date." *OA* 15 (1984): 135–46.

Müller-Karpe, H., ed. *Geschichte des 13 und 12 Jahrhundert v. Chr. Frankfurt Colloquium, February 1976* (Jahresbericht des Instituts für Vorgeschichte der Universität Frankfurt a. M. 1976). Munich, 1977.

Muhly, J. D. "The Role of the Sea Peoples in Cyprus during the LC III Period." In *Cyprus at the Close of the Late Bronze Age,* ed. Vassos Karageorghis and J. D. Muhly, 39–56. Nicosia: Zavallis, 1984.

———. R. Maddin, T. Stech, and E. Özgen. "Iron in Anatolia and the Nature of the Hittite Iron Industry." *AS* 35 (1985): 67–84.

Murnane, William. *The Road to Kadesh: A Historical Interpretation of the Battle Reliefs of King Sety I at Karnak.* Chicago: University of Chicago Press, 1985.

Musti, Domenico, ed. *Le origini dei Greci: Dori e mondo egeo.* Rome: Laterza, 1990.

Musti, Domenico. "Continuità e discontinuità tra Achei e Dori nelle tradizioni storiche." In *Le Origini dei Greci: Dori e mondo egeo,* ed. Domenico Musti, 37–71. Rome: Laterza, 1990.

Mylonas, George. *Mycenae and the Mycenaean Age.* Princeton: Princeton University Press, 1966.

Na'aman, Nadav. "Hapiru and Hebrews: The Transfer of a Social Term to the Literary Scene." *JNES* 45 (1986): 271–88.

Naue, Julius. *Die vorrömischen Schwerter aus Kupfer, Bronze und Eisen.* Munich: Piloty and Loehle, 1903.

Neumann, J., and S. Parpola. "Climatic Change and the Eleventh-Tenth-Century Eclipse of Assyria and Babylonia." *JNES* 46 (1987): 161–82.

Nibbi, Alessandra. *The Sea Peoples and Egypt.* Park Ridge, N.J.: Noyes Press, 1975.

Nougayrol, Jean. "Guerre et Paix à Ugarit." *Iraq* 25 (1963): 110–23.

———. "La 'Lettre du Général.'" In *Ugaritica*, vol. 5, 69–79.

O'Flaherty, Wendy Doniger, trans. *The Rig Veda: An Anthology.* Harmondsworth: Penguin, 1981.

Olivier, J.-P. *Les scribes de Cnossos.* Rome: Ateneo, 1967.

Ormerod, Henry A. *Piracy in the Ancient World. An Essay in Mediterranean History.* 1924. Reprint, Chicago: Argonaut, 1967.

Osten, H. H. von der. *The Alishar Hüyük: Seasons of 1930–1932.* Chicago: University of Chicago Press, 1937.

Otten, H. "Die letzte Phase des hethitischen Grossreiches nach den Texten." In *Griechenland, die Ägäis und die Levante Während der "Dark Ages,"* ed. Sigrid Deger-Jalkotzy, 13–21. Vienna: Österreichische Akademie der Wissenschaft, 1978.

Palmer, Ruth. "Subsistence Rations at Pylos and Knossos." *Minos* 24 (1989): 89–124.

Pendlebury, J. P. *The Archaeology of Crete.* London: Methuen, 1939.

———, et al. "Excavations in the Plain of Lasithi. III." *ABSA* 38 (1938–39): 57–145.

Piggott, Stuart. *The Earliest Wheeled Transport: From the Atlantic to the Caspian.* Ithaca, N.Y.: Cornell University Press, 1983.

———. "Horse and Chariot: The Price of Prestige." *Proceedings of the Seventh International Congress of Celtic Studies, Held at Oxford from 10th to 15th July, 1983.* Oxford: D. E. Evans (distributed by Oxbow Books), 1986.

Podzuweit, Christian. "Die mykenische Welt und Troja." In *Südosteuropa zwischen 1600 und 1000 v. Chr.*, ed. B. Hänsel, 65–88. Moreland, 1982.

Popham, M. R., L. H. Sackett, et al., eds. *Lefkandi I: The Dark Age.* London: Thames and Hudson, 1980.

Powell, T.G.E. "The Inception of the Final Bronze Age in Middle Europe." *PPS* 29 (1963): 214–34.

———. "Some Implications of Chariotry." In *Culture and Environment. Essays in Honour of Sir Cyril Fox*, ed. I. Foster and L. Adcock, 153–69. London: Routledge and Kegan Paul, 1963.

Pulak, Cemal. "The Bronze Age Shipwreck at Ulu Burun, Turkey: 1985 Campaign." *AJA* 92 (1988): 1–37.

Rainey, A. F. "The Military Personnel at Ugarit." *JNES* 24 (1965): 17–27.

Ramat, P. "Sul nome dei Dori." *Parola del Passato* 16 (1961): 62–65.

Redford, Donald. "The Ashkelon Relief at Karnak and the Israel Stele." *IEJ* 36 (1986): 188–200.

Reliefs and Inscriptions at Karnak, vol. 4: *The Battle Reliefs of King Sety I* (Oriental Institute Publication no. 107). Chicago: University of Chicago Press, 1986.

Ridgway, David. "Archaeology in Sardinia and South Italy, 1983–88." *AR* (1988–89): 130–47.

Risch, Ernst. "La posizione del dialetto dorico." In *Le Origini dei Greci: Dori e mondo egeo*, ed. Domenico Musti, 13–35. Rome: Laterza, 1990.

Rougé, E. de. *Extraits d'un mémoire sur les attaques dirigées contre l'Egypte par les peuples de la Méditerranee vers le xxvᵉ siècle avant notre ère*. Paris: Didier, 1867.

Rousset, D. "Les Doriens de la Metropole, I." *BCH* 113 (1989): 199–239.

Rutter, Jeremy. "Ceramic Evidence for Northern Intruders in Southern Greece at the Beginning of the Late Helladic IIIC Period." *AJA* 79 (1975): 17–32.

————. "Cultural Novelties in the Post-Palatial Aegean World: Indices of Vitality or Decline?" In *The Crisis Years: The 12th Century B.C.*, ed. Wm. A. Ward and Martha Joukowsky, 61–78. Dubuque: Kendall/Hunt, 1992.

————. "The Late Helladic IIIB and IIIC Periods at Korakou and Gonia." Ph.D. dissertation, University of Pennsylvania, 1974.

Sams, G. Kenneth. "Observations on Western Anatolia." In *The Crisis Years: The 12th Century B.C.*, ed. Wm. A. Ward and Martha Joukowsky, 56–60. Dubuque: Kendall/Hunt, 1992.

Sandars, Nancy. "The First Aegean Swords and Their Ancestry." *AJA* 65 (1961): 17–29.

————. "The Last Mycenaeans and the European Late Bronze Age." *Antiquity* 38 (1964): 258–62.

————. "Later Aegean Bronze Swords." *AJA* 67 (1963): 117–53.

————. "North and South at the End of the Mycenaean Age: Aspects of an Old Problem." *Oxford Journal of Archaeology* 2 (1983): 43–68.

————. *The Sea Peoples: Warriors of the Ancient Mediterranean 1250–1150 BC*. London: Thames and Hudson, 1978.

Sass, Benjamin. "Inscribed Babylonian Arrowheads of the Turn of the Second Millennium and Their Phoenician Counterparts." *UF* 21 (1989): 349–56.

Sasson, Jack. *The Military Establishment at Mari*. Rome: Pontifical Biblical Institute, 1969.

Schachermeyr, Fritz. *Griechische Frühgeschichte*. Vienna: Österreichische Akademie der Wissenschaft, 1984.

————. *Die Levante im Zeitalter der Wanderungen: vom 13. bis zum 11. Jahrhundert v. Chr.* Vienna: Österreichische Akademie der Wissenschaft, 1982.

————. *Mykene und das Hethiterreich*. Vienna: Österreichische Akademie der Wissenschaft, 1986.

————. "Streitwagen und Streitwagenbild im Alten Orient und bei den mykenischen Griechen." *Anthropos* 46 (1951): 705–53.

Schaeffer, C. F. A. "A Bronze Sword from Ugarit with Cartouche of Mineptah (Ras Shamra, Syria)." *Antiquity* 29 (1955): 226–29.

————. "Commentaires sur les lettres et documents trouvés dans les bibliothèques privées d'Ugarit." In *Ugaritica*, vol. 5, 607–768.

————. "Les fouilles de Minet-el-Beida et de Ras Shamra (campagne du printemps 1929)." *Syria* 10 (1929): 285–97.

Schilardi, D. "Paros: Koukounaries." *AR* (1980–81): 35–36.

Schulman, Alan. "Chariots, Chariotry, and the Hyksos." *Journal for the Society for the Study of Egyptian Antiquities* 10 (1980): 105–53.

————. "Egyptian Chariotry: A Re-Examination." *JARCE* 2 (1963): 75–98.

――――. "Egyptian Representations of Horsemen and Riding in the New King-dom." *JNES* 16 (1957): 263–71.

――――. *Military Rank, Title, and Organization in the Egyptian New Kingdom* (Münchner Aegyptologische Studien no. 6). Berlin: Hessling, 1964.

Schwyzer, Eduard. *Griechische Grammatik*, vol. 1. Munich: Beck, 1939.

Selms, A. van. "The Armed Forces of Israel under Saul and David." In *Studies on the Books of Samuel: Papers Read at 3rd Meeting of Die O. T. Werkgemeenskap in Suid-Afrika*, 55–66. Pretoria: University of Pretoria, 1960.

Shaughnessy, E. L. "Historical Perspectives on the Introduction of the Chariot into China." *Harvard Journal of Asiatic Studies* 48 (1988): 189–234.

Shrimpton, Gordon. "Regional Drought and the Decline of Mycenae." *Echos du Monde Classique* 31 (1987): 137–76.

Singer, Itamar. "The Battle of Nihriya and the End of the Hittite Empire." *ZA* 75 (1985): 100–23.

――――. "Merneptah's Campaign to Canaan and the Egyptian Occupation of the Southern Coastal Plain of Palestine in the Ramesside Period." *BASOR* 269 (1988): 1–10.

Singor, H. W. "Nine against Troy: On Epic ΦΑΛΑΓΓΕΣ, ΠΡΟΜΑΧΟΙ, and an Old Structure in the Story of the *Iliad*." *Mnemosyne* 44 (1991): 17–62.

Snodgrass, A. M. *Arms and Armour of the Greeks*. Ithaca, N.Y.: Cornell University Press, 1967.

――――. "Cyprus and the Beginnings of Iron Technology in the Eastern Mediterranean." In *Early Metallurgy in Cyprus, 4000–500 B.C.*, ed. J. D. Muhly, R. Maddin, and V. Karageorghis, 289–95. Nicosia: Zavallis, 1982.

――――. *The Dark Age of Greece*. Edinburgh: Edinburgh University Press, 1971.

――――. *Early Greek Armour and Weapons: From the Bronze Age to 600 B.C.* Edinburgh: Edinburgh University Press, 1964.

Soren, D. "An Earthquake on Cyprus. New Discoveries from Kourion." *Archaeology* 38 (1982): 52–59.

South, Alison. "Kalavasos-Ayios Dhimitrios and the Late Bronze Age of Cyprus." In *Cyprus at the Close of the Late Bronze Age*, ed. Vassos Karageorghis and J. D. Muhly, 11–17. Nicosia: Zavallis, 1984.

Spruytte, J. "La conduite du cheval chez l'archer assyrien." *Plaisirs Equestres* 129 (1983): 66–71.

Stager, Lawrence. "Merenptah, Israel, and Sea Peoples: New Light on an Old Relief." *Eretz-Israel* 18 (1985): 56–64.

――――. "When Canaanites and Philistines Ruled Ashkelon." *Bib. Arch. Rev.* 17 (1991): 24–43.

Stiebing, Wm. H., Jr. *Out of the Desert? Archaeology and the Exodus/Conquest Narratives*. Buffalo: Prometheus Books, 1989.

Stillman, Nigel, and Nigel Tallis. *Armies of the Ancient Near East, 3000 BC to 539 BC*. A Wargames Research Group Publication (photoset and printed in England by Flexiprint Ltd., Worthing, Sussex), 1984.

Strange, John. "The Transition from the Bronze Age to the Iron Age in the Eastern Mediterranean and the Emergence of the Israelite State." *Scandinavian Journal of the Old Testament* (1987): 1–19.

Strobel, August. *Der spätbronzezeitliche Seevölkersturm*. Berlin: de Gruyter, 1976.

Stubbings, Frank. "Arms and Armour." In *A Companion to Homer*, ed. A. Wace and F. Stubbings, 504–22. London: Macmillan, 1967.

Stürmer, Veit. "Das Ende der Wohnsiedlungen in Malia und Amnisos." In *Forschungen zur aegaeischen Vorgeschichte. Das Ende der mykenischen Welt*, ed. Eberhard Thomas, 33–36. Cologne: n.p., 1987.

Symons, D. J. "Archaeology in Cyprus, 1981–85." *AR* (1986–87): 62–77.

Tarragon, J.-M. de. "La pointe de flèche inscrite des Pères Blancs de Jérusalem." *Rev. Bib.* 98 (1991): 244–51.

Taylour, W. D. *The Mycenaeans*. 2d ed. New York: Thames and Hudson, 1983.

———. *Well-Built Mycenae: The Helleno-British Excavations within the Citadel at Mycenae*, vol. 1. Warminster: Aris and Phillips, 1981.

Thomas, Eberhard, ed. *Forschungen zur aegaeischen Vorgeschichte. Das Ende der mykenischen Welt* (Akten des internationalen Kolloquiums 7.-8. Juli 1984 in Köln). Cologne: n.p. ("herausgegeben von Eberhard Thomas"), 1987.

Todd, S. Randolph. "Citizenry Divisions in Ancient Greek Poleis: Military Aspects of Their Origin and Development." Ph.D. dissertation, Vanderbilt University, 1991.

Tölle-Kastenbein, Renate. *Pfeil und Bogen im alten Griechenland*. Bochum: Duris, 1980.

Tov, Emanuel. "The David and Goliath Saga." *Bible Review* (1986): 34–41.

Trump, David. *The Prehistory of the Mediterranean*. New Haven: Yale University Press, 1980.

Uchitel, Alexander. "Charioteers of Knossos." *Minos* 23 (1988): 47–58.

———. "On the 'Military' Character of the *O-KA* Tablets." *Kadmos* 23 (1984): 136–63.

Ugaritica, vol. 3 (Mission de Ras Shamra, vol. 8). Paris: Geuthner, 1956.

Ugaritica, vol. 5 (Mission de Ras Shamra, vol. 16). Paris: Geuthner 1968.

Ünal, Ahmet, et al. "The Hittite Sword from Boğazköy-Hattusa." *Müze* 4 (1990–91): 50–52.

Vermeule, Emily. "The Mycenaeans in Achaea." *AJA* 64 (1960): 1–21.

———, and Vassos Karageorghis. *Mycenaean Pictorial Vase Painting*. Cambridge: Harvard University Press, 1982.

Vernant, J.-P., ed. *Problèmes de la guerre en Grèce ancienne*. Paris: Mouton, 1968.

Waldbaum, Jane. *From Bronze to Iron: The Transition from the Bronze Age to the Iron Age in the Eastern Mediterranean* (Studies in Mediterranean Archaeology no. 54). Göteborg: Åström, 1978.

Walser, Gerold. "Alte Geschichte und Hethiterforschung." In *Neuere Hethiterforschung*, ed. Gerold Walser, 1–10. Wiesbaden: Steiner, 1964.

Ward, Wm. A., and Martha Joukowsky, eds. *The Crisis Years: The 12th Century B.C.* Dubuque: Kendall/Hunt, 1992.

Warren, Peter, and Vronwy Hankey. *Aegean Bronze Age Chronology*. Bristol: Bristol Classical Press, 1989.

Wathelet, Paul. "Les datifs analogiques en -εσσι dans la tradition épique." *REG* 104 (1991): 1–14.

Watkins, Trevor. "The Beginnings of Warfare." In *Warfare in the Ancient World*, ed. General Sir John Hackett, 15–35. London: Sidgwick and Jackson, 1989.

Wees, H. van. "Kings in Combat: Battles and Heroes in the Iliad." *CQ* 38 (1988): 1–24.

———. "Leaders of Men? Military Organization in the Iliad." *CQ* 36 (1986): 285–303.

Weinstein, James. "The Collapse of the Egyptian Empire in the Southern Levant." In *The Crisis Years: The 12th Century B.C.*, ed. Wm. A. Ward and Martha Joukowsky, 142–50. Dubuque: Kendall/Hunt, 1992.

Weiss, B. "The Decline of Late Bronze Age Civilization as a Possible Response to Climatic Change." *Climatic Change* 4 (1982): 172–98.

Wells, Peter. "Crisis Years? The 12th Century B.C. in Central and Southeastern Europe." In *The Crisis Years: The 12th Century B.C.*, ed. Wm. A. Ward and Martha Joukowsky, 31–39. Dubuque: Kendall/Hunt, 1992.

Wente, E. F., and C. C. Van Siclen. "A Chronology of the New Kingdom." In *Studies in Honor of George R. Hughes*, ed. J. H. Johnson and E. F. Wente, 217–61. Chicago: University of Chicago Press, 1976.

Wertime, Theodore A., and J. D. Muhly, eds. *The Coming of the Age of Iron*. New Haven: Yale University Press, 1980.

West, M. L. "The Rise of the Greek Epic." *JHS* 108 (1988): 151–72.

White, Donald. "The Third Season at Marsa Matruh." *AJA* 94 (1990): 330.

Wiesner, Josef, *Fahren und Reiten* (Archaeologia Homerica I F). Göttingen: Vandenhoeck and Ruprecht, 1968.

Wilson, John. *The Culture of Ancient Egypt*. Chicago: University of Chicago Press, 1951.

———. "The Royal Myth in Ancient Egypt." *Proceedings of the American Philosophical Society* 100 (1956): 439–42.

Wiseman, Donald J. "The Assyrians." In *Warfare in the Ancient World*, ed. General Sir John Hackett, 36–53. London: Sidgwick and Jackson, 1989.

Wolf, W. *Die Bewaffnung des altägyptischen Heeres*. Leipzig: Hinrichs, 1926.

Wood, Michael. *In Search of the Trojan War*. New York: New American Library, 1985.

Woolley, Sir Leonard. *A Forgotten Kingdom*. Harmondsworth: Penguin, 1953.

Wreszinski, W. *Atlas zur altägyptischen Kulturgeschichte*. Two parts (boxed sets). Leipzig, 1923–1935. Reprint, Geneva and Paris: Slatkine Reprints, 1988.

Wright, G. E. "Iron: The Date of Its Introduction into Palestine." *AJA* 43 (1939): 458–63.

Wright, H. E. "Climatic Change in Mycenaean Greece." *Antiquity* 42 (1968): 123–27.

Yadin, Yigael. *The Art of Warfare in Biblical Lands*. 2 vols. New York: McGraw-Hill, 1963.

———. "Goliath's Javelin and the מנור א׳רגים." *PEQ* (1955): 58–69.

———. "The Transition from a Semi-Nomadic to a Sedentary Society in the Twelfth Century B.C.E." In *Symposia Celebrating the Seventy-Fifth Anniversary of the Founding of the American Schools of Oriental Research (1900–1975)*, ed. Frank Cross, 57–68. Cambridge, Mass.: American Schools of Oriental Research, 1979.

————, Y. Aharoni, et al. *Hazor: An Account of the Third and Fourth Seasons of Excavations, 1957–1958*. Jerusalem: Hebrew University, 1961.

Yalouris, N. "Mykenische Bronzeschutzwaffen." *MDAI* 75 (1960): 42–67.

Yon, Marguerite. "The End of the Kingdom of Ugarit." In *The Crisis Years: The 12th Century B.C.*, ed. Wm. A. Ward and Martha Joukowsky, 111–22. Dubuque: Kendall/Hunt, 1992.

————, P. Lombard, and M. Renisio. "L'Organisation de l'habitat: les maisons A, B et E." In *Ras Shamra—Ougarit III. Le Centre de la ville: 38e–44e Campagnes (1978–1984)*, ed. Marguerite Yon et al., 11–128. Paris, 1987.

————, Annie Caubet, and Joël Mallet. "Ras Shamra-Ougarit 38, 39 et 40e campagnes (1978, 1979 et 1980)." *Syria* 59 (1982): 169–97.

————, et al., *Ras Shamra—Ougarit III. Le Centre de la ville: 38e–44e Campagnes (1978–1984)*. Paris, 1987.

Younger, John. "The End of Mycenaean Art." In *Forschungen zur aegaeischen Vorgeschichte. Das Ende der mykenischen Welt*, ed. Eberhard Thomas, 63–72. Cologne: n.p., 1987.

Yurco, Frank. "Merenptah's Canaanite Campaign," *JARCE* 23 (1986): 189–215.

————. "3200-Year-Old Picture of Israelites Found in Egypt." *Bib. Arch. Rev.* 16 (1990): 20–38.

Zaccagnini, Carlo. "The Transition from Bronze to Iron in the Near East and in the Levant: Marginal Notes." *JAOS* 110 (1990): 493–502.

Zettler, R. L. "Twelfth-Century B.C. Babylonia: Continuity and Change." In *The Crisis Years: The 12th Century B.C.*, ed. Wm. A. Ward and Martha Joukowsky, 174–81. Dubuque: Kendall/Hunt, 1992.

Index